WOMAN AS FORCE IN HISTORY

Woman as Force in History

A Study in Traditions and Realities

◊◊◊◊◊◊◊◊◊◊◊◊◊◊◊◊◊◊◊◊◊◊◊◊◊◊◊◊◊◊◊◊◊

MARY R. BEARD

OCTAGON BOOKS

A DIVISION OF FARRAR, STRAUS AND GIROUX

New York   1976

Copyright 1946 Mary R. Beard

Reprinted 1976
by special arrangement with Macmillan Publishing Company, Inc.

OCTAGON BOOKS
A DIVISION OF FARRAR, STRAUS & GIROUX, INC.
19 Union Square West
New York, N.Y. 10003

Library of Congress Cataloging in Publication Data

Beard, Mary Ritter, 1876-1958.
   Woman as force in history.

   Reprint of the ed. published by Collier Books, New York.
   Bibliography: p.
   Includes index.
   1. Women—Social Conditions.   2. Women—History.   I. Title.

HQ1121.B36   1976   301.41'2   76-39976
ISBN 0-374-90503-7

Manufactured by Braun-Brumfield, Inc.
Ann Arbor, Michigan
Printed in the United States of America

ACKNOWLEDGMENTS

To Charles Beard, my husband, I am indebted beyond my power of acknowledgment for the opportunity I have had to use freely the notes, texts, and original sources, especially on English and American legal history, which he has accumulated during long years of study in England and the United States. I am also indebted to him for criticisms respecting my drafts of this manuscript. Moreover in innumerable conversations with so thoughtful and vigilant a scholar I have deepened my understanding of the cautions imperative for any attempt to interpret history.

For my Bibliography, three women have been of invaluable aid. Marjorie White has let me take from her files many essential titles and annotations from her notes collected through years of research in the literature about women. Mrs. Henry S. Drinker has shared with me some of the major titles on goddesses, a fundamental part of her long and intensive study of women in music. Motier Harris Fisher has worked in the Congressional Library analyzing books and assembling special titles for my list.

To the following publishers my debt is great and my appreciation of their consent to my using extracts from their books is correspondingly great:

Harper and Brothers for permission to use lines from George A. Dorsey's *Man's Own Show: Civilization* (1931) and from an article in *Harper's* magazine by Dr. Grace Adams (1939) entitled "Women Are Coming Along."

G. P. Putnam's Sons for quotations from Emily James Putnam's *The Lady* (1910).

D. Appleton-Century Company for lines taken from H. J. Mozan's *Woman in Science* (1913).

Houghton Mifflin Company for rights to quotations from Henry Adams' *Education* (1918) and *Mont St. Michel and Chartres* (1936).

Charles Scribner's Sons for lines from Christian Gauss' *A Primer for Tomorrow* (1934).

Crown Publishers, as owner of the Covici-Friede properties, for quotations from Mark Graubard's *Man the Slave and Master* (1938).

Yale University Press for statements in A. G. Keller's *Man's Rough Road* (1932) and to the J. B. Lippincott Company which assumed the business of the Frederick A. Stokes Company, originally a joint publisher of this book with the Yale Press.

The John Day Company for courtesies connected with my inquiry about permission to quote from Pearl Buck's *Of Men and Women* (1941), the author's agent David Lloyd, and Pearl Buck Walsh's own gracious permission as an "express instruction" relative to such requests.

Acknowledgments

The *Yale Review* for excerpts from Dr. Ada Comstock's article in 1942 on "Women in This War."

The Macmillan Company for privileges to use materials from its works.

I also acknowledge the generosity of Dr. Maude Glasgow who granted me the right to quote from *The Subjection of Woman and Traditions of Men* (1940) to which she holds the copyright.

Earl Browder has with similar generosity allowed me to quote from his *What is Communism* (1936) to which he holds the copyright.

Nor do I pass lightly over my indebtedness to Mark Twain. His defense of the license to use capital letters and punctuation according to an author's purposes has encouraged me to express my purposes in this way. This privilege I have extended to the authors whom I quote.

Contents

Preface

Preface

THIS volume, as its subtitle distinctly states, is a *study*. In no part of it is any claim made to an all-embracing fullness or to philosophic completeness.

In the first place, it is a study of the tradition that women were members of a subject sex throughout history. This tradition has exercised an almost tyrannical power over thinking about the relations of men and women, for more than a hundred years.

In the second place, the idea of subjection is tested by reference to historical realities — legal, religious, economic, social, intellectual, military, political, and moral or philosophical.

Since American feminists have long laid emphasis on the alleged subjection of women by law, pointing to Anglo-American Common Law as expounded by Sir William Blackstone, special attention is given to (1) an analysis of his views of that law, (2) an exploration of women's property rights in mediaeval English law, and (3) an examination of the rise and growth of Equity in England and the United States. Stress is laid on Equity for the reason that it almost paralleled the development of the Common Law in time and had thoroughly riddled common-law doctrines on married women's property rights long before Blackstone published the first volume of his *Commentaries* in 1765 and more than a hundred years before the feminists of 1848 adopted Blackstone as the prime authority for their belief in the historic subjection of women.

In the third place, inasmuch as for more than a century it has been widely claimed that the idea of equality furnishes a perfect guide to women in their search for an escape from "subjection," the origin, nature, and applications of this idea, which had become traditional by 1848, are brought to the inquest.

In the fourth place, I have roughly outlined, in my analytical chapters and in my last chapter dealing with long history, the kind of studying, writing, and teaching which I believe to be mandatory if a genuine interest in understanding human life is to be cultivated. For getting closer to the truth about it, the personalities, interests, ideas, and activities of women must receive an attention commensurate with their energy in history. Women have done far more than exist and bear and rear children. They have played a great role in directing human events as thought and action. Women have been a force in making all the history that has been made.

As an aid to those who may be inclined to think that written history should be as comprehensive and realistic as possible, I have included a Bibliography, though a brief one, of some important works on women in history.

MARY R. BEARD

New Milford, Conn.,
Summer, 1945

Woman as Force in History

Chapter 1

Everybody's Interest: Man and Woman

FATEFULLY interlocked with all the visible, vocal, and revolutionary upheavals which, in our own time, have been ripping open and transforming great societies inherited from the nineteenth century and its long past are the relations between men and women. Even underground movements for counter-revolutions, revolutions against revolutions, take vitality from these relations. Thrust into the global violence which marks our age is the dynamism of women who, with men, have set the world on fire and helped to frame plans for its reconstruction.

In the war of propaganda accompanying this war of arms, women have been intransigent combatants. Their old roles of intriguing and spying have been reënacted. Millions of women have been devoting their energies for many years to feeding, clothing, and equipping with munitions the men who fight on land, from the air, on the seas, and beneath the seas. Without the enlistment of women by conscription or their voluntary support, these bitter international contests for military dominance could not have gone forward on such a scale to their fates in the morrow. As in the beginning of organized warfare, back in the aeons of unrecorded history, so in its latest forms the sanction of women is deemed essential to its terrific force.

The competition among the revolutionists for mastery in the

human world has been emphatically marked by a competition in conceptions of sex relations. Three views of perfection in these relations have been struggling for victory in this rivalry.

One is the view that the "woman's problem," a definition respecting woman's place in society satisfactory to herself, can only be solved by complete equality with men, and that the equality can only be established under Communism. A second view is that woman must find her greatest happiness and contribute most to the State by limiting her ambitions to domesticity and still more narrowly to child-bearing, in order that the population rate may be high enough to keep a given nation secure against crowded societies on its borders, and strong enough within for aggressive action when desired against neighbors or more distant communities; this is the ideology of Fascism. The third view is that woman must have the right to choose her way of life even to the point of self-centered interests; this is one among the ideologies of Democracy.

The first of the titanic revolutions of this twentieth century was launched on its course by V. I. Lenin and his wife, Nadejda Krupskaya, in 1917, after the Russian Czar had been dethroned in the midst of the first world war of this time. These two Russians had long been revolutionists and long associated in agitations for a communist uprising. Both had been exiled to Siberia and in Siberia they were married. Both had been outlawed after they left Siberia and had been compelled to carry on their propaganda beyond, if sometimes close to, the borders of Russia. When Lenin got the reins of government in his hands, with the backing of the Russian Bolsheviki, Krupskaya helped to drive home the issue of woman's rights as the significance of this revolution, for women. She had been a steadfast and zealous advocate of sex equality.

Lenin knew, as well as Krupskaya knew, that, without the ardent support of women, the communist revolt would have a brief career if any career at all. And to win their support full recognition of their "right" to full participation in the Communist regime was immediately given. Of this fact Lenin reminded women-at-large in September, 1919, during his speech delivered at the Fourth Moscow City Conference of Non-Party Women. "The Soviet government has applied democracy to a greater extent than any other country," he claimed, "even the most advanced, by the fact that in its laws not the slightest hint of any inferiority of women is left. I repeat, not a single state and no democratic legislation has done even half of what the Soviet government did for women in the very first months of its existence."

In a conversation with Klara Zetkin, indomitable German Socialist, Lenin elaborated the doctrine that "real freedom for women is possible only through Communism." Women must appreciate this and throw their energy into the Bolshevik revolution, he insisted. "The Communist women's movement must itself be a mass movement, a part of the general mass movement.... There can be no real mass movement without women. ... Unless millions of women are with us we cannot exercise the proletarian dictatorship, cannot construct on Communist lines. We must find out our way to them, we must study and try to find that way." For the "proletarian dictatorship!"

In Krupskaya's introduction to a pamphlet by Lenin on *Women and Society,* the double power of women's revolutionary agitation and the communist theory of its underlying imperative were brought out. Krupskaya said: "Ever since the beginning of Soviet rule, equal rights for women have been an object of interest not only for women, but for men as well — young men, Red Army men. I remember how surprised Mirbach, the German Ambassador, was, when, while paying an official call to Lenin in 1918, he saw one of the Red Army men who acted as Lenin's guard sitting at a table reading a book. He wanted to know what the book was and asked to have the title translated. It turned out that the guard was reading a translation of *Woman and Socialism* by [August] Bebel, a former leader of the Social-Democratic party in the German Reichstag." This book carried the gospel, derived from Karl Marx, that woman, enslaved by capitalism, must free herself by helping to set up a dictatorship of workers.

Imbued with this doctrine and envisaging utopia, Russian women in great numbers agitated and organized at home and abroad for its realization. They procured positions in Russia with the secret police and both judged and punished opponents of the Communist party. After German troops started to invade Russia in 1941 under the direction of the Nazis, women who were not members of the Communist party rushed like members of the party to defend their country. Then together

Communist women and non-party women engaged in all phases of the armed combat with their mutual foe. Russian women became guerrillas fighting from ambushes. They fought from the air in bombing planes. They fought in tanks. They fought wherever they were needed or could, by arms and by political action. They helped to open new battlefields — to make Russia the supreme power in Europe and Asia. "Hey, Slavs, in vain the depths of hell threaten!" cried Stana Tomashevich, a fiery leader in the Russian push down into the Balkans. But the women who helped to spread revolutionary fire in neighboring and distant countries overrun by German troops, and among peoples more or less amenable for other reasons to the gospel according to Marx, Bebel, Lenin, Krupskaya, Zetkin, and eventually according to Stalin, were mainly, perhaps wholly, Communists.

Whatever the destiny of this revolution may be, it can be assumed that the question of man and woman relations will remain at the center of interest, among all the people whom it affects. If the number of women in the population continues to exceed by far the number of men long after the war has stopped or declined into small local conflicts, special problems pertaining to this interest will arise in Russia and in her satellite States. At all events the rights of women to self-expression, to political positions, to paid employments, to education, and to personal liberties in respect of marriage, parenthood, or extra-legal or legalized sexual relations with men — all such issues will be matters of general concern, despite declarations of "equality" that may appear in constitutions. To no small extent the course of civilization in such areas will depend upon decisions as to the relations of men and women. How much and what kinds of liberty will women demand? How much of it can men or women in general actually have under a system of dictatorship, whatever its type? That far-reaching changes are likely to come is already foreshadowed in the new legislation on marriage relations and motherhood adopted by the Russian government in 1944.

It was within a short time after the Bolsheviks got possession of the Russian government that the second type of revolution burst forth in Europe and Asia. This occurred in Italy about 1920, in Germany some ten years later, in Japan in 1935, and in Spain in 1936. The explosion was set off in Europe by

Benito Mussolini, repeated by Adolf Hitler with the addition of organized anti-Semitism, and widened to Spain under the rebellion of Francisco Franco against the Spanish republic. All these revolutions had dictatorship as their objective. All represented in part efforts to check the spread of communism. All were intensely anti-democratic. In Italy and Spain the revolutions were called Fascist. In Germany the name National Socialism was given to the movement directed by the "Führer," Hitler. Whatever the name, whatever the slight deviations in the patterns of these revolutions, all confronted the necessity of winning the approval of women and the active aid of women, in sufficient numbers at least, to provide the sanction essential to success on the home front and in aggression abroad.

Mussolini met this vital problem in various ways. He commanded women and girls to organize supporting units in some 4,000 communities, on the models of men's units in those communities, to carry "all the obligations of those who fight for the party." For enthusiastic and competent work of this kind, women were "honored" as partners of Fascist men. At public ceremonies, moreover, mothers whose sons were conscripted for the business of fighting were lined up and "invited" to kiss the cannon already used or to be used in the execution of Italy's imperial program in Ethiopia. Believing or hoping that Mussolini and his armed followers could really halt the revolution creeping up from below, innumerable women of the upper social levels, some of whom had been radicals like Mussolini in former days, gave him their hearts, their jewels, the use of their minds, and their voices for singing his praises. The halo around the head of Mussolini in the heyday of his glamour was the gift of women as well as of men who saw in him their people's hero.

In a volume on *Italian Women, Past and Present*, issued in Rome, Professor Maria Castellani explained her allegiance to Fascism. She said: "Fascism recognizes women as a part of the life force of the country, laying down a division of duties between the two sexes, without putting obstacles in the way of those women who by their intellectual gifts can reach the highest positions." Women turned to Fascism as a protection against Bolshevism. Under the Corporative Constitution they got the equal right with men to become members of trade associations. They directed sections of the Fascist party. They held positions in the legal profession, reopened for them by Fascism as in keeping with long Italian tradition. They also occupied positions on university staffs as teachers of medicine and obstetrics, mathematics and physics, natural science, and philosophy, as Italian women had done in former times.

Capable Italian women speakers and writers represented Mussolini's aims as truly righteous. Usually they were charming members of their sex. They were clever diplomats. Several of them came to the United States where, in private conversations with influential persons and in speeches addressed to audiences for popular edification, they praised the man, at an hour when the balance between revolution and counter-revolution in Italy was quivering and in a place whence financial and "moral" aid might come to steady it.

An arduous exponent of Fascism was Margherita Sarfatti, an intimate friend of Mussolini and his official biographer. During her propagandistic tour of the United States she wrote for metropolitan dailies and women's magazines such as the *Pictorial Review*, on the women behind Mussolini. In the *New York Herald Tribune* of November 12, 1933, under the headline, "Italy is jealously guarding its women; it is giving them education, protecting their jobs, sponsoring fashions that will improve their health," she said: "Back of it all is the realization that women hold the key to Italy's future. . . . Woman! Woman! Everybody talks about her." In what way? Mainly as mother of a race looking toward imperial expansion.

The visiting Italian women who sought to interpret Mussolini to Americans were given a "'good press" by American women journalists. They also had the assistance of American women newspaper correspondents who had been favorably impressed by Mussolini during their interviews with him and wrote him up genially for the American public.

Native American women and women born in Italy or still in close contact with things Italian helped build up Mussolini as the great new Caesar whom he aspired to resemble. They raised money for him directly or sent him their rings and other ornaments of gold. In 1933, while crossing the Atlantic in a plane was still a remarkable feat and while the World's Fair was being held at Chicago, Mussolini dispatched Balbo and a convoy of flying ships to the United States to impress all the people of this country with his majesty. Many mothers of Italian origin lifted their infants in their arms to the soaring armada as if to dedicate their offspring to the service of their hero.

When in 1936 General Francisco Franco applied fascist philosophy in opening his revolutionary war on the Spanish Republic, he appealed to and won the allegiance of those Spanish women whose temperaments and interests corresponded to those of the Italian women engaged in building up Mussolini's "grandeur."

Women of the patrician élite, hating the Republic and the insurgent democracy, fearing the radicals on the far left, not only rallied to Franco themselves; they took the lead in arraying on his side women of the other classes over whom they could exert influence. Women leaders appealed to the women of the religious orders, they raised money for Falangist armies, they marched in processions, they did every kind of "women's war work," and at the end they joined in celebrating the victory of the military dictator, the Church, and the landlords over the Republic and its loyal supporters.

As in Russia, Italy, and Spain, so the revolution in Germany dominated by Adolf Hitler attained its full force through an alliance of men and women around the flag — in this case the swastika. In the beginning, when Roehm, Bäumler, and other veterans of the first world war joined Hitler, likewise a veteran of that war, there was lusty boasting by German men, so recently young soldiers in trenches, to the effect that a cyclopean masculine demonstration of force would show the world how raw brutality could play havoc with soft refinement. A men's band *(Männerbund)* was proclaimed as in process of seizing all power in Germany — proclaimed in speeches, in books, and in egoistic male programs for action. But Hitler himself soon instigated a murderous purge of men of that species and perfected plans for mobilizing women to abet his dictatorship at home and aggression abroad.

Equally with Lenin, Mussolini, and Franco, Hitler understood the force of women as an imperative in achieving and establishing a revolution. This fact Goebbels recorded in his *Diary* on March 29, 1932, with reference to a meeting of party leaders at Berchtesgaden, assembled to plan propaganda for the coming political campaign. During their all-night session, a major event took place: "In the evening the Leader developed entirely new ideas over our attitude to woman. These ideas are of the highest importance for the next electoral campaign, for it is just in that field that we were hardest hit in the first elections." Hitler's new ideas were to preach that "Woman is the companion of man in work. . . . She has always been so and always will be. . . . Formerly in the furrows, now in the offices. Man is the organizer of life, woman is his organ for carrying out plans. This conception is modern and lifts us toweringly above all the deutschvölkische Ressentiment."

To make his revolution thrive Hitler offered special rewards to the German women "of the blood" who were in a peculiar position in 1933 as members of a society that had been defeated in a frightful war. He assured such women, if unmarried, that he would provide them with husbands; and apparently they longed for husbands until they got them and found that they were soldiers primarily desirous of an eternal supply of soldiers. He also promised them shelter — at least a two-room apartment for family life — and many women, lacking even that small amount of shelter, closed their minds to the possibility that he was a dangerous demagogue, a charlatan, who could blast their hopes and ruin their country if given their aid and comfort.

Women had helped Hitler up every step of the ladder to his absolute dictatorship. When he was a penniless veteran, Helena Bechstein, wife of a rich piano maker in Berlin, supplied him with money for his organizing plans. She "mothered" the uncouth veteran of the late war, instilled in him a confidence in his own inherent genius, and introduced him to persons who could help him financially, politically, and socially. He called her "mother," and relied on her for protection. Other women early contributed to his war chest. Among them was Frau Gertrud von Seidlitz, a manufacturer, who not only gave him money of her own but got more for him from her friends in Finland. "Little Doctor" Goebbels reported in his *Vom Kaiserhof zur Reichskanzlei*, a story of Hitler's rise to power, that on January 11, 1932, "the Women's Division *(Frauenschaft)* has undertaken the financing of our coming campaigns. Within the briefest time, it will get together 50,000 marks. With that we should be solvent again."

Cosima Wagner increased his social acceptability by her personal favors. His popularity was enhanced by flaming feminine orators and writers who accepted his version of himself as a messenger of God to the German people. The votes of women were an important factor in his rise to political power. Organized in a woman's fighting band *(Frauenkampfbund),* at the behest of Hitler, clamant women shouted that they were ready, in effect, to bleed and die if need be for their Führer.

Guida Diehl, Hitler's prime evangelist, pleaded with women to remember that "the true German woman is a fighter, and a fighter out of mother love"! She recalled to them their great ancestress, Brunhild, "the woman in armor," heroine of the Nibelungenlied, who had taken up the blood revenge and was determined to pursue it to the end though it might slay all her kinsmen.

In her volume, *Die Deutsche Frau und der National Sozialismus (The German Woman and National Socialism),* Guida Diehl said in 1933: "Never did Hitler promise to the masses in his rousing speeches any material advantage whatever. On the contrary he pleaded with them to turn aside from every form of advantage-seeking and serve the great thought: Honor, Freedom, Fatherland! In his success is shown the power of great divine truths.... For us women it was almost unendurable to see the weakness of manhood in the last decades. Therefore the outbreak of the War was, despite all the hardships, a great experience for us: the upheaval of 1914 was a powerful breaking through of heroic manhood. All the more fearful to us was the breakdown. Then we called to German men: 'We implore you, German Men, among whom we have seen and admired so much heroic courage.... We long to see Men and Heroes who scorn fate.... Call us to every service, even to weapons!' "

Guida Diehl's ecstatic partisanship with Hitler and her incitement to violence were matched by many other women speakers and writers. Lydia Gottschewski marshaled her sex furiously on the side of militant men in 1934, in a book called *Die Frau im Neuen Staat (Women in the New State).* "It is a curious fact," she declared, "that pacifism ... is a mark of an age weak in faith, whereas the people of religious times have honored war as God's rod of chastisement. . . . Only the age of enlightenment has wished to decide the great questions of world history at the table of diplomats. . . . As far as this fight [of masculine solidarity among the Nazis to arouse the war spirit among men] attacked the old feminism it was rightful and healthy." And the utmost right, she went on to say, was to recover "the soul fight-readiness of the whole people" and fulfill the radiant promise that "heavy-lipped people will sing the holiest song."

To this passionate movement of German men and women, some of the most influential feminists gave more than countenance: gave their frank support. Feminism in Germany had as its background the liberal ideals of the French Revolution: liberty, equality, and fraternity. It derived its spirit and its objective largely from that revolt against despotism. But after Napoleon turned the Revolution to imperialist power, German women in general joined German men in fighting the war of liberation from his mastery. This experience had taught them the meaning of nationalism and in this lesson they had veered toward a worship of State power — of Statism. Thus the tradition was strong when the Nazis rewarmed it in their definition of a new German crisis and their design for meeting it.

It is true that German women were direct colleagues of German men in setting up the Weimar Republic at the end of the first world war. But for various reasons it collapsed and then the Nazis ordered all feminist organizations, such as the business and professional women's federation, with their liberal bent, to disband by their own action or face suppression. They did disband, and the liberal movement was seriously weakened by the wedge driven between women "of the blood" and Jewish women who had hitherto been co-members of groups associated with that movement. Though women "of the blood" did not go over en masse by any means to Hitler and his party, though they suffered martyrdom in large numbers, the desertion of the woman movement as a liberal movement or a socialist movement — it branched off in two directions — helped to shape German destiny.

This left the field wider open of course for Hitler's contention, expressed in his address to women at Nürnberg, September 14, 1934, that "Woman has her battlefield. With each child that she brings to the nation, she fights her fight for the nation." Such women as Sophie Rogge-Boerner, who called for the military training of women in the interest of recovering the old Nordic folk-rights, which made no discrimination in respect of sex and war and were in keeping with the Brunhildic tradition, were suppressed by Hitler and Goebbels in favor of women who devoted their strength and interest to child-bearing. Young women in large numbers responded enthusiastically to indoctrination on this point and entered the numerous maternity homes founded by the Nazis to promote this service, just as young men responded to indoctrination of the kind given to them. Undoubtedly countless girls who became mothers in this system were sheer victims, not volunteers. But this phase of woman's part in the German revolution cannot be ignored on that ground.

Spectacular and utterly ruthless was a country doctor's wife, Gertrud Scholtz Klink, who had been prominent in circles of feminists. She was so successful as an organizer and "fighter" in spirit that she became one of the mightiest of the Nazis. Her blond hair and general personality, combined with her zealotry as a true Nazi, brought acclaim from Hitler, who called her the perfect type of German woman. By 1941 she was governing some thirty million German women and tightening her grip on some twenty million other women in lands occupied by German troops. The dictatorial authority of this "Lady Führer über Alles" was vividly described by Peter Engelmann in an article in *The Living Age* of October, 1940, and afterward condensed for publication in the *Reader's Digest*. "Frau Klink," wrote Engelmann, "rules the lives of women in all things. She tells them how many children they must have, and when; what they shall wear, what they shall cook, and how. What they shall say, laughing, to their husbands and sons marching to war. How they shall behave, smiling, when their men are killed. Here is the responsibilty for home spirit, the core of national morale."

Engelmann could speak with authority. He had been an editor of *Deutsche Allgemeine Zeitung*, a leading German daily, before his flight from the Nazis on account of his "mixed" blood. He had watched the Women's Front *(Frauenfront)* as it began to take form, and indeed had been offered a position as her publicity agent by Frau Klink, but this he refused. It was his opinion that the "chief agency of Gertrud Scholtz Klink's power" was an "élite corps of 50,000 zealous Nazi women — the *Frauenschaft*." Long after Engelmann had been driven into exile, Frau Klink continued to gather and exercise power until at last in April, 1945, with the end of Hitler and the Nazi dictatorship in sight, according to the press report she committed suicide in Constance.

With the rise of the Axis Powers in Europe, and especially after the outbreak of war seemed imminent in Europe, American women began to manifest their will to influence the shaping of American foreign policy. By the millions they accepted the major premise, advanced by advocates of a "strong" policy, that the triumph of those Powers in Europe would mean ultimate doom for the United States; that the European war was, therefore, at bottom "our war." Women had long been prominent in the various organizations which carried on propaganda for the League of Nations. Many branded American neutrality even in time of war an evasion of moral responsibility. When the war clouds began to gather on the European horizon, those women concentrated on the advocacy of "collective security" — American participation in an international combination against aggressors.

When the war got under way in Europe in 1939, American women in huge numbers, through their national organizations and as members of special committees and associations, bent their energies to pressing for the adoption of national measures designed to supply the Powers aligned against the Axis with munitions and other sinews of war. Women were in the forefront of the agitations and activities directed to the repeal of the neutrality legislation, the enactment of the Lend-Lease law in 1941, and other bills, all called measures "short of war," though calculated by many of their promoters to put the economic and material forces of the United States actually into the war against the Axis Powers.

Late in 1941 measures short of war merged into war on the part of the United States itself. Then American women by the millions voluntarily enlisted in the service of the war on the home front and on the distant battle fronts in the European and the Asiatic theaters. They were taken into the armed forces, placed in uniform, disciplined by officers of their own sex working under military and naval authorities, accorded official ranking, honored with decorations for bravery under fire, and granted compensation according to their respective gradations of service. To release men for fighting, thousands of uniformed women substituted as secretaries, clerks, and officials. With skill and courage women served as doctors and nurses in the battle areas and in war hospitals at home; and many were killed at the fronts while working near or under fire.

In all the drives to float war loans and to raise money in aid of the armed services, women assumed leadership and served in the ranks. They labored to uphold the morale of the services at home and abroad. They toured the war areas and fronts as entertainers of the men under arms. Though not called upon to take up arms themselves or serve as guerrillas, the fighting being outside their country, they engaged in nearly all other forms of war work performed by women whose countries lay in or near the war zones. American women by the millions entered the war-production plants and made possible the output of munitions and other war supplies on a scale that astounded the whole industrial world.

"It's a Woman's War, Too" was the title of a column run in the Sunday issues of *The New York Times*.

That all the activities, agitations, tumults, and dislocations connected with "women at war" had evoked immense political excitement became evident as the time for the presidential election of 1944 approached. Were the Roosevelt policies, domestic and foreign, to be endorsed or rejected at the polls? And in terms of women's interests, what new was to be demanded for them in politics? Such questions were posed in every form of opinion, including the household and the street.

When the national campaign opened, politicians, male and female, understood that a new stage in the facts and opinions of the man-woman relationships had been reached; and politicians, who always have their ears to the ground, sensitively registered the seismic disturbances of the hour. Whether women were rejoicing in new adventures or felt frustrated by real or imagined grievances, they had the outcome of the election largely in their keeping, for they held in their hands the most votes—a number estimated at sixty or sixty-five per cent of the total voting power. And men, whether they felt cramped or free, knew this as a hard reality. But with what upshot? Would a feminine bloc appear and prove decisive in determining the results of the election, with all their implications for the fate and fortunes of the nation? Would voting women take their cue from men's plans? Would they merely reflect class and income-group alignments? Or would a serious number of voting women display indifference and remain away from the polls, letting their political power lapse?

At the conventions of both major parties women delegates were in attendance by the hundreds. Women held positions in all important committees, delivered keynote addresses, and shared in maneuvers behind the scenes. Women as women were recognized in platform pledges and acceptance speeches. With all the campaign committees and organizations, high and low, women were associated. Women were leaders and joiners in efforts to round up voters for their respective party tickets. Special appeals were made in platforms and campaign literature to interests regarded as "peculiarly feminine," as well as those common to men and women. Throughout the land politicians, male and female, spread the cry: "Get out the women or we are lost!"

When the ballots were counted, it was impossible to discover just where the weight of women's influence had fallen or how their influence had been distributed. The American way of keeping political records did not permit such knowledge. But one thing was certain. While the majority accorded to President Roosevelt was relatively smaller than it had been in 1940, he was granted a fourth term, and his policies—foreign and domestic—received an overwhelming endorsement. Contrary to predictions of many army and navy officers in previous years, American women had not become pacifists. In the main they agreed with men: that the war must go on in full force until the enemies were crushed. And their active support was proclaimed indispensable.

The cataclysmic character of this segment of a century was registered widely and deeply in every phase of economic, intellectual, and moral life. Nothing like it, in scale and intensity, had ever taken place before in the history of humanity. Not even the collapse of the Roman Empire nor the eighteenth-century social earthquakes in America and Europe were comparable to this one. Economic and political dislocations affected the highest and lowest social levels of societies in all parts of the world. The demands upon life, blood, and property became almost universally despotic. The entire population of the earth was thrown into a revolutionary turmoil.

What was and is to be the significance of this upheaval for the relations of men and women? Any answer devised, if based on knowledge, depends upon probabilities difficult to discern or imagine. If the United States should return to an economy predominantly civilian, designed to serve civilian needs and interests primarily, and another crisis in unemployment occurred, what would happen to wage-earning and salaried women? If conscription were adopted as a permanent policy and national energies were dedicated to preparations for the contingencies of another world war, the relations of men and women, economic and marital, would certainly assume forms novel to American experience. In any case, the horizon of the future was scanned with anxiety.

Professedly, American men and women alike in general hoped for a return to civilian life, and this meant a heated debate in the United States over public policies to be adopted with reference to "equality of rights" in the distribution of employments, in the competition for places and rewards in economy and society. While it was recognized that women had met heavy obligations in war production and services, while men and women both took pride in the war work of women, the very featuring of women's force and interest in the Global War reopened, in ways unprecedented, the old debate over women's "place" in society and their significance in history. Indeed the close association of men and women in war industry and in war itself added intensity to the discussion of the man-woman relationships to be retained, reshaped, or revolutionized after the war. As always the future shadowed the present.

This was recognized by the War Department. When in 1944, under the authority of the United States Government, it issued its program and booklets of instruction for the education of soldiers at round-table forums, it included one manual sharpened as if by a razor edge to invite a pointed argument: "Do you want your wife to work after the war?" In this suggestion for a warriors' discussion one side was represented by the contention that times have changed, that it is good and fitting for women to work, that they are competent in all kinds of jobs, hanker after economic independence, and are likely to hang on to a cash nexus for dear life. On the other side the argument against this thesis maintained that woman's place is in the home, that her function is child-bearing and rearing, and that men will not stand for her competition with returned veterans. Evidently the United States army felt that it could not omit from the "education" of the American soldier a reminder of woman's existence in relation to his postwar life and employment.

While men under arms were being encouraged to think of women as competitors, civilians were invited to listen to radio broadcasts, roaring from day to day, week to week, month to month, allegations, declarations, findings, and contentions pertinent to man-woman issues. Through the air sociologists, economists, and reformers, men and women alike, sped their winged words into this verbal contest. By a simple movement of the fingers the great debate came to cabins far from towns, as it came to urban tenements and fine dwellings.

Into cottages and palaces news of the events registered in the great Global War penetrated on sheets of paper — with the daily newspapers, magazines, and books. In their columns and pages were materials dealing with the heroism of men and women amid the exigencies of killing and dying — the legend of war being renewed and intensified by stories of its fantastic current impacts. The vast world beyond the desk, the hearth, the filing case, the blackboard, the professorial chair, the store counter, and the plough or poultry yard was made so vibrant with life unknown in quiet places that the desire to see and be a part of that vaster world seized the minds of countless routineers. The spirit of unrest spread to little schoolhouses, as boys and girls of the most secluded mountain notches and desert wastes caught glimpses of a world they had never imagined to exist outside their story books of Christopher Columbus. The lurid sex pictures in the press heightened the emotions of adolescent youngsters and filled them with longing to break away from the mores of their customary surroundings and escape to the allurements of the cities, the seas, the places beyond the seas where life seemed so abundant in diversities and excitements.

Girls literally in hordes decided that they could live the life of adventure, and by hook or by crook they flocked to war agencies asking for chances to enjoy a run around. If flight to the cities or from the cities to adventures elsewhere could not be managed, they could find it romantically in village movie palaces where sex and war were deliriously united, and made even more delirious than pictures, by "The Voice" crooning to them and orchestras beating out for them the rhythms of emotional ecstasy, or calls to the wild.

Youths of both sexes still privileged to attend colleges were shaken by the repercussions of the Global War and its attendant rising debate over men and women in bounds or out of bounds. Every subject in the collegiate curriculum helped to foment this debate. The purposes of education itself received a more critical examination than ever before in American history. Should men and women be educated alike? Or differently? If alike, for what end? If differently, in what respects?

Many blunt-spoken men decried the whole discussion, while they augmented it by declaring that they, not women, belonged to a subject sex loaded down with family cares and the necessity of toiling long hours and years for wages or incomes from which they received little or nothing for their personal use. If men of this temper were inclined to be imaginative, they added that they might have been "great" if it had not been for their wives and dependents for whom they had to drudge. Or if endowed with dreams of genius they could see themselves as a Henry James, a Leonardo, or a John D. Rockefeller, save for lack of proper support by women dependent upon them or lack of insight on the part of wives unable to assist in raising them to such eminence. Yet, unlike aggrieved women, they could find no consolation in the thought that an amendment to the Constitution of the United States would clear away the barriers and bring their utopia into immediate realization.

In the march of time and of debate on this theme of man and woman, the immensely popular magazine *Life* undertook an affirmation, January 29, 1945, in a full-page editorial. Said the editors: "Of all the social revolutions now abroad in the world, that of the [American] women is the least dynamic, the least predictable, the most aimless and divided — in short the most feminine." A question was propounded: "Are American women still earning the world's respect?" The editors answered the question in this fashion: "It may be doubted. As a class, they are today themselves the greatest obstacle to their own advancement.... They are simply ridiculous."

Why? Enlightenment was offered by *Life:* "American women have forgotten how women helped to create America and brought their sex worldwide prestige." The editors refrained from explaining that historians in general had failed to remind men and women about the work of the women who helped to create America. Without dwelling upon that history themselves, they resorted to quotations from Philip Wylie's *Generation of Vipers* and Amram Scheinfeld's *Women and Men,* two new books of the period.

According to Wylie, "Mom" has become a "jerk." According to Scheinfeld, woman, a simple child of nature, has been allowed by man's chivalry "rooted in his nature" to become as dependent as her natural disposition tends to make her. So men must exercise authority over women. How? "Draft them," said *Life,* and "we may come to it yet." Meanwhile it is "too bad that we can't draft their grandmothers," since living women are in such a bad state.

Many national women's organizations had been urging conscription in some form for women. But many women might regard a draft as slavery and the editors of *Life* tried to meet that objection. "To intelligent women," they went on, "a draft is not a move to enslave them. On the contrary, it would be a milestone in an age-long progress: their emancipation." A short time afterward Mrs. Eleanor Roosevelt issued a special call for a draft of women and proposed that all women up to the age of sixty-three be included in it.

Certainly the man-woman interest was being advertised everywhere, by means of every medium. Certainly all discussions of human affairs involved it, explicitly or implicitly.

Certainly special and ominous significance was given to the future of man-woman relationships by the mounting preponderance of women over men in Europe and the United States, as measured in numbers. Estimates were admittedly tentative in 1945 but they indicated that there were from eight to ten million more women than men in Soviet Russia; three million more women than men in Great Britain; approximately five women to three men in Germany; and in the neighborhood of a million more women than men in the United States. In any case the numerical superiority of women was large enough to arouse alarms and speculations as to its probable effects on the family and every other phase of sex relations in the years at hand.

Chapter 2

Attitudes of Women

IN THE democratic republic of the United States, where free speech and a free press were cherished as vital manifestations of its political principles, what views were women expressing about the relations of men and women during the long period in which revolutions and two world wars were tearing old societies asunder? What were the prevailing winds of their opinions respecting revolution or gradual evolution, war and peace, the force of arms and the force of character, the common enterprises of men and women, and their distinctive tastes and purposes? Since speech, whether censored or free, makes use of ideas and is affected by ideas, vaguely formulated or clearly defined, what were the ideas that appeared in the views and opinions of women? Every intelligent and comprehensive endeavor to advance knowledge pertaining to the man-woman relationship must be preceded by or opened with an inquiry into the stock of ideas or theories with which that relationship is discussed by women and by men representing various types of articulated activity.

When in 1944 political feminists associated with the National Woman's Party conducted the campaign which forced the two major political parties to endorse a proposal to establish equal rights for women by Federal amendment, they used as a lever an assertion on the nature and history of man-woman relations made by M. Carey Thomas. Miss Thomas had been dead for several years but her spirit still charged this party with the determination to right what it believed to be historic wrongs. Miss Thomas had been no light-hearted journalist, free and easy with speech and unlearned in the lore of men's universities. She had studied long and zealously at Cornell University and in Europe. She held the high degree, Doctor of Philosophy, won *summa cum laude* at Leipzig. From 1894 to 1922 she presided over the education of young women at Bryn Mawr College. In her time she had been widely acclaimed as a scholar and as a leader in "the progress of women."

And this was her theory of the man-woman relationship in the past, her interpretation of it in long history: "Women are born, living their lives, and dying without the justice which they have been waiting for since the time of the caveman. . . . Forever behind a woman is the mediaeval English common law which places upon her the stigma of inferiority and bondage."

In an address, delivered before the North American Woman Suffrage Association at Buffalo, in October, 1908, Miss Thomas declared: "The true objection to woman suffrage lies far deeper than any argument. Giving women the ballot is the visible sign and symbol of a stupendous social revolution and before it we are afraid. Women are one-half of the world but until a century ago the world of music and painting and sculpture and literature and scholarship and science was a man's world. The world of trades and professions and of work of all kinds was a man's world. Women lived a twilight life, a half-life apart, and looked out and saw men as shadows walking. It was a man's world. The laws were man's laws, the government a man's government, the country a man's country. . . . The man's world must become a man's and a woman's world. Why are we afraid? It is the next step forward on the path toward the sunrise, and the sun is rising over a new heaven and a new earth."

A similar idea colored Miss Thomas' formal pronouncements on "progress" in education for women. Speaking to collegiate alumnae at Boston on November 6, 1907, she referred to her early fear that women, long deprived of higher education, might not be able to master the Greek language, for instance, or have the physical hardihood to go through the rigors of college and university training. In taking this line she overlooked the fact that in the middle ages a multitude of women, in Italy and other parts of Europe, had achieved distinguished scholarship in Greek and Latin learning; and she was apparently unaware that many American women, in colonial times and for years before colleges were opened to them, had displayed the capacity to master classical learning and use it in their writings.

Ignoring such chapters in the intellectual history of women, Miss Thomas assumed that competition with men in the whole curriculum of higher learning was also a biological test — a test of women's physical power. When she discovered in the course of her college presidency that young women could "take" young men's education and come through with flying colors, she was exuberant. This was for Miss Thomas evidence that women were by nature equals of men in such important respects and were winning some justice, if slowly, at the hands of the autocratic male. Modeling educational programs for women after man's programs was a sign of "progress" for his historic slaves.

Dr. M. Carey Thomas' view of women "since the time of the caveman" received substantial support in respect of "education" by one of her younger contemporaries, Elizabeth K. Adams. The confirmation was presented in an essay on women's education published in *A Cyclopedia of Education,* the last volume of which appeared in 1913. At the time Miss Adams was professor of psychology and education at Smith College. She held the degree of Bachelor of Arts from Vassar College and the degree of Doctor of Philosophy from the University of Chicago. Before her call to Smith, she had served as a teacher at Vassar and in the College for Women in Western Reserve University. To Dr. Adams was assigned by the editor of the *Cyclopedia,* Professor Paul Munroe, the task of writing the article on the higher education of women, a historical sketch.

Conforming to the frame of reference set by the editor, like other authors of articles in this *Cyclopedia* Dr. Adams conceived education almost entirely in terms of formal instruction in schools and the educated person in terms of the formal learning acquired under professional educators. Thus a narrow circle was drawn about education and from that circle was excluded everything and everybody who did not come within the fixed pattern of training. According to that test, relatively little education had existed before the modern age and relatively few women could now be regarded as educated. This tight rule was not without exceptions but they received curt notice in Dr. Adams' essay.

The history of women's "education" in Greek and Roman antiquity Dr. Adams disposed of very briefly. "No part of the history of education," she wrote, "is so obscure as that of the education of girls. This obscurity is itself suggestive that little is known because there is little to know." Without attempting to indicate the original sources from which knowledge of the subject, such as it is, might have been gathered, she said of Greece: "Our educational institutions and practices descend from Greece *(q. v.)*. In Ionian Hellas it seems to have been an accepted dogma that no respectable girl was educated; education, including a knowledge of music, singing, poetry, and the power of conversation, was left to the *Hetæræ*. See Greece, Education in."

The author of the article on education in ancient Greece, J. P. Mahaffy, D.D., to whom Dr. Adams referred her readers for further information, likewise disposed of women in a few swift strokes: "If nothing has been said about the education of girls, it is only because nothing is known about it. Xenophon represents a bride coming into her husband's house, having lived her youth in darkness and in fear, knowing nothing but how to adorn her person and that artificially, with powder and rouge, and with enhancements of dress. The Spartan women brought up in great liberty, and freed from the strict discipline of the men, are spoken of now as specimens of bravery and patriotism, now as turbulent and mischievous to the peace and order of the state. But except that they trained openly like the boys, we know nothing of their education."

Having curtly dismissed women in ancient Greece, Dr. Adams did the same for women in ancient Rome. "At Rome," she wrote, "on the other hand, it has been positively asserted that girls received the same education as boys and attended the same schools. But the assertion is an absolute contradiction to the whole attitude of Roman law and Roman thought to women. If, however, little girls did go to the grammar schools, these were little more than preparatory schools up to thirteen or fourteen years old. . . . Some women undoubtedly were well educated, like Cornelia. . . . But it is significantly added that she was not a prig. . . . The absolute absence in Quintilian of any reference to the education of girls may be taken as conclusive that as a rule they were not educated. . . . The female philosophy lecturer, Hypatia *(q. v.)*, seems to have been a solitary phenomenon, and it is on record that she was taught by her father, himself a professor."

Although, as she came up to modern times in the history of women's education, Dr. Adams dealt with widening opportunities for women, she in effect declared that from the time of the caveman until the fall of Rome the brand of ignorance and inferiority had been stamped on women. Unintentionally perhaps, or limited by the concept of formal education, she gave the net impression that for thousands of years women had neither received nor achieved an education, as if their intellectual life, apart from the household arts, had been close to or actually at zero.

The monumental work in which Dr. Adams' article appeared, edited by a professor of Education in Teachers College, Columbia University, was for a long time a powerful instrument in the training of American teachers, the overwhelming majority of whom were women. The library of no normal school was complete without the *Cyclopedia*. It quickly became the first work of ready reference for school superintendents, principals, and classroom teachers as well as students of education in general. Probably no other single treatise of the period did more to provide the materials and theories employed by educational leaders and thinkers for a whole generation.

Another leading educator at the opening of the twentieth century, Mrs. Emily James Putnam, while a bit wary of the unqualified subjection theory, was inclined to the opinion that, with the development of wealth and refinements, women had acquired a fixed penchant for an easy life, if not dependency — especially women of the upper class. Mrs. Putnam was a scholar trained especially in classical literature and had an especial interest in Greek writing. Indeed she taught Greek literature and history before and after her services as dean of Barnard College from 1894 to 1900. Relishing Lucian, selections from whose works she translated and published in

1892, she allowed a little humor to lighten the gravity of her volume on *The Lady,* issued in 1910. In this portrayal of the grande dame from ancient times, through the middle ages, and up into the ante-bellum period of American history, Mrs. Putnam claimed, however, that there had been a rigid biological determinism and corresponding psychological response in the Lady's relation to the Gentleman.

Without going far into the documents bearing on woman in the most primitive times, Mrs. Putnam insisted on "the uncontrovertible fact of physical subjection." Whatever may have been the state of women in the earliest days of human beginnings, Mrs. Putnam said that "by degrees the woman's enforced specialisation of function affected her both physically and psychologically."

From the cautious word "affected," Mrs. Putnam moved into more deterministic language: "Her stature, weight and muscular strength became ever more noticeably less than those of the man, and to his explosive mental action she opposed her illimitable patience. As the ground of gentility came to lie more and more in superior prowess, exerted gradually not only upon women but upon the weaker men, it must have seemed to the sociologists of early barbarism that woman with her confessed and growing physical inferiority was debarred forever from the gentle class. She had it is true certain moral holds upon the veneration of the group, based chiefly on her relation to the occult and her mysterious connection with nature as the source of life. And when the gentility of the strong man became hereditary, his daughter had a theoretical share in it. But these psychological claims to social distinction for the woman were always checked by the uncontrovertible fact of physical subjection. There was no thinkable way in which the woman could emancipate herself. . . . It must have seemed to her then that the only escape from drudgery, which after all was within her strength, lay through violence and exploit which by this time were beyond it. Until changing economic conditions made the thing actually happen, struggling early society could hardly have guessed that woman's road to gentility would lie through doing nothing at all."

The theory that women had been members of a subject sex throughout long history, but coupled with a plan for their emancipation by socialism or communism, found expression with increasing force in the United States as the twentieth century advanced. Among the women who expounded this theory of woman none was more influential than Charlotte Perkins Stetson who long before her death in 1935 attained national and international fame as an exponent of a new feminism. Hampered by poverty during her youth and young womanhood, she educated herself by extensive reading in anthropology, sociology, and economics, while she supported herself by teaching art and painting advertising cards and trinkets. In her writings she ranged from light, humorous verse and witty narrative poetry, through articles gravely gay and wholly serious books, to novels. Captivated by Edward Bellamy's *Looking Backward,* published in 1888, Mrs. Stetson discovered in idealistic socialism what she deemed the clue to the emancipation of women and joined the disciples of Bellamy. Henceforward, with growing stress, she dwelt on the economic aspects of the "woman question."

Mrs. Stetson's first volume was a collection of poems, *In This Our World,* later enlarged and reissued. Her first treatise on women appeared in 1898 — *Woman and Economics* — received immediate interest, was translated into at least six foreign languages including Hungarian and Japanese, and marked her rapid rise to intellectual leadership in the woman movement.

In swift succession other volumes flowed from Mrs. Stetson's pen. These included *Concerning Children; The Home, Its Work and Influence; Human Work; The Man-Made World; His Religion and Hers;* and finally an autobiography issued after her death. So impressed by her writings was W. D. Howells as early as 1902 that he declared: "She has enriched the literary center of New York by the addition of a talent in sociological satire which would be extraordinary even if it were not altogether unrivaled among us." In 1909, several years after her second marriage, to George H. Gilman of New York, Mrs. Gilman founded an unique magazine, *The Forerunner,* and for seven years served as editor, sole contributor, and publisher.

Her belief in woman's long subjection to man was embodied in the following lines, quoted from a poem in her collection entitled *In This Our World:*

Close, close he bound her, that she should leave him never.
Weak still he kept her, lest she be strong to flee;
And the fainting flame of passion he kept alive forever
With all the arts and forces of earth and sky and sea.

But the future could be different, she believed. It had been and was woman's economic dependence on man that kept her in thrall. This was Mrs. Gilman's contention, especially, in *Woman and Economics.*

Hence, she concluded, woman — especially the mother as guardian of the social spirit in social evolution — when freed from economic bondage to her mate would achieve liberty and make her "culture" and *her* "religion" prevail over *his* culture and *his* religion. And this economic freedom was to be won through various economic institutions of a collectivist nature, especially a form of cooperative living that would ease, if not abolish, the home drudgery of woman.

To the old doctrine, so often advanced by parsons and laymen, that "woman's place is in the home," Mrs. Gilman opposed the doctrine that woman's place is in community and public life. In a poem on the assumption of male prerogatives, she stated the case in boasting words by the male:

I sing to the wide world
And she to the nest.

But Mrs. Gilman did not deride singing to the nest. She approved it and gave it social significance. She proposed, however, that henceforward there should be a common singing to the wide world, her idea being that such singing had been done by man alone.

Conservatives, on their part, asserted that the change could not be made; that it was against human nature. In a long narrative poem, "Similar Cases," Mrs. Gilman satirized resistance to change from the days of the anthropoidal ape — the burden of the lay being the old cry: "Why! you'd have to change your nature! . . . The thing cannot be done." This poem was widely enjoyed. It became a favorite of Woodrow Wilson, who in 1912 capitalized upon the progressive and socialist movements and became President of the United States.

Mrs. Gilman made much of the biological argument in framing her program for women and with considerable ingenuity affiliated it with economics, on the solid ground that life, whatever its nature, must be sustained by economic operations. But instead of accepting biological factors as inescapable determinants she maintained, in line with the teachings of her philosophic friend, Lester F. Ward the sociologist, that the human mind could control economic environment by social inventions and thus give wholly different expressions to many primary aspects of biological force.

To the tumult of talking and writing about superiorities and inferiorities of men and women, all keyed to concepts of progress or backwardness on the part of women, Olga Knopf brought opinions plainly influenced by the psychological theories of Dr. Alfred Adler of Vienna. Dr. Knopf came to New York from Vienna and in her adopted city she taught and wrote about women. In *The Art of Being a Woman,* published in 1932, she opened with a chapter on women in past and present cultures, in which she displayed her fidelity to the popular doctrine that woman had long been subordinate to man in the eyes of the law. Then she commented on the "surprising change" that had taken place in "the past fifty years," making women "in almost every Western nation" legally equal with men, on paper.

Nevertheless, she found that "the sexes are living, we might say, in a vast communal neurosis; a highly contagious neurosis which parents pass on to their children and men and women pass on to each other."

Was there a remedy? Certainly — in personal character, in "individual psychology." "I am no feminist myself," Dr. Knopf assured the public. "The freedom that women claim can only come when men and women realize in their hearts that they are equal and that their interests in this world are common interests.... Many feminists, naturally enough, have made the mistake of arguing that women are equal to men because they are superior to them; and many anti-feminists have replied, still less logically, that because women are superior they are inferior."

Dr. Knopf advocated a release from the "vast communal neurosis" by psychiatric treatment. "Health is as contagious as neurosis" if it can be attained, she said. "The art of being a woman can never consist in being a bad imitation of a man. It can consist only in being equal, independent, and cooperative; in understanding human nature and human capacities and in applying the knowledge first of all to oneself." In an effort to aid this understanding she drew to some extent on historical materials, indicating variations in the power of males and females in times and places and the similarity of power among the ancient Egyptians. Character, in short, could be in some measure developed by knowledge or thought of history.

In 1935, however, Dr. Knopf revealed what seemed to be a distinctly feminist leaning which relied less on individual psychology and more on social legislation directed to economic equality between the sexes. This trend was patent in her new book, *Women on Their Own,* in which she said: "A few years ago one could easily have taken it for granted that the battle of the 'independent woman' would end in success. . . . It is not quite so easy now to be optimistic over the progress of women. One is bound to feel that those advances are not yet stable. . . . The outer limitations to women's progress are caused by the fact that we are living in a man's culture."

Dr. Maude Glasgow, trained in medicine and a successful practitioner in New York, voiced a similar opinion respecting the long subjection of women, but expressed it in a more emphatic form, one akin to that of Dr. M. Carey Thomas. In her book, *The Subjection of Women and the Traditions of Men,* published in 1940, Dr. Glasgow presented her view of woman in history in this categorical statement: "For more than six thousand years the history of woman has been one of helpless sadness. She moved only to the clank of chains, and her vain desire for better and higher things could not find expression, for woman was by force of circumstances inarticulate. Detraction of one sex and exaltation of the other became a habit of mind expressed in law, in religion, in literature as well as in the ordinary activities of everyday life."

Yet Dr. Glasgow assumed that there had been a golden age for woman in the prehistoric past: "When new-born humanity was learning to stand upright, it depended much on its mother and stood close to her protecting side. Then women were goddesses, they conducted divine worship, woman's voice was heard in council, she was loved and revered and genealogies were reckoned through her."

What broke into this feminine Elysium and robbed it of liberty and happiness? The male of the species. "As the race grew older, rationality flourished at the expense of moral sense." It was irrational to esteem and appreciate the mother? Seemingly it was: "Man, unmindful of the mother's contribution to racial uplift and welfare, thought only of bending every energy and forcing tribute from everything and every one who could elevate himself and give him dominating power. So from the blubber consuming Esquimaux to the dusky Madagascar chief whose feet must be licked by his wives, and to the repulsive Kalmuck with his gray flat sinister face who beats his wife to submission, all demand that woman must always remain, figuratively speaking, on her knees and look up in fear and dread to this self-made god drowned in ignorance and superstition."

It was not merely in addresses by women trained in universities and holding academic positions or positions in other professions nor in books offered to a few thousand readers that the man-woman issue was discussed by American women. The issue was taken to that larger forum represented by the popular magazines and there it was turned round and round by writers whose names commanded attention. Through these journals, deliberately catering to "live" interests, thousands of readers scattered far and wide were drawn into the man-woman debate.

After publishing her novel on China, *The Good Earth,* which received the Nobel Prize, Pearl Buck, in articles, as well as books, frequently dealt with men and women in the Occident. In the summer of 1938 she announced through the pages of *Harper's* magazine that American women were really mediaeval women in their philosophy of life and ways of life. Where did she acquire this idea of contemporary American women? Naturally, from her notion of mediaeval women, coupled with her experiences as a successful author invited to the homes of prosperous business men and leisured wives. At all events, moving in that circle, she heard men cast aspersions on women and found that women resented the practice. After a time Mrs. Buck came to the conclusion that such women deserved some if not all the anathemas hurled at them, because they did not press out into the big world, compete vigorously with men, test their capacities, and show the people what they could do.

But Mrs. Buck's strictures on women and her ideal for them did not pass without resolute comment. In an article published by *Harper's* the next year a scolding was undertaken by Grace Adams, Doctor of Philosophy from Cornell University and specialist in psychology. The title of Dr. Adams' article, "American Women Are Coming Along," indicated her qualifications, but a certain amount of approval for Mrs. Buck's theory appeared in the substance of the article. The imaginary point or status in time from which women were "coming along" was evidently that described by Mary Wollstonecraft and by the American women and men of 1848 who, at their convention in Seneca Falls, proclaimed the historic subjection of women. Still there were evidences, Dr. Adams thought, that women had not come very far along.

"Whenever serious intellectuals," she wrote, "psychologists, sociologists, practicing physicians, Nobel Prize novelists — take time off from their normal pursuits to scrutinize and appraise the Modern American Woman they turn in unanimously dreary reports. They find her uninformed, intellectually lazy, lacking in ambition, and disgustingly docile in the presence of dominating males." While admitting that some of these criticisms of woman were warranted, Miss Adams then confessed "a sneaking suspicion that the intellectuals who condemn her so highhandedly on these counts are not themselves quite as alert or well-informed as they might be."

Dr. Adams was, indeed, of the opinion that nineteenth-century forerunners of the woman movement, such as Fanny Wright and Margaret Fuller, if they could see what women had achieved by 1939, "might judge us a little less unkindly than Pearl Buck in this magazine last summer. . . . Knowing the whole of woman's history, as they must by now have learned it from the hetaerae and kings' mistresses who were already old inhabitants of the particular part of hell to which they were condemned, they [the forerunners] must, I believe, feel not unsatisfied with what they were able to do for us modern American women. . . . For we . . . have . . . been . . . able to achieve the very things which Wollstonecraft herself considered most essential to a truly happy womanhood."

And what had American women achieved by 1939? "We

now have not only the affection and admiration but the sympathetic understanding and the complete confidence of the men who marry us. . . . Women in America . . . have a long way to go before they become the true professional and industrial equals of men.   But they will probably, unless America itself blows up in the meanwhile, have plenty of time in which to make the journey." In her concluding paragraph, Dr. Adams displayed more assurance: "Now that women have learned to understand men as they are, to think as men think, and to worry and laugh as they do, they have already found a firmer foundation for their eventual rise to equality than either they or their critics realize."

Women were on the march, and not "back to the kitchen," Rose C. Feld declared in a featured article in the *New York Times*. This she concluded from a kind of Gallup poll she took among leaders of business and professional women in 1935.   Despite the competitive hardships which that period of American and general depression imposed on women, their slogan was in effect: Forward to the individualistic struggle among struggling men! Unshaken was their confidence that if women kept the star of equal-right-to-compete as their guiding light their happiness would be attained.   Proletarians might have to drop by the wayside as factories closed and manual workers were thrown into the streets, deprived of wage envelopes, but "as for the individual woman, she can summon all her courage and assail the barriers, leading even though the mass of her sisters cannot follow." She can exhibit force. Remembering the feminist ideal, formulated for her incitement to "achievement" by the women of 1848, fully aware of the bitterness accompanying her attack on the barriers in many lines of endeavor, the courageous individualist was determined to "hold fast to her freedom," whatever the cost.

In 1941 Pearl Buck came back to the theme of defeated American women and methods for emancipating them — this time in a book, *Of Men and Women*. In her first chapter she accented the significance of the man-woman issue, saying that "the basic discovery about any people is the discovery of the relationship between its men and women." Unless one understands the way men and women feel toward each other and appreciates "the place each has in the life of the whole," one fails to grasp the reality of a country and its people.

As if to provide an informing background for picturing lazy and frustrated American women, Mrs. Buck made graphic delineations of Chinese women as women of personality, poise, and power. She had grown up in China where her parents were missionaries and naturally had strong impressions of Chinese life. The great Chinese family, according to Mrs. Buck, before it began to crumble in recent times, was a grand harmonious institution, a center of happiness for husband and wife, a community of like-minded and like-spirited human beings who enjoyed together the events and details of life — a system so honorable for women and felt to be so honorable by women that feminine qualities "began to be accepted as the essentials of a civilized people."

Nevertheless the Chinese woman, as Mrs. Buck described her in the great and grandly harmonious family system, was grossly ignorant. Though "even men were made an integral part of the home which Chinese women ruled," while all was happiness supreme, fathers tore their little sons from that rule to be reared by men. But woman, though grossly ignorant, was man's superior. "Long before modern China gave to women complete equality, woman in China was man's superior." Not only that: "The qualities of the feminine intelligence are exactly the qualities of the Chinese mind," she quoted from Lin Yutang.

Nor merely that. Pearl Buck applauded the change made by modern China in giving women "complete equality." She did more: "In fact, I have even suspected that when the modern revolution came he [man] was glad to insist on her becoming only equal with him at last. It was a forward step for him, and she lost by it. She had to stop being a willful creature who made the most of her ignorance and who got all she wanted by pretending to be childish and irresponsible and weak and charming while actually she was strong, tough, executively able, and mentally shrewd."

The women in the great Chinese family system got all she wanted? Pearl Buck related, à propos that story of willfulness, how many Chinese women took time off from getting all they wanted by childish wiles to make difficult trips to visit her own mother, an alien missionary in China, and confess to her "their sad stories of how the night through they have stuffed their quilts into their mouths, silk quilts, ragged quilts, so that man could not hear the sound of weeping. But they always believed their men were doing right," even when their men brought concubines into the great harmonious family to compete for the favor of their happy men. If domestic harmony required smothering the cries, were the feminine qualities which led to the smothering "exactly the qualities of the Chinese mind"?

If so, how did modern China happen to establish "complete equality" between men and women? And what did this mean for China and its mind? The answer was proffered by Mrs. Buck in these words: "It was man in China who hastened to write into the constitution that woman had to be equal with him and accept equal responsibility as an adult individual. He gladly threw open all schools and professions to her, and what must his satisfaction be today as he sees her take her gun and march beside him to battle!" A student of Chinese constitutional history might pause to ask at this point: Just what and where is this constitution that makes Chinese women the equals of men in rights and responsibilities and how enforced in various regions of China?

Taking it for granted, however, that there is a constitution and that it is enforced, there must be an upshot as far as China is concerned. As to that point Mrs. Buck referred to the old family and by implication described the ancient evils to which the new order offered such a contrast: "Thus do men always suffer when women are ignorant. They suffer more than women, not only because women are stronger than men and more resistant, but because men are peculiarly vulnerable to the damage ignorant women can do at the periods of their life when they most need intelligent and wise care: in infancy, in adolescence, in times of illness and mental and emotional crisis, and in old age. Wise China saw this, too, and endeavored to mitigate the danger by taking boys out of the care of women early in childhood." So presumably the "complete equality" in modern China has, by "the constitution," changed or removed all that once was unfortunate or evil in that general situation.

Having thus reported the striking features of happy domestic scenes in China, Mrs. Buck drew the contrasts presented in the United States as she understood them. Two classes of American women, she assumed, are successful or happy or both: talented women in the arduous pursuit of careers and women who find their vocations in the home; but their number combined is proportionately "very small." The rest of the American women are privileged, too privileged. They have the privilege of "non-competitive work," security, and privacy behind the sheltering walls of the home. They are not compelled by necessity to go out into the world, as man does, and earn their bread in the sweat of their brows in competition with him. They tend to futility. They are not reduced to subjection by man's superiority. They prefer to be little or nothing in the world. The American woman of this type is "free" to come and go; she has had an education; she is pampered rather than oppressed by man, "yet there is the same look of defeat in her eyes that there is in the Indian woman's." She is restless, silly, irritable, instable — a failure — nothing in history.

What then is the remedy? Mrs. Buck prescribed a simple formula: let women bestir themselves, cast off their lethargy, sharpen their talents, and go out like men to meet the competition of all comers in the forum of the big world. In freedom and equal opportunity — "the greatest freedom consistent with equal opportunity" — women and men will find harmony and fulfillment.

Organized feminists, as well as individual propagandists of the word, were committed to the ideal of life as a battle for place and power in the economic and political sphere. Such was the position taken by the National and International Federations of Business and Professional Women, until the opening of the year 1945. In their journal, *Independent Woman,* and their bulletin, *Widening Horizons,* these women steadily asserted their determination to get more women into positions of power and into higher places of business, industry, and the professions. From week to week they sought to strengthen their organizations, which were closely affiliated, with the objective of obtaining equal rights of combat in all fields of money-power and political influence.

This note of combat for places in "the man's world" was sounded in 1937 when the International Federation assembled in convention at Stockholm and framed a Three Year Objective. Yet this note was blended with the note of women's enthusiasm for "rendering their utmost service to humanity." There the president of the International, Lena Madesin Phillips of New York, proposed "Service" as the motto for the Federation. During the discussion of the subject Dr. Signe Svensson of Stockholm voiced the spirit of the meeting in these words: "It has been said that when the women pioneers were fighting for suffrage they forgot to teach women how to use their suffrage. I think that a part of our task must be to teach women to use the suffrage and use it in the right way." What was the "right" way? "To succeed in putting women into public office, we must educate the great body of women to take responsibility and to use their citizenship. I think it is necessary for us also to educate men to understand that we will work not only for ourselves, but for the improvement of the whole world, if we get into office. Then there need be no opposition: we can all work together."

How did these women visualize the improvement of the whole world? Both by word and by implication they took the public into their confidence. If the way were made easier and opened wider for business and professional women to "advance" from inequalities to competitive equality, women would be able to express their personalities to the good of all societies.

In February, 1945, "The World Women Want" seemed to have new aspects as speakers representing thirteen of the thirty branches of this International Federation, over an international radio circuit, again announced their aims and dreams for the world. Mme. Pierre Viennot, a member of the French Consultative Assembly which had been set up when France was liberated from her German invaders, speaking from France, and Dr. Lena Madesin Phillips, speaking from New York, were joined by Margaret A. Hickey, president of the Federation in the United States, in this broadcast. Miss Hickey declared that "the days of the old, selfish, strident feminism are over"; and she invited the women in the audience of the air to consider the special responsibility which women have as "custodians" of the moral and spiritual opposition to future wars. This, too, was an interpretation of women in history and the nature of woman.

As the Global War approached, and especially after it broke over the land, American women seized upon the occasion to review, on the platform and in the press, multiform aspects of women's relations to war and peace. In the discussion, one line of argument was followed with striking persistence: War is man's work in a man's world, now in particular the work of wicked men in foreign countries; women are by nature pacific; war, being always a foe of civilization, tends to deepen the subjection of women to men; since women are pacific by nature, they have a moral obligation to put an end to wars and hence must break into the inner circles of international conferences and lay down the law of peace, even to men who proclaim permanent peace to be the goal of their successive wars. Intermingled with argument on this line were demands that women make all the sacrifices necessary to winning the current war.

In 1940, at the World's Fair held in New York City, Mrs. Carrie Chapman Catt, addressing a receptive audience, declared that it is woman's main task to stop war. The goal could not be reached immediately, she admitted, but she expressed confidence that women could abolish war, for the reason that they are devoid of the war spirit. More than this, she maintained that "men have made all the wars in history," thus in eight words clearing women of all war guilt. With that innocence it appeared logical that women, historic and present, were inclined to peace by their very make-up and were under no necessity to cleanse their hearts and minds of a propensity to violence. Being pacific by nature and devoid of all war guilt, they could and should lead the way to peace.

Though more militant than Mrs. Catt as a leader in the suffrage movement, Alice Paul was no less certain that war sprang from men's nature and that women were under obligation to put a stop to wars. When, in April, 1941, she was interviewed on her return from Geneva, where she had spent two years directing the organization of an international movement for equal rights for women, she declared, relative to the war in Europe: "Women's instincts are constructive and tend to build and create, not to tear down." The guilt of war she laid wholly on men, saying: "This war was brought about without the women having anything to say or do about it, and now they are the greatest sufferers."

After the United States became directly involved in the war, American women had opportunities to enter the armed services in a manner and on a scale hitherto unknown to American military practice. They did not follow the example of many European women and take up arms on the front lines, but they went into the war organizations as officers and privates and thus acquired novel experiences on which presumably to base discussions of man-woman issues — past, present, and future.

For example, the president of Wellesley College, Mildred McAfee, took a leave of absence from her academic duties and assumed the burden of heading up a branch of the naval service — Women Accepted for Volunteer Emergency Services (WAVES). Soon she was awarded the title of Captain, with its appropriate insignia for her uniform. In assuming this task Miss McAfee gave a simple explanation of her action: If the men want us, that is enough for us. Back of that laconic statement may have been broader considerations derived from her study and teaching of the social sciences, but she refrained from entering upon an exposition of them at the moment. And in fact there are some grounds for believing that she had no interest in any phase of the woman movement at the moment.

Later, however, Miss McAfee gave indications of interest in women as such. In May, 1944, when she received an honorary degree at Smith College for her war service, Miss McAfee revealed the new drift of her thought in respect of women in the world and in its work. "In my inaugural remarks at Wellesley eight years ago," she told her audience at Smith, "I explained carefully that I was not interested in women as women. Education had taught us that people were more important than men or women. I have made several speeches since (or the same speech several times) explaining that the range of individual differences is more significant than group differences betwen men and women."

Thus, apparently, previous to undertaking war service, President McAfee had entertained the idea that women, as far as education was concerned, were merely undifferentiated people. They were to be treated, educated, and judged according to certain abstract standards, intellectual and perhaps moral, which were more or less measurable and had no relation to any distinct features of woman's nature.

But after Miss McAfee had acquired experience in co-operating with the Navy, a deviation had occurred in her mental direction. "And then I joined the Navy . . ." she continued in her address at Smith College. "In brief, life in the Navy has taken me out of the cloister, in which a woman was unaware of limitations on her freedom or individuality, and has thrust me into the big world where women are women, and men are men, and each individual in each category emerges into individuality out of all kinds of generalizations about the group to which he or she belongs as man or woman. . . . The achievement of any woman of responsibility for the larger purposes of the nation, the world, will speed the day which I used to think had already dawned, when women and men can be judged first as persons." In other words, Miss McAfee seemed to feel in 1944 that women were not yet fully persons, as she had once regarded them, but that nevertheless the goal of woman's ambition was to be adjudged a person in war and peace.

A more complete identification of woman with man and man's world of war was made by Oveta Culp Hobby, a newspaper woman and politician, head of the Women's Army Auxiliary Corps, subsequently the Women's Army Corps (WACS). As director of American women in the Army's branch of the war services, she could speak with authority on the value of the WACS. This she did in the Woman's Forum of the magazine, *The Woman and the Woman's Digest,* of October, 1943, where she dwelt on the soldierly qualities of the women under her command and the effects of their experience upon them: "From the four corners of the country, from every walk of life, women have joined the ranks of the WAC, to put aside their personal lives for the duration and undertake a life completely different from that which American women had ever known. . . . Each of these women is a soldier, in every sense of the word. . . . In a multitude of different ways the American women has proved her ability, her courage, and her individuality. All of these qualities are important, but there is one more which all-out war puts upon us, and that is discipline. . . . Most of all, that person who has responded to discipline will understand how to obtain discipline in others."

With what conclusions, to what end? "We know, therefore, that our women in the WAC will become better mothers for this [soldier's] training they are now undergoing. They will be better wives, for their understanding and acceptance of man's duties."

On another occasion, later in the same year, Captain Hobby, who had just returned from an inspection of women's work in the British "armed camp," in a press interview with American reporters in Washington, reaffirmed her faith in the value of women's participation in the Global War. She laid weight on the recruiting campaign which she was directing in the United States, the number of WACS already enrolled, the number in prospect, and the new types of training in process. "Three-fifths of the women we are training go to the command," she said, proud of the fact that women were getting near to the center of war.

Inspired by the discipline that British women were receiving, Captain Hobby declared that, if the training of American women could be carried out on the same lines, it would help morale. It would do more: it would give women "a chance to fit into the economic scheme after the war." Just what that scheme would or might be, she left to the imagination of the reporters and to readers who might examine their written lines. On January 8, 1945, Captain Hobby, then lifted to the rank of Colonel, was given the United States Army's third highest decoration, the Distinguished Service Medal. She was said to be the first woman to receive it and Secretary of War Stimson, pinning it upon her natty uniform, congratulated Colonel Hobby.

If Colonel Hobby's words correctly conveyed her thought, hitherto women had been less active in war affairs, but had now emerged from miiltary anonymity. They would be better prepared for wifehood and motherhood as a result of the emergence and the discipline they had received. At the same time they would be better equipped to fit into the economic scheme after arms had been laid down and the tasks of peace taken up again. Apparently a new chapter would open in the history of women and society.

In the opinion of Ada Comstock, president of Radcliffe

College from 1923 to 1943, women were gaining more than war experience in the global fray; they were widening their intellectual horizon, gathering new knowledge, making extraordinary demonstrations of power, winning high prestige. Writing on "Women in This War" in the *Yale Review* in 1942, Dr. Comstock said: "Women have had at least their share in the general growth of knowledge in this country respecting foreign affairs. Lessons in geography are still needed by all of us, but the last twenty years have seen an amazing increase of interest in other parts of the globe as political and economic forces. Through organizations such as the Foreign Policy Association, the Institute of Pacific Relations, the International Federation of University Women, through clubs and classes and the lectures for which the U.S.A. has such an appetite, much information has been diffused. At the moment, this better background of knowledge shows itself chiefly in more reading of papers and more listening to the radio."

On the basis of such gains apparently women could, with justification, plume themselves on their worldly wisdom and the world's appreciation of their having it. At all events, Dr. Comstock remarked with evident gratification: "There are, I suppose, only a very few men in the world today who command such audiences as those which listen to the interpretation of public affairs put forth by Mrs. Roosevelt and Madam Chiang Kai-shek; and Dorothy Thompson, Anne O'Hare McCormick, and Vera Micheles Dean write and speak for a public which takes little account of sex."

College girls also were becoming or doing something new. Dr. Comstock was delighted that "a college girl scales a sixty-foot ladder as easily as she used to tackle the ropes in the gymnasium, and with as little to-do. Women seem to me less self-conscious in their assumption of these new tasks [including war tasks], and men seem readier to count upon their cooperation."

While upholding the fight against the Axis Powers, Dr. Emily Hickman, professor of history at the New Jersey College for Women, urged women to fan the agitation for a place at the peace table when the war against these powers had ended. "We must get women into the international committees to plan the peace so that war will be prevented!" This, Dr.

Hickman said, was a special duty of women, for men were preoccupied with other things: "At this moment most of the businessmen and labor groups in the country are so concerned with the problems of taxation of business, termination of war contracts, and full employment, that they have no time to think of preventing another war in twenty-five years."

For a large number of the Americans who made a specialty of "foreign affairs," the Global War was not just another war, a war in the historic style — a struggle of nations for supremacy. It was a war for enduring peace, a sure thing this time, as distinguished from the failure that followed the first world war. Moreover the idea of woman as intrinsically a lover of peace was so often emphasized and repeated that makers of platforms and candidates for President in 1944 could not ignore it in their quest for votes. Franklin D. Roosevelt assured the people that "men and women" of all parties were on the staff planning for a better world; and Thomas Dewey promised that if elected he would employ the ablest men and women to be found in the country at the task of organizing the coming peace. During the political campaign and afterward, women unwilling to rely on the pledges of political parties set about consolidating their forces for the purpose of assuring the establishment of world order and permanent peace at the end of the war.

Mary Heaton Vorse had noted in her *Footnote to Folly* that women at their international conferences held after the first world war had recited the woes of war, had wept over its tragedies and sufferings, without considering their relations to the making or promotion of war or drastic means that might prevent its recurrence. Now, in the noontime of the Global War, American women, while giving the utmost support to the war and celebrating their services and recognitions, were eagerly preparing "to win the peace."

With the intention of "making enough of a rumpus" to assure places for qualified women on committees and commissions assigned to postwar world planning, representatives of twelve women's organizations began in March, 1944, a campaign to attain this end. On June 14, Mrs. Roosevelt received at the White House delegates of these organizations who had come to confer with other women on the matter of recognition for women in the form of membership on policy-forming agencies concerned with international planning. On this occasion men from the principal departments of the Federal Government were present as speakers or observers, giving a kind of official Democratic sanction to the affair. Thus "peace-loving women" had a hearing at the political capitol of the nation.

Encouraged by the event, women active in the undertaking drafted and circulated a questionnaire designed to secure the naming of women best qualified to have places of power in postwar planning for security and peace. By this process several prominent women, including Anne O'Hare McCormick and Vera Micheles Dean, were presented to the public as equipped to help as thinkers and leaders in creating the new world order and establishing the lasting peace. In line with his declaration of 1944, President Roosevelt chose Virginia Gildersleeve, dean of Barnard College, to serve as a member of the American delegation at the international conference held in San Francisco in April-June, 1945, out of which came the United Nations Charter.

While the circulation of the idea that women had long been the victims of ignorance, subordination or total subjection, but were about to lead the world to order and peace, gained in velocity, especially among the intellectuals and educated classes generally, a pressure came from an unexpected quarter. The directors of All-America Comics, Inc., in 1943, undertook to carry this "message" to the country in a form to exert a "lasting effect upon the minds of those who are now boys and girls" but maturing as a power for shaping the future.

To forward this purpose they engaged the services of Alice Marble, tennis champion in time of peace and physical trainer of women for the service of a society at war, to assist in planning and editing a comic sheet entitled *Wonder Woman*, woman conceived as a "female Superman." This effort, the corporation announced, "marks the first time that daring, strength and ingenuity have been featured as womanly qualities." It admitted that "women still have many problems and have not yet reached their fullest growth and development," thus intimating that men now have no problems and have reached their fullest growth and development. But vivaciously, *Wonder Woman* undertook "constructive entertainment for children" with its portrayal of the "female Superman."

To make more explicit its dominant idea, All-America Comics, Inc., gave prominence to the assertions of the "well-known psychologist," Dr. William Moulton Marston, printed in the magazine *Tomorrow,* in February, 1942, under the heading: "Women: Servants of Civilization." In this article Dr. Marston summarized some of the "leading thoughts" on women that were current at the time. Women had once been ruled by the harem order, but were no longer so governed. "When women eventually decided, sometime in the latter part of the nineteenth century, that the harem idea was a mistake, they began promptly, though timidly, to emerge. This emergence procedure is still going on. The first world war gave it impetus, the second should go a long way toward completing the female exodus." Emerging women are the hope of civilization: "If psychological evolution is to climb another step toward human harmony and joy of living, the emotional impetus must be furnished by women, since they have more of what it takes to love."

Man, on the other hand, is a belligerent creature: "There's no more reason for not killing humans who oppose you than for sparing the lives of mosquitoes, in the mind of a man whose self-seeking emotions are permitted to run rampant. And the average 'normal' male's personality balance tends definitely in the same direction, according to the emotion tests which I have conducted for several years in my clinic and in private consultations."

As if to prove the feminine contrast and stamp it indelibly on the minds of young admirers of the male Superman, All-America Comics, Inc., on the cover of the first issue of its magazine, represented the female of the species, dressed in a scant bathing suit, astride a circus horse, riding down Hitler and all his Nazi cohorts of men beside their war machines. Swiftly Hitler was brought to his well-deserved doom and the forces arrayed against him arrived at the grand triumph without more to-do. Such marvelous feats for democracy and civilization woman could achieve when her feeling of inadequacy was extinguished and her potentialities unleashed.

In the future, things will be different from the long past as women come into their own: "The future is woman's — as quickly as she realizes her present frustration, and her tremendously powerful potentialities ... The important thing is that a vast army of women has begun to move forward into male territory. Eventually they will conquer their own feelings of female inadequacy." With woman's feeling of inadequacy cast off and her potentialities released into full action, civilization will advance, for women have the qualities necessary for the triumph of civilization.

"The world needs more love. The world needs peace, security, an aristocracy of altruism, a new set of social values based upon what one individual can do for others and not upon what he can take away and keep for himself. Only world-mothers are psychologically capable of that great, compassionate, selfless love which should inspire the leaders of nations to forget utterly their own political ambitions, their petty hatreds and selfish interests, and give, give to their millions of slow-growing, adult children. When women rule this world they won't want to [be so mean]; they will consent to be Presidents, or Queens, or self-effacing, anonymous leaders only because they know that it is more fun to give than to receive, and that leadership offers larger opportunities to love and give themselves to others. Women are like that — don't let them fool you with their petty fears and hesitancies! When the human need signal sounds, women always have delivered — and they always will. That is why they are women. And that is why, when the world is worthy of their leadership of love, women will lead the world."

Chapter 3

Attitudes of Men

IN THE orderly and intelligent discussion of any subject, Cicero said in *De Officiis,* the terms used should be so plain that all may know and understand what the discussion is about. In the foregoing examples of American women's assertions on the subject of men and women — everybody's interest — it is perfectly clear whether they are talking about men or women. But this is not so true so often when men discuss human affairs.

Men who discuss human affairs frequently do so with an ambiguity amounting to double talk or half talk or talk so vague that one cannot be sure in every case whether they are referring to men only or to both men and women. This gives them a peculiar advantage of self-defense if the charge is made that they are not remembering women at all when they speak of "man" or "men," for they can claim that they are using these words in their generic sense. Two recent incidents illustrate this situation and its significance.

In 1944 members at large of the Laboratory of Anthropology at Santa Fe were invited by the editor of its *News Letter* to give opinions on an objection raised by one member to the customary phrase, "primitive man," employed by the laboratory in advertising its whole collection of early handicrafts and in describing primitive life. Among the prominent men who accepted the invitation were Frank Lloyd Wright and Dr. A. A. Brill.

Mr. Wright was gay and witty in his reply: "The term *Man* is used, I believe (as the professor said to his class), 'as man embracing woman.' They giggled — and Mary Beard objects — so why not say Mankind and let it go at that?"

Dr. Brill was serious and more elaborate in his reply: "I always considered the term 'primitive man,' like other similar expressions, such as 'man is the measure of all things,' etc. Fortunately, or unfortunately, for woman (I am inclined to the former), man being in the vanguard of the struggle, was always spoken of in the generic sense as representing both sexes. Also he is — at least on the surface — the more active and aggressive of the two sexes, he receiving more punishment and more honor than his equally important helpmate. The whole problems might be resolved by using the term, 'Primitive people.' "

But neither "mankind" nor "people" is always descriptively accurate, especially in dealing with human work or force when there is a division of labor between the sexes or qualities of masculine and feminine force may differ in essence or expression. Whether the problem of the little three-letter words, *man* and *men*, and a combination of man with kind in *mankind* or the obliteration of both in the six-letter word *people* is treated lightly or gravely today, the problem is really fundamental for precision in thought and its communication.

What, for instance, is meant precisely when men talk about "men of good will," as they repeatedly do today in connection with the themes of war and peace? Do they mean men as adult males, with their distinctive qualities? Or do they mean to "embrace" women of good will and treat their wills and goodnesses as the same, as equivalents undifferentiated in fact?

When Mark Twain paid his disrespect to the human race in *What Is Man?* he made it fairly evident to his readers that he was especially concerned with the male human being. A glance at the title of George A. Dorsey's *Man's Own Shadow: Civilization* might suggest that civilization is the adult male's show, but a study of Dorsey's text discovers that woman had a part in the making and running of the show. What part? Any distinctive part? And does he make it clear all the way through his text? If those are not "sixty-four-dollar" questions for the men and women who are daily, hourly, instructing the public through the press, on the platform, and over the radio, they are practical questions for members of the public who wish to know what is being talked about in discussions of public affairs. They are questions which every man or woman with the slightest concern for science or truth will want to raise and have answered.

For hundreds of years the use of the word "man" has troubled critical scholars, careful translators, and lawyers. Difficulties occur whenever and wherever it is important for truth-seeking purposes to know what is being talked about and the context gives no intimation whether "man" means just a human being irrespective of sex or means a masculine being and none other. For lawyers in particular the correct use of the term and a precise understanding of its uses may have fateful consequences; innumerable rights of person and property may turn upon the mere meaning of "man" in laws, ordinances, and judicial opinions.

Perhaps one should say that the word "man" has been making confusion in many respects for more than a thousand years. It was certainly used in the Anglo-Saxon language as early as 825 A.D. to mean specifically the human creature in general; but about the same time it was also used to mean an adult male person; while contemporaneously the word "woman" was in use as meaning an adult female human being. And persons who have occasion to study Anglo-Saxon laws and literature, if they care anything at all about exactness, have to be constantly on guard as to whether "man" means a human creature in general or an adult male. Of course if precision is no consideration, then the translation of the word *man* or *mann* from Anglo-Saxon into English may simply run riot at the will and pleasure of its repeater.

Additional ambiguities have arisen in connection with the word *man,* on account of the tendency to identify it with many other terms in common usage. As Charlotte C. Stopes says in *The Sphere of "Man" in Relation to that of "Woman" in the English Constitution:* "For centuries . . . the word 'man' was practically treated as a common noun, like freeholder, resident, taxpayer, merchant, trader, shopkeeper, pauper, prisoner, traitor, criminal, benefactor. In short, 'man' was held as equivalent to person or individual, the unit in the collective noun 'people.' "

And yet so many uncertainties appeared in the administration of the law in England, as citizens, judges, and administrators wrestled with the terms *man* and *men* that Parliament tried in 1850 to clear some of them away by legislation. A law known as Lord Romilly's or Lord Brougham's Act provided that "words importing the masculine gender shall always include women, except where otherwise stated." As a matter of fact, however, conflicts due to uncertainty of meaning did not end, even in England, respecting the use of the word *man* in statutes and judicial decisions.

Nevertheless, historians, sociologists, literary critics, and other commentators on human affairs have paid little attention to this linguistic problem — a problem of clarity in speech and writing. Yet it involves their judgments on everything human. How does one know whether any writer is using the troublesome words, *man* and *men*, generically or with reference to males only, unless the meaning is made plain by the context or a positive statement? The issue can best be defined in the form of questions perhaps. Are adult males and adult females identical in nature? Are they equals, equivalents, interchangeable parts of humanity, so that these words, *man* and *men*, may be freely used without explanations and at all times? Are the speakers and writers who use these words willing to justify their usages as self-explanatory? If self-explanatory are these words accurately used in all, many, or any cases?

This is no mere quibbling. Naturally men are deeply interested in affirmations about men with their masculine qualities. Unquestionably men are also deeply interested in women. When are they expressing their interests in themselves or in women? Sometimes they take the public into full confidence in this matter. But much of the time they lay themselves open to the accusation that they have failed to think their way through the linguistic, historical, and sociological difficulty.

This problem of clarity in thought, or the lack of it, looms large in hundreds of thousands of printed pages where the words *man* and *men* appear in bewildering profusion, as well as in common and formal speech. The wide and loose circulation of these words is one of the striking features of modern loquacity and even of modern "science." No lawyer accustomed to seeking precision in terms could possibly translate with confidence the words *man, men, person, people, and mankind*, which are strewn through and adorn the articles, books, reviews, essays, and addresses of our times. Freedom of speech allows for large liberties, but speech so free as to be inexact and unintelligible is markedly licentious — and dangerous — when such subjects as human nature, the emotions, education, science, art, democracy, government, society, literary values, history, progress, retrogression, barbarism, and civilization are brought under a discussion intended to be serious and informed.

To come to concrete cases: How is Dr. Karl A. Menninger, the eminent neuro-psychiatrist, discussing this universal interest — man-woman? Can the reader of his works be sure he had woman as well as man in his mind or whether he regarded them as identical, when he chose for the title of one of his books, *Man Against Himself?* Judging by another of his works, *The Human Mind,* he had in his memory a kind of composite personality, man-woman, with a composite mind. Yet in respect to those two books and a third volume, *Love Against Hate,* a quandary occurs. The publisher's report announced two of them as studies of the "creative energy that lies behind man's achievement in art, in science, and in living together with his fellow man." And he said of the third: "It is not offered as a cure-all for man's troubles, but it does advance the argument that the cure lies in man's essential nature, and that only as we come to understand ourselves in the light of modern psychiatric knowledge can we find our way to happiness in the better world we are seeking to create."

How, it may be properly asked, did the announcer understand his own words (or her words, if perchance a woman wrote the above lines)? Do women achieve anything in art and science? Do men live with fellow-men and also with fellow-women? Is the essential nature that is mentioned common to men and women? Or is it the nature of the male alone that is being considered? For psychiatric science itself, the query is mandatory.

Approaching the theme, love against hate, psychologically or psychiatrically, "we" may assume, may "we" not, that men and women are equally compounded of love and hate? But do we discover that by reading the book? No doubt the theme is pertinent to both sexes in their search for the proposed road to happiness. And since Dr. Menninger had the cooperation of his wife in the composition of this volume, it is possible that the term *man* was used here only in its generic sense. Yet in various types of leadership along the road to happiness, is it not possible that the two sexes display and represent forces decidedly unequal and differing in quality as well as kind and degree? Or do they? What light is Dr. Menninger shedding on this point?

Take another case as evidence of the linguistic uncertainty — the use of the word, man, in *Man the Slave and Master,* a biological approach to the potentialities of modern society (1938). Did the author, Mark Graubard, mean man, the male, in this passage: "When the authors of the Declaration of Independence declared that 'all men are created equal,' they were not speaking as biologists but as social legislators?" Or did Dr. Graubard mean to say that the authors of that document were putting women with men and declaring them equals? Dr. Graubard objects to the confusion that exists in the meaning of equality, especially as used by Fascists who make it biological only or primarily. But was he himself reckless or cautious about biological notions of equality when he listed Selma Lagerlöf among "men of genius"?

In respect of primitives, Dr. Graubard wrote: "Essentially, then, the behavior of man in primitive society was not unlike his behavior today. His biological and emotional reactions were the same. The force of conditioning was the same. His mind, like the mind of modern man, was the product of habits, conditioned emotions, responses, and beliefs." Are primitive women as well as men included in this statement? If so, were primitive men and women so nearly alike that they may be treated as one? If so treated is the word "man" sufficient? Might not "woman" do just as well?

In some places in his book and in some ways Dr. Graubard displays a definite awareness of woman as a distinctive creature. For instance he declares: "Man's earliest records indicate that the male of the species tended to adhere to the female in one manner or another to form a family in the sense commonly understood in our own civilization, namely, a closely knit economic and social group of one or more men, one or more women, and their offspring." And "women may perform agricultural tasks." He even notes that Solon placed a penalty on the sale of women for slavery. But what in many cases is he really talking about?

As another illustration of the way in which the term *man* is used indefinitely, in such a manner as to leave the existence of woman uncertain, we may take the *Primer for Tomorrow* by Christian Gauss, dean at Princeton University, published in 1934. Presumably Dr. Gauss is interested in the nature and future of all society. His book opens with comments on "The Nature of Civilization," in the course of which he criticizes Spengler's assumption that the "men" of our time are the first men to try to "grasp the nature and significance of this strictly human world about them. . . . As a matter of fact, from the beginning of human history no problem has interested man more deeply."

An elaboration of this long concern of *man* follows: "This first stage in which the mythologies are created may be said to be efforts on the part of man to explain and, if possible, to justify himself to his gods. These gods have absolute power and they themselves need no justification; man fears but does not argue with them. Adam does not argue with Jehovah; Adams accepts his prohibitions without question and then quite humanly attempts to explain and excuse his transgression. At a somewhat later stage of human development, illustrated by historians like Herodotus or Livy or Bossuet, or by poets like Virgil and Milton, man seeks 'to assert eternal Providence' and 'to justify the ways of God to man.' "

The impression seems warranted that Dean Gauss has man the male in mind. The impression is strengthened as the reader goes through the remaining pages. Consider this statement: "According to Spengler the history of civilization is the record of the struggle of man against his environment, against nature, in which nature always wins. Even if we admit with Spengler, as we must, that many civilizations have died in the past, must we admit that the challenge of nature will forever defeat the spirit of man?" Since Spengler separated men and women into distinct categories, making women history itself and man its maker, is the reader not justified in assuming that Dean Gauss presumably uses the Spenglerian distinction here?

But this *Primer* is not always sternly masculine in its conceptions. In another place the author says: "It is, of course, clear that one man alone cannot create an enduring civilization.

There must be men, women and children, continuing and co-operating generations, if man's achievement is to endure." This does seem definite in the sense that women must cooperate with men.

But what follows is not so obvious: "Man's struggle is not only against nature, but in a sense, it is against other men as well. To bring about the conditions under which his inventions and way of life can be perpetuated, man the experimenter is forced to create not only implements and tools, materialistic advantages, but he must create also ways of life, institutions, governments, religions, laws, of such a sort that the men of his group, of his own culture, will work and live together in harmony and use these implements and tools in the common interest and not against each other. For in this second case, his life must degenerate again into a meaningless struggle not against nature, but against his own kind. We must differentiate clearly between those implements, those material tools which man invents, and what we may call the spirit of his civilization."

If males who write on anthropology, sociology, mentality, love and hate, psychology, philosophy, and civilization may seem at times to take refuge with an abstract being as neither male nor female and thus appear "sound" to women who shrink from remembrance of women, what is to be said of historians? In the events they recite, human beings are the actors. Inevitably they deal with personalities and in their selection of historic events and actors, they necessarily reveal their attitudes on women as well as on men. Their very silences respecting women, no less than their accounts of women when they mention women, are evidences of the ways they interpret the past — the prologue to the present and the future.

How far then do men who write history enforce or deny the thesis maintained by living women that women were a subject sex throughout the long ages of the past? Or do they consider women something even less important than subjects of men — exactly nothing?

Naturally in order to find answers research would have to be carried very widely into the works of professional historians — an immense fact-finding and statistical expedition. But clues to the values of such research may be obtained by the examinations of general works on history which have high recognition in circles of educators and wide currency in other circles.

For example, "The American History Series," really accorded that standing, consists of five volumes long used as authoritative in American colleges and universities. One of these volumes on *The Middle Period* 1817-1858, was written by Professor John W. Burgess. In all its five hundred pages, only rare references are made to women, obviously, unmistakably, women. One cites a Virginia statute imposing heavy penalties on white women who cohabited with negro slaves. Mary Brown, who owned a slave that ran away, is mentioned in a passage on the fugitive slave law, and Ellen Crafts, a fugitive slave herself, is cited in connection with the rumor that she was concealed by "some of the most high-toned people" of Boston, presumably including some woman or women. But Harriet Beecher Stowe is not in the index and so was apparently not in the history of the middle period. Nor were other women.

To be sure, any man has a right to confine his attention entirely to the doings of men in political history if he lets his purpose be known in the title of his book or of the series in which it appears. But the series to which this volume by Professor Burgess belongs is called *history,* and on the least possible reckoning women were more than incidental to men's history in the United States from 1817 to 1858, even to their political history. And failure to admit it is an attitude with respect to women.

"Associated scholars," all men, wrote the volumes in another distinguished group, entitled "The American Nation Series." One of these volumes on *The Federalist System* is fairly representative. This was written by John Spencer Bassett who as professor at Smith College taught history to women for about a quarter of a century. In his chapter on "The State of Society" at the end of the eighteenth century, people, inhabitants, Negroes, agriculture, commerce, dancing, inns, fried bacon, and corn bread have their places, but no woman or women; not even matrimony. On a search through other chapters one may find Martha Washington, but she seems to be present merely because she was hostess at a reception. John Adams figures largely but there is no Abigail Adams in the society of his time. Nor is there mention of Mercy Warren whose history of the American Revolution so stirred John Adams' ire on account of the way she portrayed him that he engaged in a sharp epistolary battle with Mercy, long his close friend. Histories of this character, for all practical purposes of instruction in colleges and other schools for young men and women, add up to the assertion that women had been of no real importance in the making of American history.

Independent volumes, not parts of series, have been written on similar lines. *America: The Story of a Free People*, by Allan Nevins and Henry Steele Commager, runs true to form. This volume was composed by two outstanding historians and, the authors explain, was "designed to meet the need for a short narrative history of the American people." Their preface indicates their conception of the need and the nature of history in America: "The story of America is the story of the impact of an old culture upon a wilderness environment. Americans skipped, as it were, the first six thousand years of history and emerged upon the historical scene bold and mature, for the first settlers were not primitive but civilized men, and they transplanted here a culture centuries old. Yet the New World was never merely an extension of the Old. It was what its first settlers anticipated and its founding fathers planned — something new in history." The index, it is true, contains references to women in industry and with regard to the suffrage; Jane Addams, Lillian Wald, and one or two other women are listed there; but the contribution of women to the making of American history, even in helping to "settle" the new world, is overlooked by chance or deliberately as of no significance.

Brooks Adams, however, reckoned with the force of women in history. In his first significant work, *The Emancipation of Massachusetts*, issued in 1887, he paid an extraordinary tribute to Anne Hutchinson whose stand for religious liberty in the early seventeenth century led to her banishment from that colony. "The intrepid woman," said Brooks Adams, "defended her cause with a skill and courage which even now, after two hundred and fifty years, kindles the heart with admiration. . . . She shattered the case of the government in a style worthy of a leader of the bar."

Later, in his major historical work, *The Law of Civilization and Decay* (1895), he represented the female of the species as powerful in sustaining society during the early and rude stages of civilization but as promoting physical and moral decay in the stages of social decline. In this volume woman was, in his judgment, a dynamic person for weal or woe. Finally, in *The Degradation of the Democratic Dogma,* published not long before his death, Brooks Adams asserted that woman had no intellectual power and "only the importance of a degraded boy."

About thirty years after Brooks Adams' *Law of Civilization and Decay* appeared, a translation of Oswald Spengler's *Untergang des Abendlandes* was published in the United States under the title *The Decline of the West.* Spengler was not a historian but a mathematician; yet he felt able to reduce universal history to a kind of law that was in some respects akin to Adams' theory of cycles in history — from barbarism to and through civilization and round and round. Published amid the disillusionment and confusion that followed the first world war, Spengler's work had a great influence on American writing and thinking about the past, present, and future of all humanity. In a single passage Spengler declared that woman is history and that man makes history. The existence of woman in history was thus recognized, but she was represented as a mere sustaining and conserving force in history. While Spengler took that much account of woman in *The Decline,* he rubbed her out perhaps in his *Man and Technics* (1932) where he said: "Man is a beast of prey. . . . *The animal of prey is the highest form of mobile life.* . . . It imparts a high dignity to man, as a type, that he is a beast of prey." Or did Spengler here exclude woman?

The type of historical writing that in effect represents women as members of an inarticulate and subject sex in the long evolution of society up to the modern age is fairly well exemplified in Dr. Ernest L. Groves' *The American Woman* offered in 1944 as a text for the education of women. Dr. Groves is a sociologist, not a historian, but in this volume he devotes many pages to the history of woman's status through the ages. In those pages he pictures the historic life of woman as one of general subordination to man, if with rare exceptions and slight qualifications. The subtitle of the book, "the feminine side of a masculine civilization," is a digest of the author's opinion that civilization had been man's civilization at least until recent years in America, though the argument of the text is to the effect that woman should at last enter into the full enjoyment of man's civilization. Wishing women well, Dr. Groves endorses the feminist proposal for an equal rights amendment to the Federal Constitution. Still, his historical verdict stands as written: The starting point for the discussion of the modern American woman is the subjection of women through the long ages of the past.

With the slow and halting development, in late years, of what is styled "social history," male scholars, and occasionally a female scholar, have gradually manifested more consciousness that women had been *in* history and had done something, whatever it was, in the *making* of history. As to the state of things before this movement for the writing of social history was well launched, Arthur Meier Schlesinger, one of the pioneers in it, appropriately commented in his *New Viewpoints in American History* (1922): "An examination of the standard histories of the United States and of the history textbooks in use in our schools raises the pertinent question whether women have ever made a contribution to American national progress that is worthy of record. If the silence of the historians is taken to mean anything, it would appear that one-half of our population have been negligible factors in our country's history."

Although the social historians who recognized that women had been in history brought about some shift in the emphasis on man-made history, they gave many signs that they were puzzled in trying to deal with women. Many of them worked on as before, "bringing in" women here and there as if they were not really an integral part of all history; but none of them made any serious contributions to the bibliography, documentation, theory, and practice of the subject of women in history. In fact some of the social historians paid so much attention to the struggle of women for the suffrage and for "equal rights," that they helped to confirm or freeze the view that prior to the rise of feminism in the nineteenth century women had been nothing, or next to nothing, in the long course of previous history — ideed, enslaved or partly enslaved to man in a man's world or a "man's civilization." Hence despite the useful labors of the social historians and some monographs on specific phases of ideas and activities in history, the conventional view of women as negligible or nothing or helplessly subject to men in the long past continued largely to

direct research, thinking, and writing about American history.
At all events Professor Schlesinger's appeal of 1922 for some
consideration of women's contributions to the making of history effected no immediate revolution in the thinking of his
guild. How completely it could be ignored was illustrated in
1940, nearly twenty years later, in *The Course of American
Democratic Thought: An Intellectual History since 1815,* by
Ralph H. Gabriel. This work deals with thought of or about
democracy. It covers the period which witnessed the rise and
growth of an invincible movement for women's rights, inspired
by democratic theories, the tremendous agitation of thought
that accompanied the movement, drastic modifications of the
common law by legislation and equity, and the struggle that
in the fullness of time culminated in the national enfranchisement of women. It treats of an age in which thousands of
articles, pamphlets, and books on various aspects of democracy, law, and justice were written by women. Yet in the
bibliography attached to Professor Gabriel's text no work by
a woman is cited. For him, it would appear, the huge six-
volume work on the *History of Woman Suffrage,* containing
many "thoughts" about democracy, or at least what may be
regarded as a phase of it, had no pertinence whatsoever.

This is not to say that Professor Gabriel entirely overlooked
the existence of women in his intellectual history after 1815.
The names of Harriet Beecher Stowe, Mary Baker Eddy, Lydia
Pinkham, Sophia Ripley, Sarah Eleanor Royce, Carry Rand,
and Mrs. E. D. Rand, for instance, appear in the index. Note
is taken that Margaret Fuller and Sophia Ripley conferred
with Emerson about Brook Farm, though what they said to
him or he said to them on the subject is not revealed. If
women were doing any thinking in the period, it is difficult to
find out from this treatise what it was like. "Equalitarianism"
is treated in the text as if it were mainly or wholly a man's affair. Even the women's "Declaration of Sentiments" at Seneca
Falls in 1848 — a manifesto of a movement which developed
into a conquering force — escaped Professor Gabriel's attention or was discarded by him as deserving not even a page or
two in a modern work on democracy.

If one passes from obvious matters relative to women's
share in thought about democracy, which lie on the very surface of the documents for the age, to more recondite issues of

thought, one discovers that Professor Gabriel exhibits the peculiar nature of his own thought about democratic thought. There he quotes Joseph Story on the role of equity in jurisprudence. There he says that "the common law was always changing, expanding to meet human needs," and that out of the mid-nineteenth century concept of fundamental law "came ultimately the law which governed the lives of men."

Professor Gabriel devotes no paragraphs to showing that Story had demonstrated in his great work on equity jurisprudence how equity played havoc with whole branches of the common law, especially those parts which dealt with the rights of men and women in their varied legal relations. In other words, he gives no hint that Story's important historic treatise showed how the advance of thought in the democratic age was rewriting in the name of equity whole chapters of jurisprudence relative to the rights of women. But Professor Gabriel's book stands as written; as far as democratic thought is concerned, women scarcely exist; they are negligible, if not exactly nothing.

We come to political scientists and, lest it be thought that they are dragged into a matter beyond their proper sphere, their ancient mentors, Plato and Aristotle, need recalling. Like great Greek legislators, those immortal writers on society and the state, on politics and ethics, placed the Family at the very center of their political science. Plato could not solve the problem of his ideal society and state without settling the question of the Family and woman's social role. Knowing the power of the Family with its interests and ambitions, economic and political, he proposed to abolish it at least for men and women who, by their skills and talents, would come to the top of society and state as guardians. Appreciating the mental and moral force of women, Plato gave them equal position with men in the function of guarding the state.

To Aristotle a political science without attention to the Family would have been a shadowy abstraction only. He made the Family a basic element of the state and examined its nature before he erected his superstructure (Book I). He could not examine the Family and neglect to consider woman. Though it was hard for either man to regard woman as quite up to his stature mentally, nevertheless both immortal Greeks took cognizance of woman in the enormously influential works they composed on society and the state.

It has been a freakish aspect of American political science which both as theory and descriptive thinking tends either to abstraction or to thought of the male only as a factor in the state. With the rise of individualism and democracy, even society customarily drops out of this political science. Nearly all the textbooks on government, used for the instruction of young men and women in American colleges, leave the Family out of account; and beyond reporting that women now have the vote in the United States, they pay little or no attention to what women have done with the vote, to their political agitations, to their ideas of government, and their work in government as administrators and judges.

One of the very best treatises on party organization and practices, by a witty and discerning scholar whose wife, Luella Gettys, had previously written an excellent work on *The Law of Citizenship in the United States*, bears the impress of the current tendency: V. O. Key's *Politics, Parties, and Pressure Groups* (1942). This volume contains references to woman suffrage and to women's voting habits, but the long chapter on national conventions gives no idea of the number and activities of women at these great party assemblies. Yet women had been represented by delegates since 1892; at the Republican convention of 1940 there were 99 women delegates and 264 women alternates; and at the Democratic convention of that year there were 208 women delegates and 347 women alternates.

The task of inquiring into women's place in politics was left almost exclusively to women themselves. The first systematic analysis of this subject was made in 1933 by Sophonisba Breckinridge and published in her volume, *Women in the Twentieth Century*. It was two women, Marguerite J. Fisher and Betty Whitehead, who wrote for *The American Political Science Review*, of October, 1944, a brief sketch of women's participation in conventions from 1892 to 1914. The authors made no effort to "measure" the influence of women at those assemblies or to describe at length their political acumen and activities; but at a time when practical politicians, high and low, were all wrought up by the evident power of voting women, the publication of the article in this journal showed that political scientists were becoming interested in doing something about "the data" of women in politics.

More than historians and political scientists as a rule, psychologists and sociologists acknowledge the existence of woman, and inquire extensively into her nature, activities, and force or the absence of it in social development. Psychologists frequently proceed on the assumption that everybody, including women, has a mind and a will of some kind. It is true that some of them appear to be preoccupied with the mind of man, an adult male; but even these specialists, often, if not always, seem to be using the term *man* generically. At all events women as such receive much consideration in circles of psychologists, individually and collectively. For example, at its ninth spring meeting, in 1944, the Eastern Branch of the American Psychological Association held sessions on the attitudes of men and women toward women.

The meeting lasted for two days and nearly one thousand persons were reported as attending its sessions. The main discussion revolved around the results of a questionnaire submitted to an equal number of men and women and presented to this meeting by Philip M. Kitay of Teachers College, Columbia University. By means of this survey designed to explore opinions of men and women about women, the conclusion was reached by its promoters that both sexes were in "a remarkable agreement in favor of equal social rights for both sexes and a wide disagreement in evaluating the emotional stability and originality of women." Dr. Kitay said the questionnaire indictated that "the present-day attitudes toward women have been largely made by men. Since many accept prevailing opinions as facts, women as a rule fall into the same opinions as men, and therefore see themselves through male eyes."

In the discussion which followed a statement of the survey's findings, men and women participated and, according to newspaper accounts, "seven out of every ten men, and an equal proportion of women, believed that men were less influenced by emotion than women in their judgments. To the statement that 'women are more interested in trivial things of life than men,' 91.7 per cent of the men gave their assent, and 91.1 per cent of the women."

The question of extra-marital freedom was raised and on

this issue there was also general agreement among the men and the women; it is "more shameful for a married woman to have extra-marital sexual relations than for a married man." Yet the men more than the women approved greater sexual freedom for women. As large a proportion as 85 per cent of the men thought that men are more emotionally stable than women but only 44.1 per cent of the women accepted this belief. With respect to women's creative ability, 92.9 per cent of the women claimed that women possess it, while less than half of the men, 48.6 per cent, conceded it.

Dr. Kitay, a teacher of educational psychology, maintained that if men swayed women's opinions on women the men had self-interested motives — the desire to keep women from competing with men. "Thus the belief was strongly supported by men," he said, "that women were frail and delicate creatures who could not do any of the world's work that involved strain."

The discovery or assumption that women differ from men governed discussions of the subject by members of the Psychological Association which assembled at Palo Alto a few years ago, and much importance was attached to glandular differentiations.

"What is the psychological difference between a boy and a girl?" was the question on which they attempted to focus their remarks. The question had been before members of the association for meditation in advance of this meeting and those who attended it were prepared to give their answers. Indeed a report, framed by two men and one woman of Stanford University, was ready for the guidance of the discussion. Its burden was that the "original constitutional equipment" of girls and boys differs. And in women, it asserted, the whole glandular system is "more precarious" than in men. But mental balance is "superior in the male." The whys and wherefores of the divergence in mental balance were "probably" traceable to the basic physical differences, some speakers averred. As the discussion was reported in the press, its upshot was the consensus that "women in general have made no relative progress against mental irregularities since they began throwing off conventional restraints at high speed." Just when women began to do that, the press did not report as a finding disclosed at this meeting of psychologists.

For more than fifty years American sociologists drew heavily upon Herbert Spencer's *Principles of Sociology*, the first volume of which was formally published in 1876. From his work they borrowed both methods and guiding ideas. Indeed it may be truly said that Spencer was more favorably received in the United States than in England; at all events Americans took the trouble to raise money for the purpose of enabling him to carry on his monumental enterprise. At Yale University, William Graham Sumner labored for about forty years in the spirit of Spencer. Indeed many of Spencer's doctrines became so deeply embedded in American sociology that they are still revered as axioms of that "science."

Spencer recognized the fact that the man-woman relationship is at the very center of sociological interest and devoted Part III of his first volume to "Domestic Institutions." At the opening of this part, he laid down an imperative: "As full understanding of the social relations cannot be gained without studying their genesis, so neither can full understanding of the domestic relations; and fully to understand the genesis of the domestic relations, we must go further back than the history of man [human being] carries us." Proof: "Of every species it is undeniable that individuals which die must be replaced by new individuals, or the species as a whole must die." Hence it would seem axiomatic that domestic relations, if not woman as such, must be noted by sociologists and the noting must be more than casual or a display of gallantry.

Either from his own inquiries or from other sources, perhaps John Stuart Mill's *Subjection of Women*, published in 1869, Spencer derived the conclusion that "the status of women" in primitive times was one of servitude and degradation "in which they were habitually stolen, bought and sold, made beasts of burden, inherited as property and killed at will." There were exceptions to this rule, Spencer realized: among some primitive people, women were rulers and the system of descent was in the female line; but these he treated as "anomalies" to be "noticed" in passing. "Numerous examples, already cited, show that at first women were regarded by men simply as property, and continued to be so regarded through several later stages." Then he added, as if to clinch the truth of the generalization, a citation from a Chippewayan chief: "Women were made for labor; one of them can carry, or haul, as much as two men can do. They also pitch our tents, make and mend our clothing, keep us warm at night; and, in fact, there is no such thing as traveling any considerable distance, in this country, without their assistance."

Unlike John Stuart Mill, however, Spencer did not hold that woman continued to be in this or any state of subjection all the way up to the middle of the nineteenth century. On the contrary there had been advancement: "Perhaps in no way is the moral progress of mankind more clearly shown, than by contrasting the position of women among savages with their position among the most advanced of the civilized." Indeed, according to Spencer's view, things had gone too far by 1876. From an extreme of subjection "we pass to the stage America shows us, in which a lady wanting a seat stares at a gentleman occupying one until he surrenders it, and then takes it without thanking him; we may infer that the rhythm traceable throughout all changes has carried this to an extreme from which there will be a recoil."

Although A. G. Keller, who succeeded Professor Sumner at Yale, worked at the "science of society" in the spirit of Spencer and Sumner, he was no slavish follower of those elders. In his volume, *Man's Rough Road* (1932), Keller rejected the sweeping doctrine of woman's historic subjection. He ridiculed the word "status," as meaning nothing definite, and declared that "the broadest preliminary generalization about woman's rights is that when it was expedient for society that she should have them, she got them, without or despite agitation." He also maintained that woman's "actual power" had "from the outset furnished a glaring contrast" to the legal theory of her "nonentity." Moreover under the head of "Progagation," Keller devoted several chapters to marriage, status, family, and the usual sociological staples.

But in the main body of his text, in which he deals with all those vital human affairs that are not directly connected with the family and propagation, Keller usually omits woman from his reckoning, unless she is to be included with man whenever he is telling about the extraordinary things that "man" has done, in agriculture, industry, invention, government, religion, and so forth. In this large domain of human life and labor, as Keller speaks of it, "man" has been the adjuster. At the beginning "man must tackle the food question. . . . In studying mankind's experience, we start from Man and Land.

... Men who have associated and organized themselves have survived. ... Men cannot be indifferent to competition when they want the same things. ... All men and all life conditions met by them are much alike. ... Man, set down in the earthly environment, confronts a compelling truth: that the first task of life is to live. ... The tiller stays by one piece of improved land. ... He wants it also for his children. ... It is a basic fact that men start with nothing. ... Men cannot eat unless labor is done. ... Their labor turns out to be by no means the curse that some writers, ancient and modern, have misnamed it."

Yet Keller occasionally checks himself and feels moved to mention women specifically. Indeed it is difficult to imagine how he could have missed them in the vast collection of anthropological materials assembled by his master, William Graham Sumner, which he had sifted and published in four volumes. After seeming to indicate that man had done about everything in starting civilization, Keller stops to declare: "A count of the most frequently mentioned sex-occupations of about a hundred representative tribes yields the following. Men are almost the sole makers of instruments of war or the chase ... which was to be expected, as they are the fighters and hunters. Women are found to be the chief carriers, grain grinders, and 'gatherers'; they get water, make pottery, do housework, trade, prepare hides, spin, gather wood, and attend to the fire ... while the tasks calling for concentration of energy, or inventiveness, or special skill, or, above all, organizing power, fall to the men." Men also help women at tasks which call for "greater strength." Folded within these judgments of women is a curious idea of skills.

The whole course of mankind from primitive times to our own age was covered by George A. Dorsey, whose specialty was anthropology, a wide traveler and observer of peoples, in a book of 958 pages of text, *Man's Own Show: Civilization.* Like Keller, Dorsey perhaps subsumes woman under the word man, and thus perhaps has her doing about everything that man does, good and bad, from the outset to the present day. Yet in dealing with "man's" doing in his great show Dorsey, like Keller, occasionally refers to woman as if she had characteristics of her own and made specific contributions to the show. At one point Dorsey informs us: "When Cave-man left his retreats in deep rock caverns and took to a vegetable diet

in the fertile valleys, he soon became a good farmer." About
twenty pages later, he has another idea on the subject of man
and his agriculture: "Of the two greatest factors in civilization
— agriculture and language — woman contributed at least
fifty per cent of one and probably ninety-five per cent of the
other."

As to woman's historic subjection throughout the ages,
Dorsey finds himself unable to accept it, after having devoted
a lifetime to the study of human societies in nearly every quarter of the globe. He declares that "woman's status bears no
necessary relation to the height or state of civilization. The
famous code of Hammurabi showed not only a high order of
society but a high status of woman, and such recognition of
her rights as a human being as are hardly equalled on earth
today."

But he adopted the subjection theory as applicable to a long
part of English history: "English law at the time of Blackstone
practically denied woman's existence as a personality after
marriage. She had almost no rights at all. From the time of
the Norman Conquest until fairly recently, the English wife
was her husband's *liege* subject. . . . Her only redress for his
maltreatment was a church court. . . . And as for ethics, where
in all the 'savage' world can we find a standard low enough to
tolerate husbands who automatically became possessed of
their wife's property on marriage and could carry off her be-
longings, leaving her to fend for herself and her children . . . ?"

If sociologists, psychologists, and anthropologists had much
difficulty in dealing with woman — her nature, force, and work
in history — the orthodox economists were, by their own definitions, relieved of such trouble. After all, they did not claim
to be treating of human beings exactly as they were or are;
they carried on their intellectual operations with a being of
their own creation: the economic *man*. Insofar as woman had
been or was an economic being she came naturally into the
science of economics as an economic man. Furthermore, economists, especially those of the classical tradition, were not
concerned with history nor with the family nor with "propagation" as were the sociologists. They were, or claimed to be,
describing a system which is natural and timeless — unless
disturbed by errant factors — and hence involves no moral

questions of reform, save possibly to keep the "natural" system of economy intact.

With communists, however, who have utilized history, economics, and sociology for purposes of attracting women as well as men to their movement, woman has been a creature with whom to reckon. In his elementary treatise designed to make communist doctrines clear to American readers, *What Is Communism?* (1936), Earl Browder devotes several pages to the family and woman. He does not expound the simple thesis of August Bebel, that women through the ages have been members of a subject sex, but he does maintain that "the unequal status of women in the family ... characterizes capitalist society." How is woman to be emancipated? "Socialism, as the first stage leading toward Communism, places among the first items of its program, the complete liberation of women from all inequality. Not only does it give women unconditional equality with men, but it provides guarantees for maintaining that equality, by means of special protection for motherhood by the State, and by special regulations of the conditions of women's work. Equality for women is being realized for the first time in history in the Soviet Union, the land of socialism. This is substantiated, not merely by the word of Communists, but by every honest bourgeois authority who has examined the situation of women in the Soviet Union at first hand. We will cite, from a multitude of authoritative books, one only, *Women in Soviet Russia* by Fannina Halle, an Austrian writer whose large book was the fruit of more than a year of study in various parts of the Soviet Union.... We see the subjection of women as the distortion and corruption of the family. We see the family of the future based upon the complete equality of men and women."

Workers in the natural sciences also enter the forum with their pronouncements on man and woman. For example, at a large gathering of men belonging to the American Association for the Advancement of Science, held at Cambridge, Massachusetts, during a lull between two world wars, William Wheeler, professor of economic entomology at Harvard University, assured his auditors that man is the real instigator of progress. "Throughout the ages," said this profound student of ants and bees, "the aggressiveness, curiosity, unstable intelligence, contentiousness, and other anti-social tendencies which the man inherited from his anthropoidal ancestors have kept society in a constant turmoil. . . . The restlessly questing intellect, driven by the dominant impulses of the mammalian male, furnishes the necessary stimulus to progress in human societies. Feminine societies are indeed harmonious, but stationary and incapable of further development. If women ran society, as among such insects as the ants, bees and the wasps, the men merely would be tolerated as necessary for reproduction. The important difference (between insects and man) lies, I believe, in what I call the 'problem of the male,' which has been successfully solved by the social insects but not by human societies."

In that vast domain of writings and speaking known as general literature or polite letters, including both creative and critical works, the images of woman drawn by men are so varied as almost to defy classification. There the whole gamut of men's emotions, from love and admiration to neglect, hate, and contempt, is run; and it is often difficult to discover whether the portraits of woman are intended to be evaluated by standards of cleverness or by accepted evidences of truth. But whether such views of woman created by men are sampled at random or examined wholesale in any huge collection of books and reviews, one distinct type of image appears with insistent regularity. It is the image of woman as not much of anything measured by man's standards of intellectual excellence.

For example, in the symposium called *Civilization in the United States* (1922), the editor, Harold Stearns, a critic eminent in literary circles, ascribed "the poverty of intellectual things" in America largely, if not entirely, to feminine influences. Women, he said, did not or could not take part effectively in the great game of pursuing high and intricate truth for its own sake, in the disinterested manner of man. On the contrary women are too practical and do not concern themselves with philosophy — that great aggregation of conflicting systems which seem to cancel one another. No, the intellectual life of American women "turns out on examination" by Mr. Stearns, to be "not an intellectual life at all, but sociological activity. . . . What women usually understand by the intellectual life is the application of modern scientific methods to a sort of enlarged and subtler course in domestic science." Rating the philosophy of John Dewey as inferior to absolute systems of metaphysics, Stearns then contends that the popularity of pragmatic philosophy was made possible "precisely because the intellectual atmosphere has been surcharged with this feminized utilitarianism." In this respect America was a failure and Europe a success, viewed from the heights of 1922, and women had to bear the brunt of responsibility for the tragedy in the United States.

In the literary uprising against the genteel tradition supposed to mark "America's coming of age," or achievement of intellectual maturity, novelists and critics were frequently inclined to view it, in part at least, as a revolt against woman representing softness and futility, as a rebellion against "effeminacy" and, in part, as a recovery of man, the male whose virility and values were "self-evident," like the truths set forth in the Declaration of Independence. In fact the "movement" was more complex, but a reaction against the feminine principle was a striking aspect of the hostility to the genteel displayed by such writers as Jack London, Theodore Dreiser, and Frank Norris. The animus of the tendency was almost perfectly revealed in the intellectual and moral adventures of James Lane Allen, as related by Grant C. Knight in his *James Lane Allen and the Genteel Tradition,* published in 1935.

According to his reviewer, Allen, a "supersensitive, hypochondriacal, lonely man," described his own characteristics as "Refinement, Delicacy, and Grace." He aspired to be the Columbus of Southern literature, and did not refinement, delicacy, and grace form the very essence of the Southern spirit? At the beginning of his literary career, in the Victorian age, Allen explored the "feminine principle" and treated it as if it were the source and substance of the refined tradition. But in time Allen shifted his course from gentility to virility, somewhat in the vogue of Thomas Hardy in England and writers of the "realistic" school in America.

As to the "cause" of this shift literary critics have indulged in considerable speculation. Professor Knight ascribed the change to the demands made by Allen's generation on the writers of fiction. This concept of "the cause" was supported by the critic, John Cournos, in the statement: "In short Allen cannot be treated as an isolated phenomenon. He is, as his biographer demonstrates, a representative expression of the spirit of his place and time, to which it is the duty of the critic to relate him." In his final judgment Cournos declared: "On the whole, Allen emerges a bigger man than perhaps his biographer originally intended he should. The genteel epoch, however, stands convicted of making James Lane Allen a lesser man than he might have been."

Considered in a larger perspective, the genteel tradition belonged to the history of the middle class rather than the history of woman as a feminine being. Indeed this fact was often recognized by writers of the transition period. Engaged in the civilian occupation of producing and distributing goods, members of that class differed in "virility" from warriors on horseback. Only on the theory that women were basically responsible for the rise of this powerful class could its triumph for a time be correctly ascribed to the force of the feminine principle in history. In any event, no small part of the blame for gentility was laid on effeminacy and it was assumed that masculine force was its own reward and justification.

In the literary circles ruled by the doctrines of Sigmund Freud, fiction, biography, literary criticism, and essays in general were long dominated by an interpretation of human nature and human history that in sum and substance reduced woman to a servant of man's biological propensities, usually suffering from neuroses besides. When a mountain of examples from literary appraisals of woman in this vogue is accumulated and sifted, the results add up to the dogma that woman is sex, civilization is a disease, and American civilization, to use Freud's own words, is "an abortion." Although the cult entered into a steep decline before Freud's death, it exerted a wide and powerful sway over American literature for about a quarter of a century and echoes of its teachings have by no means died away.

How lightly women are frequently portrayed by men of letters is well exemplified in Van Wyck Brooks' work, *The World of Washington Irving,* published in 1944. Mr. Brooks has been widely regarded as one of the most distinguished literary critics in the United States. Certainly he does not write without spending laborious days in research. His publishers inform the reader by the jacket of this volume that he "has won every award possible for an American writer to receive," including the Pulitzer Prize. They also say: "No pedantic historian, Mr. Brooks conceives literary history as the faithful reflection of the life, thought, and social conditions of the times. . . . This technique is particularly rewarding in Mr. Brooks' penetrating analysis of Washington Irving's world — a period in which American writers first became conscious of their heritage, and in which the Jeffersonian revolution created an intellectual atmosphere that was distinctively and forever American."

This volume, which follows his works on New England, covers the rest of the country during the period from about 1800 to the early forties, and has but one chapter on New England. In its 483 packed pages, the existence of women in the intellectual and social life of America during about fifty momentous years, save in a very few cases, is recognized only casually, and then usually in no significant relation to the times.

The index contains five references to Abigail Adams, author of the invaluable letters on America and England in the Revolutionary age. It seems that her coachman once lost his way while driving from Baltimore to Washington. During her first days in the White House, the family wash had to be hung up in the audience room. There are two brief quotations in footnotes from her letters: one on the novelist Richardson and another on Canterbury, England. The fifth reference is to the fact that Abigail called Patience Wright "Queen of the Sluts."

Mercy Warren receives one gesture in less than a line cited in the index. Reference is made to "the drawing room pieces of Mercy Warren" as among the best plays of the Revolutionary era. So much for the woman who produced two of the most patriotic plays in behalf of the American cause against the Tories and then wrote a trenchant history of the American Revolution, published in 1805.

If it be said that Mr. Brooks is not here especially concerned with New England, attention may then be shifted to the Middle States and the West. Was not Lucretia Mott active in this period, speaking and writing on slavery, the rights of women, the problems of labor, the spirit necessary to sustain civilization? She is not in the index. What about Elizabeth Cady Stanton and all the other women who were to issue in 1848 at Seneca Falls a startling manifesto on the rights of women? Why should Emma Willard be singled out for a brief mention in connection with education in Greece and then given a mere footnote "as the first of all the pioneers of the higher education of women in the United States"?

Like Emma Willard, Frances Wright gets a footnote in Mr. Brooks' pages on "life, thought, and social conditions of the times." He quotes a few lines from Frances on the American farmer's love for the soil he tills. By what criterion of judgment does he fail to give at least a page or two to a woman who wrote, spoke, and agitated on religion, labor, education, marriage and divorce, law reform, slavery, and indeed almost every phase of intellectual and social life? She was highly esteemed by Lafayette, worked at Robert Owen's socialist colony in Indiana, led the movement for free thought in New York, aided in the launching of the labor movement, and discussed the current questions of economics and politics in newspapers and on the platform. Frances Wright was active and influential in Irving's world but her work and spirit find no appreciative pages in Mr. Brooks' volume on that subject.

It may be contended that the woman movement was young in the period from 1800 to the early forties and that only a feminine bias could insist on giving extended recognition to women in this account of "the life, thought, and social conditions" of that age. But thousands of articles, pamphlets, and books by women and about women of the period bear witness to the intensity of a great democratic dispute. Besides, we have some testimony from one of the most distinguished thinkers of the nineteenth century, Alexis de Tocqueville, an observer from France. Tocqueville visited Washington Irving's world, traveled East, West, North, and South, saw the country with his own eyes, talked with all sorts and conditions of people, read widely in American documentation, and wrote *Democracy in America,* the first part of which was published in 1835 and the second in 1840.

Tocqueville had barely arrived in America when he was struck by the qualities and force of American women; and after thoughtful observation and close study of American "life, thought, and social conditions," he passed a judgment on American women: "If I were asked now that I am drawing to the close of this work, in which I have spoken of so many important things done by Americans, to what the singular prosperity and growing strength of that people ought mainly to be attributed, I should reply, To the superiority of their women." If Tocqueville's attitude may be set down as an exaggeration of French gallantry, to what shall Mr. Brooks' verdict be traced?

Into a nutshell Alfred Adler, doctor of medicine and specialist in psychology, from Vienna, compressed his views on the subject of man and woman, when he arrived at the port of New York on September 7, 1935, for the purpose of lecturing in the United States. Dr. Adler had once been a member of the Freudian school but he had broken away from it about 1913 and founded a new school of his own. After his breach with his old master, he declared that Freud had laid too much stress on the drive of sexual passions in human thought and had underemphasized the influence of the lust for prestige and superiority.

Owing to the fame he had won, Dr. Adler was greeted on his arrival by a crowd of reporters eager for interviews covering the popular theme: man-woman. He seemed willing to grant them the privilege, and in the course of his remarks he declared that the idea of women's inferiority to men is an "immortal myth"; that biology refutes the theory, that the theory has been "promoted by men"; that woman's "emancipation" is mere bluff"; but "the idea is so firmly established that nothing can shake it."

"Of course, men have this inferiority, too," Dr. Adler asserted. "All this talk of suffrage, emancipation, and so forth, this is real bluff, that is all. From the very beginning they [women] are made to feel that they are not on a level with men. This, contrary to popular belief, has not been changed by the advances of women during the last few decades. As a matter of fact, the very increase in education and culture among women has made them feel their supposed inferiority more than ever. There is no biological basis for this feeling; it is merely a fictitious invention of the male sex." And men's invention, he further declared, sprang from their own feeling of inferiority — a complex from which "the majority of all people suffer at one time or another."

Is there no remedy for the suffering and misapprehension

brought about by the fictitious invention? Is the "immortal myth" too firmly established to be outlawed or changed? Dr. Adler's proposed panacea lay in the manipulations of individual psychology — not in an inquiry into the origins of the myth or into the historical experience of mankind which might lead to factual conclusions as to its validity or invalidity.

Chapter 4

The Haunting Idea: Its Nature and Origin

THERE is no need for a Sherlock Holmes to serve as a detective in a search for the controlling or influential ideas employed in modern books, articles, reviews, and published addresses dealing with men and women. Even a novice can discover one obtruding conception that haunts thousands of printed pages. It is the image of woman throughout long ages of the past as a being always and everywhere subject to *male* man or as a ghostly creature too shadowy to be even that real.

As for centuries the Ptolemaic conception of the astrophysical universe dominated discussions and "reasonings" in astronomy, so the theory of woman's subjection to man, the obliteration of her personality from consideration, governs innumerable discussions and reasonings in relation to human affairs. Here, there, and almost everywhere, it gives animus, tendency, and opinionative assurance to the man-woman controversies of our day.

There came a time, however, when the Ptolemaic idea of the starry universe was tested by patient observation and study — with the aid of scientific instruments — and declared to be a myth — a false theory. When that decision was made on the basis of more knowledge then Ptolemy possessed, rapid progress in astrophysics occurred and the art of navigating uncharted seas was brought nearer to perfection.

Out of such experiences in the natural sciences has been developed the idea that advancement in other branches of learning can be best effected by the application of what John Morley calls "engines of criticism, skepticism, and verification" to popular theories, even those held by everybody, always, and everywhere. This has become a maxim of modern science and scholarship. So it seems fair to conclude that, if learning about man and woman is to be advanced, these engines of intellectual progress must be applied to the ideas of their relations which have come from times past and are still widely current.

The value of learning lies not in sheer erudition, if there at all. Learning can provide creative guidance for civilization.

In the very nature of things historical, at the beginning of an inquiry into the idea of woman's historic subjection, four questions arise: When did this idea originate? By whom was it originated? In what circumstances was it formulated? Why did it obtain such an empire over human minds? In short, what is its real nature and origin?

BLACKSTONE EXTINGUISHED THE MARRIED WOMAN'S PERSONALITY

It is difficult, admittedly, to trace all the mental processes which converged into the idea that women were a subject sex or nothing at all — in any past or the total past — until they began to win "emancipation" in our age of enlightenment. But, if one works backward in history hunting for the origin of this idea, one encounters, near the middle of the nineteenth century, two illuminating facts: (1) the idea was first given its most complete and categorical form by American women who were in rebellion against what they regarded as restraints on their liberty; (2) the authority whom they most commonly cited in support of systematic presentations of the idea was Sir William Blackstone, author of *Commentaries on the Laws of England* — the laws of the mother country adopted in part by her offspring in the new world (see below, Chapter V). The first volume of this work appeared in 1765 and the passage from that volume which was used with unfailing reiteration by insurgent women in America was taken from Blackstone's chapter entitled "Of Husband and Wife."

That passage (7th edition, 1775) ran as follows: "By marriage, the husband and wife are one person in law; that is, the very being or legal existence of the woman is suspended during the marriage, or at least is incorporated and consolidated into that of the husband; under whose wing, protection, and *cover,* she performs every thing; . . . Upon this principle, of an union of person in husband and wife, depend almost all the legal rights, duties, and disabilities that either of them acquire by the marriage. . . . A man cannot grant any thing to his wife, or enter into covenant with her, for the grant would be to suppose her separate existence; . . . A woman indeed may be attorney for her husband; for that implies no separation from, but is rather a representation of her lord. And a husband may also bequeath any thing to his wife by will; for that cannot take effect till the coverture is determined by his death. The husband is bound to provide his wife with necessaries by law, as much as himself: and if she contracts debts for them, he is obliged to pay them; but for any thing besides necessaries, he is not chargeable. . . . If the wife be indebted before marriage, the husband is bound afterward to pay the debt; for he has adopted her and her circumstances together. . . .

"The husband also (by the old law) might give his wife moderate correction. For, as he is to answer for her misbehaviour, the law thought it reasonable to intrust him with this power of restraining her, by domestic chastisement. . . . But, with us, in the politer reign of Charles the second, this power of correction began to be doubted: and a wife may now have security of the peace against her husband; or, in return, a husband against his wife. . . .

"These are the chief legal effects of marriage during the coverture; upon which we may observe, that even the disabilities, which the wife lies under, are for the most part intended for her protection and benefit. So great a favourite is the female sex of the laws of England."

It is also a matter of historical record that for nearly a century or more Blackstone's *Commentaries* was a standard textbook for the training of lawyers, particularly in the United States. The work was written with such rhetorical persuasiveness and such display or semblance of learning, that it captivated innumerable students of law. Thomas Jefferson was scarcely exaggerating when he wrote long after the *Commentaries* appeared: "The opinion seems to be that Blackstone is to us what the Alcoran is to the Mahometans, that everything which is necessary is in him, and what is not in him is not necessary."

Whenever an American writer after 1783 was moved to instruct women on what he regarded as their rights and duties, he was almost certain to employ the authority of Blackstone, and likely to associate with the *Commentaries* expositions of divine law. For example, in 1845, eighty years after Blackstone's first volume was published, three years before the first "woman's rights" convention assembled at Seneca Falls in the state of New York, Edward D. Mansfield, A.M., "Late Professor of History in Cincinnati College, Author of the Political Grammar, and Corresponding Member of the National Institute," issued in Ohio a treatise bearing the following arresting title and descriptive subtitle: *"The Legal Rights, Liabilities and Duties of Women;* With an Introductory History of their Legal Condition in the Hebrew, Roman and Feudal Civil Systems. Including the law of marriage and divorce, the social relations of husband and wife, parent and child, of guardian and ward, and of employer and employed." In this work Professor Mansfield summarized his subject so concisely that none could miss his main points: namely, that women were subject to divine law and civil law: "The first great principle of Scripture, the unity of husband and wife, is repeated by the law. They are *in law, one person.* . . . Upon it, as observed by Blackstone, depend nearly all the legal rights, duties and disabilities acquired by marriage."

THE ANIMUS IN BLACKSTONE'S THEORIZING

Such was the nature of Blackstone's dictum to the effect that woman was civilly dead after she married, that her personality was merged into that of her husband and lord. To what extent and with what meaning was it true, if true at all? This question leads to Blackstone himself and the circumstances in which he formulated his dictum.

On his father's side Blackstone sprang from a mercantile family. His father kept a small silk shop in London. His mother was the daughter of a landed gentleman. By the assistance of his mother's brother, young Blackstone escaped from the silk shop, acquired an education at a gentlemen's university, Oxford, and entered the practice of law, at which he was a failure. Early in his course, he married the daughter of a landed gentleman and, like many a good bourgeois, settled down at a country seat where he assumed the role of a village "squire."

In politics Blackstone was an old Whig or a new Tory — a foe of reforming radicals, but not a sworn enemy of the English Revolution of 1688. Like many a commoner, Blackstone outdid the gentleman in his effusive praises of the ruling class in State and Church, with which, by fortune and ambition, he had become affiliated; his thinking and writing about law were visibly influenced by his acquired sentiment of class.

But more than this is involved in the identification of Blackstone, namely, the circumstances in which he composed his *Commentaries*. Before he became so warmly attached to the common law of England, he had tried to get a professorship at Oxford University to teach Roman civil law. When he failed in his effort he was mortified. Had he been able to get that appointment, he might have taught from his chair the domestic law of old Rome which made marriage a kind of partnership between husband and wife, each having definite property rights but using their rights for certain mutual purposes. His biographer, D. A. Lockmiller, says of Blackstone, in connection with his inability to get the chair at Oxford, that he was thus "saved . . . from the civil law of Rome and directed . . . to the growing system of common law [of England]."

The question of Blackstone's intentions in his interpretations of the common law cannot be answered beyond cavil, of course. Motives are seldom unsealed to the most careful student of personalities. But it was widely known in England that Blackstone disliked the equity jurisprudence, which invaded common-law doctrines and introduced into the laws of England principles akin to those of the Roman law in respect of married women's property rights. His love of the strict injunctions of the common law became intense. This was a matter of general knowledge in England.

BLACKSTONE'S RHETORIC AND JURISPRUDENCE TESTED BY FACTS

With these identifications of Blackstone the man, what can be ascertained about the truth of his statement of the common law respecting husband and wife? Was he technically correct? Did his philosophy of social values, of government, and his own social position and aspirations in the England of his time color his treatment of law?

First of all, in attempting to get at the correctness of his statement, one must consider the language in which it was expressed. Blackstone was not a scholar exceedingly cautious about his choice of words. On the contrary he was a rhetorician and indulged at times in "elegant" language which lent itself to the verdict of "brilliance." Thus he was "easy reading" and "convincing" to persons who were in a hurry to learn what was known about the laws of England, including the common law. When he declared, for instance, that by marriage "the husband and wife are one" and that "she performs everything" under his wing and cover, he was using metaphors; he was not speaking in any exact terms but in the sparkling fashion that intrigues readers who detest "dry facts."

Is Blackstone's statement true or what is its real nature? For the moment it may be said that there are some truths in it, that it contains a great deal of misleading verbalism, and that in upshot it is false. We must remember, moreover, very distinctly, that he was, at this point in his *Commentaries,* dealing solely with the rights or rightlessness of the married woman only, with her position, as he said, "in law." Now the words "in law" actually meant in common law. Blackstone so understood it and understood it as a qualification on all the passage. So did his readers who were trained in law.

The common law was, however, only one branch of English law, one of the laws of England, or bodies of law. Other bodies of law were acts of Parliament often drastically modifying the common law and old customs left undisturbed by the common and statutory laws; and, as Blackstone remarked casually, "over and above" these laws was Equity, "frequently called in to assist, to moderate, and to explain the other laws."

It was Equity administered by a special court, having no jury, that provided, in the name of justice, remedies for wrongs for which the Common Law afforded no remedies. Equity enforced trusts and other understandings that assured to married women rights of property denied to them by the Common Law. (For the revolutionary nature of Equity in the United States and England see Chapters VI and VIII.)

Besides, there were the private practices and agreements of men and women in the ordinary affairs of daily living, which as a rule prevailed undisturbed unless perchance they became involved in actions before the courts and were declared illegal, contrary to law or good morals. Only when such practices and agreements were notoriously contrary to law or good morals or the men or women who were parties to such practices and agreements were entangled in litigation was any kind of "law" applied to them. In fact the number of human actions and understandings which ever come before courts of law is small in comparison with the vast number that make up the complex of family and social life.

Yet when Blackstone spoke of the husband's rights over the real and personal property of his wife and of her disabilities "in law," he was technically correct, within fixed limits. On its face the statement meant that, in case of litigation, the husband asserts certain rights over the real and personal property of his wife and, if the wife contests them or the said rights are otherwise drawn in question at common law, the common-law courts will enforce the husband's common-law rights *unless the husband and wife have made agreements to the contrary before and after marriage or the father or other friend or relative of the wife has safeguarded the wife's rights by the creation of a trust or otherwise, which agreements and trusts made in due form are valid in equity and will be enforced by courts of equity.* In other words, *in the absence of valid agreements and actions to the contrary,* the husband may, if he so desires, or his creditors or other litigants may, assert a husband's rights over the wife's property within the limits set by specific rules of the common law, and common-law courts will enforce them in case of litigation.

In this highly restricted and technical sense, and subject to reservations he did not set forth and explain in detail, Blackstone's statement on husband and wife contained several correct sentences. But of all the men and women who for generations cited his statement as evidence of women's subjection, few were well trained in the technicalities of law. Most of them were unable, therefore, to comprehend the severe limitations imposed on it in fact and the exact sense in which the statement could be regarded as true, particularly in view of the metaphorical style which Blackstone used.

Did Blackstone willfully intend to mislead his readers into believing that the legal status of married women in England in 1765 was correctly and fully described in his statement on husband and wife?

Whatever his intentions Blackstone could have avoided the charge of distortion by including in his chapter on husband and wife another statement correctly presenting the rules of equity jurisprudence under which the wife could be fully protected in the enjoyment of her separate property rights. Had he done this he would have carried the qualifications of the common law along with his assertions and informed his readers immediately that common-law doctrines were only common-law doctrines; that under principles of equity jurisprudence a married woman's separate status in respect of her property rights could be, in the event of litigation and in innumerable cases was being, protected by a branch of law "over and above" the common law, namely, Equity.

Informed English lawyers knew that Equity afforded protection to arrangements which safeguarded married women's separate property rights. So did informed American lawyers. The great American commentator, James Kent, as if alert to the peril of misunderstanding in regard to the married woman's status, immediately followed his own exposition of the common-law doctrines by an exposition of the equity doctrines under which the application of the former could be avoided, as far as the married woman's property rights were concerned. But Blackstone did not see fit to provide this safeguard against a misunderstanding by dealing fully with Equity either in the section on husband and wife or anywhere else in the *Commentaries*. As a result, generations of men and women, untrained in law and equity, accepted Blackstone's statement on husband and wife as the whole truth of the married woman's status. In these circumstances it is not surprising that the statement became a main support, indeed the very basis, of a great fiction — the fiction that women were, historically, members of a subject sex — "civilly dead," their very being suspended during marriage and their property, along with their bodies, placed under the dominion of their respective "lords" or "barons."

In some measure the most demoralizing effects of Blackstone's tyranny over lawyers and law were due to his laudation of the Common Law, his dislike if not contempt for Legislation, and the slight consideration he gave to Equity. To Blackstone the common law was a magnificent system of human justice, deserving all praise. There might be some blemishes in it but they were to be deemed slight. The Civil Law of Rome, with its provisions for the equality of husband and wife in the marriage partnership, was, in comparison with the English law, "a mild and rational system of laws," scarcely deserving mention, in his opinion.

Attempts to introduce the Roman law into England he ascribed largely to the efforts of "the monkish clergy (devoted to the will of a foreign primate)," the Pope at Rome. Although Blackstone confessed that it was far from his desire to derogate the study of the Roman law considered as "a collection of written reason," he proposed to uphold English veneration of Alfred the Great and Edward as against Theodosius and Justinian — "the free constitution of Britain, as against the despotic monarchy of Rome and Byzantium."

To the modification of the common law by legislation, Blackstone was openly hostile. He referred with scorn to the "rash and unexperienced workmen" who "have ventured to new-dress and refine, with all the rage of modern improvement." Reformers who tried to improve the common law, he alleged, had frequently destroyed its symmetry . . . for specious embellishments and fantastic novelties." Few of the legal problems of England could be laid at the door of the common law: "To say the truth, almost all the perplexed questions, almost all the niceties, intricacies, and delays (which have sometimes disgraced the English, as well as other courts of justice) owe their original not to the common law itself, but to innovations that have been made in it by acts of parliament ... penned or corrected by men of none or very little judgment in law."

The confusion introduced by unlearned and ill-judging legislators decried by Coke was lamented with equal passion by Blackstone. Indeed one of his avowed purposes in writing his *Commentaries* was to instruct English gentlemen in the arts of governing the country (under a constitution which excluded most of the English people from any share in the government), so that gentlemen so trained would uphold the magnificent system of the Common Law and avoid any fundamental alterations in it. This was, of course, heady wine for American lawyers who looked with fear and disgust at the uprising of democracy in 1800 and during the triumph of the populace in the Jacksonian era.

BLACKSTONE'S MISREPRESENTATION OF ENGLAND'S "LAWS"

Convinced that the Common Law was so perfect in its symmetry and in the quality of its justice as to bar tinkering by legislators, Blackstone was opposed to the inroads made upon that law by Equity jurisprudence. In one of the greatest understatements ever made in historical writing, the cautious scholar, Frederick W. Maitland, long afterward declared that "Blackstone, like other common-law lawyers, was not very fond of the chancery [equity]. The view of the thinking English lawyer of his time seems to have been that the chancery was a necessary evil." Indeed Blackstone was hardly willing to concede that the "evil" was even "necessary."

At all events, considering the role of Equity in the development of justice in England, and the immense volume of equity law in his own time, Blackstone treated it in such a brief, cursory, and inadequate manner as to give his readers the impression and induce the conviction that they need pay little serious attention to equity, save in some particulars. The great subject of equity which dealt with trusts, so important in correcting, even obliterating, the property "disabilities" of the married woman, he dismissed in pages so relatively few as to give no adequate key to the revolution wrought by equity in this domain of marital relations.

In effect, therefore, Blackstone deceived generations of lawyers and laymen of both sexes by the manner in which he treated the disabilities of married women and pronounced their "civil death" at law. He did not immediately follow up his disquisition on husband and wife with a section showing how the disabilities of married women, in respect of their property, could be and were frequently nullified by uses, trusts, and other arrangements which were valid and enforced in equity. He did, it is true, in scattered parts of the *Commentaries*, show how the common-law disabilities in such respects were avoidable by private agreements among men and women, among men, and among women. For example, in Book II, Chapter 20, he dealt extensively with uses and trusts — instruments employed to nullify in effect the restrictions at common law on married women's property rights. In this section he told of the battle between Common Law, Statutory Law, and Equity. He remarked that at one time the courts of law "greatly curtailed and diminished" the power of the court of chancery over landed property and then by "one or two technical scruples" restored that power "with tenfold increase."

In that chapter Blackstone, with some asperity, also spoke of a "species of conveyance, called a *covenant to stand seised to uses*." This, he explained, is an instrument "by which a man seised of lands, covenants in consideration of blood or marriage that he will stand seised of the same to the use of his child, wife, or kinsman; for life, in tail, or in fee. Here the statute executes at once the estate; for the party intended to be benefited, having thus acquired the use, is thereby put at once into corporal possession of the land, without ever seeing it, by a kind of parliamentary magic. But this conveyance can only operate when made upon such weighty and interesting considerations as those of blood and marriage."

These were, of course, the very considerations to which men and women could and did resort in those numerous arrangements with which to create and protect the property rights of married women. In other words, if the qualifications of Chapter 20 in Book II and similar relevant passages had been inserted in Blackstone's chapter on husband and wife, the false notion of the married woman's civil death could scarcely have been started on its brain-storming course through English and American agitation relative to "women's rights."

Through the long legal struggle between the common law on the one side and statutory and equity law on the other ran the eternal struggle of life — not of individuals, but of men *and* women united by their inexorable relationships — to survive and provide safeguards for each other and for their children, under the law or in spite of it. Here the strength and permanence of the family was an objective. In legal essence this struggle, amid every variety of being and experience, involved conflicts with the precision, rigidity, and certainty of common-law rules, which were ceasing to fit the ever-changing conditions of life and economy, and with the strivings for more freedom to make adjustments to the new necessities and aspirations. And in England, Equity was the jurisprudence, or branch of law, in general to which men and women could look for relief from the "wrongs" inflicted by the common law. Blackstone was aware of this and did not wholly neglect equity.

In Section 2 of his Introduction, he referred to Equity in general as a "method of interpreting laws, by the reason of them" and to the treatment of the subject by Hugo Grotius, the Dutch author of the great treatise on *The Law of War and Peace*. Of this equity, as universal reason used to correct the deficiency of the law, Blackstone then wrote: "Equity thus depending, essentially, upon the particular circumstances of each individual case, there can be no established rules and fixed precepts of equity laid down, without destroying its very essence, and reducing it to a positive law. . . . Law, without equity, though hard and disagreeable, is much more desirable for the public good, than equity without law." There was some good in equity, he admitted, but he thought that, if pushed too far, it would, like legislation, introduce confusion into the perfection of the common law.

When Blackstone came to a survey of the sources of the laws of England, Section 3 of his Introduction, he devoted about thirty pages to the subject. He was careful to treat fully the Common Law as the great fountain of law and justice. He did not, indeed could not, ignore the statutes of Parliament; but he boldly asserted that acts of Parliament, productive of "absurd consequences, manifestly contradictory to common reason," were, as regards these consequences, null and void. In this fashion, with nothing more than a shadowy authority, if any authority at all, Blackstone proclaimed that common-law judges could, in these "absurd" cases, declare acts of Parliament that were contrary to common reason invalid and hold them of no effect.

At the very end of his discourse on the sources of English laws, Blackstone dedicated one of these thirty pages to Equity. He did not, indeed could not, in making commentaries on the *laws* of England, wholly ignore equity law, for it was certainly one of the sources of those laws. He remarked: "What equity is, and how impossible in its very essence to be reduced to stated rules, hath been shewn in the preceding section." But then he sought to reduce the role of Equity in English law to its simplest, severest, and most restricted terms, minimizing with a mere gesture the great part it had played and was then playing in the humanizing of the common law.

"I shall therefore only add," he went on, "that (besides the liberality of sentiment with which our common law judges interpret acts of parliament, and such rules of the unwritten law as are not of a positive kind) there are also courts of equity established for the benefit of the subject, to detect latent frauds and concealments, which the process of the courts of law is not adapted to reach; to enforce the execution of such matters of trust and confidence, as are binding in conscience, though not cognizable in a court of law; to deliver from such dangers as are owing to misfortune or oversight; and to give a more specific relief . . . than can always be obtained by the generality of the rules of the positive or common law. This is the business of our courts of equity, which however are only conversant in matters of property." This was about the least that Blackstone could say of equity if he was to notice it at all.

Of his chapter on the courts of the realm, about thirty pages, Blackstone devoted ten to the high court of chancery. In the main he confined his record to a bare recital of certain outstanding facts in the history of Equity. On the final page of this section, he at last unbent to pay tribute to the work of the Earl of Nottingham who, toward the close of the seventeenth century, opened the period of modern Equity. He said: "The reason and necessities of mankind, arising from the great change in property by the extension of trade and the abolition of military tenures, coöperated in establishing his [Nottingham's] plan, and enabled him in the course of nine years to build a system of jurisprudence and jurisdiction upon wide and rational foundations; which have also been extended and improved by many great men, who have since presided in chancery. And from that time to this, the power and business of the court have increased to an amazing degree." In view of this clear, though brief, tribute to Equity, the scant consideration given to the *substance* of Equity in other parts of the *Commentaries* is the more amazing, to those familiar with the role of Equity in law as practice.

Well aware that in their practice many lawyers would have to take account of the equity remedies accessible to their clients, Blackstone assigned a chapter of Book III to proceedings in the courts of equity. Here he mentioned particularly equity law for infants, idiots, lunatics, charities, and bankrupts, and omitted any extended consideration of trusts in general or the privileges open to married women as against the rigors of the Common Law.

In dealing with equity proceedings, he was for the most part, and with justification, concerned with technicalities. But he went far out of his way in combating the idea that it had been and was the business of Equity to abate the harshness of the Common Law, and asserted that "no such power is contended for" by equity. He labored to break down distinctions between Equity and Common Law in favor of the Common Law. To accomplish this aim, he asserted that "the judgments of the courts of law are guided by the most liberal equity." If then, he asked, the parity of law and reason governs both equity courts and common law courts, what then is the essential difference? He gave the narrowest possible answer: "It principally consists in the different modes of administering justice in each; in the mode of proof, the mode of trial, and the mode of relief." The qualifying word "principally" saved him from the just charge of utterly disregarding the very nature and substance of equity, of which he certainly was "not very fond." Even so, his treatment of equity in general was both superficial and misleading.

Most astounding of all to students of equity is Blackstone's plea in defense of the scant treatment he accorded to Equity — the plea of ignorance. In a passage on the subject, he said: "Let us next take a brief, but comprehensive view of the general nature of *equity,* as now understood and practised in our several courts of judicature. . . . As nothing is hitherto extant, that can give a stranger a tolerable idea of the courts of equity subsisting in England, as distinguished from the courts of law, the compiler of these observations cannot but attempt it with diffidence; those who know them best, are too much employed to find time to write; and those who have attended but little in those courts, must be often at a loss for materials." Thus the reader is left to infer that Blackstone had at his command no supply of treatises and documents on which to base an appropriate and comprehensive treatment of the equity under which the common-law restriction on women had been, could be, and was being eradicated in England.

This inference is wrong. Blackstone, through ignorance, indifference, abhorrence, or carelessness, in this passage of the *Commentaries,* misrepresented the facts in the case. As the distinguished modern historian of English law, Sir William Holdsworth, remarked in an article on "Blackstone's Treatment of Equity," in the *Harvard Law Review* for November, 1929, the author of the *Commentaries* had available, when he wrote the above passage, "several series of equity reports" (from 1557 to 1766), two volumes of abridged equity reports, at least two textbooks on equity, and several works dealing with the practice, procedure, and pleading of the court of Chancery. In short he had easy access to at least twenty-two collections of equity reports extending over about two centuries and at least twelve treatises and textbooks. Furthermore he had at his command Richard Francis' *Maxims of Equity: Collected from and proved by cases, out of the Books of the Best Authority in the High Court of Chancery,* published in 1728. In Francis' *Maxims* alone Blackstone could have found all the first principles of equity jurisprudence, then and later applied in the interest of a kind of justice which common-law courts did not provide for guiding the adjustments of many vital relations between men and women, and between parents and children, in the interests of the Family.

With ample justification Holdsworth decided that Blackstone, "when dealing with the equity administered by the court of Chancery . . . presents a picture of equity and its relation to the law which was highly speculative when he wrote it, and is positively misleading in the light of the subsequent development of equitable and legal doctrine." Thus through Blackstone's selective jurisprudence and his treatment of equity, thousands, perhaps millions, of men and women in England and the United States were led to accept the idea of women's historic "subjection" into "civil death," as the whole truth. That is, they adopted a fiction about human behavior.

Various reasons may be given for Blackstone's dislike of, or lack of fondness for, equity, but it is not necessary to ascribe it to any personal animosity toward women. Generosity may well plead his ignorance as a sufficient explanation. Devotees of the common law may seek to account for his operations by referring to his overweening fondness for the common law. Technologists in law may, with justice, point out his affection for the precision and certainty of common-law doctrines and his fear of the vagaries, variety, and uncertainty in the practices of men and women allowed and enforced by equity. Equity did indeed seem to be permitting men and women to do almost as they pleased in safeguarding their mutual responsibilities and their separate property interests under agreements and understandings of their own making.

Under such agreements and understandings, the titles to a vast amount of property were afloat. In an age when agreements, even if written, were not matters of public record open to lawyers and inquiries, it was often impossible, under equity practices, to find out who owned what, for innumerable apparent owners had only a nominal possession under a trust, while the income and other advantages of the property might go to wives, daughters, or other beneficiaries of trusts. In such circumstances, it was difficult for creditors to discover whom to sue in case of indebtedness and for lawyers to straighten out the titles to property entangled in trust arrangements, unrecorded, and perhaps nowhere written down.

That Blackstone may have objected to the rights conferred

upon English women by family arrangements enforceable in equity is possible. Objections of the kind were often expressed in the eighteenth century. For example, "A friend to the Sex," who wrote *Sketches of . . . the Sex,* republished in Boston in 1807, complained: "It is no uncommon thing, in the present times, for the matrimonial bargain to be made so as that the wife shall retain the sole and absolute power of her own fortune, in the same manner as if she were not married. But what is more inequitable, the husband is liable to pay all the debts which his wife thinks proper to burden him with, even though she have abundance of her own to answer that purpose. He is also obliged to maintain her, though her circumstances be more opulent than his."

Blackstone may have had some such ideas in mind when he said that the female sex was a favorite of English laws. But whatever excuses may now be found for Blackstone's neglect of equity, it can in no way offset the fact that his great dogma respecting husbands and wives has played havoc with the minds and relations of countless men and women from his day to ours.

Blackstone not only gave scant consideration to equity jurisprudence, which led to drastic modifications in the binding character of the common-law doctrines formulated in his *Commentaries;* he was often inaccurate in handling details of English legal history. An example in respect of women's status appears in Book II, Chapter 5. There he dealt with Clause 6 of Henry III's reissue of the Great Charter — a clause that pertains to control over the marriage of heirs (*haeredes*). The words *haeredes maritentur absque disparagatione* he construed as "meaning certainly, by *haeredes,* heirs female, as there are no traces before this to be found of the lord's claiming the marriage of heirs male; and as Glanvill expressly confines it to heirs female." Thus as to the period in question he expressly denied that the lord had control over the marriage of the male ward, and confined the control to females.

Here we have an excellent illustration of Blackstone's method and the kind of original sources on which he relied for evidence. If he had searched in the voluminous records in London, he would have found numerous documents showing that male heirs were treated in respect of the lord's control over marriage substantially in the same way as female heirs. But he relied for authority upon Ranulf de Glanvill, an English legist of the twelfth century, who had held high office under the king and had written a treatise on English law, particularly with reference to procedure in the king's court. In other words, without examining the sources themselves, Blackstone simply took as adequate a comment from a twelfth-century commentator to the effect that early law discriminated against females by providing a different rule for males.

There is no doubt that Glanvill did make the comment in question and it is strange, too, in view of the fact that he had no sons and that his own heirs were three daughters, to whom his estate passed by inheritance. As chief justiciar under Henry III Glanvill could easily have avoided his error by investigating the legal records on which his statements of law were presumably based, for in those records were many instances of male wards disposed of by their guardians.

To give an example: "Ralph of Normanville offers [to the king] one good destrier [war-horse] to have the custody of the land in his fee which belonged to Richard Labbe in Empingham with [the right to control] the marriage of the son and heir of the same Richard . . . until the heir be of age; and the sheriff [of Rutland] is commanded to allow him to have that custody." Again, "Henry de Redeman offers forty marks to have the custody of the land and heir of Roger de Hedon, and to have the marriage of the same heir to the use of his daughter."

Although the records of appeals to the king's officers and of decisions respecting the overlord's right to dispose of male heirs in marriage do not seem to be as numerous as those pertaining to female heirs, they are sufficiently numerous to invalidate Blackstone's dictum that such right of disposition in early law was confined to "heirs female." If the dictum had been true it would have meant that the early law did in fact discriminate against female wards, subject to the proviso, constantly repeated, that the overlord could not force them into unworthy marriages — a proviso also applied to male wards. But the dictum was false to the records of English legal history, and Blackstone's error in this instance permits a suggestion that additional research might invalidate other dicta confidently expressed in his *Commentaries* and later accepted as true and binding by generations of lawyers and judges in England and the United States.

MARY WOLLSTONECRAFT REINFORCES BLACKSTONE

To the vogue of the Blackstonian doctrine, respecting the nothingness of women, Mary Wollstonecraft contributed, perhaps unwittingly. In the midst of the French upheaval, she issued in 1790 a reply to Edmund Burke's strictures — a volume which she entitled *A Vindication of the Rights of Men*. Two years later, in 1792, and twelve years after the death of Blackstone, while the strife over his legal conservatism was raging in England, when the "rights of man" was challenging all restrictions on human freedom, she published her *Vindication of the Rights of Woman*.

In arguing for the rights of woman she made use of the writings of philosophers, moralists, educators, and agitators rather than the works by lawyers. She depended most on Rousseau for the doctrine of "natural" rights. The objects of her special aspersions were customs and opinions, not specific provisions of law affecting women, married and single. She attacked the *"divine right* of husbands," and expressed the hope that it might be contested "without danger." Here she was not speaking of the dominion exercised by Blackstone's "lord" or "baron" over the *feme covert*. Rather she was dealing with mental and emotional attitudes. But in her portrayal of the alleged social tyranny exercised by man over woman, she helped to vitalize the doctrine that married women were civilly dead, members of a subject sex in effect, nothing in history save perhaps obsequious playthings or furtive intriguers trying to make their way out from under man's domination.

In the manipulation of this theory of life one fact is outstanding and immediately germane to all thought about the subject. This fact is that Rousseau who set the Western world aflame with the doctrine of equality and democracy for men also formulated and put into circulation a doctrine claiming that woman should be content to please man and get very little in return. "Woman," he declared in *Émile*, "is expressly formed to please the man: if the obligation be reciprocal also, and the man ought to please in his turn, it is not so immediately necessary: his great merit is in his power, and he pleases merely because he is strong. This, I must confess, is not one of the refined maxims of love; it is, however, one of the laws of nature, prior to love itself. If woman be formed to please and to be subjected to man, it is her place, doubtless, to render herself agreeable to him, instead of challenging his passion. The violence of his desires depends on her charms; it is by means of these she should urge him to the exertion of those powers which nature hath given him."

Yet Rousseau did not deny that woman had power and was a force in history. Nor did he reduce her qualities to those of mere futility. On the contrary, he ascribed to her extraordinary endowments for discernment and judgment. "A woman," he asserted, "who is naturally weak and does not carry her ideas to any great extent, knows how to judge and make a proper estimate of those movements which she set to work, in order to aid her weakness; and those movements are the passions of men. The mechanism she employs is much more powerful than ours, for all her levers move the human heart. She must have the skill to incline us to do everything which her sex will not enable her to do herself, and which is necessary or agreeable to her; therefore she ought to study the mind of man thoroughly, not the mind of man in general, abstractedly, but the dispositions of those men to whom she is subject either by the laws of her country or by the force of opinion. She should learn to penetrate into their real sentiments from their conversation, their actions, their looks and gestures. She should also have the art, by her own conversation, actions, looks, and gestures, to communicate those sentiments which are agreeable to them, without seeming to intend it. Men will argue more philosophically about the human heart; but women will read the heart of men better than they. . . . Women have the most wit, men have most genius; women observe, men reason. From the concurrence of both we derive the clearest light and the most perfect knowledge which the human mind is of itself capable of attaining. . . . The world is the book of woman."

Rousseau's doctrine that woman's duty is to please man fitted neatly, not only with Rousseau's personal egotism but also into the genteel theory respecting woman which was then spreading among the middle classes in England. In short form, this theory maintained that if woman would exercise the faculty of gratifying and deluding men, God or providence would assure to her a good father, a protective husband, economic security, and freedom from the responsibility of fending for herself in the struggle for existence. To attain this "fortunate" position, woman needs only to practice the arts of apparent submission and actual cunning, and to refrain from challenging man by a resort to learning, the acquisition of worldly knowledge, and the use of reason. If she should willfully leave the sphere thus assigned to her, she would fail to achieve the idea of irresponsible comfort so highly cherished in a bourgeois society.

It was this vision of modesty, or gentility, fortified by the pronouncement of Rousseau, that Mary Wollstonecraft assailed in her *Vindication of the Rights of Woman.* In contending for the rights of woman she appealed to reason, justice, and virtue. She did not inquire how far and in what respects the genteel theory conformed to innumerable known facts about women in contemporary society or in deeper history. Perhaps it never occurred to her to do that. At any rate Mary Wollstonecraft conceded the central point of the genteel theory with these words: "That woman is naturally weak, or degraded by a concurrence of circumstances, is, I think, clear." In effect she took over Rousseau's thesis, and phrased it in her fashion: Woman is everywhere in chains but I propose to show her the road to freedom.

In Wollstonecraft's view, the idea that woman was formed to please man and could govern him by the use of sex charms "is the philosophy of lasciviousness," an offense against virtue, reason, and respectability — against everything that gives dignity and value to human life. The educational ideal of the doctrine, she held, is to deprive girls of the physical exercise necessary to bodily strength, to restrain them in the use of the reason with which they are endowed, to deny them access to the knowledge which belongs of right to human beings and is indispensable to women in the discharge of the responsibilities that fall upon them in actual life. Law, custom, education, and opinion, she contended, sustain this false ideal for woman, force her to regard her subjection as her proper lot in life, and mold her in the image of the tradition. Thus not only is woman subjected to tyranny and degraded, but man is encouraged to cultivate his worst passions and prejudices, to grow in arrogance, and to applaud ignorance.

The genteel business, Wollstonecraft declared, flouts all the virtues that give worth to human character and works against civilization itself. Is not truth the same for men and women? Is not the exercise of reason by women as desirable as the exercise of reason by men? By what just and intelligible principle are women denied free access to knowledge? If freedom is a value, by what right are women deprived of it? "Women," she granted, ". . . may have different duties to fulfill; but they are *human* duties, and the principles that should regulate the discharge of them, I sturdily maintain, must be the same. To become respectable, the exercise of their understanding is necessary; there is no other foundation for independence of character; I mean explicitly to say that they must only bow to the authority of reason, instead of being the *modest* slaves of opinion."

That under the sway of the genteel impulse women could exercise great powers Wollstonecraft did not deny: "Women . . . sometimes boast of their weakness, cunningly obtaining power by playing on the *weakness* of men; and they may well glory in their illicit sway, for, like Turkish bashaws, they have more real power than their masters." But exercising power in this manner is an evidence of degradation: "Virtue is sacrificed to temporary gratifications, and the respectability of life to the triumph of an hour." Thus, in Wollstonecraft's theory, even the very power exercised by women in history — the force in history which she had readily conceded — symbolized their subjection, and it was only by breaking the tyranny of custom and opinion which degraded them that women could escape from the status so assigned to women in history.

Neither a trained psychologist nor a student of history, Mary Wollstonecraft speculated freely in thinking about the relation of men and women. One of the many loose generalizations which stand out conspicuously in her volume reads: "It is wandering from my present subject, perhaps, to make a political remark; but as it was produced naturally by the train of my reflections, I shall not pass it silently over. Standing armies can never consist of resolute robust men; they may be well-disciplined machines, but they will seldom contain men under the influence of strong passions, or with very vigorous faculties; and as for any depth of understanding, I will venture to affirm that it is as rarely to be found in the army as amongst women. And the cause, I maintain, is the same. It may be further observed that officers are also particularly attentive to their persons, fond of dancing, crowded rooms, adventures, and ridicule."

Then in a footnote she asked these questions: "Why should women be censured with petulant acrimony because they seem to have a passion for a scarlet coat? Has not education placed them more on a level with soldiers than any other class of men?"

Going back to the main identification of women with soldiers as "well-disciplined machines," Wollstonecraft averred that in the case of soldiers, "like the *fair* sex, the business of their lives is gallantry; they were taught to please, and they only live to please. Yet they do not lose their rank in the distinction of sexes, for they are still reckoned superior to women, though in what their superiority consists, beyond what I have just mentioned, it is difficult to discover."

Scattered through *Vindication of the Rights of Woman* were innumerable opinions equally preposterous. Yet the boldness of the book, like the experiments in living which the author undertook, attracted attention, friendly and adverse, to this ardent advocate of human "rights." Mary Wollstonecraft's unrepressed thrust at conventions was issued in an American edition at Boston the same year of its publication in England. Her name entered the stream of consciousness in which other names of social rebels floated near the surface or deeper in memory. To this day she is a near-saint of countless feminists, most of whom have probably never read a line of her pamphlet on women critically at least.

LIBERALS AND SOCIALISTS CARRY THE IDEA THROUGH UNIVERSAL HISTORY

Although Wollstonecraft's *Vindication* appeared in the United States shortly after publication in England, it attained no very great sale in this country, either then or later. After all, she had left her argument unfinished and had given to women no program of legislation guaranteed to bring about their "emancipation." However that may be, leaders of the woman movement in America formulated their own statement on the subjection of women at Seneca Falls in 1848, in terms more economic and political than Wollstonecraft's effusion and definitely in accord with Blackstone's legal thesis. Subsequent formulations at other women's conventions merely amplified and enlarged upon the Seneca Falls declaration of their historic servitude and their will to independence. And there is good reason for believing that American statements of this kind helped to crystallize insurgent opinion in England along similar lines and to bring the Blackstone creed forcibly to the attention of English feminists and their friends among men as the warrant for adopting the theory of total subjection on which to base a demand for freedom and equality.

At all events the following facts have a distinct bearing on the acceptance in England of the Blackstone formula of subjection as the starting point for the feminist argument. First, Blackstone never acquired in that country the tyranny over the legal mind which he exercised in America; from the very beginning powerful critics, led by Jeremy Bentham, assailed his underlying philosophy with devastating effect and English scholarship made inroads upon the soundness of his treatise in detail. Second, the first great textbook for the English feminist movement, written by John Stuart Mill, in cooperation with his wife, and published in 1869, was entitled *The Subjection of Women* and was based on the acceptance of the Blackstone formula as an irreducible datum applicable not only to married women but to all women. How did Mill happen to choose this title and take this line?

Some pertinent facts may provide the answer. Mill, the economist, political philosopher, and sometime Liberal member of the House of Commons, had long been associated with Harriet Taylor, whom he finally married in 1851. Under the influence of this friend, later his wife, his views on economics and social affairs in general were profoundly modified. As his autobiography discloses, it is also certain that Mrs. Mill was interested in the woman movement in the United States as well as in England; and it is said that the report of an American convention, held in Massachusetts in 1850 for the promotion of women's rights, published by the *New York Tribune* in 1851, "aroused her to active thought on this question." That very year Mrs. Mill published in the *Westminster Review* a comprehensive article on the convention and on the general subject of women's social and political rights. It is also recorded that John Stuart Mill's *The Subjection of Women* was "thought out and partly written in collaboration with his wife."

In the call for the Massachusetts convention, reference was made to the theory of woman's annihilation and enslavement as Blackstone had expounded it, and it was declared that women were in the "condition of a disabled caste." In her article in the *Westminster Review*, Mrs. Mill declared that "there are indications that the example of America will be followed on this side of the Atlantic," Mr. and Mrs. Mill, in *The Subjection of Women*, certainly followed the American example in taking Blackstone's creed without qualifications and in making it a dogma of history to be accepted by everybody, everywhere, as if established by irrefutable knowledge.

In the first paragraph of the first chapter the premise stands stark: "The principle which regulates the existing social relations between the two sexes [is] the legal subjection of one sex to the other." From that position the argument proceeds: Laws "always begin by recognizing the relations they find already existing between individuals." And what are the real relations of men and women? "In early times the great majority of the male sex were slaves, as well as the whole of the female." In this summary fashion Mill, or the Mills, disposed of the beginnings of civilization. The contemporary subjection of women (in 1869), the argument continued, "is the primitive state of slavery lasting on, through successive mitigations and modifications occasioned by the same causes which have softened the general manners, and brought all human relations more under the control of justice and the influence of humanity." After these generalizations come detailed statements on the status of women in the very terms which Blackstone had employed in the eighteenth century.

Having historicized the Blackstone creed and stripped it of all its qualifications in law and equity, the Mills provided a moral antithesis in the form of women's revolt against their status. Then to perfect the argument the Mills set up the synthesis: The emancipation of women from the tyranny of history can only come by abolishing all the legal signs of this subjection and putting women on a legal equality with men in competition for place, security, and advancement in society.

The Mills conceded that practice did not exactly coincide with the legal theory which they accepted as if true: "I have described the wife's legal position, not her actual treatment. The laws of most countries are far worse than the people who execute them, and many of them are only able to remain laws by being seldom or never carried into effect. If married life were all that it might be expected to be, looking to the laws alone, society would be a hell on earth. Happily there are both feelings and interests which in many men exclude, and in most, greatly temper, the impulses and propensities which lead to tyranny; and of those feelings, the tie which connects a man with his wife affords, in a normal state of things, incomparably the strongest example. The only tie which at all approaches to it, that between him and his children, tends, in all save exceptional cases, to strengthen, instead of conflicting with, the first."

But for feminists of the middle class the Mills' treatise on subjection became the "authority" in respect of woman's status in law, history, and society as the nineteenth century passed its meridian. In the contest to free women from a long list of common-law disabilities and attain enfranchisemen, feminists used *The Subjection of Women* as a veritable bible.

The Mills' references to the qualifications induced by practice were easily overlooked by those who read the book or readily forgotten in the urge for agitation and for simplified ideas to be used in popular propaganda. Had Mill not swept them aside himself when he declared that woman's subjection to man had been a fact even if ninety-nine marriages out of a hundred had not been hellish for women? He took E. E. Schwabach's position that the thesis of subjection was confirmed if the hundredth marriage "is a hell and is legalized as a hell." The severe simplification of woman's status into the dogma of her historic subjection was for innumerable feminists in England, the United States, Germany, and other countries a primary source of concepts about their sex in the past.

To the doctrines of Blackstone, American feminists, and the Mills, pertaining to woman in law and history, Marxian Socialists added a revised version near the middle of the nineteenth century. What Blackstone had done for British patricians in respect to law and order, what Wollstonecraft and the Mills had done for the bourgeoisie in respect of manners, law, and history, the Marxists did for the proletariat in their interpretation of woman, law, and history.

In two fundamental respects the Socialist thesis of woman's status differed from that of Wollstonecraft and the Mills. In primitive times, it asserted, women had not been subject to men: they had either governed the community or been equals of men in it. Once dominated or equal, women had been driven, however, into subjection by the appearance of private property and the beginning of capitalism. "The overthrow of mother-right," wrote Friedrich Engels, "was the world-historical downfall of the female sex." Since the subjection of woman has been due to the rise and tyranny of private property, not merely to man's lust of power over woman, it follows, the Socialist thesis concluded, that woman's emancipation lies not in the equal competition of women with men for wealth and employment but in the socialization of the instruments of production and in the provision of employment for all.

This version of woman's historical subjection to man was presented to the German public and indeed, through translations, to the whole modern world by many writers, but first in systematic form by August Bebel, a leader of the German Social Democrats from about 1865 until his death in 1913. Among Bebel's writings on this subject two became classics or bibles for socialists all over the world. The first, *Die Frau und der Sozialismus,* which appeared in 1879, was subsequently revised, republished in fifty-seven German editions by 1926, and translated into all leading languages. The second, *Die Frau in Vergangenheit, Gegenwart und Zukunft,* came out in 1883 and, although it did not have the popularity that marked the career of *Woman and Socialism,* also served to spread the doctrine of women's subjection far and wide among working women who might never have heard of it otherwise.

When the first of Bebel's works on women came out in 1879 bourgeois feminists were stirring in Germany. For their benefit *The Subjection of Women* by the Mills had been translated into German shortly after its publication in 1869 and had quickly gone into a second edition. The Communist Manifesto of 1848 on the contrary had declared: "Differences of age and sex have no longer any distinctive social validity for the working class. All are instruments of labor. . . . The bourgeois sees in his wife a mere instrument of production." The Manifesto had called upon the proletarians of the world to unite and win emancipation through a socialist revolution. It was Bebel's task to formulate the doctrine of subjection and emancipation in the effort to counteract the bourgeois appeal to women made in the name of laissez faire economy.

Bebel's socialistic creed for women employed without question the thesis of woman's historic subjection to man in all the ages since primitive times, ascribed the subjection mainly to the tyrannical features of capitalism, and offered complete emancipation through the overthrow of the capitalist system and the ushering in of the socialist society.

Bebel supported, it is true, the struggle of German women to win the legal and political rights which feminists in general demanded, but in his view woman's "spring into freedom" was to come only with the triumph of the working classes over capitalism. In anticipation of that triumph, he favored the march of women by the millions into industry. Thus, he maintained, women would be freed from the backwardness and submission of the historic, rural, patriarchal family, would become individualized and educated for the revolution, and would be prepared for the universal freedom to be achieved under socialism.

Under the stimulus of this doctrine, women's socialist societies for equal rights were formed in Germany, women were drawn in large numbers into the socialist movement, and publications to advance their interests were launched. As socialist and communist propaganda spread around the world, the doctrine of woman's subjection, her nothingness in history, also spread to the four corners of the earth, affecting the ideas and beliefs of the Orient and coming back in novel versions to the Occident. Thus this world-image of women throughout history became almost universal in its sweep.

Each construct or version of this doctrine fitted into the requirements of some political party or faction as a convenient instrument of agitation for the vindication of traditions or for the reform or overthrow of social and economic institutions. The doctrine in it totality or special phases of it were utilized in all media of literary expression — polite letters, historical treatises, sociological surveys, economic and political works, and educational philosophy, programs, and critiques. It haunted the dreams of Freudian disciples and incited women to brave police and prison in passionate struggles for equality with their historic "masters."

In the whole intellectual history of human beings there is surely nothing more extraordinary — and fateful — than this dogmatic summarizing of all women's history from antiquity to recent times under the head of "subjection."

Chapter 5

Sway of Blackstone in the United States

MANY circumstances after 1776 fortified in the United States the doctrine of woman's legal subjection to man as set forth by Sir William Blackstone, and gave it a large command over American minds, rendering them susceptible to the dialectical elaborations provided by Mill and Bebel.

One was the position of the common law in America. Except as altered and adapted to conditions in the English colonies, the common law of England had been in effect in all the colonies except Connecticut. Nor was it wholly abolished with the revolt against Britain and the creation of the republic. The extent and character of its sway in the United States were carefully considered by Jefferson in a memorandum written in 1812. Some of the colonial legislatures, he noted, at an early time in their development had by express act of their own adopted "the laws of England as they stood at that date [of settlement], comprehending the common law, statutes to that period, and the chancery law [equity]." Other colonies, without resorting to a formal adoption, continued to operate under the English laws and thus by practice and tacit consent gave effect to those laws. In the case of Connecticut, however, "they did not adopt the common law of England at all as their basis, but declared by an act of their own, that the law of God, as it stood revealed in the Old and

New Testament, should be the basis of their laws, to be subject to such alterations as they should make."

Yet in adopting, either by express action or practice, the common law of England, the early colonists claimed and exercised the right to modify, by legislation of their own, the rules of that law and to fit it to their own needs and conditions. "In all the cases," said Jefferson, "where the common law, or laws of England, were adopted either expressly or tacitly, the legislatures held of course, and exercised the power of making additions and alterations."

Owing to this mode of adoption, the common law as accepted in America varied from colony to colony. "As the different States," wrote Jefferson, "were settled at very different periods, and the adoption for each State was the laws of England as they stood at the moment of the adoption by the State, it is evident that the system [as] adopted in 1607 by Virginia, was one thing, as by Pennsylvania was another thing, as by Georgia, in 1759, was still a different one. And when to this is added the very diversified modifications of the adoptive code, produced by the subsequent laws passed by the legislatures of the different States, the system of common law in force in any one state [in 1789] . . . was very different from the systems in force at the same moment in the several other States."

Hence the common law in force in the American republic at the end of the eighteenth century varied materially from state to state as to its extent and nature; so lawyers who practiced in more than one state were confronted by various forms of common law, not necessarily *the* common law of England as expounded by Blackstone. Moreover in some states this common law, as taken over, was qualified by coupling with its acceptance provisions of English statute law and equity jurisprudence likewise incorporated in the local body of law.

Nevertheless there were die-hards in America who shared Blackstone's distaste for opening any gate to progressive legislation. In 1776, eleven years after the first volume of his *Commentaries* was issued, a planter of Virginia, Edmund Randolph, seriously proposed to make the *Commentaries* the framework for the whole body of private law in Virginia. In that year a committee of five Virginians, of which Jefferson was a member, working for the provisional legislature of that state, took under consideration the drafting of a revised colonial code of law with the object of reducing to a single text the common law as applied in that state, the English statutes adopted in Virginia, and other forms of local law then in effect. Edmund Pendleton, like Edmund Randolph, a conservative of the old political school, advocated the use of Blackstone as the foundation of this entire revision and consolidation of Virginia law; but he was blocked if only by a single majority vote.

LAWYERS IN AMERICA BOW DOWN TO BLACKSTONE

Jefferson was against this subservience to Blackstone. He viewed it as a neglect of legal science. In describing the committee problem, in after years, he wrote that "Pendleton proposed to take Blackstone for that text, only purging him of what was inapplicable or unsuitable to us. In that case, the meaning of every word of Blackstone would have become a source of litigation, until it had been settled by repeated legal decisions. And to come at that meaning, we should have produced, on all occasions, that very pile of authorities from which it would be said he drew his conclusions, and which, of course, would explain it, and the terms in which it is couched. Thus we should have retained the same chaos of law-lore from which we wished to be emancipated." It was on such grounds, as well as due to the bustle of the times, that the committee was deterred from attempting the reduction of Virginia law to a simple text. Of one thing a majority was certain: Blackstone was not to be taken as the basis of the new text, if it was to be made.

But with the growth of commerce and the increase of litigation, lawyers had multiplied in the colonies and had won a position of respectability in American society that had not been granted them in England. Lawyers were important leaders in the American Revolution and, with the outcome in independence and the federation of the states, lawyers steadily forged to the front as politicians and legislators. They became authors of statutes and they might have modified more drastically than they did the terms of the common law inherited from England. But it was not to their professional interest to have the law simplified and the jargon of the common law, so advantageous in mystifying clients, supplanted by language made easy for laymen to understand. Moreover as edition after edition of the *Commentaries* was printed for American usage, American lawyers became more and more imprisoned in Blackstone's system of dogmas — legal, political and economic.

To lawyers, at the end of the American Revolution, Blackstone's *Commentaries* was a veritable godsend. It reduced to a moderate compass, digested, organized, and expounded a vast mass of old laws, rulings, and precedents. Moreover, for a law work, it was written in free, flowing, and popular style, so that any literate person of a little more than ordinary intelligence could by a few months' close study make himself master of its leading principles. With relief, law students could neglect the qualifying provisions of Equity and put aside the more difficult texts of Littleton tenures, Coke's commentaries on Littleton, and Coke's institutes — all of which called for hard work if they were to be mastered. In short students could get their legal "education" from "the elegant Blackstone," with relative ease.

In a letter to John Tyler in 1810, even Jefferson said that he still lent his "counsel and books to such young students as will fix themselves in the neighborhood. Coke's institutes and reports are their first, and Blackstone their last book, after an intermediate course of two or three years."

Throughout the country, ordinarily, ambitious young men who aspired to fame and fortune at the bar usually read Blackstone at the beginning of such legal education as they undertook for themselves and then made Blackstone their staunch authority for the conduct of their law business. Judge Simeon Baldwin, at the opening of the twentieth century, speaking of the age of the American Revolution, declared: "Law books were largely imported. It is believed that more copies of *Blackstone's Commentaries,* during the eighteenth century, were sold in America than in England. Their elegance of literary form appealed more strongly to our bar."

As the nation expanded toward the Pacific Ocean, Blackstone's treatise went west in its wake. Abraham Lincoln, early in his manhood, bought a copy at an auction and immersed himself in the study of law as outlined and defined by Blackstone. By the middle of the nineteenth century, the *Commentaries* constituted the prime legal work for instruction in the United States, except in Louisiana where the French code of law was entrenched. Near the beginning of his public career as a lawyer, Oliver Wendell Holmes, Jr., became so enamored of the common law through its "elegant" exposition by Blackstone that he almost enslaved his mind to its alleged perfection.

This servitude Jefferson and lawyers inclined to his views had never approved. Jefferson had realized the full significance of the tendency among American lawyers to exalt Blackstone as an authority binding American conscience, law, and practice. In harmony with "radicals" of his time, he insisted that Americans abandon the citation of British legal sources subsequent to 1783 — the year in which American independence was formally recognized by Great Britain. On this matter he unburdened himself June 17, 1812, to John Tyler, who had then become the federal judge for the district of Virginia, as follows: "The exclusion from the courts of the malign influence of all authorities after the *Georgium sidus* became ascendant [1783], would uncanonize Blackstone, whose book, although the most elegant and best digested of our law catalogue, has been perverted more than all others, to the degeneracy of legal science. A student finds there a smattering of everything, and his indolence easily persuades him that if he understands that book, he is master of the whole body of the law. The distinction between these, and those who have drawn their stores from the deep and rich mines of Coke and Littleton, seems well understood even by the unlettered common people, who apply the appellation of Blackstone lawyers to these ephemeral insects of the law."

Jefferson had read extensively in history and philosophy but a large portion of American lawyers in the early nineteenth century had undergone no training in legal history or philosophy, and accordingly they were in no position either to understand or to criticize the animus of Blackstone's *Commentaries,* or the class structure of English society reflected in its pages, or the purposes to which its argument was bent. Most of them were probably equally ignorant of contemporary English law and thus unable to discover how far Blackstone's doctrines actually failed to represent English law and practice in the age of which he wrote. Furthermore, there is good reason for believing that few American lawyers understood, if they ever heard of, the attack begun on Blackstone by the great legal reformers such as Jeremy Bentham and John Austin, shortly after the *Commentaries* appeared, and continued until huge segments of English law were recast.

At all events, few American lawyers who labored so mightily to impose Blackstone on the American people knew that Blackstone had made it his business to discover and expound reasons for justifying the existence and rightness of the English class order to which he, as a conservative politican, was warmly attached. They did not know that "through his own timidity and subserviency as a man and a politician, he is always found to be a specious defender of the existing order of things" against the reformers, and that the reformers were then doing battle for a greater equality of rights and greater justice in the inherited law of England stamped by class doctrines of property. For hundreds of American lawyers the sheer ability to quote Blackstone sufficed as a way to fame and fortune.

By the 1820's, the "Blackstone lawyers" had demonstrated that they were not the "ephemeral insects" which Jefferson had hoped they would be. Despite the many changes which reforming legislators had wrought in the common law, American lawyers had managed to impose on large sections of the country, as "good, sound law," the stark outlines of Blackstone's chapter "Of Husband and Wife." Some of them did, it is true, make genuflections to the exceptions provided by Equity, but, like Blackstone, the majority of lawyers seemed to have had little use for such forms of justice. As a rule, they stuck close to the text of what Jefferson called "the Alcoran." The great commentators Kent and Story, as we shall see later, gave Equity its due place in American jurisprudence, but the rank and file of lawyers appeared to accord it slight recognition in their teaching and practice.

By 1840 Blackstone's supremacy was unshaken, at least for the ordinary practicing lawyers and for the writers of small texts on law. When, for example, Edward D. Mansfield, to whom reference has already been made, wrote his work on *The Legal Rights, Liabilities and Duties of Women,* published in 1845, he recited the Blackstone ritual. "As the marriage creates a unity," he averred, "and the husband is religiously the head of the family, the law declares, that the external powers of this family, in respect to property and government, shall vest in the husband." For this judgment, he gave the authority of Blackstone. After a brief reference to the wife's rights in case of a trusteeship, Mansfield proceeded: "This *merging,* as it is called, of the wife's rights of property and person in the husband, has been called little less than downright slavery. In this respect the Roman law was much more liberal than the English or American. For that law considered marriage as a sort of *partnership,* in which each partner had equal rights of property. We consider here, however, not the propriety, but the facts of the law; in order that women may know what it is."

A convincing display of the tyranny which Blackstone exercised in the United States was made by the American Bar Association as late as 1924. By that date the profound researches of British scholars had revealed the specious pleadings of Blackstone; scholars of the first rank, such as Maitland and Holdsworth, had reconstructed the history of English law — the history which Blackstone had so often oversimplified and so distorted. By that time, British reformers, after more than a century of laborious work, had legislated out of existence much of the common law which the *Commentaries* had celebrated with such verbal flourishes, and brought English law more closely in harmony with the enlightened ideas of justice and reason combated by Blackstone in his day. Yet in the year 1924, during the administration of President Calvin Coolidge, the American Bar Association presented to the law courts of London a statue of Sir William Blackstone "to mark the influence which the great commentator had had over American jurisprudence."

As the statue had not been executed in marble at the time of the presentation in 1924, the American lawyers then merely unveiled a "giant plaster model." The commission to execute the statue in marble was given to the American sculptor, Paul Bartlett, whose artistic leanings had been toward the historic. Years before Bartlett undertook this commission he had made a portrait bust of Elizabeth Cady

Stanton who, amid no little derision from American lawyers, had battled valiantly against Blackstone's dictum that woman was a favorite in English law and had lived to see many triumphs over common-law doctrines in the enactment of married women's property acts in state after state. But, according to a biographer, "Never had the sculptor developed his teeming ideas with greater zest than in this tribute to British jurisprudence. A successful statue, yet a difficult one, since in less capable hands the subject's greatness might have been smothered under circumstantial wig and robe." Bartlett died before he had brought his statue of Blackstone to completion, and the finishing touches were given to it by his wife. The statue was placed in position in the Royal Law Courts in June, 1928.

AMERICAN FEMINISTS BOW DOWN WITH THE BLACKSTONE LAWYERS

If possible, the dictation which Blackstone's oversimplification of English jurisprudence exerted over the leaders of the woman movement in the course of the nineteenth century was even more autocratic than it was in the case of most competent lawyers. On what does this assertion rest? Although many of the "Blackstone lawyers," whom Jefferson called "insects," may have known little or nothing of Equity or the evasion of common-law doctrines for which equity had provided, centuries before Blackstone became an authoritarian exponent of the common law the better-educated American lawyers were more or less familiar with Equity, and many dispensed justice as equity judges. Jefferson knew very well how to protect the property of wives against improvident husbands by the creation of trusts which equity would enforce. So did other Americans.

After about 1835, American lawyers had for their better understanding of Equity and its development the *Commentaries on American Law* by James Kent, who had served in courts of Equity and had given in his treatise an extended consideration to Equity. About this time also they had at their command the monumental *Commentaries on Equity Jurisprudence,* written by Joseph Story, a careful student of this branch of the law. By 1840 there was no excuse for the ignorance of American lawyers respecting the inroads which equity had made on common-law prescriptions relative to the married woman's property rights. If lawyers failed to realize that Blackstone himself had indulged in hyperbole or had been deliberately propagandistic in his statement on the rights and obligations of husband and wife, if they did not know that equity had riddled his common law long before he published the first volume of his *Commentaries* in 1765, the fault was theirs, in view of the great mass of materials on equity easily accessible to them.

As for the women engaged in starting the organized movement for "women's emancipation," their leaders were not as a rule careful students of jurisprudence, to put it mildly. Legal training was not available to women in American colleges when the woman movement was formally launched in 1848. Even if it had been and women had studied law at institutions of learning, they, like so many men, might have become "Blackstone lawyers" themselves. At any rate, leaders in the woman movement took Blackstone's metaphorical words about the civil death of the married woman as inescapable law, took it to heart as if it were the supreme truth for marital relations, and advertised it throughout the Western world; yes, even as far as the Orient.

Furthermore, the women emphasized some particular formulas of Blackstone's statement which happened to be correct in common law and neglected to discover, or to point out if they made the discovery, that Equity had long made it possible to escape from the "disabilities" imposed by the most severe of these formulas. Consequently the women who followed this course were parroting and giving currency to dogmas about woman's legal history which were in part false when Blackstone uttered them and, insofar as they had been correct at common law in 1765, were not generally applicable in the United States or, when applicable, were avoidable by a resort to practices enforceable in Equity.

As a matter of fact, after the American Revolution, nearly all the states recognized Equity in some measure and all of them made modifications in their laws governing the distribution of intestates' estates, following, often line by line, an old English statute governing personal estates. Before 1850, James Kent could record: "In a majority of the states the descent of real and personal property is to the same persons and in the same proportions, and the regulation is the same in substance, as the English statute of distributions, with the exception of the widow, as to the real estate, who takes one third for life only, as dower. In Georgia, the real and personal estate of the intestate is considered as altogether of the same nature and upon the same footing, both in respect to their statute of distributions and the descent of property. ... Such a uniform rule in the descent of real and personal property gives simplicity and symmetry to the whole doctrine of descent. The English statute of distributions, being founded in justice and on the wisdom of ages, and fully and profoundly illustrated by a series of judicial decisions, was well selected as the most suitable and judicious basis on which to establish our American law of descent and distribution."

In other words, Blackstone's ornate dictum that "the very being or legal existence of the woman is suspended during marriage, or at least incorporated and consolidated into that of the hubsand: under whose wing, protection, and *cover,* she performs everything" — false when made — was no universal rule of American law in 1840 or earlier, and Equity had long been shooting holes in the list of the married woman's disabilities. But leaders of the woman movement in the United States did not take these facts into full account. On the contrary, in the 1840's they adhered tenaciously to Blackstone's maxim which represented married women as historically subject to their husbands and as still subject in the United States. Taking this as a starting point, especially when there were crowds to address, they often associated with the alleged subjection of wives the subjection of all women, whether single or married. Not content with attacking legal discriminations against women in detail, they adopted a myth and made a frontal assault on that.

With constant reiteration, for example, the acclaimed legalist of the woman movement in the nineteenth century, Mrs. Elizabeth Cady Stanton, an outstanding pleader for women's rights before law-making bodies, spoke and wrote as if Blackstone's account of English law was in fact the law of the land — supreme law — in nearly all vital man-woman relations. It is true that Mrs. Stanton mentioned from time to time the gains which women had been making and were making in their struggle against formulas of the common law; but she repeatedly resorted to wholesale generalizations which treated Blackstone's sweeping generalizations as still binding in law, even to her day in the United States.

In her address to the legislature of the state of New York in 1854, for instance, Mrs. Stanton declared that on entering wedlock the woman met "instant civil death." The woman signed her own death warrant when she put her name to the marriage contract: "The woman who but yesterday was sued on bended knee, who stood so high in the scale of being as to make an agreement on equal terms with a proud Saxon man, to-day has no civil existence, no social freedom." Although later in this address, Mrs. Stanton conceded that the wife had been recently "redeemed from her lost condition" by new state legislation respecting her inherited property, the keynote for her argument was the Blackstone precept about the death of the married woman in the eyes of the common law.

Six years afterward, in another address to the New York legislature in support of a woman-suffrage bill, Mrs. Stanton again made use of the Blackstone fiction. She said: "Blackstone declares that the husband and wife are one, and learned commentators have decided that that one is the husband. In all civil codes, you will find them classified as one. Certain rights and immunities, such and such privileges are to be secured to white male citizens. What have women and negroes to do with rights? What know they of government, war, or glory?"

The chance for oratory was irresistible and Mrs. Stanton made the most of it: "The prejudice against color, of which we hear so much, is no stronger than that against sex. It is produced by the same cause, and manifested very much in the same way. The negro's skin and the woman's sex are both *prima facie* evidence that they were intended to be in subjection to the white Saxon man. The few social privileges which the man gives the woman, he makes up to the negro in civil rights. The woman may sit at the same table and eat with the white man; the free negro may hold property and vote. The woman may sit in the same pew with the white man in church; the free negro may enter the pulpit and preach. . . . It is evident that the prejudice against sex is more deeply rooted and more unreasonably maintained than that against color. As citizens of a republic, which should we most highly prize, social privileges or civil rights? The latter, most certainly. . . .

"Look over all his laws concerning us, and you will see just enough of woman to tell of her existence; all the rest is submerged, or made to crawl upon the earth. . . .

"Man is in such a labyrinth of contradictions with his marital and property rights; he is so befogged on the whole question of maidens, wives, and mothers, that from pure benevolence we should relieve him from this troublesome branch of legislation. We should vote, and make laws for ourselves. Do not be alarmed, dear ladies! You need spend no time reading Grotius, Coke, Puffendorf, Blackstone, Bentham, Kent, and Story to find out what you need. We may safely trust the shrewd selfishness of the white. man, and consent to live under the same broad code where he has so comfortably ensconced himself. Any legislation that will do for man, we may abide by most cheerfully."

Blackstone's declaration respecting the civil death of married women haunted many other outstanding leaders in the woman movement of the middle period. Although Matilda Joslyn Gage tried to meet it by a curious display of logic, she regarded it as a statement of the law. "After marriage," she declared in 1852,· "the husband and wife are considered as one person in law, which I hold to be false from the very laws applicable to married parties. Were it so, the act of one would be as binding as the act of the other; . . . were it so, a woman could not legally be a man's inferior. Such a thing would be a veritable impossibility. One-half of a person cannot be made the protection or direction of the other half. Blackstone says 'a woman may indeed be attorney for her husband, for that implies no separation from, but rather a representation of, her lord. And a husband may also bequeath anything to his wife by will; for it cannot take effect till the coverture is determined by his death.' After stating at considerable length the reasons showing their unity, the learned commentator proceeds to cut the knot, and show they are not one, but are considered as two persons, one superior, the one inferior, and not only so, but the inferior in the eye of the law as acting from compulsion "

At the Woman's Rights Convention held in Syracuse the following year, 1853, Mrs. Gage recurred to the subject and spoke as if equity and legislation had made no changes in the "disabilities" of married women at common law. She affirmed that "the legal disabilities of women" are numerous; that they are only known to those who bear them; that they "are acknowledged by Kent, Story, and many other legal authorities." Without directing attention to those pages of Kent and Story which set forth at length the equitable principles by which common-law rules could be and often were nullified, Mrs. Gage went on with her oration: "A wife has no management in the joint earnings of herself and her husband; they are entirely under control of the husband, who is obliged to furnish the wife merely the common necessaries of life; all that she receives beyond these is looked upon by the law as a favor, and not held as her right. A mother is denied the custody of her own child; a most barbarous and unjust law, which robs her of the child placed in her care by the great Creator himself. A widow is allowed the use merely of one-third of the real estate left at the husband's death; and when her minor children have grown up she must surrender the personal property, even to the family Bible, and the pictures of her dear children. In view of such laws the women engaged in this movement ask that the wife shall be made heir to the husband to the same extent that he is now her heir. . . .

"The present law of divorce is very unjust; the husband, whether the innocent or the guilty party, retaining all the wife's property, has also the control of the children unless by special decree of the court they are assigned to the mother."

For the gentle Quaker, Lucretia Mott, one of the most persuasive American women of her time, Blackstone was no less an unquestioned authority than he was for Mrs. Stanton and Mrs. Gage. After hearing Richard H. Dana deliver a lecture in 1849 ridiculing "the new demand of American womanhood for civil and political rights," Mrs. Mott also delivered a lecture, in reply to the Boston orator. In her discourse appeared the inevitable Hamlet of the play.

In the solemn resolutions of women's conventions, as well as in speeches, lectures, and articles, rose the specter of Blackstone, pronouncing the married woman as civilly dead.

When leaders of the woman movement assembled in Ohio in 1850 to formulate a program of demands to be made upon the coming constitutional convention in that state, they concentrated fire on Blackstone's doctrines. "We believe," they declared in their memorial and address, "the whole theory of the Common Law in relation to woman is unjust and degrading, tending to reduce her to a level with the slave.... At the marriage-altar, the law divests her of all distinct individuality. Blackstone says: 'The very being or legal existence of the woman is suspended during marriage, or at least incorporated or consolidated into that of her husband.' Legally she ceases to exist, and becomes emphatically a new creature, and is ever after denied the dignity of a rational and accountable being. The husband is allowed to take possession of her estates, as the law has proclaimed her legally dead.... She can own nothing, have nothing, which is not regarded by the law as belonging to her husband.... Slaves are we, politically and legally."

While recognizing the fact that certain important reforms had been made in respect of married women's property rights in the state of New York, women of this state assembled at the state capital, Albany, in 1854, taking Blackstone's interpretation of English law as the whole picture of English jurisprudence and its American counterpart, among their resolutions passed this one:

"*Resolved,* That the fundamental error of the whole structure of legislation and custom, whereby women are practically sustained, even in this republic, is the preposterous fiction of law, that in the eye of the law the husband and wife are one person, that person being the husband; that this falsehood itself, the deposit of barbarism, tends perpetually to brutalize the marriage relation by subjecting wives as irresponsible tools to the capricious authority of husbands; that this degradation of married women re-acts inevitably to depress the condition of single women, by impairing their own self-respect and man's respect for them; and that the final result is that system of tutelage miscalled protection, by which the industry of women is kept on half-pay, their affections trifled with, their energies crippled, and even their noblest aspirations wasted away in vain efforts, ennui, and regret."

In order that the widest possible circulation might be given to the Blackstone creed of the married woman's complete subjection, leaders in the American woman movement incorporated it in their literature of propaganda. For example, after asserting that women had been utterly subjected to men under Hindu laws as long ago as 2000 B.C., *The Woman's Rights Almanac* of 1857 published a list of modern grievances in the West. This list started with the inevitable passage from Blackstone, forever ringing like a bell to summon women to a wailing wall or to gird themselves for battle; it was characterized as "scarcely" varying "in principle" from the barbaric laws of the ancient Hindus. "By marriage," the characterization as quoted from Blackstone read, "the husband and wife are one person in law; that is, *the very being or existence of the woman is suspended during the marriage,* or at least is incorporated and consolidated into that of the husband, under whose wing, protection, and *cover* she performs everything; and is, therefore, called in our Law-French a *feme-covert,* is said to be *covert-baron,* or under the protection and influence of her husband, her baron, or lord; and her condition during her marriage is called her *coverture.* Upon this principle, of an union of person in husband and wife, depend almost all the legal rights, duties, and disabilities that either of them acquire by the marriage."

After citing another long passage from Blackstone and additional examples of man's inhumanity to woman, the compiler of the *Almanac* commented on changes in common-law doctrines in a manner which implied that these changes were only of recent date: "Signs of the Times. 1857. It is obvious that the English common law, as above stated, is scarcely a step beyond barbarism. Yet this law remained almost unaltered in the United States, as respects woman, till the year 1848 — the year of the first local Woman's Rights Convention. . . . Since then every year has brought improvements, and even those who denounce the Woman's Rights Movement admit the value of its results." From this statement it would seem that to feminists of 1857 Blackstone's view of the law had long been the absolute law of the land and that equity and a huge volume of state legislation, some of it enacted before the women's convention met at Seneca Falls in 1848, had made no material alteration in the force of the common law, which was "scarcely a step beyond barbarism."

From these examples taken from the literature of the woman movement near the middle of the nineteenth century it is clear that the full-fledged thesis of woman's historic subjection to man was grounded on the belief in Blackstone's doctrine. Older than that doctrine, of course, were the preachments of many theologians, clergymen, and moralists to the effect that woman is evil and *ought to be* subject to man, but Blackstone afforded sanction for the feminist manifesto that woman had been *in fact* subject to man throughout the long history of Anglo-American law — and, indeed, of all law. Here was the original construct that was to give forms and twists to endless writing and speaking, even that alleged to be scientific, and to bedevil women and befuddle men in years to come in all parts of the world.

Chapter 6

The Challenge of Legislation and Equity

THE Common Law, as multitudes of American lawyers saw it through Blackstone's narrow eyes, was powerful. There is no doubt of that. But it could not gain undisputed mastery in America.

Resistance to the English common law had begun in the English colonies even before Blackstone published his laudation of that system. And this early resistance in America grew out of many circumstances — out of economic and political realities and developments. It took many forms, moreover. On an almost uninhabited continent, where land was cheap and often so free that any person or family could have it simply by "squatting" upon it, where the vast natural resources could sustain life if human beings were at all inclined to exert themselves, the English common law with its feudal characteristics was not accepted complacently by colonists at large. In the nature of things American, it could not be generally applied.

The mounting democratic spirit, associated with the comparatively wide distribution of freehold land ownership and the love of liberty underlying the migration of many Europeans to the new world, did not comport with the aristocratic servitudes of old feudal land tenures. This American distinction of economy and spirit was early manifested in colonial struggles with great landlords who in one way or another, usually by grants from the English Crown, had acquired huge estates. Furthermore, at the end of the colonial period, freehold farming families, owning and tilling the soil, outnumbered by far all the owners of great manors, estates, and plantations.

In the circumstances peculiar to the new world, immigrants to America began to cast off the restrictions of English law as soon as they had reached these shores and commenced to parcel out the land among themselves. And throughout the colonial era three stringent rules were applied to the acceptance of the common law as binding on the founders and builders of American civilization. First, it was only the common law existing at the time of the founding of the particular colony which was to be treated as binding upon the inhabitants. Second, only those principles of the common law were adopted in any colony which were "suited to the conditions" of that colony, as the lawyers admitted. Third, very early in its founding and development each colony had a legislature, and American legislatures soon began to pour out statutes that revised in numerous respects the doctrines of the common law which otherwise might have been applied by the courts of law.

THE AMERICANS WAGE WAR ON THE COMMON LAW

In the documents of the period following the American Revolution were registered many protests against the theory that the common law generally prevailed in the states of the Union. On this point Jefferson said, in 1812, in the course of a letter to Judge John Tyler of Virginia: "On the other subject of your letter, the application of the common law to our present situation, I deride with you the ordinary doctrine, that we brought with us from England the *common law rights*. . . . The truth is, that we brought with us the *rights of men;* of expatriated men. On our arrival here, the question would at once arise, by what law will we govern ourselves? The resolution seems to have been, by that system, with which we are familiar, to be altered by ourselves occasionally, and adapted to our new situation. . . . But the state of the English law at the date of our emigration, constituted the system adopted here."

Owing to the fact that the general domain of civil law was left to the determination of the several states after the Revolution and even after the adoption of the Federal Constitution, there was no uniformity in the extension of equity jurisprudence or in modifications of the common law in that direction. This did not mean, however, that in those states which gave little force to equity the common law as expounded by Blackstone was fully accepted. The extent to which equity was accepted and enforced varied from state to state but the degree and nature of its usage gave distinction to American jurisprudence.

In an opinion written in 1819, Judge Peters of Connecticut objected to the contention of the majority of the state supreme court to the effect that a common law of crimes had existed in that state. "I have sought in vain, in the history and legislative acts of our ancestors, for a confirmation of this doctrine. But it is apparent to my understanding that their sole object was to found a pure government in church and commonwealth, 'surely bottomed on the word of God,' and that they brought with them no more affection for the common law than the canon law, the court of star-chamber, and the high commission, from which they fled with horror and detestation." Although Judge Peters' opinion was a minority opinion in that court, it represented the attitude of countless Americans toward attempts to make the common law govern generally in the United States. American legislation did not consist merely of statutory amendments and rejections of the common law.

When it is said, therefore, as it must be said on the basis of historical records, that, in the middle years of the nineteenth century, Equity was enthroned only to a limited extent in Maine, Massachusetts, New Hampshire, and Rhode Island, a caution must be added. Such a statement does not tell the whole story. In colonial times the legislatures of New England turned out statutes in large volume. Under the laws of the Plymouth colony, the high court of assistants was given jurisdiction over "such matters of equity as could not be relieved at law." Although no such general jurisdiction was ever conferred upon the colonial courts of Massachusetts,

Rhode Island, and Connecticut, these three colonies, by legislation, made innumerable laws of their own, touching the law of proper.y and crimes. Not until the history of legislation in colonial and later times has been written will it be possible to discover how far equity principles or other more enlightened principles had been "digested" by statute law before 1850. Hence the following table, which illustrates the rapid spread of equity jurisprudence by the middle of the nineteenth century, by no means reveals the full extent to which the common law had been supplanted by other principles through legislation and judicial decisions.

Of the original thirteen states, by 1850 several had recognized or adopted equity jurisprudence and had vested jurisdiction over cases in equity either in special courts of Chancery or in the ordinary courts of law.

Virginia. The constitution of 1776, in force until 1830, empowered the legislature to appoint judges in chancery, as well as judges of other high courts. Lower courts of equity were created in 1802. Under the constitution of 1830 general judicial power was vested in a supreme court and inferior courts, including county courts and the justices of the peace. Thus the same set of judges had jurisdiction over laws and equity.

North Carolina. The constitution of 1776 instructed the legislature to make provision for the salaries of "the judges of the supreme court of law and equity." The jurisdiction and proceedings in chancery were extensively covered by legislation.

South Carolina. The constitutions of 1776 and 1778 made provision for chancery courts. The constitution of 1790, in force until the civil war, vested judicial powers in such superior and inferior courts of law and equity as the legislature might direct and establish. In 1850 equity powers were still vested in and exercised by separate tribunals on the English model.

Maryland. The constitution of 1776 had provisions relative to the chancellor and the court of chancery. Later a mixed jurisdiction in law and equity was conferred on Maryland courts.

Delaware. After trying a mixture of law and equity under the constitution of 1776, Delaware, by the constitution of

1792, established a special court of chancery, required to hold sessions in the several counties of the state.

New Jersey. Under the constitution of 1776, New Jersey long relied upon the common law as modified by legislation in which law and equity were blended; but by the constitution of 1844 New Jersey provided for a separate court of chancery, and made the chancellor a member of the court of errors and appeals.

New York. The constitution of 1777 provided for a chancellor. In 1823 the office of chancellor was abolished and equity distributed among law courts and vice-chancellors' courts. In 1846 jurisdiction over law and equity was vested in the regular courts of law, high and low.

In the remaining original states, six in number, the use of equity was limited, either particularly or loosely.

Pennsylvania. Under the constitutions of 1776 and 1790 regular courts had grants of a few specific equity powers. These were extended greatly in 1836 and 1840 but not made broad and universal.

Georgia. Ordinary courts of law were given equity powers over all cases where the common-law remendy was inadequate.

Connecticut. James Kent noted in his *Commentaries:* "In the revised Statute Code of Connecticut, published in 1784, p. 48, and again in 1821, p. 195, the courts having jurisdiction of suits in equity are directed to proceed according to the rules in equity, and to take cognizance of such matters only wherein adequate remedy cannot be had in the ordinary course of law. But, under this general grant, the equity system in Connecticut appears, in practice, to be broad and liberal."

Rhode Island. The constitution of 1842 authorized the legislature to confer equity powers on the supreme court but on no other court to any greater extent "than is now provided by law." In practice the exercise of equity powers by the courts was closely limited.

Massachusetts and New Hampshire. Chancery powers in general were strictly limited in Massachusetts and New Hampshire; but in relation to trusts created by will, the performance of contracts concerning land as against heirs, and some other matters, the supreme judicial court in Massachusetts had ample equity powers.

As new states came into the original Union, the equity powers conferred upon courts varied from extremely limited to broad and general; and in practice the application of equity by courts varied in the same way, often according to the quality of the judges chosen to enforce law and equity. In Vermont, equity powers were severely limited. Tennessee in 1796 empowered the legislature to vest judicial powers in superior and inferior courts of law and equity. The Ohio constitution of 1803 vested the judicial power "in matters of law and equity" in the supreme court, courts of common pleas in each county, justices of the peace, and such other courts as the legislature might establish. The supreme court heard appeals in common law and equity. The Indiana constitution of 1816 gave the judicial power "both as to matters of law and equity" to the supreme court, circuit courts, and other inferior courts which the legislature might establish from time to time. Under the Michigan constitution of 1835 "a separate court of equity was established, with plenary powers and jurisdiction"; the state was divided into circuits and the chancellor held sessions in each circuit; appeals from the chancellor's court came under the equity jurisdiction of the supreme court. In other states of the West and South equity jurisdiction was generally limited, but equity proceedings were distinct from proceedings in law and appeals were heard by the supreme court. Louisiana, whose law was based upon the French civil code, was the one state in 1850 in which the distinction between law and equity in the English sense apparently was not recognized at all.

An impetus to the spread of equity in the United States was given by the adoption of the Federal Constitution and the establishment of the federal judiciary in 1789. The third article of the Constitution provided that the judicial power shall extend to "all cases arising in law and equity" under the Constitution, laws, and treaties of the United States. Thus, as Judge Story wrote in his *Commentaries on the Constitution of the United States,* in 1833, when any case was a suit in equity, no less than in law, and involved any federal question, it came within the judicial power of the federal courts. Where equitable remedies were properly demanded by parties to suits, the principles of the decision were to be derived from equity sources. Since federal courts also had jurisdiction over suits between citizens of different states, often involving not federal law but state law only, the federal courts, when issues of equity were raised, confronted the necessity of applying, even developing, the principles of equity.

The Federal Judiciary Act of 1789, drawn to carry into effect the article of the Constitution relative to judicial powers, provided that, in equity suits properly arising under the Constitution, proceedings shall be according to the principles, rules, and usages which belong to courts of equity as distinguished from courts of law. Speaking in 1819 of a case in equity which rose in Massachusetts, where equity was extremely limited, Chief Justice Marshall declared: "As the Courts of the Union have a chancery jurisdiction in every State and the Judiciary Act confers the same chancery powers on all, and gives the same rule of decision, its jurisdiction in Massachusetts must be the same as in other States." Confirming this view in 1869, Justice Davis, of the Supreme Court, asserted: "The Equity jurisdiction conferred on the Federal Courts is the same that the High Court of Chancery in England possesses; is subject to neither limitation nor restraint by State Legislation, and is uniform throughout the different States of the Union." Although the range of federal equity was limited to specific types of cases, its application in such cases extended throughout the Union and even Blackstone lawyers in search of remedies in federal courts for their clients were remiss if they knew no equity as developed by federal courts.

While the makers of state constitutions were establishing or empowering legislatures to establish separate equity courts or mixed courts having jurisdiction in law and equity, legislatures in the states were sweeping away whole sections of the common law, particularly in respect of the property right of married women, and substituting new law based on or going beyond equity principles. This is what Thomas Jefferson hoped that his fellow citizens would do, as he made evident in the letter already mentioned: "For, however I admit the superiority of the [Roman] civil law over the common law code, as a system of perfect justice, yet an incorporation of the two would be like Nebuchadnezzar's image of metals and clay, a thing without cohesion of parts. The only natural improvement of the common law, is through its homogeneous ally, the chancery, in which new principles are to be examined, concocted and digested. But when, by repeated decisions and modifications, they are rendered pure and certain, they should be transferred by statute to the courts of common law, and placed within the pale of juries."

STATE LEGISLATION OVERRIDES COMMON LAW DOCTRINES

In no respect was the swiftness and radicalism of this new movement more evident than in modifications of the land laws, particularly with regard to primogeniture and entail, both features of the feudal law incorporated in the common law. The rule of primogeniture prescribed that, if the father died without making a will, his lands passed to the eldest son, if there was one, or through a daughter or daughters, to eldest sons. Under the law of entail, a landed estate could be irrevocably vested in a man and his legitimate descendants, according to arrangements which the maker of the legal instrument might devise, within limits. Both primogeniture and entail formed the basis of the English landed aristocracy. But they were early resented in several of the American colonies and after 1776 they encountered revolutionary opposition.

The situation in New England was peculiar, for the leveling spirit was strong among the Puritans. Their laws gave landholders a considerable freedom in distributing their property by gift or will among their children — sons and daughters. Nevertheless, owing to their attachment to the Mosaic law, they generally provided that, in case a landowner left no will, an exception to equal distribution must be made: the eldest son was to have a double share of the estate. Primogeniture once existed in Pennsylvania and Maryland, but it had been abolished there before the Revolution. So had entails in South Carolina. In 1776, however, primogeniture and entails were still well entrenched in New York, New Jersey, Virginia, North Carolina, and Georgia.

"Then came the Revolution," as J. Franklin Jameson says in *The American Revolution Considered as a Social Movement.* "In ten years from the Declaration of Independence every state had abolished entails, excepting two, and those were two in which entails were rare. In fifteen years every state, without exception, abolished primogeniture and in some form provided for equality of inheritance, since which time the American eldest son has never been a privileged character. It is painful to have to confess that two states, North Carolina and New Jersey, did not at once put the daughters of the Revolution upon a level with the sons. North Carolina for a few years provided for equal distribution of the lands among the sons alone, and not among the daughters save in case there were no sons. New Jersey gave the sons a double share. But elsewhere absolute equality was introduced."

Of the Virginia movement for the revolution in land tenure, Thomas Jefferson was the leader, and he was proud of his accomplishments. From the outset he insisted upon equal distribution among sons and daughters. When one of his colleagues, Edmund Pendleton, proposed to "adopt the Hebrew principle, and give a double portion to the elder son," Jefferson replied: "If the eldest son could eat twice as much, or do double work, it might be a natural evidence of his right to a double portion; but being on a par in his powers and wants, with his brothers and sisters, he should be on a par also in the partition of the patrimony." Thus Jefferson advanced the democratic principle of equality against common-law doctrines held by Blackstone lawyers in America.

Long before 1850 practically all vestiges of feudal land tenures had been abolished in the original states and one tenure had been substituted as basic, namely, freehold tenure in fee simple; and the principle of equal distribution among children, saving the widow's special share, had become the general rule applicable in cases where the owner died intestate. As feudal tenures were never introduced in the Western states, the rule of freehold tenure in fee simple and the principles of equal distribution were more easily established there as a matter of course.

In this legal development the daughters of land owners became land owners in increasing numbers. Besides, owing to the amount and cheapness of land, unmarried women could acquire and did acquire, by various methods of purchase, inheritance, and devise, land holdings in all parts of the country, especially in the West. In this way their economic power was enlarged, and additional reasons were provided for modifying the common-law rules respecting the power of the husband over the wife's real and personal property. An ever greater number of fathers and mothers had manifest grounds for protecting their daughters against selfish or improvident husbands through a resort to the safeguards of equity, in case modifications had not already been made by legislation in the common-law rules expounded under the Blackstone fiction.

So much for landed property. With reference to the distribution of personal property of persons dying intestate — furniture, jewels, money, goods, stocks, bonds, notes, and evidences of indebtedness in general — the rule of equal distribution among children, saving the wife's share, was adopted earlier and prevailed even more easily. This was partly due to the growing importance of commerce and industry as against agriculture and the ever-increasing proportion of personal property in the total national wealth, and partly to the fact that American colonists had quickly grasped the significance of the English statute of 1671 for the distribution of personal estates. That statute, enacted in the reign of Charles II, covered in great detail the distribution of personal property in all cases of intestacy. The colony of New Jersey adopted it ten years after its passage, that is in 1681, and other colonies brought it into application, subject to various qualifications. Blackstone had taken note of it and American lawyers who studied the *Commentaries* could hardly miss it.

The English statute of distributions provided that, after the discharge of the intestate's debts and other proper obligations, the remaining goods and personal estate should be divided as follows: "one third part . . . to the wife of the intestate, and of the residue, by equal portions, to and amongst the children of the intestate and their representatives." For cases in which there was no widow or children or children's descendants, the act made elaborate provision in detail for distribution among other relatives of the intestate. Although Blackstone insisted that the statute bore a close resemblance to the "ancient English law" and, in his regular manner, minimized its resemblance to Roman civil law, the substance of the act was borrowed from Justinian's novels and, except in certain instances expressly mentioned, was to be construed and applied according to the rules of Roman civil law. In short, it came from a primary source of equity and in fact was written by a specialist in Roman law.

Since the equal distribution of personal property among sons and daughters increased the number of women, single and married, who acquired property, it made still more objectionable to men and women involved in the process the common-law doctrine which, in the absence of other arrangements, vested the married woman's personal property in her husband during marriage. And men and women were often equally concerned in avoiding the proscriptions of the common law as applied to any particular woman. The father and mother, brothers and sisters, and other relatives, male and female, had interests, affectionate and practical, in safeguarding a woman's rights before and after her marriage. The woman herself, holding property or knowing that property would come into her possession at some time, could scarcely be indifferent to the disabilities she could incur in respect of her property under common-law rules. In anticipation of marriage or afterward, if informed at all, she knew that her personal property, in case of misfortune to her husband, might be swept away for the benefit of his creditors and a part, if not the whole, of the family support be destroyed. Moreover, a husband, in his regard for his intended or his actual wife, if not in his own interest, if informed at all, knew that, in case of misfortune to him, under the common-law rules his wife's estate as well as his own might be seized for the benefit of creditors.

For such men and women there was only one unfailing recourse until the abolition of the common-law doctrines respecting married women's property was effected by legislation: that was to ante-nuptial and post-nuptial arrangements authorized by equity jurisprudence and enforced by courts of equity. As time passed resort to such arrangements became more common; and Blackstone's feudal law was more and more civilized by the spread of equity jurisprudence in the United States. Indeed it is scarcely too much to say that the moral revolution in respect of married women's property rights had occurred before 1840 and that the married women's property acts, which completed the revolt against Blackstone, merely transformed generally accepted equity principles into provisions of statutes.

From decade to decade, as the nineteenth century advanced, the battle between Equity and Blackstone for possession of the law intensified. From the seaboard to the frontiers of the United States, thousands of courts, independent and mixed, on petitions in due form and at the insistence of equity lawyers, applied Equity to the correction of common-law discriminations against married women, establishing more and more the equality of rights which had prevailed in the civil law of Rome in the age of Roman enlightenment. Leaders in the woman movement joined men in the war on Blackstone and demanded from legislators the enactment of statutes designed to obliterate common-law rules and to safeguard the property rights of women in general and bring them into more accord with the spirit of the age.

GREAT AMERICAN COMMENTATORS ON LAW AND EQUITY BEGIN
TO BREAK THE TYRANNY OF BLACKSTONE

Another factor in the disintegration of the Blackstone dogma was the publication of great treatises on American law in which Equity received a recognition denied to it in the *Commentaries on the Laws of England*. It is true that American editors who brought out fresh editions of Blackstone from time to time inserted notes calling attention to some legal departures in the United States; but they treated the changes on the whole in a cavalier fashion. It was American writers of law books, writing for American readers, who first devoted serious attention to modifications in the common law by American statutes and by the inroads of Equity. If in the early age of the Republic of the United States, when the allegiance to Blackstone was so tenacious, the average Americans who stood out as leaders of opinion had excuses for being unaware of the nature and force of equity as practice, their heirs and successors had no such grounds for justifying their ignorance in the time of Andrew Jackson and the rise of American democracy. Books for the appraisal and correction of Blackstone as master of jurisprudence were then in the public bookshops and in many private libraries.

Two men trained in Blackstone's version of English and

inherited American law led the way in this intellectual revolution: James Kent and Joseph Story.

The first great treatise of the new age was James Kent's *Commentaries on American Law* in four volumes. They were published from 1827 to 1830, and the work was received with so much enthusiasm that five new editions came from his pen by 1848. In many ways Kent was peculiarly fitted to make this monumental survey of American law and equity. He had begun his career as a disciple of Blackstone; of this experience he later said that the reading of Blackstone's four volumes had "inspired me, at the age of fifteen, with awe, and I fondly determined to be a lawyer." From the practice of law in New York, he rose high in the administration of justice. From 1796 to 1798 he was dispensing Equity as a master in chancery; from 1798 to 1814 he was a judge of the New York supreme court; from 1814 to 1823 he served as chancellor of the New York chancery court.

After his retirement, Kent lectured on law at Columbia College and devoted himself to the study of law as historically developed and practiced. His extraordinary learning, his ease with foreign languages and his study of Roman and Continental law, combined with his special knowledge of American law, qualified him for the immense undertaking he assumed. As a Federalist in politics and hostile to the democratic equalitarianism of the age, Kent in legal theory followed the Federalist line, but his political predilections did not lead him to bypass or belittle Equity in the style of his early mentor, Sir William Blackstone. He preferred, he confessed, the common law to the civil law of Rome on "paternal and conjugal relations," and he did not go as far as he could have done in treating equity principles in that respect. Nevertheless, in his sections on the property rights of women in American law, he demonstrated that equity had in practice extensively shaken the force of the common-law doctrines.

True to common-law traditions, Kent opened his chapter on husband and wife with a statement of the Blackstone summary on husband and wife. But he then dealt with modifications of the common law in America. And, unlike Blackstone, he immediately took up at length, in the very same chapter, the wife's capacity in Equity and showed how most of the "disabilities" which prevailed at common law had been or could be voided in Equity.

After making this demonstration of equity's power, Kent called distinct attention to the differences between American law and equity and the provisions of Roman and Continental civil law in respect of the rights of husband and wife. "Our law concerning marriage settlements," he remarked, "appears to us at least to be quite simple, and easy to be digested, when compared with the complicated relations of the community and partnership system between husband and wife prevailing in parts of Europe and the state of Louisiana." He added that "doubts may arise in the mind of a person educated in the school of the common law, as to the wisdom or policy of the powers which, by the civil law and the law of those modern nations which have adopted it, are conceded to the wife in matters of property." But he noted that the civil law of Rome in the age of its enlightenment and of the modern countries which had followed this law conferred "equality and dignity upon the female character."

Six years after Kent published the last volume of his *Commentaries on American Law*, Justice Joseph Story brought out a great work in two volumes, entitled *Commentaries on Equity Jurisprudence as Administered in England and America* and devoted entirely to the development and nature of equity in England and the United States. After his appointment as an associate justice of the United States Supreme Court in 1811, Story, who as Kent had done started his legal training with a study of Blackstone, dedicated spare time to independent research, combining it with work as a professor of law at Harvard after 1828.

Well versed in European history and law and given to wide ranging explorations, Story early encountered the deep imprints which Equity had made upon the Common Law, including that part of it concerned with the rights and obligations of married women. He spent years in examining the decisions and opinions in equity cases, English and American.

The results of his researches he employed in formulating and expounding the first principles of equity jurisprudence, supported by citations of specific cases settled in courts which enjoyed chancery jurisdiction. After the first edition appeared in 1836 no educated man or woman in the United

States, who wished to discourse on the rights of women with knowledge and intelligence, had any just grounds for overlooking the drastic changes which equity had wrought in the common law or for treating Blackstone as the supreme legal authority. Story's treatise went through many editions, the fourteenth edition coming out in 1918, at the end of the first world war.

Although Joseph Story, in his *Commentaries on Equity Jurisprudence,* was cautious and gentle in dealing with the curt way in which Blackstone handled equity, he entered a strong dissent as to Blackstone's statement pertaining to the nature and substance of equity. Story, like Blackstone, rejected the extravagant claims of those writers who insisted that equity dispensed freely a kind of omniscient justice based on principles of universal and everlasting ethics. Like Blackstone, he conceded that equity had become a type of law fixed in many respects by long lines of precedents established by equity courts through the centuries. But Story challenged Blackstone's narrow enumeration of the functions performed by equity. He chose an enumeration by Lord Redesdale as "far more satisfactory as a definite enumeration." In Redesdale's summation, equity must intervene "where the courts of ordinary jurisdiction are made instruments of injustice"; and "where the principles of law, by which the ordinary courts are guided, give no right, and upon the principles of universal justice the interference of the judicial power is necessary to prevent a wrong and the positive law is silent"; . . . and "to put a bound to vexations and oppressive litigation, and to prevent multiplicity of suits." Thus, in effect, Story repudiated Blackstone's illiberal views as to the very substance and duties of equity and accorded to it the flexibility for doing justice, which Blackstone and his school of lawyers sought to withhold from it.

At the opening of his chapter on "Married Women," Story described the position of married women under the common law as expounded by Blackstone, beginning with the famous doctrine that husband and wife are "one person" — the husband — under that law. But he qualified that doctrine by indicating that even under the creed itself they were not "one" in all respects. Then Story proceeded to show in what fundamental respects equity modified, overrode, voided for particular purposes the common-law doctrines and substantiated the rights of married women in their persons and property.

Did a woman, after all, cease to exist at law in respect of her property rights when she married? Story answered: "Courts of Equity for many purposes treat the husband and wife as the civil law [of Rome] treats them, as distinct persons, capable (in a limited sense) of contracting with each other, of suing each other, and of having separate estates, debts, and interests. A wife may in a Court of Equity sue her husband and be used by him. And in cases respecting her separate estate, she may also be sued without him, although he is ordinarily required to be joined, for the sake of conformity to the rule of law, as a nominal party whenever he is within the jurisdiction of the court and can be made a party."

Do contracts made between a man and a woman before their marriage become utterly extinguished after they are married? It depends upon the nature of the contracts. "Courts of Equity ... will, in special cases in furtherance of the manifest intentions and objects of the parties, carry into effect such a contract made before marriage between husband and wife, although it would be voided at law. An agreement therefore entered into by husband and wife before marriage for the mutual settlement of their estates, or of the estate of either upon the other upon the marriage, even without the intervention of trustees, will be enforced in equity though void at law; for equity will not suffer the intention of the parties to be defeated by the very act which is designed to give effect to such a contract. . . . 'In equity it is constant experience that the husband may sue the wife or the wife the husband' . . . Where a husband convenanted before marriage with his intended wife that she should have the power to dispose of £300 of her estate, he was afterwards held bound specifically to perform it." The same rule in equity was applied in cases where the woman bound herself to give her intended husband any portion of her estate.

But what of the woman's contractual rights after marriage, when her separate personality "ceased to exist" at common law in such matters? "Courts of Equity will ... under particular circumstances give full effect and validity to post-nuptial contracts. Thus, for example, if a wife having a separate estate should bona fide enter into a contract with her husband to make him a certain allowance out of the income of such estate for a reasonable consideration, the contract, although void at law, would be held obligatory, and would be enforced in equity. So if the husband should after marriage for good reasons contract with his wife that she should separately possess and enjoy property bequeathed to her, the contract would be upheld in equity.... Nay, if an estate should be devised to a husband for the separate use of his wife, it would be considered as a trust for the wife, and he would be compelled to perform it."

In general the husband, in Equity, could make gifts to his wife, although according to Blackstone she had no separate existence: "Courts of Equity will uphold them in many cases where they would be held void at law, although in other cases the rule of law will be recognized and enforced. Thus, for example, if a husband should by deed grant all his estate or property to his wife, the deed would be held inoperative in equity as it would be in law; for it could in no just sense be deemed a reasonable provision for her (which is all that the Courts of Equity hold the wife entitled to), and in giving her the whole he would surrender all his own interests. But on the other hand if the nature and circumstances of the gift or grant, whether it be express or implied, are such that there is no ground to suspect fraud, but it amounts only to a reasonable provision for the wife, it will, even though made after coverture, be sustained in equity."

Not only will reasonable post-nuptial settlements made by a husband upon his wife in return for proper consideration be enforced at equity, but a married woman may acquire and possess a separate estate subject to her own power and interests. "It is well known that the strict rules of the old common law would not permit the wife to take or enjoy any real or personal estate separate from or independent of her husband. And although these rules have been in some degree relaxed and modified in modern times, yet they have still a very comprehensive influence and operation in Courts of Law. On the other hand Courts of Equity have for a great length of time admitted the doctrine that a married woman is capable of taking real and personal estate to her own separ-

ate and exclusive use, and that she also has an incidental
power to dispose of it. The power to hold real and personal
property to her own separate and exclusive use may be and
often is reserved to her by marriage articles or by an actual
settlement made before marriage; and in that case the agreement becomes completely obligatory between the parties
after marriage and regulates their future rights, interests, and
duties. In a like manner real and personal property may be
secured for the separate and exclusive use of a married woman
after marriage, and thus the arrangement may acquire a
complete obligation between the parties."

But in the equity of the middle ages in England it was
necessary to put property designed for the separate and exclusive use of a married woman in the hands of trustees
obligated to manage it in her interest, subject to her scrutiny
and her power to institute legal actions against them. Was
this the absolute rule of equity for modern times? Story informed his readers that it was not: "It was formerly supposed
that the interposition of trustees was in all arrangements of
this sort, whether made before or after marriage, indispensable for the protection of the wife's rights and interests. In
other words, it was deemed absolutely necessary that the
property of which the wife was to have the separate and
exclusive use should be vested in trustees for her benefit;
and that the agreement of the husband should be made with
such trustees, or at least with persons capable of contracting
with him for her benefit. But although in strict propriety
that should always be done and it usually is done in regular
and well-considered settlements, yet it has for more than a
century been established in Courts of Equity that the intervention of trustees is not indispensable; and that whenever
real or personal property is given or devised or settled upon
a married woman either before or after marriage for her
separate and exclusive use without the intervention of trustees,
the intention of the parties shall be effectuated in equity, and
the wife's interest protected against the marital rights and
claims of her husband and of his creditors also. In all such
cases the husband will be held a mere trustee for her; and
although the agreement is made between him and her alone,
the trust will attach upon him and be enforced in the same
manner and under the same circumstances that it would be if

he were a mere stranger. It makes no difference whether the separate estate be derived from her husband himself or from a mere stranger; for as to such separate estate when obtained in either way her husband will be treated as a mere trustee and prohibited from disposing of it to her prejudice."

In numerous cases in equity involving the rights of the married woman in the enjoyment of property dedicated to her separate and exclusive use, equity made various discriminations. In each case the Court of Equity had to be on guard against loose claims made by the husband or the wife. In particular it had to be watchful lest the husband and wife had entered into collusion in this respect for the purpose of defrauding his or her creditors. For such reasons equity insisted that the instruments relative to the married woman's property should contain precise language or terms showing that a separate and independent estate was actually intended by the parties to transactions and settlements in the premises. But in construing the rights of the married woman to her own property, Courts of Equity were generally liberal in that they sought to give effect to the intention of the parties respecting any such arrangement, settlement, or understanding.

Such arrangements respecting the separate existence and the rights of the married woman to the enjoyment of her own property, and the income derived from it, could be and were readily carried into effect in rural regions where most of the property was in land and in chattels associated with the operations of agriculture. Men and women could make innumerable agreements between themselves in various relations, as husbands and wives, and as fathers or mothers in connection with their sons and daughters. The major portion of such arrangements were carried out by mutual understanding and never came before any court of law or court of equity for adjudication. But if litigation did arise involving equitable rights, courts of equity were prepared to enforce the rights of women as well as the rights of men in respect of reasonable agreements and separate holdings, if free of any taint of collusion intended to defraud the creditors of either husbands or wives.

What, however, of the right of the married woman, in the modern age of expanding commerce and industry, to engage in separate occupations on her own account? At common law the single woman could, of course, buy and sell, make contracts, sue and be sued, hold and transfer property at will in the same manner as the single or married man. But at Common Law the existence of the married woman was supposed to be "suspended" during marriage; she could not make independent contracts, buy and sell at her pleasure, sue or be sued, and hence she could not engage in business transactions on her own account.

What did Equity have to say about this domain of the married woman's liberty? Story carefully considered this matter and replied: "By the custom of London a married woman may carry on trade within the city as a sole trader and be liable as such." Yet as a rule in England and the United States the practice raised many ticklish questions for both husbands and wives. If the wife was successful in trade, perhaps few issues arose, except as to the disposition of her accumulated property after her death. If, on the other hand, she was unsuccessful in trade and became heavily involved in debts, where then did the husband stand in case litigation arose between her and her creditors? In this situation equity, in justice to both husband and wife, had to be circumspect, and inquire whether the husband was involved in the affair and/or had given his consent.

Story took into account the position of the married woman in business as far as equity was then concerned. "The right to carry on trade on her sole account," he said, "may independently of any such custom [as prevailed in London] be established by an agreement between the husband and wife before or after marriage. When such an agreement is entered into before marriage, it stands upon a valuable consideration; and therefore, if there is the interposition of trustees, it will be maintained against the husband and his creditors as well at law as in equity. In such a case the trustees of the wife will be entitled to the property assigned and to the increase and profits thereof, for her sole and separate use and benefit. . . . Even if no trustees are interposed, the property will in the like case be protected in equity, against the claims of the husband and his creditors, and excepted out of the general rules which govern in cases of husband and wife."

If the agreement for a separate trade by the wife occurred

after marriage and was made in due form, both Equity and Law would enforce it for the protection of the wife's interest against the husband and his creditors. "If it is a voluntary agreement, it will be good against the husband only, and not against his creditors." But, of course, the wife in trade had to be careful as to the form of her transactions lest, through neglect, the husband enforce against her his rights in her property allowed to him by common law.

The wife, whether in trade or not, could have her separate estate in real and personal property and use the income of it for her sole and exclusive purposes. What of her right to dispose of it? Story also dealt with this question: "It may be laid down as a general rule that all ante-nuptial agreements for securing to a wife separate property will, unless the contrary is stipulated or implied, give her in equity the full power of disposing of the same, whether real or personal, by any suitable act or instrument in her lifetime, or by her last will, in the same manner and to the same extent as if she were a *feme sole*. And in all cases where a power for this purpose is reserved to her by means of a trust which is created for the purpose, she may execute the power without joining her trustees, unless it is made necessary by the instrument of trust."

In the case of post-nuptial agreements respecting the wife's separate estate, numerous fine distinctions appeared, particularly as to the rights of her husband and her heirs in her separate property. Many technical rules were therefore applied in relation to the right of the woman to dispose of separate property acquired after marriage. She could enjoy it for her own purposes but she could not sell, give, or bequeath any way she liked. In this connection it is important to know and remember that neither could the husband so dispose of his own property to any extent or in any way that suited his pleasure or convenience. The protection of the family through its property was at stake.

In numerous other cases, mounting upward into the hundreds by the time Story wrote his great work on *Equity Jurisprudence,* the rights of the married woman were protected by equity as against common-law doctrines. Of her dowry rights in her husband's estate or their combined estates, so complicated and extensive in nature, there is no room to speak here, except to say that equity sought to maintain them as they stood at law and in equity, against the husband and all other claimants upon him. He too, of course, had his rights in her estate, exclusive of any portion assigned to her and her heirs for separate use. This was of necessity a certain outcome of the very marriage union which men and women voluntarily entered, thus assuming obligations which neither of them could morally or legally avoid at their pleasure afterward. Even if they desired or agreed to do exactly as they wished in their own relations, personal and propertied, both law and equity perforce had to intervene if other parties, such as creditors and heirs, instituted litigation against the husband or the wife or the two jointly or their estates. And equity courts, as well as common-law courts, in rendering decisions, had to consider the rights of outsiders, no less than the rights and obligations of the husband and the wife, and to enforce these rights in proper cases against husband and wife.

In cases at law and in equity, therefore, it was not often, if ever, a question whether the rights of the husband and wife were "equal." It was usually a question of the rights and obligations attached to each party to the marriage and to both of them, by virtue of their act of marriage and the continuance of marital relations in varying circumstances of life. Equity sought to follow the common law in certain cases, the precedents of equity, and in final analysis the prescriptions of reasoned justice. Exact equality or exact justice to husband and wife and creditors and heirs was difficult to define — and still is; but an examination of Story's volumes, to say nothing of other records of the time, reveals valiant efforts on the part of equity courts to attain the ideal of justice.

By way of illustrating this broad generalization another citation from Story may be given: "If it is apparent from the state of the case that the husband must remain in future without funds to maintain his wife, and there is an equitable fund belonging to her within the reach of a Court of Equity, it will decree the income of the whole fund to be applied primarily to the maintenance of the wife during her lifetime, and after her death the principal to be divided among her children. Thus if the husband has become insolvent and has taken advantage of an Insolvent Act, which discharges his person but not his future effects, there a Court of Equity will secure the whole fund in the manner above mentioned, for the benefit of the wife and children."

Not only did equity protect the married woman against restraints of common law in innumerable relations. It protected young unmarried men and women against various kinds of fraudulent and coercive acts on the part of each other or their parents or outside persons. Equity did this on the general principle that all conditions and actions against the liberty of young men and women to choose their own mates were unlawful, void and unenforceable. For example, a gift or grant based on the condition that a person did not marry until reaching the age of fifty was void. So was a condition that a girl should not marry a lawyer or a physician or any person not a member of a particular craft or trade. On the other hand, many conditions were held valid, such as the condition to marry or not to marry a person or persons specified by name.

Anyone who runs through hundreds of equity cases involving restraints on the right of young men and women to marry (or widows and widowers, as well) will discover problems put up to equity courts that might well defy the wisdom of omniscient justice to settle according to rules of universal right and equality. Yet anyone who makes a survey of this kind must be deeply impressed by the reasonableness and humane spirit of Equity, as it broadened through the years.

Since such were the rights of women in Equity as things stood in 1836, fortified by a long line of precedents stretching back through the centuries, it seems perfectly plain that the dogma of woman's complete historic subjection to man must be rated as one of the most fantastic myths ever created by the human mind.

Chapter 7

Equality as the Escape from Subjection

WHILE JUDGES presiding in courts of equity were administering justice, guarding the interests of family cohesion or protecting the property of women as of men from seizure by undue process, zealous efforts were being made outside the courts, in the nineteenth century, to introduce spacious principles of justice into law by legislation — by the enactment of statutes. Women reformers thus directed their attacks against those features of the common law which they called tyrannical to women — their judgment being derived from Blackstone's over-simplification respecting the common law conception of marriage.

Given this acceptance of the Blackstone emphasis on the common law, it was natural that women reformers, who concentrated on the task of substituting liberty for tyranny in law, should pay little heed to the methods provided by equity. Taking equality between men and women, not equity, as their slogan, they forged ahead, hewing to a straight line of agitation based on a narrow interpretation of history. Their line gave an intensity to their declarations and a single track to their program for action that made their revolution against the "status" of women "at law" take on the fury of a storm. It provided the satisfaction of a "fight" for women possessing great physical energy and oratorical power. It also offered the more or less dubious satisfaction of bringing "sleeping dogs" to the bark and the bite.

WOMEN PROCLAIM SUBJECTION AND DEMAND EQUALITY —
IN 1848

An organized movement for wholesale reform in the interest of "sex equality" started at Seneca Falls in the state of New York, in 1848, when a convention of women and men accepted woman's historic subjection to man as a fact and declared her equality with man to be the goal of their ambitions. The Declaration of Sentiments adopted at that convention asserted without qualification: "The history of mankind is a history of repeated injuries and usurpations on the part of man toward woman, having in direct object the establishment of an absolute tyranny over her. To prove this, let facts be submitted to a candid world."

Having made the broad change against man, the convention then presented a list of grievances to support it, patterning them on the American men's Declaration of Independence submitted to a "candid" world as well as to the British government in 1776. Though the women found it somewhat difficult to match the exact number of grievances which had been assembled in the men's Declaration of 1776, as Elizabeth Cady Stanton later confessed, they finally accomplished the feat and specified the "abuses and usurpations" of which man was guilty in gaining his object — "the establishment of an absolute tyranny over her [woman]."

What principle or idea or assumption or dogma was to guide women in escaping from man's "design to reduce them under absolute despotism"? The convention set it forth in a solemn declaration: "*Resolved,* That woman is man's equal — was intended to be so by the Creator, and the highest good of the race demands that she should be recognized as such."

In the principle of Equality the rebellious woman of 1848 thus established their warrant for waging war on man's tyranny and in the same principle they fixed the object of their revolt. They affirmed their faith that "equality of human rights results necessarily from the fact of the identity of the race in capabilities and responsibilities." Here they set forth for themselves and for generations of women to come the ideal that freedom from tyranny required complete and unconditional equality with man — with the male creature who had, throughout history, pursued as a "direct object the establishment of an absolute tyranny over" woman. It is true that in coupling responsibilities with capacities and rights, especially in many of their ensuing public speeches, the "new women" struck a social note which was absent from most of men's great documents on their own struggle for equal rights among men. Yet in the prolonged contest for equal rights with men, leaders of the woman movement steadily fixed their attention on legal and political equality rather than on women's force, potentialities, and obligations.

Unquestionably there was dynamism in the slogan: Equality! Here was a formula of perfection, hoary with age and ringing with revolutionary associations. The women of '48 did not invent the word or the idea behind it. They adopted a conception older than Christianity, an ideal pagan in origin. The utter simplification of historic processes, the propagandistic convenience, and the flavor of utopian grandeur represented by equality furnished fuel for a fiery crusade.

THE IDEA OF EQUALITY — HISTORY AND NATURE

The English word equality was derived, in the fifteenth century, from the old French word, *égalité,* which then had merely a mathematical meaning — equality of time, equality of space, equality of distance. But during the revolutionary upheaval of the seventeenth century in England the meaning of equality was given a social significance. From its old French usage as signifying uniformity or "exactly the same in measure, amount, degree, value, or quality," it came to signify what is right, proper, just, and reasonable.

In this broader usage the idea of equality corresponded to a matured Roman concept of social justice — to the Latin verbal form, *aequalitas.* As Roman governors and jurists were compelled to deal with the inhabitants of conquered provinces adeptly, if they were to retain control, and with all sorts and conditions of people who were not Roman citizens, they learned that all peoples have certain things in common and out of this knowledge they established the

famous *jus gentium,* or the common law of peoples in the
Roman Empire. Finally the Romans reached the conclusion
that nature had originally decreed human equality and that
disobedience to this mandate of nature had marred the
"natural law" of equality. It was this ancient Roman theory,
legal and philosophical, which Rousseau was to reaffirm in
the eighteenth century with his declaration that men were
born free but were everywhere in chains — the chains to be
severed by a return to "natural" rights.

In the broadening of Roman thought beyond the confines
of the tribal state, a continuous and treasured belief was
held in the essential oneness of humanity, despite glaring
discrepancies in human customs. Epictetus, an enslaved
Greek, insisted that human beings are all children of God
and are duty-bound to cherish love for, and practice forbear-
ance toward, one another. Weakness has its claims and
strength its moral limitations, he maintained. While in Roman
history no assembly proclaimed the rights of man, as did
the Continental Congress of the American colonies in 1776
and the French Revolutionary Assembly of 1789, all the
elements of such a declaration could be gathered by students
of classical literature from the writings of Roman philosophers and moralists. Though neither the American declaration of rights nor the French bill of rights proclaimed the
rights of women, specifically, the women of 1848 could feel
that they were operating in a great tradition when they proclaimed equality as a right of women and as offering an
escape from "tyranny."

In Roman writings had been foreshadowed the teachings
of Jesus Christ respecting the oneness of humanity. Seneca
had said: "We are all akin by nature which has formed us of
the same elements and placed us here together for the same
end." To a similar conclusion the meditative emperor, Marcus
Aurelius, had arrived: "If our reason is common, there is a
common law. . . . And if there is a common law, we are fellow
citizens; if this is so, we are members of some political community — the world is in a manner of State." And in this
evolving philosophy the moral worth of the human personality
and the principle of human equality were clearly and cate-
gorically asserted in the teachings of Christianity: "Of one
blood are all nations of men. . . . There is neither Jew nor

Greek, neither bond nor free, neither male nor female; for ye are all one in Jesus Christ."

From the flowering of Christianity in the later ages the idea of human equality was never absent. It is true that many Christian writers and teachers, recognizing the force of woman in society, inveighed against woman, declared her a source, if not the source, of evil in the world, and proclaimed in bitter language that she *ought to be* in all things subject to man. But such teaching was utterly different from the contention that *as a matter of fact* woman had been throughout the past subject to man and still was. Moreover it is possible to assemble from other Christian teachings quotations giving entirely different views of woman; and in any case the doctrine of human equality continued to be asserted amid the storms and strains of the centuries. Among the early Christians there were many writers who maintained that this equality should extend to community of goods. Even after the triumph of feudalism in the middle ages of Christendom, the idea of equality retained a strong grip on the thought of the plain people and its power was demonstrated in the peasants' revolts which menaced the dominance of lay and clerical landlords.

The idea of equality was revived with renewed zest after the unity of the Catholic Church had been broken by the Protestant Reformers and the unity of succeeding Protestant State Churches had been shattered by the assaults of dissenting sects. The idea of equality was upheld and preached with vehemence by the Levellers who supported the Cromwellian revolution against Charles I of England and overthrew the British monarchy in 1649. Among the Levellers, Baptists were outstanding leaders but other dissenting sects in England also promoted the egalitarian doctrine.

In one of the Levellers' tracts it was declared: "By naturall birth all men are equally and alike born to like propriety [property] liberty, and freedom . . . every man by nature being a King, Priest and Prophet in his owne naturall circuite and compasse." In another tract it was asserted that originally men and women were "by nature all equall and alike in power, digny [dignity], authority, and majesty, no one possessing any right of dominance except by mutual consent."

Though the monarchy was restored in England in 1660,

the doctrine of equality was not extinguished. It is true that in the pronouncements of men, equality among men was emphasized and the larger equality of men and women was commonly ignored. Nevertheless the idea of equality was kept in circulation for the benefit of men at least and women could recover its significance for themselves and put it into circulation whenever their purposes were to be served.

For the men's purposes primarily, Thomas Hobbes set forth this formulation in 1651. He was personally attached to the monarchy but in his *Leviathan* he offered a wider view of mankind: "Nature hath made men so equal in the faculties of body and mind, as that . . . when all is reckoned together the difference between man and man is not so considerable, as that one man can thereupon claim to himself any benefit to which another may not pretend as well."

This broad statement of equality John Locke, however, did not support. Nevertheless his influence in America penetrated to the firesides of nearly all literate men and women in the new world directly or through the work of Jefferson. This was the way in which Locke put the case for equality: "Man being born . . . with a title to perfect freedom and an uncontrolled enjoyment of all the rights and privileges of the law of nature, equally with any other man, or number of men in the world, hath by nature a power not only to preserve his property . . . but to judge of and punish the breaches of that law in others." While accepting the thesis of the equality of men "by nature," Locke did not say that men are equal in fact or are born *in* it. He merely maintained that they are born *to* equality. If this means anything, it means that in the imaginary original society — imaginary because it cannot be known as it actually was — called "natural," men were entitled to equality by some moral concept.

Nor did Jefferson adhere to Hobbes' doctrine that men are substantially equal in mind and body. He was more akin spiritually to Locke. In the famous Declaration of Independence with which his name is linked as framer, he asserted only that "all men are created equal." When he added that all men "are endowed by the Creator with certain unalienable Rights, that among these are Life, Liberty, and the pursuit of Happiness," he did not say that these rights are equal in form and substance. No less cautious had been the Virginia

Declaration of Rights proclaimed a short time before by the Virginia assembly. It announced merely that "all men are by nature *equally free* and *independent.*" To conservative defenders of chattel slavery and the class orders so obvious in American society in 1776, when those two bold declarations were given out to the public, the doctrine that all men are *created* or are *by nature* equal was a meaningless and glittering, if not a positively dangerous, generality which did not correspond to known facts in the case and was impossible of realization. Yet the doctrine persisted. Inspired by it as ideal, American men moved toward equality among themselves in several respects, notably in voting rights and in the abolition of chattel slavery.

Insofar as the doctrine of equality, whether for men only or for men and women together, represented simply an opposition of Nature to the established institutions, ranks, classes, and special privileges of society as it existed in times and places when the doctrine was preached, it was essentially negative in its practical applications. Insofar as the theory of equality was derived from a theory of a golden age in the dim and distant and unknown past, it was altogether romantic, especially when used to urge the restoration of a golden age never to be recovered as an experience identical with that of original men and women.

In its negative aspect, the idea of equality was directed primarily to the destruction of all special privileges enjoyed by specific persons and classes in society — in Europe particularly the privileges of King, Aristocracy, and Clergy. As against such privileges, the French Revolutionists proclaimed Liberty, Equality, and Fraternity!

But the doctrine of equality also represented from time to time positive aspirations. As upheld by the Levellers it maintained that every human being was a peer of a king and a priest, and a master of property in his own bailiwick or province. For women it often meant, simply, taking the stature of man as the measure of excellence and endowing woman with his qualities, aims, and chances in the world for personal advantages.

Efforts to give constructive concreteness to the idea of equality as the years of the nineteenth century passed led far and wide into sociology and economics, and thus into a maze of perplexities. Jeremy Bentham had sought to work out the implications of equality by devising some standard of measurement. If "everybody is to count for one, nobody for more than one," for what is everybody to count? What is the substance of equality desired for all? Bentham decided that the substance is happiness and that the aim of legislation should be to assure the greatest happiness to the greatest number of people in some proportion of equality. As John Stuart Mill, famous author of *The Subjection of Women* and proponent of their emancipation through equalizing legislation, interpreted the principle of measurement, Bentham had simply assumed that "equal amounts of happiness are equally desirable, whether felt by the same or different persons."

Although the doctrine which Bentham taught was ridiculed as "the greatest happiness principle" and "the calculus of pleasures and pains," especially by adherents of old systems of thought and social arrangements, in fact Bentham did more to humanize and rationalize the criminal and civil laws of England than any other single individual in the nineteenth century. He also aided in kindling a similar reforming spirit on this side of the Atlantic in his time.

Yet, when everything had been said that could be said about the idea of equality in happiness, at least for the greatest number of human beings, the idea was still a shadowy guide to practical applications. It was comparatively easy to provide that each man, or every man who met certain broad tests, should have one vote, and thus become a political equal at the election polls. It demanded no great acumen to write into constitutions or statutes the principle that all men or all persons including women shall be equal before or under the law. But the idea of equality in property rights, as between men and women, which the American women of 1848 were disseminating, if actually reduced to legislation, would involve the definition and acceptance of some fundamental system of ownership and economic practice about which their notions were exceedingly hazy, judging by their speeches and printed works in 1848 and afterward, if discernible at all.

This question of property ownership and economic practice had been recognized from ancient times by reflective thinkers who pondered on the nature and applications of equality.

Plato a pagan and many early Christians had considered this matter and had decided that only by communism — the community of goods — could the philosophy of equality be actually applied. After the French revolutionists of the eighteenth century had adopted the idea of equality, François Babeuf and his followers declared that equality called for a still greater revolution than the one in process in France: "something more sublime, more equitable . . . common property." Conservative American critics of Jefferson's theory of equalitarianism prophesied that it would lead to similar demands for the leveling of property rights in the United States. In 1848, the year of the woman's rights convention at Seneca Falls, the phantom of communism had raised its head in Europe and seemed to be raising its whole body in a general European revolution. Nor were wide-awake Americans indifferent to that fact.

But the communist theory of equality as practice attained no great vogue in the United States, notwithstanding the large number of communistic colonies founded in various parts of this country in the first half of the nineteenth century. To Americans at large it made little appeal. Their continent was not yet occupied and exploited in 1848 when women assembled at Seneca Falls to denounce special privileges for men and "civil death" for women in marriage, in an answer to the Blackstone thesis of privilege and perfection. Equal opportunity for the exploitation of natural resources and for business and professional careers seemed the easiest thing in the world to have and enjoy.

Communism ran counter to the insurgent theory of individual liberty and individual rights, associated with the rise of capitalism in the modern age and marking the advance of democracy in the United States during the Jacksonian upheaval. It was widely realized that, if property were held and effectively operated in common, the other rule of communism would have to come into force if real equality were to be established: "from each according to his abilities and to each according to his needs." In other words, the strong individual would be subjected to the necessities of the weak and obligations would be superior to rights or, at all events, materially limit them. Thus a paradox appeared: the idea of equality leads to communism and the inequalities of the strong and the weak under communism are to be obviated by the subjection of the strong to the weak.

The paradox troubled most Americans not at all. If writers and speakers in general knew of its existence, they betrayed slight, if any, consciousness of it, deeming it academic or worse. They were committed to other views of equality defined principally in political, libertarian, or social terms.

During the nineteenth century the system of economic thought which triumphed over other systems in the United States was that known as laissez faire, or individualism. English in origin, the theory took root in the new world and won strategic positions in seats of the higher learning, in the press, and on the platform. Under this system of economic thought the functions or obligations of the state and the community were reduced mainly to the maintenance of order and the protection of private property. This was the political concept of the state as a police state. Under this state, each possessor of property was to do whatsoever he wished "with his own" and individuals were to enjoy full liberty and equality to compete with one another for the possession of property and prestige.

As far as it was logically applied, the creed was atomistic in its social effects. It split families, communities, and society at large into units, into individuals, having equal rights to engage in the pursuit of happiness and property. The family, the community, the larger society embracing families and communities were played down. The individual was exalted and the competitive urge among individuals was regarded as a natural and socially wholesome human attribute.

It was admitted that equal right or liberty to compete did and would result in great inequalities of wealth and of opportunities for acquisition and enjoyment. But it was assumed that, as Adam Smith, regarded as the father of the competitive principle, said, the process would redound to the general good under "the invisible hand" of Providence. The fiercer the competition, the larger would be the production of wealth. In the struggle of individuals for a foothold and survival, the family and even society in the large would in some mysterious way take care of themselves, while individuals, lifted to the privilege of free competition with one another for the possession of all things they held dear, enjoyed their liberty.

VICISSITUDES IN THE IDEA OF EQUALITY

As the discussion of equality went forward, efforts were made to explore it anew in its historical and sociological concreteness; and in this exploration women were made the center of new inquiries respecting their nature and talents and social role or function. Old questions were reformulated in the light of findings or sheer assumptions in anthropology, psychology, and sociology. Were all men exactly identical with all men in physical nature, mental interests, and aspirations? How far could proclamations of rights and prescriptions of law introduce exact equality of men with men, of women with women, of women with men, where, as alleged, equality does not exist? Is it possible to make all men and women equal in rights or in goods? If so, by what laws and institutional arrangements?

Some answers became as controversial as the theory of equality itself. Some were documented by knowledge and experience. Others were merely logical deductions from asserted premises having feeble or no roots in knowledge or experience.

On the issue of physical, mental, and moral equality among men, the general verdict was negative. In self-evident respects men varied widely as to physical strength, intellectual powers, manners, and moral character.

On the issue of women's equality or identity with men the verdict could not be reached as easily. Like discussions of witchcraft in the seventeenth century, so in this discussion in the nineteenth and on into the twentieth century, ludicrous contradictions carried the matter far out of the bounds of reason. Confusion was scarcely less confounded among women who talked on the theme of sex equality than among men who discoursed on the subject.

For example, leaders of the woman movement at some times and in some places stood fast by the contention in the Seneca Falls Declaration of Sentiments that the overweening object of man had been to hold woman in servitude to him and that the "history of mankind" is a history of "man's repeated injuries and usurpations," at least as far as women are concerned. At such times and places they represented women as rightless in long history and passive in that condition. Yet at other times and places, confronted with the question as to how a creature who had been nothing or nearly nothing in all history could suddenly, if ever, become something — something like man, his equal — a few leaders in the woman movement used history to show what force women had displayed in history.

This contradiction is manifest in the volumes of the huge *History of Woman Suffrage* put together from the archives of the campaign for woman's enfranchisement from 1848 to the 1880's by Susan B. Anthony, Elizabeth Cady Stanton, Ida Husted Harper, and other workers in that movement. In the first volume the dilemma is disclosed. The first chapters of that volume deal almost entirely with the great "achievements" of women in times past, from the Abbess of Whitby in the ninth century to George Sand, Florence Nightingale, and Clara Barton in the nineteenth century. The second chapter is devoted entirely to women in journalism and it presents historical facts about important women editors, publishers, and writers from colonial times in America to the very moment when the very doctrine of subjection was being stoutly asserted in the best Blackstonian style. In Chapter IV, so closely following the accounts of women, single and married, who were not mere victims of men's "tyranny," occurs the Seneca Falls Declaration against man the tyrant and the attendant Resolutions of resistance to his mastery. Yet throughout the mammoth volumes of this *History of Woman Suffrage,* a record setting forth women's labors in this cause, are scattered extensive references to women as writers, speakers, agitators, business enterprisers, doctors, teachers, and other types of non-domestic activists, most of whom were wives and mothers living on good terms with their husbands and sons.

With this logical dilemma a few outstanding leaders of women wrestled. They had some familiarity with the attempts of philosophers in preceding centuries to reduce the issue of human equality to such precise formulas as equality before the law, equality in respect, equality in freedom of expression. With meager or no reference to those ancient mental struggles, however, women reiterated their formulas during the nineteenth century in the United States: formulas which rang round the world. These included such phrases as equal protection of the laws; equal opportunity in all "fields of endeavor"; equal suffrage; and equal privileges and immunities, including the right to hold public offices. But the favorite line of assertion was simplified to the absolute and unconditional demand for "equal rights" and "no discrimination on account of sex" anywhere in any relation.

Women were eloquent and effective in exposing innumerable instances of horrifying abuses that had arisen under the common law to which so many American lawyers clung. They were incisive in portraying, often with wit and humor, the arrogance of those men who asserted and boasted of their superiority as members of the masculine sex, while paying tribute to the superior virtues of women in language more maudlin than authentic. But women were open to cutting thrusts from the other side, when they displayed indifference to or ignorance of the actual terms of law and equity in their own times and places, as well as in other ages and places.

Moreover, the laws, rules, and interpretations against which women protested were not all rigid like fossils in a museum. Practices under them had direct bearings on the sentiments and habits of living men and women pursuing their daily affairs. New kinds of controversies involving the property rights of husbands and wives, and claims of their creditors and children, were constantly taxing the ingenuity of judges. New decisions and opinions were pouring out in torrents from courtrooms. As soon as a new statute affecting, even in a slight degree, the rights of husband or wife was passed, unforeseen consequences and disputes appeared; judges, often having in the law no clear guidance for such special cases, rendered decisions which were regarded as violating the ideal of equality; and new reforms were instantly demanded. Thus law reform and law practice revolved together in an endless cycle through the years.

EFFORTS AT REALIZING EQUALITY BY LEGISLATION

It was in such circumstances that leaders in the woman movement set out to criticize existing laws respecting married women's property rights, to break what they called the

yoke of subjection, and to consider the kinds of new Legislation which would realize the ideas of independence and equality they had formulated in general terms. To cover all the
Legislation which grew out of the reforming zeal of these
women and their aides among men would require many
volumes of a comprehensive encyclopaedia of statutory law.
All that is possible here is to present some illustrations of a
single type of Legislation, and the type chosen consists of laws
loosely known as married women's property acts — acts
which in the main merely reduced to statutory law or applied
universally certain rules or equity devised by men as chancellors or equity judges in the course of the preceding centuries.

About 1830, long after Equity had emancipated millions
of women from the rigidities of the Common Law so admired
by Blackstone and his disciples, a widespread demand arose
for married women's property acts. Such an act meant the
abolition of numerous common-law rules respecting the right
of the husband to control his wife's real estate and take
possession of her personal property, in case no pre-nuptial or
post-nuptial settlements or arrangements intervened. Rights
which prudent parents had long secured for daughters under
Equity were now to be extended to all married women as a
matter of written law. In upshot, the distinction between
Common Law and Equity, which had led to so much misunderstanding in relation to married women's rights, was
eliminated by legislative acts; and special precautions in the
form of elaborate legal documents, drawn by skilled lawyers,
were no longer necessary to assure the possession of property
to the married woman as against her husband and his
creditors. Henceforward, as to future marriages at least, in
states which passed this legislation, the husband had no common-law estate in his wife's real property; and his rights to
her personal property, including her chattels, money, and
choses in action, went by the board. In this way the doctrine
of the separate estate for married women, which had been
a creation of Equity, was embodied in the express terms of
statutory law and put beyond the reach of the Blackstone
lawyers.

A married women's property act was, therefore, simple
in principle. But in applications the terms of such an act
were difficult to draw. Despite the theory of independence and

equality which was supposed to furnish guidance in drafting the act, law-reformers and law-makers actually confronted a paradox: "The wife is to be treated as if she were a single woman in respect of her property, but in marital relations she has obligations not assumed by single women and is no more of a single person than her husband is; for both are entangled in a network of duties not imposed on single persons." Is the wife to be free to use her property as she pleases while the husband is in straits to support her and their children? In what, if any, circumstances is the wife to be under obligations to support the family in part or whole? Is the owner of the home, whether husband or wife, to be allowed to sell it at will, without the consent of the other party to the marriage contract, and turn the family out of it? These and a hundred other questions taxed the adroitness of law-makers and were answered by women and by men in many different ways. No mere declaration of equality could dispose of them in a few words. At no time or place did it prove possible to write one married women's property bill which could settle all these questions.

But long before the close of the nineteenth century disciples of Blackstone were in full flight before new legislation. In some states men took the lead in framing and driving reform bills through legislatures; in others, women took the initiative; in others men and women cooperated.

In the North, New York broke the path for a thorough reformation of the law relative to the property rights of married women. As early as 1836 a proposal to effect this change was introduced in the legislature but not until 1848 was the married women's property bill enacted into law. With the passage of the bill in 1848 the agitations of women apparently had little to do. According to the records printed in the *History of Woman Suffrage,* the measure was drawn by a member of the legislature who was eager to safeguard the rights of his wife, and it was vigorously pressed by another member equally eager to protect the interests of his daughter. The bill was introduced in January; it passed in April and was quickly signed by the governor. In the Senate the vote on the bill was: ayes 23 and nays 1. In the lower house of the legislature the vote was: ayes 93 and nays 9. During the whole proceeding only one petition favoring the bill was presented to the legislature and that petition was instigated by one of the members especially desirous of having the bill passed. So little did the leaders of the woman movement know about the history of the bill that years afterward one of them wrote to a member of the legislature asking him for information as to the origin and passage of the measure.

Perhaps the most remarkable thing about the New York Act was the ease with which it was carried through the legislature. The proposal was, from the point of view of Blackstone lawyers, radical and dangerous. As George Geddes, a sponsor of the bill in the Assembly, afterward wrote: "The measure was so radical, so extreme, that even its friends had doubts; but the moment any important amendment was offered, up rose the whole question of woman's proper place in society, in the family, and everywhere. We all felt that the laws regulating women's, as well as married men's, rights demanded careful revision and adaptation to our times and to our civilization. No such regulation could be perfected, nor has it been since. We meant to strike a hard blow, and if possible shake the old system of laws to their foundations, and leave it to other times and wiser counsels to perfect a new system. . . . We had in the Senate a man of mature years, who had never had a wife. He was a lawyer well-read in the old books and versed in the adjudications which had determined that husband and wife were one person, and the husband was that person; and he expressed great fears in regard to meddling with this well-settled condition of domestic happiness. This champion of the past made long and very able arguments to show the ruin this law must work, but he voted for the bill in the final decision."

The New York law of 1848, as its sponsors had foreseen, was soon found to need amendments, and in time many amendments were passed. For example, an act of 1860 provided that "any married woman may bring and maintain an action in her own name for damages against any person or body corporate for any injury to her person or character." The same statute also declared that "every married woman is constituted and declared to be the joint guardian of her children, with equal powers, rights, and duties in regard to them, with her husband."

Two years later, in 1862, the New York legislature was

again moved to make modifications in the rights of married women and men. Over this act, however, a heated dispute arose. Leaders in the woman movement asserted that the act marked retrogression and not progress in the development of married women's rights. Judge Charles J. Folger, who had been chairman of the judiciary committee of the New York Senate, in which the bill originated, took great pains to explain that, in his opinion, the new act gave greater powers and freedom to married women in most respects, while in others it enlarged the property rights of the husband. Whatever the merits of this controversy, it effectively illustrated the difficulty of settling, by egalitarian legislation, all at once and for all time, every issue pertaining to the respective rights and obligations of husband, wife, children, relatives, and creditors with reference to the ownership, use, partition, and disposition of property.

The next Northern state to make a drastic revision of the old law and confer new property rights upon married women was Massachusetts. Here leadership in the opposition to Blackstone doctrines and in the movement to secure new legislation was taken by women, with Mrs. Mary Upton Ferrin in the forefront. She enlisted the support of other women and the assistance of many able men as early as 1848. For six successive years she presented petitions to the legislature. In 1850 Mrs. Ferrin made an address to the judiciary committee of the legislature in which she presented an informed and well-organized argument against the old laws and in favor of a comprehensive bill enlarging the property and personal rights of married women. Four years later, in 1854, still prodded by Mrs. Ferrin and her associates, the Massachusetts legislature passed an act securing to every woman, married after the act, control over her property, the power to make a will without her husband's consent (except as to one-half her personal property), and certain fixed rights in the property of a husband dying intestate. In 1855 the divorce law of Massachusetts was amended in the interest of more equal rights for women.

It was with justice that the authors of the *History of Woman Suffrage* paid tribute to Mary Upton Ferrin, "who for six years, after her own quaint method, poured the hot shot of her earnest conviction of woman's wrongs into the

Legislature. In circulating petitions, she traveled six hundred miles, two-thirds of the distance on foot. Much money was expended, besides her time, and her name should be remembered as that of one of the brave pioneers in this work."

While Mrs. Ferrin was making her drive on the Massachusetts legislature, Robert Dale Owen was pleading with the people and law-makers of Indiana for legislation which would, as he had phrased it in 1832, abolish "the barbarous relics of a feudal, despotic system" and assure to women all the personal and property rights demanded by "the good sense and good feeling of this comparatively civilized age."

For more than thirty years a citizen of Indiana, and often a member of the state legislature, Owen labored in this cause. As a member of the State Constitutional Convention in 1850 he sought to write the principles of a married women's property act into the new state constitution then under discussion. He was defeated in this attempt by lovers of the common law who declared that heaven, home, and mother would be outraged by this innovation, but Owen persisted in his agitation. Within a few years, by various amendments to the statutes and novel provisions of law, Indiana adopted the principal features of an "ideal" married women's property act.

After the civil war, when Connecticut finally came around to a serious consideration of the laws affecting the personal and property rights of women, it was largely, if not principally, under the influence of forceful women that the hearts and minds of legislators were turned to the enactment of a married women's property bill. Most active, steadfast, and indomitable among them was Isabella Beecher Hooker, daughter of the Reverend Lyman Beecher and wife of Thomas Hooker sixth in descent from Thomas Hooker, memorable leader among the founders of the colony in the seventeenth century. While her husband was a young lawyer, she had learned the doctrines of Blackstone in his office and instinctively revolted against the creed that woman's existence was suspended during marriage. Encouraged by her husband, who shared her views, Mrs. Hooker adopted the principle of woman suffrage and began a campaign for a married women's property bill.

By 1869 the agitation for such a bill had advanced so

far that Marshall Jewell, a wealthy manufacturer who had just been elected governor of the state, sent a message to the legislature calling for a revision of the laws affecting the rights of married women. He called attention to the fact that such laws had been amended from time to time in recent years with a view to securing for them "in a more ample manner their property held before or acquired after marriage," but he reminded the legislators that "yet we are still considerably behind many of our sister states, and even conservative England."

For a time the legislature delayed action. But Mrs. Hooker and her supporters redoubled their efforts. At last in 1877 they were successful. In that year Governor R. D. Hubbard, in a forthright message, informed the legislature that "the property relations of husband and wife do not to-day rest upon any just or harmonious system," and urged the immediate enactment of new legislation on the subject. A bill prepared by Mrs. Hooker's husband was introduced in the legislature and quickly enacted into law.

By the Connecticut act of 1877 provisions of previous legislation which had left untouched the right of the wife to property acquired before marriage were amended and new principles established in law. The new act, incorporating the views and sentiments of Mrs. Hooker and her husband, was broad in its range. The burden of supporting the family was placed upon the husband. In respect of all future marriages the wife's property and her earnings were to be her sole property; she could convey her personal and real property to others without the consent of her husband; her property was to be liable for her debts but not for his; the husband was not liable for any of her debts except those incurred for the support of the family. As to purchases made by either party, they were presumed to be on the account of the party in question but both were liable where purchases actually went to the support of the family. In order that the duty of the husband to support the family could be strictly enforced, his property was first to be applied to the satisfaction of this liability, and the wife was entitled to indemnity for the use of her money to satisfy any such claims against him. On the death of either, the survivor was to be entitled to the use for life of at least one-third of the other's estate. Special provision was made authorizing men and women already married before the passage of the act to surrender their rights under the old laws for the rights provided by the new law. This they could do by a mere registration of such a contract in the records of a probate court. Not without reason did the editor of a newspaper comment that under such legislation "in some respects the woman is now the more favored party."

So far had the movement for property rights advanced by 1856 that Lucy Stone could report to the seventh National Woman's Rights Convention: "Now almost every Northern state has more or less modified its laws." Maine, Massachusetts, Vermont, New Hampshire, Rhode Island, and New York had gone far in the new direction. "Ohio, Illinois, and Indiana have also very materially modified their laws." Michigan and Wisconsin had also satisfied most of the demands of women in this regard. From Nebraska in the distant West news of coming victories was proudly hailed. "In England, too," Lucy Stone concluded, "the claims of women are making progress." In time Blackstone's formula on the "civil death" of married women was blasted throughout the Union by written law.

But in some of the states a different form of regulating the property relations of husband and wife, known as "the community system," was adopted instead of the type represented by married women's property acts. Under the influence of Spanish and French laws, bearing traces of the ancient Roman civil law, Louisiana remained from the outset a "community property" state; and for various reasons Texas, New Mexico, Arizona, and California chose that form of marital property relations. Furthermore, Nevada, Washington, and Idaho, where Spanish influences had been non-existent or at least negligible, deliberately chose that type in preference to any of the statutes enacted in the Eastern sections of the country. And, as a matter of fact, even in the old common-law states, before and after the passage of married women's property acts, the rules of community property, the property of husband and wife, reigned to a large extent in practice.

Neither at the close of the nineteenth century nor at any time afterward was it possible to summarize in a few statements, necessarily more or less abstract, the principles governing married women's property under acts modifying the common law or establishing a system of community property. The general rules governing the rights of the husband or wife in separate property and their rights to separate actions relative to the use and disposition of such estate were fairly clear in both systems; but they were qualified on one side or the other, in the interests of the community obligations entered into by the man and woman by the voluntary act of marriage. In addition they were further qualified in the interest of children born to the couple, for the appearance of children raised questions as to their rights of support and inheritance in the property of the mother or the father or both.

In their efforts to clear away anachronisms and to bring the law abreast the advance in civilization, legislators did not, indeed could not, treat a man and a woman who had chosen to marry and bring children into the world as if they were perfectly free and entitled to be wholly whimsical with their respective properties and earnings, without regard for obligations due to each other. Nor could legislators overlook the rights of their children, their creditors, and their more or less distant relatives. All law-makers recognized the fact that husband and wife had to surrender some freedom by virtue of their very marriage contract. How much and what kinds of freedom?

On this question men were divided and women were divided. So were and have been legislators and it is likely that they will ever be. In consequence, statutes declaring the general principle of freedom varied widely as to the detailed expression of that freedom and as to the limitations imposed in the interest of the family as a community. It was the same with the general principle of equality. It too found expression in detailed provisions bewildering in variety. Were the husband and wife equal if each had to consent to the disposition of property by the other? Were they equal if the husband was bound to support the wife and she could dispose of her property as she pleased? On the point of how to realize the ideal of equality men differed and women differed and provisions of law running into hundreds of pages reflected their doubts, uncertainties, and aspirations.

Furthermore, after statutes were enacted, the application

of the principles incorporated in them to human controversies which arose in law and equity led to a positive riot of variations. The more general the principles the more difficult it was for men and women as litigants and for courts as tribunals of adjudication to agree on the meaning of the principles as governing concrete cases. Especially was this true of novel cases not specifically contemplated or provided for in the written law. And novel cases were and are perennial and striking features of life and law.

WHEN IS EQUALITY ATTAINED?

How far married women's property acts and kindred legislation fell short of covering in concrete anticipation the numerous problems that arose under them is indicated by the following types of questions raised and adjudicated in various jurisdictions of the United States after the process of abolishing common-law doctrines had been started. In order that readers may decide for themselves, if they can, how these questions should have been answered under the theory of separate property rights and equality, the answers given to these questions by the judges in affirmative opinions, negative opinions, and diversities of opinions are left to the readers' imaginations.

May the wife require the husband to pay rent to her for the house she owns separately, in which the family lives?

Does the provision of law authorizing the wife to contract, to sue, and to be sued permit her to make contracts for family and personal necessities which the husband, under his obligation to support the family, must fulfill by payments?

If the wife leaves the husband without good reason and returns home voluntarily at a later date, is the husband bound to pay the bills which she had incurred for her support during her absence?

Is the wife's separate property liable for the payment of domestic servants engaged in doing the household work of the family?

May the wife dissipate or give away her separate property during the marriage relation so that on her death nothing will be left to provide any share for the husband and the children?

May the husband avail himself of the wife's separate estate to lighten his load of supporting the family?

If the wife has separate property, is the husband bound to support her in complete idleness out of his property and earnings?

Must the husband give outright to his wife the clothes, furniture, and other things necessary to her support or is the law satisfied if he merely lends them to her for her free use in such a form that she cannot sell them or give them away?

Does an ante-nuptial contract that the wife is to live with her husband's relatives relieve him of the obligation to support her in a separate home if his relatives destroy her comfort and peace of mind by uncivil language and actions?

May the husband require the wife to earn all she can to help support the family?

If the wife has voluntarily contributed to the support of the family out of her property and earnings, may she, in the absence of any agreement to that effect, secure reimbursement from the husband?

Is the separate estate of the wife liable for any property or money received from the husband in case he and she are sued by his creditors in efforts to collect money from him?

If the husband incurs a debt or debts in improving his wife's separate property or in building a house on her land, is her separate property liable for the said debt or debts?

Is the husband liable under modifications of the common law for debts incurred by his wife before their marriage?

Does the married women's property act relieve a husband of obligations to support his wife, even if he has become bankrupt and she is earning money?

Is the failure of a husband to support his wife, save in case of his sickness or of extremely extenuating circumstances, to be regarded as a punishable crime after the enactment of the married women's property law?

Can the wife lawfully waive the husband's liability to support her with a view to helping him pay his debts to creditors?

If the husband employs his wife at wages otherwise payable to someone else, may she be deprived of the money or the property in which it is invested on the ground that it is actually her husband's?

If a woman earns money by keeping roomers and boarders

in a house owned by her husband, are her earnings all her own and beyond reach of his creditors?

Are the husband and wife each free to deed to a third party an estate separately owned, even the family home, without the consent of the other spouse?

If the husband leases his wife's land for a term of years and she accepts a down payment on the rent, is she stopped from declaring the lease void as a violation of her rights in her separate estate?

Do ornaments and jewels given to the wife by her husband during marriage belong, after her death, to him or to her estate shared by her children?

Where the law permits the wife to enter a business partnership with third parties at will, may she enter into such partnership with her husband?

May the wife pledge her separate estate as surety for her husband in case of family need?

May the wife assign her separate property to discharge a note against her husband, which she has voluntarily signed in his interest?

Is the wife liable to provide from her property or earnings necessaries for herself and children or must creditors first sue the husband and exhaust all remedies in efforts to collect from him?

If the husband has supported the wife during her married life and pays her funeral expenses after her death, may be collect the amount of the said expenses from her separate estate?

If the wife carries on a business under an assumed name, may she bar a suit against her in that name by claiming that her real name is her husband's name and that she is married?

May a wife take her separate property, enter business, and, without his consent, compete wtih her husband who is legally liable for her support?

Where under a new statute the husband is forbidden to use even gentle force to restrain his wife, may he lawfully restrain her from committing a crime?

If the husband carries on a gambling business in his wife's house, may she be liable for his crimes committed therein?

Chapter 8

Theory of Subjection Tested by Long Legal History

ALTHOUGH the movement to bring doctrines of equity respecting the rights of women into statutory law made sweeping advances and the principle of equal suffrage was gaining in acceptance, the theory of woman's historic universal subjection to man continued to exercise a curious fascination. Even the appearance of the word "matriarchy" about 1880 to characterize presumptively the earliest form of human government and a widespread adoption of that idea as correct did not entirely dispose of the subjection dogma; for those who conceded priority to the matriarchy often insisted that it was only a passing system and that very early in history it was completely supplanted by the patriarchal system. Hence, it was "reasoned," while woman ruled man in the most primitive times, man dominated woman through all the following ages, up to the beginning of feminist reforms. Even the alleged sciences of anthropology and sociology were captured, more or less, by such simplifications in the closing years of the nineteenth century. What the women of 1848 asserted, science now seemed to confirm.

A WORD ON THE LAW OF CLASSICAL ANTIQUITY

For example, in a few pages of his *The Evolution of Marriage,* written near the end of the nineteenth century, Charles

181

Letourneau portrayed women as members of a subject sex during all the known ages of Greek and Roman antiquity: "Throughout the historic period, the Greco-Roman world is patriarchal. In Greece and at Rome woman is despised, subjected, and possessed like a thing; while the power of the father of the family is enormous. . . . At the commencement of Roman history . . . the family is possessed by the *pater familias;* he is the king and priest of it, and becomes one of its gods when his shade goes to dwell among the manes. In this last case, the family simply changes masters. Something very similar existed in Greece. . . . The long duration of Greco-Roman society enables us to follow the whole evolution of the family in it. It would be going beyond the facts to affirm the existence of a still confused consanguinity in the ancient *gens;* but it seems very probable that this *gens* first adopted the maternal and then the paternal family, which last became somewhat modified, in the extension of feminine rights. This extension was slow, and it was not until the time of Justinian [483-565 A.D.] that equal shares were given to sons and daughters in succession, or even that widows were entrusted with the care of their children."

So much for the theory of woman's historic subjection as derived by M. Letourneau from his study of Roman law. Is it supported by an adequate documentation and by modern scholarship? No documents, no history, no scholarship, no critical evaluation and interpretation of the evidence; just inferences, speculations, and "convenient" theories. Here we may take as a guide Professor H. F. Jolowicz, specialist in Roman law, for ten years at the University of Oxford and then at the University of London, author of the article on Roman Law in the *Encyclopaedia Britannica* (1941). From the mythological beginnings of Roman history, about 750 B.C. to the Twelve Tables (451-450 B.C.), remarks Professor Jolowicz [Italics supplied], *"we have really no evidence but unreliable tradition and inference from later institutions."* For the next "period," that is about 450 B.C. to about 150 B.C., "apart from fragments of the Tables and from historians, who are of course chiefly of use for constitutional law, *our evidence is not a great deal better than for the previous period when it comes to detail. . . .* However, we know of some laws passed, of the existence of certain legal institutions, and

the names of some professional lawyers, *though no professedly legal work has survived,* and indeed few were written."

And what sources of law do we have for the last hundred
and fifty years of the Republic — to the birth of Christ?
We have *"a few quotations from legal writers* of the time
[which] survive in Justinian's digest; we have Cicero, in all
of whose works there are numerous references to legal matters, and we have other non-legal literature from which information on law can be deducted. We have too the text of a
few laws in inscriptions."

Such are the scant documentary evidences for the wholesale
generalization of Letourneau, the anthropologist, that woman
was "despised, subjected, and possessed like a thing" throughout the historic period of the Roman world. Now what does
modern critical scholarship have to say about the status of
women in the law of the Roman world after a minute examination has been made of the available documents relevant
to the subject?

There are marked traces of mother-right in the earliest records of Roman law, even if they do not wholly warrant Bachofen's broad conclusion that they indicate a definite stage of
mother-right in primitive Roman history. There is no doubt
about the existence of the *patria potestas* — the power of the
father over his children — *in certain circumstances and subject to specific conditions.* There is also no doubt that this
autocratic power of the father over his sons and daughters was
also wielded over the wife *in the case of marriage with manus,*
that is, with subjection; but such marriage occurred only in
certain cases among patricians and others, for reasons at best
obscure. How common was this type of marriage?

Professor Jolowicz answers: It "was rare already in the
late republic . . . had disappeared long before Justinian. . . .
It *may be that at one time* marriage with *manus* was the only
form of union recognized at all, but by the time of the XII
Tables [451-450 B.C.] this was apparently no longer the
case, for it is clear . . . that it was possible to be married
without *manus.* In any case marriage without *manus* was
*by far the more common in all periods of which we have
any real knowledge. . . .* Divorce was always possible at the
instance of the husband in cases of marriage with *manus,* and

in marriage without *manus* it was free to either party to put an end to the relationship at will; . . . any manifestation of intention to end the relationship made clear to the other party and accompanied by actual parting was all that was legally necessary." Certainly in the later development of Roman law marriage was treated as a species of partnership, with community of property interests; and divorce continued to be easily acquired.

Thus Letourneau's generalization respecting the despised and subject status of women, in a relatively brief period of universal history restricted to the Roman world, crumbles into dust, becomes under the scrutiny of modern scholarship in Roman law a gross misrepresentation.

Even more destructive has been the effect of recent scholarship in anthropology and sociology upon nineteenth-century generalizations about the "successive stages" in all human history and the subjection of women at one or all stages up to the "enlightenment" of the modern age. Anthropologists and sociologists of competence and standing no longer believe it possible to reduce the development of all the human societies that have existed on the earth to a common pattern, marked by "stages," each characterized by given institutions respecting the status of women. They are certainly not agreed that the primitive societies now surviving and directly studied actually represent any primordial form or forms of human society everywhere. Likewise generally abandoned by such scholars is the once popular theory that each of the so-called "periods" of history, or "stages" of social evolution, represented a total "break" with the preceding period, or stage, a complete revolution. So in this contemporary movement of thought the idea of woman's personal subjection to man during definite stages or periods in human history falls to pieces and is rejected by scholarship as untenable in the light of the available evidence.

Before we move from such conjectures as Letourneau's respecting the subjection of women through Greek and Roman antiquity to a study of that English law from which the Blackstone doctrine was supposed to stem, a warning must be given about methods of historical research and generalization. It has long been a favorite practice of incautious historians, sociologists, and propagandists to select from the documents of the past a few or numerous citations to "prove" this or that about men and/or women. Often such pieces of alleged "evidence" are chosen from records of peoples scattered through fifty or more centuries and of peoples distributed over the vast surface of the globe.

It is possible to assemble thousands, no doubt tens of thousands, of extracts from whole or fragmentary documents illustrating profusely (a) the inhumanity of men to men and/or women, and (b) the inhumanity of women to women and/or men. It is also possible to assemble thousands, no doubt tens of thousands, of extracts illustrating (a) the humanity of men to men and/or women, and (b) the humanity of women to men and/or women.

No practice has been more common among writers who stoutly maintain the doctrine of women's historic subjection to men than that of collecting numerous quotations from the works of travelers, missionaries, historians, and sociologists and treating the quotations as proof that the subjection of the wife to the husband was the custom at least in all the ages prior to our own.

More is involved in the ascertainment of truth, however, than the number of procurable quotations from printed pages. The knowledge of the writers, their preconceptions, their interests, their education, and their discriminative judgment as independent observers and thinkers all enter into the question of their competence. In any case a collection of illustrations is only good as far as it goes. This fact Herbert Spencer, for instance, failed to recognize, when he decided, on the basis of many disjointed and widely distributed references assembled by his assistants, that the historic subjection of woman to man was the general rule and dismissed contrary evidence from similar sources as incidental or episodal.

Edward Westermarck in this affair was more wary in his day and generation. In his chapter on "The Subjection of Wives," included in his work on *The Origin and Development of the Moral Ideas* (1906), he said: "Among the lower races, as a rule, a woman is always more or less in a state of dependence." As if to verify this statement, he gave a number of illustrations. But on the very next page he began to qualify the statement and he ended with limitations and contrary evidence which destroyed its validity, declaring: "We must distinctly reject as erroneous the broad statement that the lower races in general hold their women in a state of almost complete subjection. . . . In several cases she [woman] is stated to be his [man's] equal, and in a few his superior." Thereupon Westermarck added about eight pages of fine print consisting of extracts from more than a hundred different sources as demonstrating the case for the equality or superiority of women among the lower races.

Suppose we had all the thousands or tens of thousands or more extracts that could be gathered on the points of subjection, equality, and/or superiority and could put them into three parallel columns classifying them under those heads. What case would be proved? The negative case that the historic subjection of woman has been no general rule. What then has been the general rule? Any doctor who feels qualified to handle such symptoms of behavior may make his own prescription, but searchers for the truth of universal history in this matter will at least be careful.

REALITIES IN MEDIAEVAL ENGLISH LAW

Inasmuch as a theory of woman's historic subjection under universal law includes English law, it must therefore apply to this part of such universal law. Indeed, it was from Blackstone's treatise on English laws that the systematic formulation of the subjection theory was derived by the American women of 1848. It would appear, accordingly, that, as far as England is concerned, the validity of the subjection theory can be and should be adequately tested on appeal to the historical records of English law. These records from the sixth century A.D. onward are voluminous and varied. In fact, it is highly probable that no other country in Europe or Asia has such a rich store of legal records covering its legal development from early time to the modern age.

Fortunately, for the study of these records until the reign of Edward I (1239–1307), we have the help of one of the most learned and exacting scholars of the late nineteenth century, Frederick William Maitland, who wrote the major portion of *The History of English Law* with Si·· Frederick Pollock as his collaborator. Maitland's knowledge cf English legal records was immense and precise. In addition, he made himself well acquainted with the history of Roman and Continental law, for he knew that English law did not originate and develop in insulation from the history of Europe, especially Western Europe. Besides commanding all this erudition, Maitland was familiar with the great legal and political theories, ancient and modern, and constantly on his guard against reading modern ideas of any kind into the law of England before and after the Norman Conquest in 1066. In Maitland, therefore, we have a guide to early and medieval English law so authoritative as to challenge all comparison from any quarter.

When Maitland, in 1884, began his career as student and teacher of law in Cambridge University, there were in general circulation two theories respecting the first form of social relations among men and women, expressed in customs — the sources of the earliest law. According to one, that form was marked by the dominance of the husband and father, to which the name "patriarchy" was beginning to be generally applied. For proof of its correctness advocates of this theory usually pointed to the Biblical account of human origins, to the customs of the ancient Jews, and to the *patria protestas* of Roman law. The second theory, later in origins, had been definitely formulated by Johann Bachofen, specialist in Greek and Roman antiquities, and published in 1861 in a path-breaking book, *Das Mutterrecht*. After long and patient research Bachofen came to the conclusion that, amid the promiscuous relationships of primitive societies, descent had been traced through the female line, that the mother was the original center of the family, and that as such she had assumed a dominant role in primitive associations or communities. To this form of family connections the name "matriarchy" was soon loosely applied, and Bachofen's word *Mutterrecht* was often translated as matriarchy rather than mother-right or mother-law.

Familiar with the theory of patriarchy, Maitland was at pains to inquire whether the earliest English laws set down in the documents at his command conformed to the dogma of father-law; and he soon discovered that the man and the male line were not the supreme considerations in those laws. For example, if in early English society a man was killed, the murderer and his family group had to pay a given sum of money to the family group to which the dead man belonged — not to his male heir or heirs. Part of the money went to persons related to the dead man through his father, and part of it to persons related to him through his mother. Again, if a man committed murder, his maternal as well as his paternal relatives had to join in paying the price or sum of money due to the paternal and maternal relatives of the dead man. The complicated nature of the family group mentioned in the laws, taken for granted by the writer of the laws, could not be clearly discerned in the language of the laws.

But in those far-off times it was true that, whatever the nature of the family group, the woman did not pass entirely into her husband's family or under his personal control. At an early period land was being inherited directly through women; and some women were leaving their husbands and "taking" their land and children with them. After a woman's marriage her kinfolk continued to be responsible for her misdeeds. If she was murdered, her price or *wergeld* did not go to her husband but to her kinsfolk. Apparently the husband could not remove his wife from the region inhabited by her kinsfolk without binding himself to treat her well and in specific matters to recognize the rights and claims of her kinsfolk.

In other words, Maitland found in the earliest legal documents of England evidences of mother-right, as well as father-right, and he warned his readers that the evidences of mother-right presented grave obstacles to any thesis that "would start with the patriarchal family as a primitive datum." While he evinced discontent with the vagueness of the word, matriarchy, and did not jump to the conclusion that it was the primitive datum, he was firm in his insistence that the practice described in the first English legal records did not square with the idea of patriarchy as the controlling rule of law.

What lay beyond the times in which the provisions of those old legal documents were in effect, Maitland left to speculative anthropologists and sociologists who deal with human arrangements unrecorded in history. Whatever they might say, it was indubitably certain that the oldest recorded laws of England did not show that, in her personal and property rights, woman was subject to the regime of a patriarch or was regarded in law as a mere member of a subject sex — a nobody.

When Maitland came down in his history of English law to the period of his special emphasis — the thirteenth century — he had to deal with an order of society and government in fundamental respects different from that of the early Anglo-Saxon age. England had long been ruled by a line of strong kings. The State was then powerful. Feudal civil wars had practically disappeared. Peace reigned generally through the realm. Territorial bonds — realm, counties, hundreds, manors, and towns — had for many purposes supplanted blood bonds. Royal judges were traveling up and down the land, trying lawsuits and developing in positive form that body of selected and ordered customs which became known as the common law. Commerce was increasing. The volume of money was expanding and its circulation was more rapid. The amount of movable or personal property had been increased.

Of this mediaeval English order, status under the crown was a prime characteristic. Practically every person — man or woman — had a status in the hierarchy extended downward from the king, through the major and minor barons, the knights of the county, and the freeholders, such as there were, to the serfs at the bottom of the scale. In rural regions only outlaws and stray persons were without standing in this order. Residents of towns, it is true, had no regular position in the feudal hierarchy; they had rights, privileges, and liberties; they had more freedom of movement and association; but every town had an overlord — the king or a powerful landlord — from whom its legal privileges were derived, under whom its customs were allowed to prevail, subject to his rights.

The overwhelming majority of the people lived on the land and, in terms of fact and economic support, belonged to some level in the hierarchy of positions headed by the king. The legal rights of person and property were related to status — a class status, not a sex status. The rights and obligations or "disabilities" of all before the law — men and women alike — conformed to the requirements of their class status. All were "subjects" of the king. All members of the lower ranks from the serfs upward were immediately subject to some

overlord, and the highest overlords were immediately subject
to the king. In this hierarchy neither men nor women as
such had a status. Such "discriminations" as were imposed
on women in respect of rights and obligations pertaining to
property, like those imposed on men, rested on the fact that
land was held by military tenure; that is, estates in land,
roughly according to their size, were bound, no matter who
held them, to render certain degrees and kinds of military
service in war at home or abroad. To this general rule there
were many exceptions in customs and practices but they were
incidents rather than compelling features of the feudal regime.

In this society, the primary datum as to landholding and
the personal property of landholders was the military service
due to the State represented by the king. This service governed
the holding, descent, transfer, inheritance, and use of the
land. Since each estate had to furnish its fighting man or
quota of fighting men, the law of property was bent to that
fact. Here discriminations appeared. But they did not apply
to women alone. Although women, as a rule, were not expected to put on armor and fight in wars, they were not, as
women, assigned a subject status. The law of descent in
respect of property in this hierarchy was not through males
alone. The eldest male, on whom military service fell, excluded the younger brothers and all the sisters; saving the
rights of the widow. But if the eldest son had no son, his
property at his death did not pass to his brothers if there were
any alive or to any other male members of his patrilinear
line; it passed to his daughter or to his daughters as co-
heiresses, if he had a daughter or daughters. If the eldest
son of the eldest son was dead when the father died and there
was a granddaughter by the eldest son living, she inherited to
the exclusion of the father's younger sons and all other male
relatives. Thus the so-called patriarchal preference for descent through males only, if it ever did exist among Anglo-
Saxons, was unknown to the law of England in the middle
ages.

Although it may be inferred from many written histories
dealing with the middle ages that practically all the great
estates of England were kept unified and intact in the hands of
the eldest sons or daughters, as the case might be, this was by
no means an absolute rule. In the case of descent to daugh-

ters, many estates were split into parts. As Maitland relates, the estate of the great Earl of Chester "fell among the spindles" twice within a few years. The inheritance of the mighty William Marshall, Earl of Pembroke, regent of England during the youth of Henry III, passed through many vicissitudes. He succeeded to his title through his marriage with Isabel, daughter of Richard, Earl of Pembroke. On the death of William, his estate "fell among the spindles," and was divided into thirty-five parts, "for one of his daughters was represented by five daughters." How common such divisions actually were, in the absence of full records, must be one of the imponderables. Nor can we discover how many daughters remained unmarried during their entire lives. May not one suspect that few eligible women endowed with large property stayed long in the state or status of single blessedness?

While many women acquired estates through failures in direct male lines, others held property through gifts or devises. Under an application of Norman law adopted in England, a daughter could demand from her father a share of his land as a marriage portion, and the father, either by direct gift or will, could turn it over to her without asking the consent of his sons. In Normandy, the father could thus transfer to his daughter or daughters at least one-third of his estate; whether this limitation as to the amount transferable prevailed in England seems uncertain; but the practice of endowing daughters was common in England. In case the father made provisions for his daughter or daughters, such estates generally returned to the male line in case of an end to the female line or lines.

Another usage must be noted. This was the discrimination of wardship. If on the receipt of his inheritance a young man was a minor, his overlord had the wardship of the estate unitl he became of age, and enjoyed the rents and profits during the period of minority, subject to the necessity of making provision for the maintenance of the youth. When the heir was a woman, the overlord had a similar right of wardship until she became of age or married with the consent of the overlord. And on her marriage, as explained above, her husband, who assumed all the military obligations attached to her land, enjoyed the rents and profits subject to the obligation to maintain her in the style of her class. What was done with the surplus of income, if any, that remained after provision for his military services and her maintenance was a matter of adjustment between a man and his wife.

If on the marriage the husband thus in some respects became her "lord," it is to be remembered that by the same transaction he himself became the subject of her former overlord. When he assumed control over the income of the marriage "portion" which she brought with her, he likewise undertook to discharge the obligations of military service attached to her holding or holdings. Nor was the male minor in wardship to an overlord any freer to marry without his lord's consent than was the young woman. How many marriages were "forced" upon young men and young women in the middle ages can only be a riddle of history. What basis is there for any solution?

So far we have spoken of men and women in what we may call for convenience the noble classes of England. Similar rules were often applied to the property relationships of men and women among the servile classes and non-noble freeholders. Yet here variations were numerous and bewildering, owing to the varieties and tenacity of the local customs which existed and were accepted by courts as law locally valid. But nowhere in the law or laws applicable to theses classes does Maitland find women as such treated as mere members of a sex subject to men. To illustrate the point, Maitland gives a citation from a verdict of jurors as to the custom of two ancient manors in the year 1224: "If any tenant has three or four daughters, and all of them are married outside their father's tenement, save one, who remains at the hearth, she who remains at the hearth shall have the whole land of her father, and her sisters shall recover no part thereof; but if there are two or three or more daughters and all of them are married outside their father's tenement with his chattels . . . the eldest daughter shall have the whole tenement and her sisters no part." As long as one daughter was unmarried, she retains the whole tenement transmitted by the father.

Nor did women in the middle ages always leave the management of their affairs in the hands of men. When we turn from Maitland to the actual records of, let us say, the thirteenth century, which cover petitions and actions before the king's *curia* and administrative officers, we find women active in the protection of their rights and interests in respect of their property and personal obligations. This is especially true of unmarried women and widows with regard to wardship and marriage. Since every estate in land and chattels owed military obligations to the king or to some overlord between the holder and the kind, it was a matter of vital interest to the State and overlords that some man capable of rendering military service and providing military supplies be made responsible for the discharge of that war duty. At all times the king had to be on guard against allowing any maid or widow to marry a powerful feudal lord who was his personal enemy or likely to take up arms against him. Women as well as men struggled against being victimized by it, and in the exercise of control over marriage cruelty and exploitation were possible but, whatever the control was, female wards as well as male wards were subject to it.

On this point the records of the thirteenth century, especially under the tyranny of King John, are illuminating. Take the following entries, for instance:

Richard de Lee offers the king one hundred marks for license to have the widow of Stephen de Falconbridge, with her inheritance and dowry; but the petition is canceled because the said widow of Stephen offers more money to escape the said Richard, that is £100.

Hugh de Haversham offers the king 100 marks to have the custody of the land and heir of William de Clinton; canceled because Isabel de Clinton offers 300 marks for the same.

Margaret de Lucy offers the king 40 marks to have her dowry and inheritance and to have the privilege of remaining a widow as long as she pleases.

Sebilia de Tingera offers the king 200 marks to have certain land and a "license to marry whomsoever she pleases."

Nichola de Emingford, wife of William Rufus, offers the king £100 that she may not be constrained to marry; but if of her own accord she pleases to marry, she will take counsel of the king in so doing.

Gilbert and Alicia, his mother, offer the king 80 marks and two palfreys that Gilbert may have his father's land

and that he may marry according to his own pleasure, with the advice of his mother, and that the same Alicia may follow her own counsel in marrying him off.

When we leave the property rights of women under the rules of descent and come to the property rights of married women in general, we meet more warning from Maitland. He tells us that we must at the very outset beware of the false generalization that history is the record of the progressive attainment of property rights by women from primitive ages forward; beware of the assumption that the position of women in the middle ages was higher than in preceding ages or lower than in what was called the "enlightened age" of Blackstone who treated the female sex as such a "favorite" of the law. He advises us to be on guard against any simplification of the mediaeval law which reduces a variety of customs and usages to the stark terms of the common-law rules as Blackstone stated them.

In the legal records of early English society is indubitable testimony to laws and customs which do not square with common-law doctrines of the middle ages or any later period in English history. In the oldest written laws of England, those of King Aethelbert, who was baptized by Augustine in 597, were passages which should have given Blackstone pause if he ever read them. For example, "If she [the wife] bear a live child, let her have half the property, if the husband die first. If she wish to go away with her children, let her have half the property. If the husband wish to have them, [let her portion be] as one child." With reference to this provision Maitland comments: "On the extreme verge of our legal history we seem to see the wife of Aethelbert's day leaving her husband of her own free will and carrying off her children and half the goods." In the great Doomsday Book of 1086 stands an entry similar in spirit; the local jurors in one community declare of a certain married woman called Asa that she holds her land separately and free from the power of her husband and that after they in fact separate she goes away with all her land and possesses it as mistress (*ipsa habuit terram suam separatam et liberam a dominatu et potestate Bernulfi mariti sui. . . . Post eorum vero separationem, ipsa cum omni terra sua recessit, et eam ut domina possedit*). In the light of such earlier documents it would appear that under the feudal law, which formed the basis of the common law, married women possessed less freedom than was accorded to them in times deemed more primitive and unenlightened.

It was with the rise of the powerful military State under the Norman conqueror and his successors to supremacy in England that older customs, widely diverse in nature, were subordinated to the special rules of "common" law — that is, the law common to the realm. It was then that landed estates were subjected in a systematic manner to the necessity of furnishing military services to the king and that the strength and will of men and women, single or married, were bent to the requirements of those services. It was in relation to those services that the obligations of married women in respect of property were made more or less rigid. It was then that the landed estates of the wife passed under control of her husband and that her personal property went into his possession, subject to numerous restraints and limitations; including the obligation to protect his wife and their children against economic misfortunes and to hold her dower rights in his own property intact. This was not a situation which all men of the several landed classes created by acts of their own will for their own benefit. Most of them were subdued to the requirements of the military State above them as were their wives to the restraints imposed upon their lands and chattels.

When a woman who held property, through descent or otherwise, married, her husband, of necessity and often as a real burden, assumed responsibility for the military services owed by her land to the king. In so doing, he took over the management of her landed estate and, in the absence of agreements to the contrary, entered into possession of her personal property. In the feudal age this personal property or chattels (derived from the word "cattel") consisted largely of beasts of burden, tools, and implements used for the production of wealth on her land — not of money, stocks, bonds, jewels, and other movables.

Since, in the discharge of his military obligations, the husband had to supply the king or his overlord with war horses and to raise money for paying taxes and dues owed to the king, or overlord, he often had to dispose of or sell stock or other property from his wife's estate, as well as his own if he had any. If his wife had enjoyed and exercised the unrestricted right to dispose of her personal property at her own pleasure for her own uses, she could have stripped her estate of the property absolutely necessary to meet the military services and charges ultimately due to the king as chief overlord. Thus a rule, which long afterward often worked a grave injustice to married women and had to be endured or circumvented, was in its origins an essential part of the law which compelled the husband to discharge efficiently all the obligations owed to the State from his own and his wife's property in land.

But with swift and shattering strokes Maitland destroys, as far as mediaeval law is concerned, the fiction that "by marriage, the husband and wife are one person in law: that is, the very being or legal existence of the woman is suspended during the marriage, or at least incorporated and consolidated into that of her husband." He shows that the theory of "unity of person" was little more than rhetorical glitter and that in fact the law treated the wife as a person, in various relations, if in certain relations under the guardianship of the husband who carried the obligation of the military services for her land as well as his own. Blackstone's reference to the husband as the wife's "baron" or "lord," Maitland disposes of with precision and humor. The wife of a feudal magnate would naturally speak of her husband in public as "mon baron," just as naturally as he would speak of her as "ma dame." When Blackstone lawyers in America deemed it fitting, if not necessary, for the wife of a free farmer who tilled fifty acres of her land to speak of her spouse as her "baron" or "lord," they approached the climax of absurdity.

A formula of the common law in the middle ages decreed that the wife should not oppose her husband's will. But Maitland shows the falsity of the scheme as fact. He brushes the dictum aside as invalid, in a generalization derived from his long and close examination of mediaeval law documents, and then adds numerous unimpeachable pieces of evidence from the records of law. "We cannot," he says, "even within the sphere of property law explain the marital relationship as being simply the subjection of the wife to her husband's will. He constantly needs her concurrence, and the law takes care that she shall have an opportunity of freely refusing her assent to his acts. To this we must add that . . . there is a latent idea of a community between husband and wife which cannot easily be suppressed." Then follow nearly thirty pages crowded with illustrations revealing legal expressions of the wife's independent personality at law alone, irrespective of domestic customs and usages. A few of his illustrations are given here:

The husband is not wholly seized of her land as long as the marriage endures. If the seisin is not vested in a third person, then "husband *and* wife are seised in the right of the wife."

In certain litigations, the husband can vouch his wife as his warrantor; she can appear in court for him; and the law treats her "as an independent person whose voice should be heard."

If the wife does not appear in person, she may appoint her husband or a third person to speak for her. And upon occasion the husband appoints his wife as his attorney.

If the husband made default in the administration of his wife's land, she could go into court and defend her title in person.

The husband had no right to exclude the wife from the enjoyment of the advantages of her land to which she was entitled. If he tried to do this, she could go into an ecclesiastical court and by establishing her case could secure a decree against him ordering him to allow to her the benefit of her tenement. If he did not comply with the decree, the king's court would send him to jail until he was ready to discharge the obligations respecting her property and person imposed upon him by the civil and church law.

The mediaeval husband was not free to alienate land by deed or gift as if he were an independent man in whose personality that of his wife was utterly merged — as if she did not exist. In deed of the twelfth century it is often difficult to discover whether the land being conveyed belongs to the husband or the wife. Sometimes the husband gives with the consent of the wife; sometimes husband and wife join in making the gift. "Throughout the twelfth century and into the thirteenth we habitually find married women professing to do what according to the law of a later time they could not have done, effectually. . . . Often the price [of land], if price there be, is said to be paid to the wife and husband jointly; sometimes a large payment is made to the husband, a small payment to the wife."

Save in very extraordinary circumstances, the wife could not be deprived of her dower rights in her husband's property unless she freely consented. The old law gave to the widow an aliquot share of the chattels left by her deceased husband.

As to the married woman's chattels in general, mediaeval law was not as definite and harsh as the later law which transferred them outright to her husband. In English mediaeval law were traces of other practices akin to those under Continental law respecting "community of movables," but under the pressure of common-law judges and lawyers indefinite powers of the husband over the wife's movables became a definite power of possession at law — that is, in the absence of pre-nuptial settlements and trusts (see pp. 139, 201).

As to the rights of married women in towns, customs differed and records are fragmentary. But it is well known that in some towns married women carried on trades and could be sued for any debts they contracted as traders. This custom prevailed in some places although, under the common law of later times, the married woman could not make contracts on her own behalf during marriage; she could do this, however, as her husband's agent.

In relation to all this, and more that could be said about the rights of the married woman as a separate personality, it must be borne in mind that the common law, though based on old customs varying widely from locality to locality, was law formulated by royal judges serving a highly centralized military State. The underlying local customs had grown up naturally in the cooperative life of families and communities; and in this cooperative life the needs, nature, and force of the woman, whether married or unmarried, entered into the making of the customary laws and rules which governed family and community living.

The formulation of the common law, which selected and emphasized some customs to the exclusion of others, was taken over by men alone — judges and lawyers. Simple and exigent as it later became, it was applied only in anticipation of, or in actual, litigation before the common-law courts. Innumerable family and community usages and customs which, as James Kent pointed out in his *Commentaries,* constitute about nine-tenths of the substance of life, continued undisturbed, side by side with the common law and equity (see p. 136), yielding only to legislation by Parliament. Hence the mediaeval common law must be regarded as covering only one phase of the rights and obligations belonging to husbands and wives.

WOMEN IN THE GREAT CHARTER

Such conclusions resting mainly on Maitland's study of mediaeval law furnish a fitting background for considering briefly the Great Charter, *Magna Carta,* wrung from King John in 1215. This famous document has long been treated by many historians as if it was in fact a men's charter of liberty and in no way concerned with the rights, privileges, and obligations of women. Yet historians familiar with the Latin language of the document and the technicalities of mediaeval law have long known that many passages in the Charter, besides those relative to the rights of widows, concerned women without mentioning women as such.

For example, Chapter IV of the Great Charter declares: *Custos terre hujusmodi heredis qui infra etatem fuerit, non capiat de terra heredis nisi racionabiles exitus, et racionabiles consuetudines, et racionabilia servicia, et hoc sine destructione et vasto hominum vel rerum. . . ."* As a rule these Latin words are translated: "The guardian of the land of an heir who is thus under age shall take from the land of the heir nothing but reasonable produce, reasonable customs, and reasonable services, and that without destruction or waste of men or goods." Here no woman is mentioned.

But the word *heredis,* the possessive form of *heres,* so translated as heir, in fact applied to women as well as men in the same condition; and the protection against tyrannical actions by an overlord accorded to men was, by the very language precisely understood, also accorded to women in the same condition. Often mediaeval scriveners, to make sure that there would be no misunderstanding, added to the word, *heres,* the explanation "either male or female" (*sive sit masculus sive foemina*). But the authors of *Magna Carta* evidently regarded here explanation as superfluous; they understood the meaning of *heres* or *heredes* in its context as referring to males and females.

Nor indeed does the *hominum* in Chapter IV of the Charter refer to men alone. The guardian is not to waste men or goods belonging to the estate of an heir. Certainly the female serfs on the estate were by this provision as well protected as the men. At all events the guardian could not waste them any more than they could waste the men or things.

Two provisions of the Charter — Chapters VII and VIII — deal explicitly with the rights of a large and important class of women and their property rights. In English they run as follows:

"A widow, after the death of her husband, shall forthwith and without difficulty have her marriage portion and inheritance (*maritagium et hereditatem*); nor shall she give any thing for her dower, or for her marriage portion, or for the inheritance which her husband and she held on the day of the death of that husband. . . ."

"Let no widow be compelled to marry, so long as she prefers to live without a husband; provided always that she gives security not to marry without our [royal] consent, if she holds of us, or without the consent of the lord of whom she holds, if she holds of another."

Merely to illustrate the technicalities and ramifications of these chapters we may refer to two words used in Chapter VII — *dos* and *maritagium*. Here we have the guidance of the great authority, W. S. McKechnie, expert on *Magna Carta*. Respecting the *dos*, or dowry, he says: "It was customary from an early date for a bridegroom to make adequate provision for his bride [against the hazards of widowhood] on the day he married her. Such a ceremony, indeed, formed a picturesque feature of the marriage rejoicings, taking place literally at the door of the church, as man and wife returned from the altar."

As to the woman's *maritagium*, McKechnie comments: "It was customary for a landowner to bestow some share of his property as a marriage portion (upon his daughters), that they might not come to their husbands as empty-handed brides. The land so granted was usually relieved of all burdens of service and homage. Hence it was known as *liberum maritagium,* which almost came to be recognized as a separate form of feudal tenure." But the *maritagium* was by no means always granted in view of immediate marriage; it was often granted to the daughter for the express purpose of affording her protection against any contingencies that might adversely affect her power to maintain herself in the style to which she was accustomed.

When we pass from the various provisions of the Charter, which protected the rights of men and women in the upper ranges of the class hierarchy, and come to the famous Chapter XX which protects persons against unjust and unduly heavy fines, we find that women are not specified: "A freeman (*liber homo*) shall not be amerced for a small offense, except in accordance with the gravity of his offense, saving always his 'contenement' (ancestral lands). . . ."

As far as this chapter of the Great Charter applied to fines for offenses against the criminal law, it applied to women in respect of offenses for which they were responsible. And in later interpretations of the term "contenement," which was to be protected against royal exactions, crown lawyers considered how much a man could pay "saving his own sustenance and that of his wife and children."

Volumes could be written on the private rights of person and property which the Charter was designed to secure to women of the various gradations in the feudal hierarchy. Indeed a full exposition of the Charter would call for an examination of all private rights of women of all classes which the Charter was expected to protect and uphold. And not until this examination is made should one speak with assurance respecting discriminations against women as such. That innumerable positive rights were guaranteed to them is beyond all question.

WOMEN RECOGNIZED AS PERSONS

If one tries to epitomize the testimony contained in thousands of mediaeval records respecting the rights and position of women in mediaeval society, one is bound to enter in the summary the following facts:

Women of all classes, from peasants at the bottom of the scale to the highest level of nobility, had some rights in property, by law and custom. Women of no class were absolutely rightless in this respect or in the case of serfs more rightless than the men, though it is true that all serfs, men and women alike, held their property by a precarious tenure which often approached a condition of rightlessness.

Women of the upper classes, townswomen of the merchant and craft classes, and many women of the peasant class had money in their own possession and disposed of it at their discretion. Patrician women often had command of large sums, as the records of the Crown show, for they were continually buying privileges or rights from the king. As members of craft gilds, religious gilds, and social gilds, women — married, single, and widowed — paid fees and dues in cash.

The harshness of wardship, to which women as minors or widows as well as men under age were subject, was mitigated by rules of law against disparagement; and women frequently secured the right to marry or not as they pleased and to hold their portions of their inheritances undisturbed, save as to feudal dues, such as there were, owing to the overlord or Crown directly or indirectly.

In the towns, women were active participants in all the affairs of the craft, religious, and social gilds to which they belonged, made gifts to gild endowments, and received the pecuniary benefits of the association, where such accrued from membership.

Women of the nobility took advantage of their general freedom to carry petitions and cases before the king's judicial and administrative officers, to be heard, and to claim and receive recognition of rights, personal and property.

Women of the feudal hierarchy had a status, as did all men, but it was a class status, not a status of women as members of a subject sex.

The obligations of State laid upon women as minors, widows, unmarried adults, and wives in the upper feudal hierarchy bore a direct relation to the feudal services imposed upon their real and personal property and assumed by guardians or husbands. Their property so burdened was not in fact at the free disposal of their guardians or husbands. No such obligations were imposed on women as women. All were obligations attended to landed estates and their appurtenances.

"After the Norman conquest," says Maitland, "the woman

of full age who has no husband is in England a fully competent person for all the purposes of private law; she sues and is sued, makes feoffments, seals bonds, and all this without any guardian."

It is, therefore, with the justification of evidence that Maitland writes of single women, spinsters, and widows during the twelfth and thirteenth centuries: "Women are now 'in' all private law, and are the equals of men. The law of inheritance, it is true, shows a preference for males over females; but not a very strong preference, for a daughter will exclude a brother of a dead man, and the law of wardship and marriage, though it makes some difference between the male and the female ward, is almost equally severe for both. But the woman can hold land, even by military tenure, can own chattels, make a will, make a contract, can sue and be sued. She sues and is sued in person without the interposition of a guardian; she can plead with her own voice if she pleases; indeed — and this is a strong case — a married woman will sometimes appear as her husband's attorney. . . . As regards private rights women are on the same level as men, though postponed in the canons of inheritance."

Turning to married women, Maitland shows that they "are in a different position." But here he refers his readers to the large and complicated sections on family law. If she was married, the mediaeval woman of the landed classes usually had her *maritagium* and dowry; she had some command over money and the right of proper maintenance in her style; but as her husband assumed the obligation of discharging the military services and dues attached to her estate, he had the use of her land and command over her chattels. By marriage, in short, woman entered into a vast and complicated network of law bearing on the family, inheritance, and possession which yields to no simple generalization in terms of equality or inequality. In that domain the rights of men and women were deeply entangled in, if not balanced by, heavy obligations on both sides — the sword and the spindle sides.

All this pertained to private law. But what of public law — the law of government? On this point Maitland said: "In the camp, at the council board [of the king], on the bench, in the jury box there is no place for them." Yet in high matters of government, diplomacy, and war, which were mainly outside the purview of public law, women exercised immense power in and through their family relations (see Chapter XII).

ECONOMIC AND LEGISLATIVE CHANGES (1239-1765)

During five hundred years, from the accession of Edward I in 1239 to the publication of Blackstone's first volume in 1765, the whole *raison d'être* of the English military State with its military tenures of property and corresponding family relations, the very basis of mediaeval property law, practically disappeared. An increase in the volume of money in circulation made it possible for serfs to transmute their payments to landlords, formerly made in personal services and kind, into cash payments of rents. Serfdom gradually dissolved. By the opening of the seventeenth century only remnants of it remained. In time serfs by the thousands were driven from the soil, as wool growing became more profitable than tillage. The common lands of the villages were enclosed and made the property of landlords. Meanwhile commerce expanded. Personal property in goods and notes, bonds, mortgages, and other paper claims to wealth approached and finally exceeded in value all the property in land. Old cities increased in population and new cities came into being, as domestic manufacturing assumed an ever-larger role in the production of commodities for commerce.

Economic transformations were accompanied by political and military changes. After the rise of Parliament in the thirteenth century, the landlords of the rural regions and the burgesses of the towns, represented in that body, strove to curtail the power of the king by the enactment of laws which drastically modified the ancient customs which lay at the base of the common law. At length, near the end of the seventeenth century, as an outcome of the Puritan Revolution, the supremacy of Parliament over the Crown was firmly established.

After the invention of gunpowder and firearms a standing army of regular troops, supplemented by the county militia, finally took the place of the old feudal array — barons, knights, esquires, and retainers — which had served as the king's army in his wars at home and abroad. Thus landlords were personally relieved of military servitudes which their ancient tenures of land had involved — by which their tenures had been justified. Since they now had large cash incomes from rentals, it was easier for them to pay taxes for the support of the royal army and navy than to supply their own weapons and take to the battlefield themselves. At length in 1660, by one of the most drastic forms of class legislation in history, members of the English landlord class in Parliament forced through an act abolishing practically all the old military and other obligations. For the former tenure from the king, conditioned on the fulfillment of duties to the king, they substituted tenure in "free and common socage," that is, in effect, outright ownership.

Having struck off their feudal burdens and deprived the Crown of a huge revenue, many of the landlords in Parliament declared that, as winners in the "great deal," their class should substitute for the old dues a compensatory tax on lands held in chivalry; but by a small majority that proposal was defeated. Instead of a land tax, Parliament then imposed a hereditary excise on beer and certain liquors — a tax on consumption. So, when Blackstone began to write his *Commentaries* nearly a hundred years later, the very substance of the feudal tenures, by which the common law had once found its moral justification, had in truth been destroyed, though he did not like it or admit it.

In this economic and legal transformation, women certainly were participants, beneficiaries, or victims, according to their class and individual fortunes in English society. In town and country, they were producers in industries and agriculture and contributed to the growing volume and circulation of wealth that dissolved the rigid order of the middle ages. Women of the former servile class, freed from serfdom and often driven from the land of their ancestors, like the men of that class, if fortunate, found a place in urban industries; if unfortunate they joined the throngs of paupers who wandered in the highways and byways of England or huddled in the slums of the towns. Women of the mercantile and domestic-manufacturing class, steadily growing in numbers, shared the fortunes and opportunities of their class, took part in its activities, and derived benefits from its achievements. As to the women of the upper landed class, whose rights and obligations had been reflected in the common law of the middle ages, they, like the men of their class, gained advantages from the abolition of feudal burdens in 1660 and held their old economic privileges intact.

Meanwhile, for the benefit of the propertied class in general, Parliament continued from year to year to grind out new statutes imposing savage punishment upon men and women convicted of even the most trivial offenses against property — until the criminal law of England in the eighteenth century, including common-law and statutory crimes, put to shame the barbarities of the middle ages, condemned as "benighted." Between 1660 and 1820, no less than 180 offenses were added to the list of crimes for which men and women could be executed, making in all 250 capital crimes registered in the law books.

THE SIMPLIFIERS AND DOGMATIZERS OF THE COMMON LAW (1239–1765)

The five hundred years between 1239, the year of Edward I's accession to the throne, and 1765, the year in which Blackstone's first volume of *Commentaries on the Laws of England* was published, had brought many great changes relative to the legal position of women. The phrase, "common law," had come into general use early in the fourteenth century, the word "common" in this connection meaning general throughout the realm.

Common law was marked off on the one side from royal ordinances and from statutes enacted by Parliament, and marked off on the other side from special and local customs or laws. Common law was the general law worked out by men "learned in the law," the king's justices, as they heard cases in various parts of the kingdom and were instructed by professional lawyers. It consisted, in short, of customs evolved into a coherent system of laws. It froze, so to speak, the feudal rights, obligations, and disabilities of men and women, in respect of the real estate and personal property of which they were seized. In its well-rounded form it treated men and women not as owners in fee simple, able to do what they wanted to do with their property, but as temporary possessors holding their estates from overlords as long as they discharged the military and other state services laid upon the land — roughly, according to the acreage of their holdings.

In the course of time the common law, as known to early royal justices and professional lawyers, was simplified and given rigid form in textbooks by great writers on the subject. Among the earliest of these texts on the common law was Thomas de Littleton's *Treatise on Tenures,* written in law-French and published about 1482. To the various kinds of land tenures Littleton gave careful definitions and then he classified them according to the rights of landholders. He not only digested rulings of the courts on his subject. He sought to introduce more order by deducing great principles from the diverse cases scattered through the centuries and thus gave a fund of "logic" to the law. At bottom Littleton's work was concerned with the English land law of the middle ages, although he was aware of the existence of a new kind of law known as Equity. His treatise was written with such exactitude and force that it became for centuries the standard text of English lawyers. Men who were to serve as royal justices were trained in it. Generations of lawyers were brought up to swear by it as the final word.

A little more than one hundred years after Littleton, another commentator on the common law, Edward Coke, lawyer and royal judge, took the *Treatise on Tenures* as the foundation for another great restatement of the common law, known as Coke's *Institutes.* The first volume of this work is known as *Coke upon Littleton.* Widening his interest beyond tenures, Coke sought to give an ordered view of all common law, for him the *summum bonum* of English jurisprudence. A lawyer, prosecutor, judge, and writer, he fought bitterly to keep out everything that interfered with the traditional rules of his precious common law. With equal fervor, he did battle against royal encroachments in the name of high prerogative and also against equity which modified the common law in the interest of justice, common sense, and the changing conditions of English economic and cultural life. As a judge he was often forced to yield to the demands of equity, but as a writer and opponent of Stuart prerogative he was almost savage in his adherence to the common law — the feudal offspring of a feudal State built upon communities and families with customs which originated in far older times.

When the long and complicated processes of practice and rationalization, by which the common law reached its climax in the systems of Coke and Blackstone, are critically surveyed, certain conclusions seem inescapable. The old customs of English communities on which the common law was originally based varied materially from region to region. These customs had grown out of the practices of men and women in families and villages in adjusting their relations, including property relations. When royal judges, serving the interests of the centralized feudal State, began to build up their system of common law, these practices and usages by no means conformed to the rules of the common law as finally reduced to the simple dogmas which so delighted Coke and Blackstone. The documented pages of Maitland make this abundantly evident. For instance, to cite a single passage, he says, after dealing with property rights of husband and wife: "If we patiently examine the records of the thirteenth century, we may be persuaded that there was an age in which our law had not decisively made up its mind against a community of chattels between husband and wife. We see rules which, had our lawyers so pleased, might have been represented as an outcome of this community."

In the course of this legal development, the common law, at the hands of the simplifiers and foes of "papistical" jurisprudence, took on its "finished" form. In so doing it became more severe and discriminative against women in respect of property rights than were the customs and usages of the early middle ages out of which it was supposed to have sprung. As to the partnership and community rights for husband and wife, to be found in the *Corpus Juris Civilis* of enlightened Rome and in primitive customs in regions of Western Europe, scattered from Iceland to Portugal, the "finished" common law was even more hostile. It was, therefore, with good reasons, founded on critical scholarship, that Maitland warned his readers against the pleasing delusion that the growth of the common law inevitably meant improvement in the status of women — until, as Blackstone rhetoricized it, they became the "favorites" of the laws of England. If it had not been for the growth of Equity, the position of women before the law in the eighteenth century would have been lower in many respects than it had been in the thirteenth century; and the Blackstone lawyers in England and America were certainly no warm friends of Equity.

COMMON LAW RIDDLED BY EQUITY LAW (1239–1765)

While common-law jurists, judges, and writers were systematizing, simplifying, and trying to save the common law from foes, a second line of changes respecting the legal position and relations of men and women was going forward. This was the development of Equity — a kind of law distinct from the common law and administered by a different set of judges.

One of the early rights of English subjects was that of petitioning the King for relief, favors, or extraordinary privileges — "for the love of God and in the way of charity," as the old formula ran. Often petitions were made for relief from one or more burdens imposed by the common law and for the right to make property arrangements either forbidden by or not recognized by the common law.

In time it became the custom to refer all such petitions to the King's Chancellor. The business of examining petitions and petitioners and granting or denying petitions grew enormously with the spread of commerce, the decline of the feudal order, and modifications of feudal manners and customs.

By the end of the fifteenth century the Chancellor's office became a formal Court of Chancery. To that court went appeals for departures from the fixed rules and formal procedures of the regular common-law courts. In both hearing and deciding cases, the Chancellor dealt informally with petitioners and assumed considerable liberty of deciding causes according to his own notions of right and wrong.

At first the Chancellor was an ecclesiastic, not a secular lawyer, and he often knew little about common law and perhaps cared less. At any rate Chancery developed a body of precedents and law which was concerned with "justice" rather than prescriptions of the feudal State. In vain did common-law judges and lawyers fight against it or ignore it in their opinions and treatises. Even before the end of the fifteenth century, equity was authorizing many actions and procedures respecting the property rights of men and women which overrode and riddled the rules of the common law.

Thus equity jurisprudence grew up by the side of the common law, not as a part of it, and steadily gave to petitioners remedies contrary to the rules which the common law had early prescribed and continued to prescribe on the ancient theory of feudal tenures. When a man or woman found, or felt convinced, that the common law could afford no redress for grievances, he or she could appeal to the Chancellor of the realm for redress and was often granted it. The outcome of such appeals varied with the character, humanity, learning, and sympathy of the successive chancellors; but in any case the sources of law, learning, and humanity upon which the Chancellor drew to instruct his conscience and deepen his sense of justice were different from the technical, traditional, rigid opinions and treatises on the common law.

In the early days of equity, when chancellors were usually ecclesiastics, many rulings in equity were drawn from the Canon Law of the Church, particularly in respect of rights growing out of marriages and wills disposing of property. But most of the cases in equity, particularly as the middle ages drew to a close, were secular cases, involving little or no religious sanction. Then the chancellors drew heavily for instruction upon the Civil Law of ancient Rome, as developed at the high point of its civilization. In this Roman law, chancellors learned that marriage was a type of partnership between husband and wife, in which the two partners had property rights substantially equal in character. In the recorded statements of later chancellors were often entered "entire texts from the [Roman] *Corpus Juris Civilis,* with their terms unaltered, though their origin is never acknowledged."

Still later in the development of equity, chancellors resorted, for the guidance of their consciences, to "the mixed systems of jurisprudence and morals constructed by the publicists of the Low Countries" and there they found other reasons for giving sanction to equity — in effect, legalizing the practices of men and women, single or married, which the common law did not recognize. By applying great principles derived from such sources, chancellors were thus able to keep equity jurisprudence somewhat in harmony with the advance of civilization in England, while the common law, always looking backward, clung to the law and conventions of old times.

In making his decisions, drawing his decrees, and formulating his opinions, the Chancellor, it is true, had to conform in various respects to the terms and technicalities of the common law; but, as Sir Henry Maine wrote, the Chancellor always had at his command "a body of comparatively novel legal principles claiming to override the older jurisprudence of the country [England] on the strength of an intrinsic ethical superiority."

Drawing upon a vast range of civil and moral law outside the domain of the common law, equity was thus inspired to follow the trends of sensitive opinion as economic and political changes transformed English society from a feudal into a modern commercial and industrial society. From about 1650 forward the development of English judge-made law was mainly through equity, aided in many respects by parliamentary legislation, while the common law remained anchored in its old moorings and found increasing difficulty in making adjustments to meet the new conditions of English life and economy. At length in the nineteenth century it could be said that "Equity includes, perhaps, half the body of law relating to property."

Nothing less than a law encyclopaedia could present all the manifold ways in which equity affected the rights of women, married and single. But in the revolutionary eighteenth century, and fifty years before Blackstone wrote, the following principal matters are strikingly treated by the Court of Chancery: "(1) Chancery enforced rights which were unrecognized at Common Law: trusts were peculiarly its care, and the subjects of administrations, charities, separate estate, and equities of redemption were closely connected with the preservation of trusts; (2) as a Court of Conscience it interfered where a legal advantage had been unjustly gained by fraud, accident, or mistake, and granted relief according to the true intent of the parties, as it understood it, in cases of joint indebtedness and suretyship, by its doctrine of contribution; (3) where a right was recognized at law, but was there imperfectly protected or secured, it stepped in to decree specific performance, to take accounts, to allow set-off, to enforce dower or partition and to quiet and end rival claims by interpleader and bill of peace, by its injunction to secure quiet possession and to afford protection from threatened wrongs, and by discovery to give assistance in aid of proceedings at law, and to perpetuate testimony in danger of being lost."

The significance of equity for women may be vividly illustrated by reference to its treatment of the married woman's property rights existing under Trusts. By the middle of the fifteenth century it had become a general custom for men and women who held property at their disposition to create "trusts" for the use of some person or persons. That is, A (man or woman) would convey an estate to B, whom A trusted, on the understanding between them that, although B was to be and remain the legal holder of it, all the advantages of the ownership were to go to A or some other person or persons designated by A.

This was a practice unsanctioned by the common law and hence there was no means at common law by which to compel the trustee to fulfill his obligations to the person or persons for whom he held the property in trust. Indeed at law the trustee was bound only in conscience and morals to discharge the trust vested in him by the donor, in the interests of the donor or the donor's beneficiary or beneficiaries. But very early in the history of trusts the Chancellor, administering Equity, assumed jurisdiction over trusts and, if necessary, compelled Trustees to carry out to the letter the intentions of the donors and to transfer to the beneficiaries of trusts the money or other advantages of estates held in trust.

Fully protected Equity, fathers and mothers could with confidence transfer property to their daughters, whether single or married, in trust for them and their heirs; and the bridegroom, before marriage and, at a later period, after marriage, could transfer property in trust to his bride or wife for the benefit of herself and her heirs. By innumerable forms of stipulation the particular advantages accruing from the property in trust could be assured to the married woman, and the property in trust was withdrawn from the controls of the common law which otherwise vested in the husband an ownership or dominion over the wife's property not so placed to her use by a trust.

As the centuries passed in England the number of trusts increased. In the opening years of the nineteenth century it was estimated that about one-half of the property in England was held in the form of trusts. What proportion of this property was in trust for women there is no way of knowing, but it is known that the trust was commonly employed by men and women to safeguard the interests of single and married women. Indeed, it has been said that this system of protecting women's interests was far more often used in England at that time than in the United States.

At all events, long before Blackstone wrote on the "disabilities" of the wife at Common Law, the practice of creating Trusts for the benefit of single and married women under the protection of Equity had taken millions of pounds' worth of property out of the common-law domain as to disabilities. Informed men and women of property, either in ownership or in anticipation of it, knew that the disabilities of married women in respect of property under common law could be avoided by a resort to trusts, and that equity, liberally construing the rights of such women, would protect them and their heirs in the enjoyment of the rights so vested. In short, equity made it possible for men and women to put as much of the remaining property of England as they liked beyond the reach of the common law as to disabilities.

Naturally, lawyers devoted to the inelastic common law disliked, to put it mildly, the corroding attacks of equity upon their legal domain. The law which they championed had the advantage for practice of traditional certainty and reverence for precedents. Equity, on the other hand, though it acquired respect for its own precedents, could be flexible. It could place reliance on moral principles and be guided by an understanding concern for the rights of individuals and for family interests. It could give more consideration to the motives of the persons whose rights and actions came before it for settlement than to the mere legal forms in which such motives might be expressed. Equity could advance rapidly to meet the changing conditions of life and economy which made old laws unjust or discriminative.

SUMMARY

In summary, what does modern critical scholarship find in the long review of English legal history prior to 1765? It finds men and women, in many fundamental respects, on a similar footing with regard to their property holdings under the requirements of a strong feudal State. It finds men and women making powerful efforts, individually and together, to protect their families against the encroachments of that State. It finds an early and persistent recognition, especially with the development of Equity, of justice as the ideal for adjusting and determining the relations of men and women as members of families and communities, and as individuals.

This is not to deny that there were discriminations between men and women in the feudal law — civil and criminal — which were in various cases carried forward through the centuries. There were many discriminations against women in both branches of the law; but many responsibilities, which may in some instances be called "unfair" discriminations, were imposed on men, independently and in connection with discriminations against women. To the enlightened conscience of modern times, several of the discriminations against women, such as the right of the husband to inflict punishment on his wife, are barbaric; but even as to that it must be remembered that the husband was at law responsible for his wife's behavior and women were by no means all peaceable by nature. Other discriminations associated with the feudal state and manners — now deemed forms of tyranny — should more properly be regarded as anachronisms. Yet all of the discriminations combined do not add up to the utter subjection of women, single and married, under the sovereign power of men at law, to say nothing of practice, in feudal economy or as it was revolutionized and feudal impulses were checked by changes in economy and improvements in morals.

Chapter 9

Woman in the Age of Faith — "Judge of Equity"

How essential the thought of justice and humaneness — the sources of equity — was to the people of France in the twelfth and thirteenth centuries and how intimately it was related to feminine force is explained in Henry Adams' account of *Mont-Saint-Michel and Chartres,* first privately printed in 1904 and then published for general circulation in 1913. In an introduction to this intensive study of that time and that society, Ralph Adams Cram, architect and enthusiast for the period, declared that this volume represented a fusion of "all the theology, philosophy, and mysticism, the politics, sociology, and economics, the romance, literature, and art in that greatest epoch of Christian civilization."

More concretely Henry Adams affirmed in this volume that "in order to feel Gothic architecture in the twelfth and thirteenth centuries, one must feel first and last, around and above and beneath it, the good faith of the people, excepting only Jews and atheists, permeating every portion of it with the conviction of an immediate alternative between heaven and hell, with Mary as the *only* court in equity capable of overruling strict law."

To Our Lady of Pity, whether called Virgin or Mary or

Madonna, were built in those centuries scores of churches and cathedrals in a spontaneous outburst of French ardor for a feminine arbitrament of cases requiring a sympathetic response to appeals for aid and comfort. In the designs and decorations of these churches and cathedrals every detail expressed the infinite respect and adoration for the Virgin which moved the people. At Chartres the rivalry of great families for dynastic supremacy was painted into the very windows — evidences that their claims, contentions, and sanctions were being submitted to Mary for adjudication. There Pierre de Dreux and Blanche of Castile, regents and guardians for heirs to the scepter of State, "carry on across the very heart of the cathedral," Adams said, their struggle for power, while Mary, high on her throne, holding her Holy Child on her knees, presides over her court, listening calmly, serenely, to pleas for justice, mercy, or favor in behalf of their sons.

Thus the Virgin signified to the people moral, human, or humane power as against the stern mandates of God's law taught and enforced by the Church. As such, her position made trouble for the Church; but the Papacy, if it had been so minded, could scarcely have suppressed the urge of the people to Virgin worship, however successful it was in excluding women from the priesthood and the musical services of its choir. In the popular devotion to Mary was asserted a passionate attachment to the feminine qualities so directive in the long history of the human race.

"Without understanding movement of sex," Henry Adams declared in his autobiography, *The Education of Henry Adams,* written in 1905 and published in 1918, "history seemed to him mere pedantry." By what process had Adams come to this conclusion? Its inner nature is veiled, but some hints may be obtained by a study of his life and letters.

Adams taught history for several years at Harvard and after his retirement from that institution he wrote many volumes on American history, without displaying in any of his pages this particular interest in woman as force in history. In 1893, in the midst of a great panic that threatened the disruption of American capitalism, Henry Adams renewed his intimate associations with his brother, Brooks Adams, who was then working on the manuscript of his *The Law of*

Civilization and Decay. Brooks' volume was a study in history as force or energy directed by human qualities, such as fear and greed, and in this history woman appeared as force in the rise and fall of human societies. After spending days and weeks on Brooks' manuscript, Henry Adams likewise became absorbed in both force and woman in history.

At his home in Washington he observed the representatives of American society, urban and rural, engaged in politics, and the army of government employees, men and women, running in and out of offices. Supplementing his previous travels in the Old World and the Orient, Henry went on almost endless journeys in the Americas, in Europe, Africa, and Western Asia, studying human beings at first hand and reading books and documents that recorded the doings of humanity. Amid such circumstances and experiences he reached the conviction that history without woman was pedantry and that the force of woman in history was a subject deserving all the solicitude that critical scholarship could give to it.

By 1905 when his autobiography, *The Education of Henry Adams,* was written, Adams had come to this conclusion: "The task of accelerating or deflecting movement of the American woman had interest infinitely greater than that of any race whatever, Russian or Chinese, Asiatic or African. . . . He [Adams] was studying the laws of motion, and had struck two large questions of vital importance to America — inertia of race and inertia of sex. He had seen Mr. de Witte and Prince Khilkoff turn artificial energy to the value of three thousand million dollars, more or less, upon Russian inertia, in the last twenty years, and he needed to get some idea of the effect. He had seen artificial energy to the amount of five-and-twenty million steam horse-power created in America since 1840, and as much more economized, which had been socially turned over to the American woman, she being the chief object of social expenditure, and the household the only considerable object of American extravagance. According to the scientific notions of inertia and force, what ought to be the result?"

Henry Adams believed that no result of the artificial pressure on Russia was discernible in his time, "because of race and bulk," but he thought that the results of artificial energy spent in America on women were "evident and undisputed."

Undoubtedly, he declared, the American woman had been "set free." But was she happy? She was not, he affirmed. Women were as "hungry for illusions as ever in the fourth century of the Church; but this was probably survival, and gave no hint of the future. The problem remained — to find out whether movement of inertia, inherent in function, could take direction except in lines of inertia. This problem needed to be solved," he asserted, "in one generation of American women, and was the most vital of all problems of force."

He defined it in this way. Behind all the "shifting visions" — "swarms" of tourists encountered in all the resorts of the world, on floating palaces and in the streets of Paris or Jerusalem, and other swarms like the "grave gatherings of Dames or Daughters" at the American Capital — "behind them in every city, town, and farmhouse, were myriads of new types —or type-writers — telephone and telegraph girls, shop-clerks, factory-hands, running into millions of millions, and, as classes, unknown to themselves as to historians. . . . All these new women had been created since 1840; all were to show their meaning before 1940."

Yet when it came to the issue of understanding the modern American woman, Adams confessed that he was baffled. While he realized that American women, especially of the middle and upper classes, occupied a peculiar position in history and were in conflict with traditions, he could "draw no conclusions" respecting them as force and "suggest nothing" to them or about them, he said. Nevertheless he did in fact decide and suggest — that "the Marguerite of the future" could only choose "whether she would rather be victim to man, a church, or a machine."

Of woman's force Adams had no doubt: "The idea that she was weak revolted all history; it was a palæontological falsehood that even an Eocene female monkey would have laughed at. . . . One's studies in the twelfth century, like one's studies in the fourth, as in Homeric and archaic time, showed her always busy in the illusions of heaven or of hell — ambition, intrigue, jealousy, magic." At times, he confessed, he wondered whether woman's force, like that of man, could not be brought under the mathematical formulas of thermodynamics — generalizations concerning physical force which interested him intensely.

Convinced that she was a, if not the, determining force in the rise and decline of civilization, Adams fumed against the kind of history-writing which prevailed in his time. "American history," as he knew it, "mentioned hardly the name of a woman, while English history handled them as timidly as though they were a new and undescribed species." Since written history, in the prevailing American and English style, scarcely mentioned women, Adams pronounced a critical judgment on this literature: "The study of history is useful to the historian by teaching him his ignorance of women; and the mass of this ignorance crushes one who is familiar enough with what are called historical sources to realize how few women have ever been known. The woman who is only known through a man is known wrong.... The American woman of the nineteenth century will live only as the man saw her; probably she will be less known than the woman of the eighteenth; none of the female descendants of Abigail Adams can ever be nearly so familiar as her letters have made her; and all this is pure loss to history."

Deeply cognizant of his own ignorance of woman's force in history and stirred by the neglect of the subject among professional historians, Henry Adams took up the study of woman in history — manifestations of her power in every relation, from economy and social affairs to war, politics, and philosophy. His search for knowledge led him far afield into paths "long and tortuous," drawing him at last into "the vast forests of scholastic science." His quest seems to have started in earnest at the great Exposition in Paris in 1900 where the power of the machine was almost fiercely exhibited. From that point in time he went far back into time, far beyond the capitalistic age, into the eleventh, twelfth, and thirteenth centuries of French history, looking for another kind of power in history — the force of woman. In his volume on *Mont-Saint-Michel and Chartres* he set forth his discoveries, illustrated and supported by a fabulous wealth of details.

As if to provide a true historic setting for his consideration of woman as force in the middle ages, Adams opened with a study of Mont-Saint-Michel, that massive testament to the man of war, to his militant Archangel whose sign of force was the uplifted sword. In every line of that huge structure, masculine force and warlike aspirations were typified. In every stone of the knight's great hall, "the masculine, military energy of Saint Michael lives still," Adams wrote. Here the "warlike emotion" is incarnate. Lines, curves, and upward thrusts, lights and shadows, every "centimetre" of the work, reflects it. The very Chanson de Roland, associated with the time and the spirit of Mont-Saint-Michel, "is so masculine" that, despite its length of four thousand lines, only one Christian woman is mentioned — Alda, the betrothed of Roland — and perhaps this is a later fabrication. In Mont-Saint-Michel, man the warrior, a masculine principle, Church and State militant, were symbolized in stone and form for the age of William the Norman Conqueror.

To this part of his volume Adams devoted forty-five of his three hundred and seventy-seven pages. For his purposes that was enough. In other writings, both Catholic and Protestant, man militant had been profusely celebrated. Adams could be sure that the men and women who read his pages were reasonably familiar with man as force, in man's feuding world.

Having dealt with man's warlike energy symbolized at Mont-Saint-Michel, Adams took up his main theme — the symbolization of woman as force in cathedrals, songs, and writings, honoring the Virgin, and the role of women in the making of French history during two eventful centuries. Fearing that American readers steeped in the Protestant tradition might regard his entire report as coming under the head of religious imagery or even "superstition," Adams endeavored to make it clear that he was concerned with far more than "the last and greatest deity of all, the Virgin." He insisted and demonstrated that he was also portraying living and working men and women, with their ideals of woman, with their interest in the man and woman relationship, with their conceptions of the feminine principle as a mighty force. He explicitly stated that "the study of Our Lady . . . leads directly back to Eve, and lays bare the whole subject of sex."

For the realities of social and economic life in those centuries, Adams relied partly on the writings of modern authorities but chiefly on original sources of the time. Out of his researches he evolved fundamental conclusions, such as the following. In that age men and women were more alike in manners and conduct than they are in the modern age. Women could swear and talk in ribald language; men, without shame, could weep "like a woman." On the intellectual level, "women appeared distinctly superior." They were grave and clever and not in the "rude state of civilization" to which men belonged. They were less impulsive, more given to controlling momentary passions. If on the whole they were more Christian in habits, they could be even more perfidious than men in the arts of crime. In the education of sons, the influence of women was powerful, often predominant, and the superiority of some men over their contemporaries was frequently due to maternal influences.

After studying exhaustively the poetry of that time, Adams found that "always the woman appears as the practical guide; the one who keeps her head, even in love. ... The man never cared; he was always getting himself into crusades, or feuds, or love, or debt, and depended on the woman to get him out. The story was always of Charles VII and Jeanne d'Arc, or Agnes Sorel. The woman might be the good or the evil spirit, but she was always the stronger force. The twelfth and thirteenth centuries were a period when men were at their strongest; never before or since have they shown equal energy in such varied directions, or such intelligence in the direction of their energy; yet these marvels of history — these Plantagenets; these scholastic philosophers; these architects of Rheims and Amiens; these Innocents, and Robin Hoods and Marco Polos; these crusaders, who planted their enormous fortresses all over the Levant; these monks who made the wastes and barrens yield harvests; — all, without apparent exception, bowed down before the woman. Explain it who will! We are not particularly interested in the explanation; it is the art we have chased through this French forest, like Aucassins hunting for Nicolette; and the art leads always to the woman. Poetry, like the architecture and the decoration, harks back to the same standard of taste."

Yet Adams in fact proffered several explanations, not so defined. "Without Mary," he said, "man had no hope except in atheism, and for atheism the world was not ready. Hemmed back on that side, men rushed like sheep to escape the butcher, and were driven to Mary; only too happy in finding protection and hope in a being who could understand the language they talked, and the excuses they had to offer."

Skepticism, he went on to say, would have shattered French society at that time: "The thirteenth century could not afford to admit a doubt. Society had staked its existence, in this world and the next, on the reality and power of the Virgin." She was no creature solely of the imagination: "How actual Mary was, to the men and women of the Middle Ages, and how she was present, as a matter of course, whether by way of miracle or as a habit of life, throughout their daily existence" was attested by the "enormous money value they put on her assistance, and the art that was lavished on her gratification." It was also signified in "the casual allusion, the chance reference to her, which assumes her presence." French society "had invested in her care nearly its whole capital, spiritual, artistic, intellectual, and economical, even to the bulk of its real and personal estate."

Yet another essential feature enters into the explanation of Mary's enthronement as the judge of equity. This is the fact that she was closest to the common life as the Great Mother: "To the Western mind, a figure like the Buddha stood much farther away than the Virgin. That of the Christ even to Saint Bernard stood not so near as that of his mother." Abélard stated the case this way: "After the Trinity, you are our *only* hope; ... you are placed there as our advocate; all of us who fear the wrath of the Judge, fly to the Judge's mother, who is logically compelled to sue for us, and stands in the place of a mother to the guilty."

It was to the Virgin, as the greatest humane force, that the minds and hearts of French men and women paid tribute in this period of the middle ages; they sustained their ardent faith in her against all the strenuous efforts of powerful men in the Church hierarchy to uphold, as superior, masculine conceptions of God, the trinity, the law, and theological systems. It is true that no small part of the Virgin's hold on the people came from the firm belief that, as mediator with

God and Jesus Christ, she could more easily open the way for eternal salvation in the world to come.

Yet that was by no means the whole source of her power. An immense, if immeasurable, portion of it sprang from the fact that she was regarded as the most convincing expression of civilized aspirations and ways of life, in the feudal ages which followed the breakup of the Roman Empire and the barbarian invasions of Mediterranean regions. At all events she steadily gained mastery as a civilizing force during mediaeval times, while barbarism was being brought under the sway of Christianity.

This advance in the power of Mariology, Adams pointed out, can be traced in the documents of the succeeding centuries, after the launching of Christianity, and graphically with dates in M. de Fleury's *Iconographie de la Sainte Vierge*. Admitting that those Americans, who had a penchant for literal exactness, would want proof, Adams indicated where it could be found. As "God-mother" and "Pathfinder" and under other names, the Virgin was "the chief favorite of the Eastern Empire." In the royal chapel at Byzantium, at the head of processions, and on the walls of hovels and cottages, her picture or image was to be found from generation to generation. In the West she was increasingly worshiped and in the age of the crusades "she began to overshadow the Trinity itself."

Abundant evidence indicates that the rise of the Virgin in prestige and power was to a large extent due to popular forces outside the hierarchy of the Western Church. "Papal Rome," says Adams, "never greatly loved Byzantine empresses or French queens. The Virgin of Chartres was never wholly sympathetic to the Roman Curia." Some part of her force was due to the fact that "she was popularly supposed to have no very marked fancy for priests as such; she was a queen, a woman, and a mother, functions, all, which priests could not perform." Nor was Mary supposed to care much about the theology and scholastic system-making which engrossed so many learned men of the Church and awakened grave criticism among the "mystics," notably St. Francis, who had doubts about the ability of the human mind to unravel the riddle of the universe.

Whatever may have been the orthodox conception of

Mary's place in the hierarchy of ecclesiastical power, her popularity with all classes of the people of the time was indisputable. Many monks and monastic orders were warmly attached to her. The gilds, says Adams, "were, if possible, more devoted to her than the monks." In French cities, the bourgeois manifested their attachment by lavish gifts of money to her monuments. "Most surprising of all," Adams continued, "the great military class was perhaps the most vociferous." It seemed to Adams that it was almost blasphemous for men to call on the Queen of Mercy and Pity to lead them into battle; but the fact was undeniable. For at least five hundred years warriors, in innumerable combats, invoked the aid of Notre Dame. Even the soldiers of the Pope were said to cry, "Notre-Dame-Saint-Pierre!" At length scholastics bowed to the clamor and conceded that Mary "possessed perfectly the seven liberal arts." At Chartres all the fine arts including music were identified with her protection. For a time it seemed as if innumerable French men and women were bent on "making the Mother the Church, and Christ the Symbol."

WOMEN—EARTHLY QUEENS

In his wide-ranging examination of mediaeval documents, searching for the manifestations and nature of woman's force in history, Henry Adams also discovered earthly women of great power in the government and civilization of France and chose three of them for special treatment. Attracted by their personalities, energies, qualities, and activities he studied the source materials bearing on their lives and times and undertook to give an account of their characters and operations in the age of the Virgin Mary's great ascendancy.

The first was Eleanor of Guienne who was born in 1122 and died in 1204. The second was Mary of Champagne, 1145–1198, the daughter of Eleanor by her first husband, Louis VII, king of France. The third was Blanche of Castile, 1187–1252 — granddaughter of Eleanor by the line of her second husband, Henry II, king of England.

As Eleanor began her active public life when she was fifteen, on her marriage with Louis VII in 1137, and as her granddaughter, Blanche of Castile, wife of Louis VIII, king of France, mother of Saint Louis, was actively wielding her imperious scepter in France till the time of her death in 1252, the era of their regal influence extended over a century of demiurgic history of France and England — a century fateful for the relations of France and England in ages ahead.

Although these women, whom Adams call "The Three Queens," engaged in sturdy contests with men and other women in the quest for, and the maintenance of, power in the State for themselves and for their families, they were not mere duplicates of the fighting men celebrated at Mont-Saint-Michel. All of them, Adams declared, in a statement disclosing his own sense of refinement, employed both terror and tenderness "to tame the beasts around them." This they did in part by dedicating talents and strength to formulating and establishing codes of manners and morals, and to enforcing the codes in their school which they called their "Court of Love." In their search for high sanction to sustain gentler manners and more civilized practices, they paid tribute to the Virgin, invoking her aid in their struggle against the barbarism that still flourished in the age of Mary's high command over French faith. For example, in verses of the time inspired by courts of love, Count Thibaut called upon the Virgin to intercede with God for mercy, and thus protect mortals against the wrath of His stern justice. It seemed as if "the three queens" could attain their aims only with the help of a woman above them — "the Queen of Heaven."

How could the force of the three queens in the private and public affairs of Western Europe be measured or appraised? That it was pronounced and wide in its ramifications was scarcely to be questioned. But measurement was difficult. Adams remarked at the opening of his chapter dealing with them: "The proper study of mankind is woman and, by common agreement since the time of Adam, it is the most complex and arduous." So he confined himself to a sketch in thirty-two pages which, valuable as it is, presents only fragments of the story narrated in the documents.

Two of these women, Eleanor and Blanche, who were queens in fact, have not entirely escaped the attention of professional historians. Some recognition is occasionally accorded to them in the general histories of mediaeval times, but the recognition so awarded is among the seven wonders

of modern historiography. When Eleanor, Mary, and Blanche
do appear, they do so usually as mere shadows accompanying
Louis VII, Louis VIII, Louis IX, Henry II, Richard the
Lion-Hearted, and John — the villain in the drama of *Magna
Carta* — in their exploits, wars, state-building operations, and
crusades. If the energies and power of Eleanor and Blanche
are recognised, they are apt to be ascribed to their "masculine"
qualities, as the sensibility of men is often ascribed to their
"feminine" qualities. That is to say the existence and activities of the three queens are treated as accidents or incidents
among the doings of men.

Take, for example, John Richard Green's *Short History of
England*, in which about forty pages are given to the period
from the accession of Henry II, second husband of Eleanor,
in 1154, to the conflict of the barons with her son, John,
over *Magna Carta*, in 1215. In these pages Eleanor is mentioned four times. Note is made of the fact that, through
his marriage with Eleanor, Henry II "added Aquitaine to
his dominions." What Henry added with her rich dominions
is left untouched. Note is made of the fact that Henry was
luckless in a war to enforce by arms the claims which his
queen, Eleanor, had on Toulouse. Green also granted that
John, on his accession, secured Aquitaine through "its duchess, his mother," and that on her death in 1204 the bulk of
Aquitaine fell to Philip Augustus, king of France. But that
was just that.

As a rule authors of large histories of France are consid-
erate enough to treat Eleanor as a little more than an owner
of valuable real estate — the greatest dowry any French
woman had yet brought to the crown; but authors of smaller
works can be very blind. For instance, Amman and Coutant,
in their little *Histoire de France* for *Cours supérieur, Cours
complémentaire,* and *Ecoles supérieures*, make short shrift of
Eleanor. Writing of the reign of her husband, Louis VII,
they say: "On his return [from a crusade] he repudiated
his wife, Eleanor of Aquitaine. She was a naughty wife; but
the king had to give her all the provinces that she brought to
him as her dowry . . . and this was a great loss."

After dismissing Eleanor as "naughty," what do Amman
and Coutant say about her granddaughter, Blanche, wife of
King Louis VIII? "The new king, Louis IX," they wrote,

"being only twelve years old, his mother, Blanche of Castile, exercised the regency during his minority. This minority might have put in jeopardy the whole work of Capetian royalty, the great vassals profiting by the occasion to ruin the royal authority. Blanche was its savior; she was a remarkably strong queen, who had the courage of a man in the heart of a woman."

If we turn from the portrayal of the three queens as in general histories, large and small, to the actual records pertaining to their history as lived and enacted, we get at sources of information, rumor, allegations, and recrimination respecting Eleanor and Blanche, abundant and realistic enough to reveal Eleanor and Blanche as dynamic and competent persons in their own characters.

Is it a question of State — form, powers, policies, actions?

Is it a matter of manners and morals?

Is it the great debate between the mystics and the humanists on the one side and, on the other, the hard and puritanical logicians seeking to turn Christianity into sheer theology and absolute law?

Is it the conflict between the male principle and the female principle that rages in the disputes over the Virgin Mary and efforts to subject her to Jahweh?

Is it a matter of arts and letters in their diverse forms of expression and the interests they represent?

Is it, above all, a question of civilization — the elevation of the capacities inherent in human beings to the modes, uses, and amenities of civil life?

If so, then every informed, comprehensive, or "balanced" history of the century under consideration must reckon with the ambitions, ideas, and activities of Eleanor and Blanche. As for Mary of Champagne, although she was no queen by title, she was, as Henry Adams said, "a queen in social influence," especially in "the literature of courteous love."

Readers may call extravagant many of the conclusions respecting the three queens which Henry Adams reached at the end of his study in the sources. They may resent his contention that "the scientific mind is atrophied, and suffers under inherited cerebral weakness, when it comes in contact with the eternal woman." But the documentation of his brief is so full and so explicit that if Adams had gone further into

the political and military history of the times — into the
intrigues, wars, and settlements — he could have expanded
enormously the narrative of Eleanor's and Blanche's deeds
in relation to the making of great history. He could have
described Eleanor stirring up her sons in their rebellion
against her husband, Henry II, and as "a political person of
the highest importance" in shaping the careers of her sons,
Richard the Lion-Hearted and John. He could have shown
Blanche organizing naval forces at Calais in a vain design to
conquer England for Louis after the death of King John in
1216. Or he could have written the history of her reign and
guardian of her children, defeating the league of nobles
formed against the Crown, raising men and money for crusades and war, holding the kingdom of France together for
her son against ambitious war lords who threatened a return
to feudal anarchy.

But Adams went far enough to establish on the basis of the
authentic documentation the fact that woman — both the
earthly creature and the popular conception of her as divinity
— displayed titanic energies in the making of everyday history and Great History.

Chapter 10.

Force of Woman in Mediaeval Economic and Social Life

AFTER the dissolution of the Roman Empire, nearly all the economic activities connected with the production of food, clothing, and shelter were carried on in rural villages and their outlying fields everywhere in Western Europe. Whether the village was a free community or property belonging to the estate of a great feudal lord or lady, it was largely self-sufficing; its inhabitants supplied nearly all their needs for the maintenance of life. Furthermore, the industries of households and fields were not like the modern "heavy industries." Women could handle nearly all of them alone or with some aid from men.

Thus there was no sharp division of labor as a rule. Men and women worked together for the most part. If the major responsibilities for spinning, weaving, and cooking were women's tasks, if wood-cutting and ditching were generally men's tasks, men and women commonly worked side by side in the fields to a considerable extent in all the processes of transforming raw materials into commodities for use. Whether the toilers on the land were bond or free, men and women labored under similar conditions and enjoyed similar liberties of choice such as they were. Though women gave birth to the children, both parents had the services of children to help them in their work. In the records of mediaeval rural life that are available in our age, no specially onerous burdens are found to have been laid on women as women by men as men. On the contrary the records show a sharing of the toilsome tasks on about the same terms.

In the rude castle or grand establishment of the feudal lord, the mistress of the household was usually no languid lady or mere attendant ministering to the wants of an imperious male. The manuals and other documents which treat of domestic economy in the middle ages show the lady discharging onerous duties connected with the management of a large household, besides instructing boys and girls in the etiquette of their class and often in reading and writing. When the lord was absent at war, as frequently happened, or was dead, the lady's burdens were multiplied. It is true that the work in fields, forests, and barns was directed by a bailiff or seneschal, but the cautious wife or widow scarcely dared to leave everything to him even there. And she was warned against doing so in a thirteenth century instruction book written about 1240 for Margaret, widow of the Count of Lincoln. The Countess was therein advised not to trust such matters entirely to the seneschal, but to learn what the estates were producing, so that she could manage her household with due reference to the output of agricultural and other commodities and to her total income. The castles, with their villages and cottages, belonged to a self-sufficing economy, mainly at all events, though some commodities, principally luxuries, might be imported from the outside world.

After the flood of barbarian invasions subsided and large areas of fairly settled life were more secure, commerce was renewed, and cities rose in all parts of Western Europe. In the cities, specialization became a feature of economy. Some merchants dealt in woolen goods, others in silks, metal wares, or spices. Similarly, in the crafts, metalworking was separated from woodworking, tanning from leatherworking, and so on through the long list of craft occupations.

But neither merchandising nor manufacturing was taken out of the urban household. The merchant's shop and warehouse were a part of the family establishment. The crafts remained, as of old, domestic industries carried on by members of the household, if now with the aid of apprentices. In manufacturing at the several stages, women, married and single, participated — if with varying degrees of freedom and subject to various regulations according to time and circumstances, including in some cases the desire to protect women from injury.

In this urban economy, as barter diminished and money transactions took its place, a new class of men and women was formed, known as the bourgeoisie, and it was destined, in widening areas, to challenge, win concessions from, dominate, bore within, or overthrow the landed nobility and become itself a governing élite. In this connection the law of personal property and practices under it or running parallel to it, as adjustments were made to meet the growing power of business enterprise, comes into review as a test of the doctrine that women were members of a subject sex, nothing, or of no force, in mediaeval economy.

While the ownership, barter, purchase, and sale of town lots and buildings, with rights in the same, continued to be financially important, transactions connected with the ownership of tools, other implements, stocks of goods, and money gained in volume and in significance for the life and position of multitudes, especially after the discovery of precious metals in the new world. Money was to become a giant power and in time to break the rigidities of status, that is, the fixed position of all classes of men and women in the feudal hierarchy. Freer enterprise and civil liberties were in the process of creation.

MEMBERSHIP AND ACTIVITIES IN GILDS

Meanwhile, in the mediaeval period, manufacture and distribution were strictly regulated by merchant and craft gilds in large regions of Europe and the British Isles. The gild system of economy was more local than international in emphasis. It was everywhere social — not individualistic in the correct sense of that very modern word. It became a fundamental institution of urbanism as towns and cities emerged from the economy of agriculture. Though commerce was in some measure separated from production, it was likewise widely controlled by rules formulated by associations, or gilds, of merchants.

Besides the merchant and craft gilds, yet made up of members of those gilds in part, rose religious and benevolent gilds concerned with the morals, manners, health, and general welfare of communities. They provided social insurance for their fellowship in the form of provisions for sickness, poverty, and burial. They were solicitous about prayers for the unfortunate and Masses for the dead. They erected standards of decent behavior for men and women prone to remain in or revert to a state of barbarism. They upheld religious conformity in matters of faith and raised funds for supporting church institutions such as hospitals, orphanages, and homes for the aged or other needy folk. In the social work women were active and prodders, thus continuing and developing the humane interests which had been among the interests of women from the dawn of human time.

Fundamental to the operations of the religious and benevolent gilds was the productive economy of the city. And that was ordered under the rules of craft gilds, nearly everywhere in Western Europe for centuries. It was protected by the ordinances of city authorities who had rights of self-government incorporated in charters, obtained from the Crown or from a local landlord, lay or clerical, the possessor of the territory in which the town or city was located. In the local government, gilds were often so authoritative as to be almost indistinguishable from the government itself. Gilds of weavers, fullers, dyers, smiths, cordwainers, cloth workers, grocers, tanners, clock makers, bakers, fishmongers, glaziers, glass blowers, lace makers, and merchants but illustrate the long list of organizations engaged in producing, promoting, buying, and selling various lines of manufactured goods.

And what was the relation of women to the economic gilds? Were they excluded from membership and treated in the charters, government ordinances, and practices as persons belonging to a sex having no place or force in gild management and leadership? The early age of the gilds is commonly called "the dark age." Was its darkness a pall over women? How shall we answer this question so germane to the whole theory of woman's nothingness, her passivity, in the long past?

We might drop the question after reading the article on "European Guilds," in the *Encyclopaedia of the Social Sciences,* as a foolish one to raise. The article was written by a distinguished Belgian scholar, Henri Pirenne, accredited master of the sources and secondary writings on the subject of gilds. He says nothing about women in connection with European gilds.

This is the more remarkable when we note that A. E. R. Boak, who writes the section on "Late Roman and Byzantine" gilds for the same *Encyclopaedia,* says positively that "women as well as men were considered as belonging to the gilds even when they could not personally carry on the professional duties of the members."

Like Henri Pirenne, another writer on the subject for the *Encyclopaedia,* Louis Massignon, furnishes no information as to the participation of women in the later Islamic gilds. Nor does Vera Anstey give information in her section on Indian gilds with respect to the women of India who for centuries worked at handicrafts, as they still do. Since the long-enduring gild system of China was in part certainly associated with household industries, one may infer that women in families engaged in spinning and weaving, for example, and were naturally members of such gilds; but Harold M. Vinacke gives no positive assurance one way or the other in his account of Chinese gilds. G. C. Allen, dealing with Japanese gilds, is no more helpful with regard to the relations of women to such organizations.

If one expects the *Encyclopœdia Britannica* to display more interest in women's relations to gilds, one will be disappointed in reading the article on "European Gilds," written by Charles Gross, one of the greatest scholars in that subject. Though he was a specialist in this "field," at no point in this article does he even hint that women had any place whatever, equal or subordinate, in European gilds. In the bibliography attached to his article, Gross cites the work by J. T. Smith, *English Gilds,* but surely he had never read it carefully. Otherwise how could he have escaped observing the voluminous data there assembled on women's activities in English gilds?

In the volume edited by Smith is a wealth of material showing the extent and nature of the fellowship which women enjoyed with men in numerous English gilds. This volume is a collection of original documents, largely fourteenth-century records, published by The Early English Text Society, giving essential facts about the constitution, membership, proceedings, rules and by-laws of gilds functioning during the middle ages in England. They were taken from the English Public Record Office in London where they had been shelved for several centuries undisturbed. Though the analytical introduction to this collection of sources throws little or no light, not even twilight, on the participation of women in gild affairs, the documents themselves shed strong daylight on this matter.

The majority of these documents were reports from local governments and gild authorities prepared in response to an act of Parliament calling for information on the nature, government, and practices of gilds composed of "bretheren and sisteren" in every shire of England in the year 1389. The types of gilds represented are of many patterns.

A large majority cited in the documents belonged to the class of social and religious organizations. But numerous craft gilds are also described in the records; for example, barbers, pelters, tailors, carpenters, tilers, merchants, saddlers and spurriers, shipmen, scholars, bakers, cordwainers, and fullers. The gilds covered in the reports were scattered among towns and counties: London, Norwich, Lynn, York, Beverly, Kingston-on-Hull, Chesterfield, Lincoln, Stamford, Worcester, Stratford-on-Avon, Coventry, Birmingham, Cambridge, Exeter, Bristol, and Reading, for instance.

While in some of the records the details are lacking, Smith's *English Gilds* contains accounts of the structure, membership, functions, and proceedings of about eighty-five gilds. In at least seventy-two of them women were members on an equal basis with men. That is surely a large proportion. In some of the other gilds a slight qualification was placed on widows; they were accepted if their husbands had been gild men. Lest the idea of sheer generosity or friendship for the deceased be adjudged the reason for admitting widows to gilds, let it be remembered that, in innumerable cases, widows carried on the craft in which their husbands had been active, being directly familiar with it as a household industry at which they had themselves labored or in connection with which they had borne responsibilities for training and directing apprentices.

The reports of only nine gilds in this collection are in such form and language as to warrant the conclusion that they were composed entirely of men. There were no women, apparently, in the Gild of Young Scholars at Lynn, who may have been preparing for the priesthood. No women are mentioned as members of the gilds of shipmen at Lynn, smiths at Chesterfield, fullers at Bristol, tailors, cordwainers, and bakers at Exeter. But widows of gild men who had belonged to the organization of tailors at Exeter were admitted in later years.

Women were full and equal members of the following craft gilds, listed in this collection: barbers, furriers, carpenters, saddlers and spurriers at Norwich; fullers, tailors, and tylers at Lincoln; joiners and carpenters at Worcester. At Berwick-upon-Tweed, where the town burgesses compelled all gilds to combine, women as well as men were members, and daughters as well as sons of gild members were eligible to membership.

To the religious and benevolent gilds women also belonged. Of twenty-two founders of the Gild of the Blessed Virgin Mary at Kingston-on-Hull, twelve were women; of the forty-three founders of the Gild of Corpus Christi, eighteen were women. On the roll of the Gild of St. George at Norwich were the names of fifty women most of whom, but not all, were wives of gild men.

Few of the documents in this collection give clues to the proportion of men and women in the membership of the gilds. Actual names are so rarely inserted as to make an estimate impossible. But a large number of cases in the records are full enough to give some distinct information respecting the role of women in the gilds to which they belonged. It seems to be a fact that their rights, privileges, and responsibilities were the same as those of the men. Women took part in the proceedings, helped to elect officers, were under the same penalties for neglect of duties, and discharged the obligations imposed on all gild members. Evidently also they were outspoken in asserting their opinions and strenuous in arguments, for frequently the rules of a gild forbade disorderly or contumacious debates and expressly stated that the "sisteren," no less than the "bretheren," must keep the peace and will be punished by fine of the gild if they fail to comply with the rule.

On the Continent, likewise, women were frequently members of the gilds to which men belonged and often had gilds of their own for the promotion and protection of their special crafts. To Georges François Renard, well-known French writer on economic subjects, we are indebted for information about Continental women. In his *Guilds in the Middle Ages*

(1919), he says: "It was in Flanders, in Italy, in the 'Imperial Towns,' in the trading ports, wherever, in fact, the central authority was weak or distant, that they [the gilds] received the strongest impetus. They prospered more brilliantly in the Italian Republics than at Rome under the shadow of the Holy See."

And those which prospered did so usually with the direct aid of women. If in many Continental towns women could not become gild masters in cases where gild membership conferred political rights and military duties, otherwise women were not excluded from the gilds. "It would be a mistake," declares Renard, "to imagine that the woman of the Middle Ages was confined to her home, and was ignorant of the difficulties of a worker's life. In those days she had an economic independence, such as is hardly to be met with in our own time. In many countries she possessed, for instance, the power to dispose of her property without her husband's permission. It is therefore natural that there should be women's gilds organized and administered like those of men. They existed in exclusively feminine crafts: fifteen of them were to be found in Paris alone towards the end of the thirteenth century, in the dressmaking industry and among the silk-workers and gold-thread workers especially."

Yet women were not restricted to their separate gilds. The mixed gilds of Paris in the thirteenth century were about eighty in number. In these Paris gilds, as in English gilds, a master's widow had the right to carry on her husband's workshop after he had died. Yet men were not always generous in this relation to women and at times men tried to wrest from women some of their craft rights. The bakers of Pontoise are named by Renard as offenders; they wanted to get a monopoly of bread-baking and they argued that women were not strong enough to knead the bread themselves. But a French Parlement refused to prohibit the customary baking by women and declined to back up the men's opposition to the women. A French parliamentary decree even accorded some gild women rights frequently denied to English widows; it ruled that a widow could retain her membership in a gild even if she took as her second husband a man who did not work in her craft.

In France some legislation of another kind was enacted as a precedent for modern "protective legislation" for women.

For instance a prohibition was ordered against women's working in the craft of "Saracen" carpet-making. The purpose was to prevent injury to mothers during pregnancy.

Respecting inner management, Continental gilds ranged, according to Renard, from more or less democratic forms among the humblest craftsfolk to autocratic government by powerful personages, commercial and political, especially in the merchant gilds. Some of the latter even forbade their paid representatives in branch houses outside their homeland to marry, the idea being to hold their loyalty to the domestic interests. As time passed, Florentine merchants handling woolen goods sought the good offices of the Church in teaching working women to be humble of spirit and careful about dressing too elegantly in wool, thereby "wasting" material which could be more profitable to merchants if sold in the better markets.

GLIMPSES OF ECONOMY IN GILDS IN FLORENCE AND VENICE

The attitude of rulers was often crucial to the prosperity and government of merchant and craft gilds. For example, Matilda (1046-1115), Countess of Tuscany, sole heir to the richest estate in all Italy, took a genuine interest in the fortunes of the gilds in her leading city, Florence, protected them, and promoted their prosperity. Her mother, Beatrice of Bar, had given much thought to her education and Matilda was talented as well as an eager student. She spoke Italian, French and German readily, and wrote many letters in Latin, having need of Latin particularly in her dealings with the Holy See. She assembled a library of considerable size. She supervised an edition of Justinian's *Pandects*. She has been noticed by historians mainly for her support of the papacy against the temporal power impersonated by Henry IV whose penance before Gregory VI was in large measure brought about by her manipulations. But she did not lose sight of economic strength in Tuscany and she was both adept in winning cooperation from the merchant gilds and sagacious in guarding the security of the craft gilds.

"That women were not disqualified by their sex from enjoying the rights of membership in the Guilds is proved by many entries in the articles of matriculation and the records of association," declares J. Edgcumbe Staley in a volume in 1294 sought and obtained membership in the company of Belt and Girdle Makers after she had paid the entrance fee and had sworn to observe its rules and regulations.

He tells far more about women in connection with Italian gilds in his fascinating volume entitled *The Dogaressas of Venice,* with whom the fortunes of the gilds were so intimately associated. In the story of these gilds the vitality and the weakness of the gild system were dramatically enclosed. Venice rose from the marshes by the sturdy labor of fisherfolk and refugees from mainland cities who had fled to its tiny islets for safety from barbarian invaders then plunging pell-mell into Italy, looting or occupying all the best land. Women helped to make the bags for the earth which was used to create and extend the little islands by filling up the swamps. Women helped to build the bridges which enabled the people to move from isle to isle. And when the "Queen of the Adriatic" won her triumphant place as a great imperial city, women continued to help in directing Venetian affairs.

"In the election of a Doge of the Most Serene Republic of Venice, the personality of his spouse had often as not considerable weight in the decision of the Lords of Council," says Staley, by way of introduction to his notable study of Venice. Though the Doges sat extensively for their portraits, less than a dozen of the dogaressas seem to have been immortalized on canvas. Great painters were commissioned to portray divine Venuses rather than mortal wives. But the wives could have ordered artists to paint them. Why didn't they do this as much as the Doges had themselves represented in paint?

Staley offers this as explanation: "Women of every age and clime care very little about the Fine Arts so called; they are themselves the finest of the Fine Arts, and their sympathy goes out rather to the artistic Crafts, in search of objects to add, if may be, to their own charms." If extreme as a generalization respecting women's indifference to the Fine Arts, and pointedly so in view of Isabella d'Este's patronage of the Fine Arts at the time when the Venetian ladies were making themselves works of art, certainly the Venetian Dogaressas were firm and energetic sponsors, promoters, and defenders of Venetian crafts.

"In Venice," Staley says, "the 'Fragilie,' or Trade-Guilds, were directly under the patronage of the Dogaressas, and we shall find their personal attributes in the beautiful and fragile glass of Murano, and the delicate and chaste point-lace of Burano, in the lovely and costly ornaments of the goldsmiths, in the superb brocades of silk and velvet and the splendid tissues of gold and silver of the costumers, and in the endless fascinating adjuncts of the toilet and the table."

If this implies that the Dogaressas were themselves fragile, that is a great error. In truth they could love dainty or ponderous products of the workshops and be very hardy themselves; they could and did love the handicrafts and yet were exceedingly public-spirited and energetic in other affairs for a long span of time; they could be foolish and many were; they could be very wise and several were unmistakable stateswomen. Some were viragoes, strong-willed and iron-hearted, richly endowed at marriage with goods and chattel slaves to whom they clung despite the anger of popular resentment against slavery — an innovation which came in the wake of princesses from Byzantium and other Eastern places.

The wife of one Doge introduced the bull fight to Venice. Another introduced the Greek fork, refined Greek cooking, dainty table manners, and eunuchs to carve and serve delicacies in the menu. Costly wines and liqueurs from Syria and the further East succeeded, in the mansions of the governing élite, the heavy beverages to which the people of the lagunes had been accustomed. The change was fostered by brides from the East. Perfume became a Venetian obsession derived from the newcomers. Extravagance stamped the living of the ruling household as Venice grew in economic wealth.

Venetian products, staples and luxuries, found markets far and wide and her craft gilds grew in number and strength. And it was with the support of reigning ladies that the city became honored from the Near East to England as "the nursery of the Fine Arts and the boudoir of the Graces, as well as the Patroness of the Crafts." Eventually it was feared as the center of great Sea Power.

According to Staley, "As the First Lady of the Commonwealth the Dogaressa had many responsibilities which were greatly expanded when her Consort was away. If she had no position with respect to the Council of State and had nothing whatever to do with politics, there were numerous duties which devolved upon her. The patronage and direction of charities of all kinds — whether eleemosynary or educational — the maintenance of the Ducal hospitalities, the reception of ambassadors, the claims of family, and the encouragement of the arts and crafts gave her Serenity much to devise and do."

While the sixth Grand Doge Giacomo Tiepolo was absorbed, around 1242, in settling factional disputes and jealousies and carrying on naval and military expeditions, his spouse, Valdrada, Staley tells us, gave her whole time to the patronage and support of the trade corporations. All the Dogaressas who came after her gave them attention if not in every case to the same degree; but the tendency towards love of imported finery, set in motion by foreign brides brought home to Venice by merchants and fighting men, gained momentum, to the irreparable injury of Venetian economy and independent life.

That women had money of their own and for self-indulgence if so inclined is indicated in Italian archives. In the time of the Doge Tiepolo a compilation of laws, "Il Statuto di Giacomo Tiepolo," or "Il Statuto Veneto" as it was also called, was made and designed for the "amelioration and moralisation of manners." According to these laws, "the husband was required to render an account to his wife of his use of her dowry, and the capital sum remained in her power to will as she chose. An unfaithful wife forfeited her dower, but a widow enjoyed her husband's patrimony till her second marriage or death. If ever a couple decided to renounce secular life and enter Religion, the united property was shared equally, each being free to do what he or she liked with the money. Children, if any and under age, were provided for equally by each parent."

But sometimes the doge and his consort were thrifty and deeply interested in promoting home industries. In 1340–1341, for instance, the Dogaressa Agnese and her husband, a poor man elected to the supreme office in one of the democratic uprisings of the city, supported the development of the local silk industry, while discouraging the importation of Oriental brocades and tissues. Foreign trade was stopped for a time. This Doge was in power only one year, however; he was not political-minded.

His successor, Messir Giovanni Sorenzo, was a warrior and

belonged to an old and wealthy family. Under his patronage and that of his wife, Franchesina, the importation of mirrors from Germany and hanging-lamps from Greece was checked, the Venetian glass industry reached the height of its reputation, and the cost of living for the general public was held within practical bounds, though in the palace splendor characterized official entertaining. In this regime the arsenal was so extended that it could fully equip 40,000 men.

For a hundred and fifty years, up to the fifteenth century, under the solicitude of the Dogaressas, the fine Venetian crafts "attained both perfection in the details of their several interests, and also a dominant position in the social economy of the State." Moreover the Fine Arts and Literature were beginning to be cultivated after long neglect. Venice was also renowned for its naval exploits. But all was not as sound as outward appearances might suggest.

Intercourse with the East brought in its train terrible plagues which lowered the physical vitality of Venetians. Commercial opulence led to a decline in industrious habits. Fun-loving nabobs founded the Company of the Tights, *Compagnia della Calza,* to which women associates were freely admitted. With the tight-fitting pants and petticoats went the garish use of pearls and other gems, rings and chains, short cloaks of elegant materials lined with furs, and all the splendor of spectacular pageantry. Imposing ceremonies attended the inauguration of Marina Nani-Foscari in 1427 as Dogaressa when the jewelled *Corno* was placed on her head. The fashion of "conspicuous waste" was making history in Venice.

At the middle of that century, the fifteenth, Venetian grandeur was so astounding as to amaze even such a visitor as the Duchess Beatrice d'Este of Milan. She had come on a diplomatic errand — to draw Venice into the league with Milan against Charles VIII of France. Her retinue was so large and numbered so many princes and ambassadors of high social position that three palaces were placed at her disposal. That was the time of Doge Agostino Barbarigo. His spouse, Elizabetta, a member of the Banco family, one of the proudest ruling houses in Venice, entertained the guest and her entourage superbly.

While the Duchess d'Este was executing her mission successfully, she was also writing to her husband, Duke Lodovico il

Moro, about the Venetian scene. Staley said she compared the older nobles and their ladies to "great dolls" or "Stately Deities" and commented on the abbreviated dress and unguarded manners of the girls. She noted that "they are clothed in pearls and gold chains from head to toe, but little else . . . cloth of gold is as common here as fustian is with us." The Duchess was herself acclaimed as a beauty and her imperious temper was beyond dispute. What she might have seen at Venice, but perhaps without recognizing it, was the ebbing of economic strength from all the pores of the Adriatic city, while battles at sea were being lost in steady succession.

A new form of preëminence, nevertheless, was to add to the laurels of Venice, when it became a center of printing in the middle of the fifteenth century, under the sponsorship of Donna Giovanna Dandolo, wife of the Doge Pasquale Malipiero. Service books for the churches had been printed from wooden blocks in Venice as early as 1441, but the venture into printing with the newly invented molded type began about 1469, and then classical works, Bibles, and pretentious books on Morals were offered in the shops. The first illustrated book ever seen in print anywhere, we are told by Staley, was turned out in Venice in 1480 — *Hypnerotomachio*, or *The Dream of Love*. Many of the early books carried expressions of gratitude to Donna Giovanna Dandolo for her leadership in publishing; and her family, the Dandolo, was kept long in memory on account of Giovanna's practical interest in writers. For two centuries after her death, Venice was the chief center in Europe for books, publishers, and printers.

If Giovanna Dandolo was "Empress of Printing," she was also "Queen of Lace." Her interest in the craft girls who made the lovely Burano lace, designed by a young Italian, named Bella, from a coral model, spread the renown of this lace far and wide and helped to extend the fame of other kinds, notably Honiton, Valenciennes, and Alençon.

Setting her course sternly against the introduction of foreign goods, Dogaressa Cristina, though a great spendthrift, insisted that the workers in the crafts at Venice must improve both the materials which they used and the manner of conducting their industries. As the fifteenth century drew to its close, however, at public slave auctions in the Rialto foreign boys and girls were being sold as workers in the trade gilds, especially to carpet-weavers, makers of cloth of gold and silver tissue, and armorers. The same practice appeared at Florence, and Madonna Alessandra negli Strozzi of Florence recorded in her *Letters* that swarthy Tartars with dark hair were in demand in her city as "best for work and the most simple in their ways," whereas in Venice, "fair-skinned, auburn-haired Circassians" were preferred for their skill in making artifices of the toilet.

Marriage with slaves was forbidden to Venetians but extra-legal associations paved the way for the rise to power of courtesans from alien peoples. From their ascent to high places, concern with the promotion of Venetian domestic economy, with the protection of men and women who worked in the crafts, with security on the home front, lost caste. Even the verve of "gallant companies" of La Calza (The Tights) weakened after defeats were suffered by Venetian arms.

"What sort of a wife has he got?" Staley says this was "the constantly recurring question" which, upon the death of a doge, was brought up in the Council of Forty in respect of his successor. Individuality and initiative in the consort were prized for a long time; and when they diminished, shadows closed in on the lagunes, the elegant gardens, the handsome palaces, and the workshops of men and women skilled in industrial arts.

Cloth of gold from India, porcelain and glass from Sevres, earthenware from Birmingham also helped to destroy important local gilds. By 1547 the great gild of glass workers of Murano was facing annihilation. Its members were being invited to come to distant lands for employment but the very idea of deserting Venice was abhorrent to them and to the whole community besides. Nevertheless these craftsfolk could not live by tradition alone. So the masters of the gild described their plight to the Dogaressa Alicia Giustiniana-Donato, who had tried to hold back the tide of disaster to Venetian industries by giving employment to builders, decorators, and painters. Through her influence in 1550 parties of Murano glass-blowers were granted the privilege of going to England, Flanders, Spain, and France. Henry VIII had been collecting fine specimens of Murano glass. He welcomed these workmen and set them to teaching the English how to make that glass.

In 1569 when the harvests failed in Italy and in neighboring countries, famine and plague multiplied the woes of the Venetians. Their celebrated arsenal burned that year. Philanthropy was the only offset to dire misery. But philanthropy could not check the ravages of the plague. More substantial succor was given to Venice, in its agonies of disease, by Loredana Marcello-Mocenigo, a woman of wealth and noble family, a writer and a classical scholar — a "new woman" interested in intellectual attainments, whose botanical researches proved of value to physicians during the plague. She herself died of the plague in 1572 but her formulas and recipes for healing were applied to other sufferers with excellent effects.

As the century advanced, spurts of renewed vigor and signs of strength marked great State banquets and festivities on the Canal, especially during visits of illustrious foreign rulers, princes of state, and powerful women of merchant-prince families. In 1597 when Morosina Morisini-Grimani, possessor of a combined noble and commercial family tree, made her entry as Dogaressa, her coronation exceeded anything yet witnessed in Venice. "Every craftsman and craftswoman" in Venice went to work with might and main, contributing magnificence to this occasion. Sumptuary and other restrictions were lifted. "The Forty and Ten raised no barriers" against splendor. Poets, orators, and publishers welcomed commissions to laud the First Lady. Four hundred noblewomen attended her. Noble lords paid respects to her and she bestowed upon each a fine gift. Charitable, as well as "elegant, refined, and witty," she went out on the balcony of her palace and showered coins on the populace below in the Piazza. Within doors the Doge and Dogaressa dined foreign princes and ambassadors on forty-seven courses of food, finishing the feast with "apples of Paradise." For days and days the banqueting went on. In the rejoicing no one seems to have been overlooked; crowds of working men and working women were invited to share the viands served at the court.

Already, however, Venice had entered upon that long, though slow, descent which ended in her extinction as an independent republic at the hands of Napoleon Bonaparte.

MEDIAEVAL WOMEN RAMPANT

Just as women took part and carried full loads of work in agriculture, domestic industries, and trading, just as they participated in the activities of craft, trade, and social gilds or corporations, so they shared and expressed themselves in all the forms of social life in town and country. In everything human their qualities and force were expressed — from religious and secular festivities, sports, games, and riots to the discussion of religious and moral questions and the management of charitable undertakings. In castles and cottages, in fields and in gild halls, on village greens and in church-yards, in towns and on city streets, in taverns and at market fairs they sought release from the rigors of earning a livelihood, from burdens of domesticity, or responsibilities belonging to the status of their class, whatever it was.

When knights held tourneys to display and test their prowess, it was largely for the purpose of winning the plaudits of the lady spectators. Jongleurs, strolling actors, and troubadours singing songs of heroism and love helped to divert lords and ladies in castles, "country bumpkins" in rural communities, and crowds in towns. At fêtes, banquets, and in robust enjoyments such as "pagan routs" following dances around the pole on May Day, women were present in force to eat, drink, dance, shout, and carry on in many ways that testified to exuberance of spirit. Their gustful tempers found outlets in arguments over matters private, public, and religious; in disputes about property, trade, marriage arrangements, and family difficulties; in quarrels about tastes, habits, and manners high and low.

Like many men of the time, many women were muscular and tough. In speech and deeds they were often libertarian, if not libertine, as the documents clearly show. Even de la Tour Landry's *Le Livre du Chevalier (The Book of the Knight of the Tower)*, written in 1371 for the instruction of his daughters in good manners — for girls of the upper class — contained so many stories now to be regarded so obscene that no modern publisher could reprint it in the United States or England without the risk of prosecution. Robert Briffault's *The Mothers* is full of materials on the likeness-of-kind which characterized innumerable men and women of the middle ages. In such source materials actual women come to life out of ghosthood and proclaim the fact that they were not uniformly demure or subject to men, priestly or secular. Although the word "emancipation" was not in vogue, liberties were taken as the mood dictated.

In the code of chivalry modern literary commentators have seen the nursery of private and public virtues such as service to others without price, protection of the weak by the strong, kindness to the poor by the rich, and especially the devoted championship of feminine chastity against wicked and cruel males. Thus Professor F. J. C. Hearnshaw, an Englishman, in an essay on "Chivalry and Its Place in History," taking the English gentleman as a standard of measurement, declared that in England chivalry "set that tone which has been perpetuated in the Public School tradition." And what could be better than "the old School tie"? At the opposite pole chivalry has been represented as a hypocritical fraud covering brutality, savagery, and gross lechery so shocking to refined sensibilities in modern times as to defy description for publication in the English-speaking world. If the records which alone furnish us positive knowledge of chivalry are consulted, it must be said that the "truth" lies somewhere between the extremes and on the whole closer to the description of chivalry as brutality and lechery than to the description of it as purity and gentility.

With no intention of playing up the grossness of human nature in some of its aspects, indeed with regret that such aspects exhibit themselves, the student must admit that women of the chivalric age were not all quiet Griseldas passively watching the exploits of pure-hearted knights. A single extract from the English chronicler, Knighton of Leicester, describes a scene that scarcely fits either the Public School tradition or the Ladies' Academy tradition of chivalry: "In those days [1348] there arose a huge rumour and outcry among the people, because when tournaments were held, a band of women would come as if to share the sport, dressed in divers and marvellous dresses of men — sometimes to the number of 40 or 50 ladies, of the fairest and comeliest (though I say not, of the best) among the whole Kingdom. Thither they came in party-coloured tunics, one colour or pattern on the right side and another on the left, with short hoods that had pendants like ropes wound around their necks, and belts thickly studded with gold and silver — nay, they even wore, in pouches slung across their bodies, those knives which are called *daggers* in the vulgar tongue; and thus they rode on choice war-horses or other splendid steeds to the places of tournament. There and thus they spent and lavished their possessions, and wearied their bodies with fooleries and wanton buffoonery, if popular report lie not."

Yet, in Knighton's view, God was not to be mocked: "But God in this matter, as in all others, brought marvellous remedy; for He harassed the places and times appointed for such vanities by opening the floodgates of heaven with rain and thunder and lurid lightning, and by unwonted blasts of tempestuous winds. . . . That same year and the next came the general mortality [the Black Death] throughout the world."

Anyone who desires more precise details bearing on the nature and actions of mediaeval women can find them luxuriant in G. G. Coulton's *Mediaeval Panorama* and his four volumes of documents, *Life in the Middle Ages*. In the pages of these works mediaeval women stand out as they were seen and heard by their contemporaries. At one point a woman and her daughters are lustily engaged in a general brawl with relatives and neighbors. In another passage a woman is described as "an animal prouder than the lion, the fiercest and proudest of the brute creation; more wanton than the ape; and more venomous than an asp; more false and deceitful than the syren." Women display their independence by drinking and merrymaking and singing in taverns. A woman is cited as a leader of village dancing. Perverse women wash clothes on Sundays and Holy Days. A woman steals her husband's money and runs off with a monk. Women are found dancing under the leadership of the Devil. A stout woman merchant smashes a knight with a sword. Two women beat each other up in a jealous rage. Women are so accustomed to swearing that they could hardly speak a word without an oath.

Not even in churchly affairs were mediaeval women all meek and silent. The records testify that many of them were quite otherwise. Illicit relations of women and priests were disclosed by witnesses at official inquests. Rebellious nuns defied men's orders. Wicked women cast spells. Women were unmannerly in churches. Women joined men in tossing a priest into a pit. Women crowded into the cloisters of a noble monastery, along with men, and made hubbub there.

That women were not always expected to treat priests with respect, no matter what the clerics did, is indicated in a story told by Thomas of Chantipré in Brabant, a distinguished Dominican preacher and suffragan bishop of the thirteenth century. Once when Thomas was in Brussels, a comely maiden of lowly birth told him that a priest had tried to ravish her, that she had bloodied his nose; thereupon the priest informed her that for this she had to make a pilgrimage to Rome. Thomas could scarcely withhold his laughter but he solemnly instructed her that, if this or any other priest made improper approaches to her, "then thou smite him sore with thy clenched fist, even to the striking out, if possible, of his eye; and in this matter thou shalt spare no order of men, for it is as lawful for thee to strike in defense of thy chastity as to fight for thy life."

In the numberless mediaeval records which indicate men's ideas of women, all kinds of formulas appear again and again. Thus, women are cleaner and better than men; by their virtues they lift men above masculine grossness, vulgarity, and brutality; they bear the heavy burden of civilizing men. Again, women are inherently sinful and wicked, the originators and abettors of evil; they are forward in their insolence; they have commerce with the Devil, resort to magic, and in general must be subdued to the ordinances of the priests if not of other men; they should be humble and obedient to their husbands; and it is not meet for them to invade man's domain. Also, repeated again and again and again in mediaeval documents was the idea that women had been better, if not ideal, "in the good old days," but were now given to luxury, assertiveness, display, love of worldly goods and pleasures. Hence it would appear that the newest clichés are not so new after all.

Such citations, illustrations, and facts (and all that might be added to them) certainly do not show that the women of the middle ages were all on the side of civilization — or all against it. The number of men who actually fought in the endless battles and wars of the time doubtless outnumbered women; and men do seem in the light of archives to have been on the whole more brutal, cruel, and gross. Yet women, as queens or in other posts of power, ordered men to battle; women marshaled troops; women often fought side by side with men; and, besides being guilty themselves of innumerable cruelties, women aided and approved the worst. In short, mediaeval women conformed to no "type," in respect of mentality, possessions, activities, tastes, interests, or, to use that now-popular but misleading word, "status." They were certainly not all tame in the "man's world."

All mediaeval women were not cowed when marriage arrangements and settlements were made or by marriage itself. Apart from legal texts, decrees, commentaries, and decisions, mediaeval documents relative to women and marriage are bewildering in number and variety. They include letters, copious extracts from chronicles, passages from royal and ecclesiastical official inquests, sermons, chivalric romances, miracle plays, ballads, tales, books for ladies, and snatches of gossip and recollections. Although a large number of them refer principally to women of the upper classes, others give glimpses into the life and practices of peasants and serfs toiling under the jurisdiction of overlords, male and female. Anyone who pores for only a few weeks over these records will shrink from making any single generalization purporting to cover the marital practices of the middle ages, particularly on "the position of woman."

Beyond all question the weight of documentary evidence is against any simple conclusion that men handed women around like chattels; that boys were free to make their own choices of mates, while girls were helpless creatures at the disposition of men. After the rise of the centralized state, no one, male or female, was actually "free," save perhaps the king or queen as highest lord, and even members of royal families had to be on guard against actions likely to stir up revolt among underlings. As a matter of fact, fathers and mothers of the middle and lower classes, as well as lords and ladies, took part in arranging the marriages of both boys and girls under the almost universal rule of "convenience." The boy apparently had no more choice than the girl. There are records indicating that boys and girls sometimes made vigorous protests without avail; other records show that their protests were effective. But the general rule of marriage for convenience long prevailed.

Whether fathers or mothers, men or women, usually dominated in the making of matches is a matter buried in the silence of unrecorded history, but there is abundant proof that women were active in the business and were no less circumspect or ruthless than men at the business. Women looked about for marriageable boys and girls to be convenient mates for girls and boys in their own families. Maidens were inclined to be shrewd and insistent — that is, "practical" — in marrying men with property, when they had any chance of selection, as they often did. Mothers were zealous in procuring for their daughters men who had property and in making sure that the property was good, and carefully guarded by proper legal titles. In other words, the marriage of convenience was no one-sided affair in which fathers and sons "had their own way" with the women concerned in it.

In a book of illustrations for sermons designed to teach moral lessons, a Franciscan friar, who had been a fellow-student of Roger Bacon, wrote, about 1275, a story of a greedy woman who was punished for demanding a mate who had money. "A certain great lady," he said, "being left a widow by the death of her husband, and wooed by many for marriage, one of her many suitors was comely to see, doughty of his body, practiced and renowned in arms, but poor. When, therefore, he besought her instantly, seeking to bend that lady's mind to consent to the marriage, seeing also that his body pleased her while his poverty (according to the way of the world) displeased her, she gave him one day the following answer: 'Beloved sir, how could I, being such a lady as I am, take thee who are so poor a man and of so slender substance? . . . If thou hadst a fief I would gladly take thee." Thus rebuffed the suitor went away, found a rich merchant on a public road, slew him, stole his money, and returned to the lady loved. Though he confessed to her that he had got his sudden riches by murder and robbery, she accepted him, with his ill-gotten gains, as her husband. Then after many years both met a terrible fate. While the story may be fanciful in some respects, it undoubtedly reflects a conception of human conduct deemed probable in such times.

Documentary evidence wholly conclusive in nature and showing women's participation in arranging marriages appears in the famous *Letters* of the Paston family written in the fifteenth century. One of the letters gives a warm picture of a negotiation. About 1449 Elizabeth Clere wrote to her cousin, John Paston, Jr., with reference to fixing up a match for his sister and the way the mother of the girl tried to rule her with an iron rod. Elizabeth told John that a man, Scrope, was looking for a wife, that she [Elizabeth] had examined his [Scrope's] legal rights to his property, and that he would make a good match for the girl in question, "without ye might get her a better." Elizabeth warned John, however, against letting others know about her maneuvers: "Cousin, I pray you to burn this letter, that your man nor none other may see it; for if your mother knew that I had sent you this letter, she should never love me."

Among the peasants, servile and free, the marriage of convenience was, if possible, still more a matter of sheer economic interest. In the control of overlords, girls and widows were often treated as if they were property, but peasant boys seem not to have fared any better. The overlord wanted strong and husky workers of both sexes, male and female, on his estates, and either he or his bailiff frequently forced the marriage of boys and girls, no matter what they or their parents said or did. For instance, on the manor of Liestal, near Basel, a rule was laid down in 1411 that "every year before Shrove Tuesday, when folk are wont to think of holy matrimony, the bailiff shall bethink him what boys and girls are of such an age that they may reasonably betake wife or husband, so that he may then allot to each his mate, as husband or wife." If in such cases the girls were regarded as chattels, the same could be said of the boys. The line of subjection was clearly a class line, not a sex line.

In general, marriage ties in the middle ages, particularly during the early centuries, were at best loose and confused, and the conception of marital virtues was low as compared to the highest modern standards. Innumerable marriages were consummated without the blessing of the Church. Extralegal relations of men and women were common. But in the course of time Church authorities, for many reasons, tried to regularize marriages and wedded life. Despite the dissoluteness of many ecclesiastics, a large proportion of the clerics labored to establish more refined and humane relations between men and women. In numerous cases the motive of an ideal was supplemented by the desire to provide means of tracing legitimacy in descent, for the purposes of apportionment of property among legal heirs and heiresses and of preventing marriages between boys and girls who might be too closely related by known or unknown ties of blood. At all events, mediaeval sermons against sinful females, indicating the desirability of their subjection, were accompanied by sermons exalting their virtues and condemning men for masculine grossness, brutality, and irresponsibility.

That husbands were allowed by common and ecclesiastical law to beat their wives cannot be gainsaid. Although numerous cases of wife-beating appear in the records, the actual extent of the practice is unregistered and it is certain that priests often tried to mitigate the abuse. Men were frequently punished for cruelty to their wives.

The origin of the custom and law as to wife-beating is obscure. But from glimpses of mediaeval society afforded by documents, family life was commonly rough and boisterous. Women, as well as men, were free with their fists, assisted by their children and relatives. Miracle plays, pageants, and village tales with striking frequency depict women as outwitting their husbands by shrewdness, if not shrewishness, and it often happened that men resorted to their ancient device, violence, when their psychological resources were not equal to the occasion. Nor is it to be overlooked that wives were sometimes aggressors: Chaucer's Wife of Bath tore three pages out of her clerkly husband's book and clouted him on the cheek with her fists.

In the Chester *Deluge Play*, to which Chaucer referred with obvious zest, Noah is exhibited in a dispute with his wife and as conceding that he was defeated. When his wife refused to heed a command, Noah exclaimed: "Good wife, do as thou art bid." She snapped back:

> *By Christ, no! ere I see more need,*
> *Though thou stand all day and rave.*

Noah then lamented his plight:

> *Lord, how crabbed are women alway!*
> *They are never meek, that dare I say . . .*
> *Good wife, let be all this trouble and stir*
> *That thou makest this place here,*
> *For all men think thou art my master*
> *(And so thou art, by St. John!)*

Closely related to marriage, inheritance, descent, and wills, all through the middle ages, were practices connected with the ownership, use, and disposition of property under or outside the law. In respect of property neither men nor women stood alone. As to property in agricultural land, little or none of it was held outright, save as far as the highest lord or king could be said to have owned a principality or realm. Landed property was everywhere as a rule subject to feudal services, whether nominally in the hands of men or women. And, as we have seen, women, married and single, had extensive rights in property under the law of England in the middle ages.

What the law indicates is confirmed by a large variety of sources entirely apart from purely legal documents. Women made large gifts of land, money, and chattels to church institutions. They founded nunneries, monasteries, hospitals, orphanages, and asylums. They bought benefices for their sons, and places for their daughters in convents. They received property by will or descent from fathers, mothers, brothers, and sisters. Women engaged in trading operations, haggled in the markets over prices, and were denounced by priests for being parties to the practices of usury, pawnbroking, and price manipulations by which consumers were cheated. They bought "finery" recklessly and were criticized by priests for their luxury and pride. With money at their disposal they traveled far and wide through Christendom, as far as the Holy Land. It is impossible to discover the proportionate number of women who so disposed of property or carried on trade or made long journeys for various reasons. But an abundant documentation destroys the fiction that women were in matters of property solely dependent on the rules or whims of men.

Legal records even reveal women of those distant times selling men and women, as men sold men and women, into forced labor. For example, the widow of John the Leech announced in a formulary that "I . . . have sold to the Abbot of Bruerne, for twenty shillings, Richard the son of William de Eastend of Kingham, my man, with all his chattels and livestock. . . . And, that none may doubt this I have published these deeds present, sealed with mine own seal, for a testimony." Again, Audrina, widow of Robert de Driby, sold to Henry Cole of Boston, "Agnes, daughter of Hordan Blanet of Baston, and simon Calf her son dwelling at Stamford, with all their chattels and live-stock . . . and all claim of serfdom and villeinage which I or my heirs have or might have therein."

In these, as indeed in other evidences from social and economic life in the middle ages, class lines are sharply marked. But sex lines, such as there were, if prescribed in law, were abundantly defied in practice and in any event cannot be brought within the scope of any single formula on the "status" or the "function" and "role" of women.

Chapter 11

Evidences in Mediaeval Educational and Intellectual Interests

In the Protestant world, where the "rights" of women were first formally proclaimed in manifestos, it has been generally assumed, at least until recent times, that the Catholic Church was absolutely opposed to the education of lay people, and that the education of women in convents and by nuns is to be viewed as of little or no import in the development of Western civilization. How did this misunderstanding occur?

To some extent it was due to the fact that formal education in its upper ranges, particularly in mediaeval universities, was confined largely to the training of men for the priesthood and that men who enjoyed that privilege wrote so many treatises, chronicles, and works on theology. Apart from the tendency of Protestant critics to paint the "dark ages" as blacker than they really were, this conception was also due in no small measure to the neglect of woman by historians, both Catholic and Protestant, and their persistent habit of publicizing men as if they had made all the history worth noting. In these circumstances it is difficult to see the tree of women's education in the forest of controversial and masculine literature.

It is true that many students of the middle ages have noted that women in the convents were educated by some process and often conducted schools for the training of nuns and the education of daughters of the upper classes in the neighborhood in the interest of domestic life and courtly society. Yet relatively slight consideration has been given to the larger place which educated women held in the mediaeval period.

Although it is easy to select from the bulky writings of clerics, early and late, passages which treat women as dangerous, if not inferior — a being to be kept down and away from learning — such passages can be easily paralleled by other mediaeval writings which demonstrate that this was not a universal theory of the Church and was indeed far from according with the practices of the middle ages. There were numerous Catholic writers and teachers of the time who held other ideas of woman's "place" in society. Among the Dominican mystics were many men who made a special point of teaching women and encouraging them to aid in awakening the public to the importance of a deeper religious life. Pierre Dubois (c. 1250–1312) for instance argued that, since crusades had failed to conquer the Infidel by violence, girls should be taught theology and medicine and sent out as missionaries to overcome the Infidel by the sword of the spirit and service.

William Occam, the great English schoolman who was often in collision with Church authorities, believed that intuition was the basis of knowledge; that will — not intellect as the scholastics conceived intellect — was the primary faculty of the human soul. He had faith in natural moral intelligence. He demanded that the Church be ruled by world councils instead of autocratically and he asked why women, who have souls to save, should not be allowed to vote in such councils. It is fair to infer that if Occam deemed women worthy of membership in such assemblies, he thought of them as possessing the intellectual and moral powers requisite to the responsibilities involved.

In some respects, certainly, the customary way of dismissing the intellectual life of women in the middle ages, with that of the masses in general, has been due to mediaeval writings, especially for the early centuries of the period. As Samuel Dill remarks in his *Roman Society in Gaul in the Merovingian Age*, speaking of the life of the common people, the fragmentary chronicles of the time were chiefly concerned with kings, their great officers, and nobles; only here and there from the scribes, particularly in their lives of the Saints, are to be caught glimpses of the people-at-large and their conditions.

For centuries books that were available even to the great scholars were few in number. The distinguished Bernard of Chartres who died about 1130, called "perhaps the greatest classical teacher north of the Alps during the middle ages," had a collection of only twenty-four books which he bequeathed to the cathedral library. Most books were written by members of the higher clergy and dealt mainly with matters theological or the doings of kings, princes, saints, and to some extent the upper classes generally. The intellectual and moral interests of the people were expressed orally for the most part and carried along in the steam of time mainly by memory and recitation.

Before the fourteenth century, the chief written works made available to the people were psalters and manuals of devotion. But as modern investigations have discovered there was an increasing numbers of books, fragments, and fugitive pieces in circulation as the centuries passed, especially after the invention of printing. Laymen and lawwomen singly and in groups were then reading more and discussing more kinds of books.

THE EDUCATION OF WOMEN A REALITY

Whatever was the weight of Church authority against the education of women and their right to an intellectual life of their own, records of the middle ages, though as yet meagerly exposed for this particular kind of information, certainly reveal women, high and low, receiving an education by some process, pursuing intellectual interests, reading, writing, expounding, and corresponding with one another and with learned men. Voluminous writing was done by women, particularly those associated with the mystics. A specific citation, from among many, gives concreteness to the generalization: in the documents of Coulton, *Life in the Middle Ages,* are letters from the correspondence between Christina von Stommeln, born in a farming family in 1242, with Peter of Sweden, a Dominican friar, and with Brother Maurice, an undergraduate at Paris. The letters deal mainly with matters of religious experience. But they convey two striking facts relative to woman's role in the intellectual life of the middle ages: here was a gifted woman with genuine talent for literary expression; and it seemed to be taken as a matter of course that she should be engaged in correspondence with two brethren of the Church dedicated to intellectual pursuits.

That the education of women was going on far and wide in Europe is demonstrated in innumerable documents. One may find, as items of evidence, stories like the following. In the early years of the eleventh century, Hadwig, daughter of the Duke of Bavaria and after the death of her husband Duchess of Suabia, acquired, by the aid of tutors, proficiency in the Greek language. Then she took up the study of Latin literature; and later employed the famous monk Ekkehard to give her additional instruction at her castle, Hohenwiel. In recounting a thirteenth-century miracle Thomas of Chantipré in Brabant noted that a mistress of a village taught "the daughters of the rich." Moreover, it was a common practice for the lady of the castle to give instruction not only to girls, but also to boys committed to her care.

For girls Geoffrey de la Tour-Landry's fourteenth-century book on chivalry became an exceedingly popular text, indicative of the number of young and older women who could read. It was in time translated into German and English and by the middle of the sixteenth century it had passed through seven editions in three languages. It advised brides to honor and obey husbands and taught them ingenuity in obedience: how to win wealth, power, and prestige by discreet methods in dealing with men and their relatives. The large circulation gained by the book was not only a sign that women were reading in the late middle ages. It also signified that in "the days of chivalry" women were interested in "getting on in the world."

In the life and writings of Geoffrey's contemporary, Jean Froissart, who was born in 1338 and lived until about 1410, is another testament in respect of mediaeval women and their education. In his autobiographical work, Jean tells of his own education in a little school at his town in France. He states that he was often beaten at school and in turn he beat up other boys. But he was particuarly interested in commenting on the girls who sat on school benches with him. That girls were there was not strange, for coeducation in the lower schools was often the case in his time. He liked to exchange apples, pears, and trinkets with the girls; and, when he was about the age of fourteen, Jean fell in love with a girl whom he found sitting under a tree reading a romance. They read for a while together, and she asked him whether he would lend her other romances. He had one and granted this favor after slipping between the pages a ballad of his own by way of commending himself to her. In vain. She married another man and on meeting Jean at a garden party she tore a lock out of his head with such violence as to convince him at last that their affair was at an end.

Evidently girls studied at schools in the fourteenth century. They might marry to suit themselves; and, if a suitor was objectionable, the tender and timid creature might tear the hair out of his head. Surely this was no picture of the modest female who, Geoffrey de la Tour-Landry seemed to think, had once existed, lived no more, but might be resurrected by reading the book he wrote for the education of his daughters.

Available documents permit no comparative judgment as to the nature and extent of women's education in the countries of the Western world. Those to which access is easy may be interpreted to mean that German or Italian women had the best education of the middle ages. The convents were centers of education of a formal kind. The number of women's religious orders in parts of Germany exceeded the number of men's orders and one might infer from this that numerous German women were formally educated.

HUMANIZING EDUCATION — INDIVIDUAL, CIVIC, AND PHILOSOPHIC

Many things conspired to give leadership and acclaim in education and letters to the women of Italy, earlier than to women of other countries. Italy was the original home of the revival of the Latin classics and it was to Italy that the choicest of Greek classics were brought from Byzantium, before and after the fall of Constantinople to the Turks in 1453. To Italy came able scholars and tutors straight from the Near East; and at their hands, or under their influence, Greek and Latin grammars and texts of the classics were issued in profusion.

With the revival of classical learning came the humanizing of intellectual interest, knowledge, and public measures; that is, thought and action were directed by this learning to human concerns, as distinguished from the divine, and to the human race in general, as distinguished from individual salvation and particular peoples. Now educated men and women in Italy had at their command, for example, the great histories written by Greek and Roman authorities in antiquity and were attracted by the difference between these human and secular works and the monkish chronicles which, besides being fragmentary, twisted the story of the past to fit theological conceptions of the universe. Now Italian men and women were in possession of literary and philsophic works dealing entirely with the great human and nature subjects, without regard for those "ultimate causes" with which theologians occupied themselves on the basis of theories and convictions respecting the nature and designs of God. Moreover, instead of the degraded Latin so often employed by monkish chroniclers, Italian men and women now had models of writing by Greek and Roman thinkers and stylists, inviting them to lofty aspirations and lucid expressions whether in poetry, letters, the arts, history, philosophy, or politics.

In the promotion of the new learning, two tasks had to be carried out. The first included the recovery of additional classical works, the preparation of critical editions, the reissue of the best in manuscript form and, after the invention of printing, in book form, and critical study of the new texts. The second was the dissemination of the knowledge derived from this critical study.

The number of women who devoted themselves to scholarship was by no means as large as the number of men, for reasons other than the lack of talents; but in the fifteenth century and early sixteenth century many Italian women displayed the highest technical competence in the study, interpretation, and exposition of the revived humanist learning. Some of them, for example Isotta Nogarola, we are told by Dr. G. R. Potter in *The Cambridge Mediaeval History* (Volume VIII, Chapter XXIII), "could hold their own in matters of scholarship with the best of their male contemporaries and . . . were accepted and even acclaimed everywhere."

According to Dr. H. J. Mozans' *Women in Science,* women took "an active part in the great educational movement inaugurated by the revival of learning" and won "the highest honors for their sex in every department of science, art, and learning. . . . The universities, which had been opened to them at the close of the middle ages, gladly conferred upon them the doctorate, and eagerly welcomed them to the chairs of some of their most important faculties. . . . Cecelia Gonzaga, pupil of the celebrated humanist, Vittorino da Feltre, read the gospels in Greek when she was only seven years old. Isotta and Ginevra Nogarola, pupils of the humanist, Guarino Verronese, likewise distinguished themselves at an early age by their rare knowledge of Latin and Greek. . . . Livia Chiavello, of Fabriano, was celebrated as one of the most brilliant representatives of the Petrarchian school. . . . Cassandra Fidele, of Venice, deserved, according to Poliziano, the noted Florentine humanist, to be ranked with that famous universal genius, Pico de la Mirandola. So extensive were her attainments that in addition to being a thorough mistress of Latin and Greek, she was likewise distinguished in music, eloquence, philosophy, and even theology. . . . But for the extent and variety of her attainments, Tarquinia Molza seems to have eclipsed all her contemporaries. Not only did she excel in poetry and the fine arts, she also had a rare knowledge of astronomy and mathematics, Latin, Greek and Hebrew. So great was the esteem in which she was held that the senate of Rome conferred upon her the singular honor of Roman citizenship, transmissible in perpetuity to her descendants."

In nearly every great intellectual center of Italy women were lecturing on literature and philosophy, and religious faith could not escape impacts of the new knowledge. They were studying medicine and natural science in the light of pagan learning in these subjects. Great Italian women teachers of the awakening "sent forth such students as Moritz von Spiegelberg and Rudolph Agricola to reform the instruction of Deventer and Zwoll and prepare the way for Erasmus and Reuchlin."

Some of the women crossed the Alps themselves, as the ancient learning was said to do when Erasmus and other returning students bore back to outlying countries the knowl-

edge gleaned in Italy. One of the most distinguished classical scholars of the age, Olympia Morata, for example, meeting difficulties as Renée's court where the duchess and all her
friends were persecuted by the Duke for their religious independence, fled to Germany, with a young Bavarian student
of medicine and philosophy, and was planning to continue
her teaching of the classics in Heidelberg, to which she had
been invited, when an untimely death closed her career.

In the dissemination of the new learning among the Italian
people, especially among the rich but including some not as
well off in this world's goods, five methods were widely and
intensively employed: tutoring and self-directed study in
families, education in schools, humanist lecturing, conversations in small private groups and larger coteries, and correspondence.

As soon as the Renaissance had got under way, Italian
women in the rich commercial cities and at ducal or princely
courts, such as Ferrara and Urbino, turned with avidity to
the study and discussion of Greek and Roman literature.

While men of the governing class were away from their
castles fighting in wars, women and girls of their families
thus "improved their minds" and displayed their accomplishments to the warriors when they came home on furloughs.
French officers and Spanish ambassadors who were guests
in the great houses from time to time were so impressed that
they let their own women relatives and friends know how
backward they were and how advisable it would be for them
to catch up with Italian women. When Erasmus, Grocyn, and
Colet joined in the student pilgrimage to Italy early in the
sixteenth century, they found women immersed in the ancient
languages and lore, surrounded by poets, artists, scholars, and
writers from near and distant places as companions in the
new intellectual movement.

This linguistic and literary development was not confined to
the ruling circles, however. Classical schools for girls and
boys were opened in Italian cities, giving to the business and
professional circles, as well as to patricians, opportunities to
acquire knowledge of the ancient languages and the natural,
or secular, philosophies embodied in Greek and Latin literature. Here entered the insurgent bourgeois influence which
Henry Adams, looking back from the twentieth century and

his vantage point within it, concluded was an invincible menace to the throne of Mary, Queen of Heaven.

Among the outstanding Italians of the fifteenth century who promoted education, letters, and arts were Gian Francesco Gonzaga II and his wife, Paola Malatesta, who brought to Mantua in 1425 the exceptional humanist, Vittorino da Feltre, and established him there as the teacher of their sons and daughters. The Gonzagas took it as a matter of course that their daughters should have the same kind of instruction as their sons — in an age when women, according to a tradition of our time, were supposed to have no education at all. It was with the full support of both patrons that Vittorino was to devise and execute a program of education that made his school one of the most creative in the Italy of the Renaissance.

In Chapter XVI, Volume I, of *The Cambridge Modern History*, Sir R. C. Jebb describes the new type of civic education created by Vittorino at his school in Mantua under the patronage of Gian and Paola Gonzaga in 1425 and carried on until his death in 1446: "His aim was to develop the whole nature of his pupils, intellectual, moral, and physical; not with a view to any special calling, but so as to form good citizens and useful members of society, capable of bearing their part with credit in public and private life. For intellectual training he took the Latin classics as a basis; teaching them, however, not in the dry and meagre fashion generally prevalent in the mediaeval schools . . . but in the large and generous spirit of Renaissance humanism. Poetry, oratory, Roman history, and the ethics of Roman Stoicism, were studied in the best Latin writers. . . . By degrees Vittorino introduced some Greek also. . . . He provided for some teaching of mathematics, including geometry . . . arithmetic, and the elements of astronomy. Nor did he neglect the rudiments of such knowledge as then passed for natural philosophy and natural history. Music and singing also found a place. . . . With great insight and tact, Vittorino saw how far social education could be given in a school with advantage to morals and without loss to manliness; he inculcated a good tone of manners, and encouraged the acquirement of such social accomplishments as the age demanded in well-educated men."

It was not only as scholars, tutors, lecturers, members of

coteries, participants in the work of academies, and patrons of schools that Italian women led and cooperated in the dissemination of the humanist learning. They carried on extensive correspondence with men and other women engaged in spreading humanist knowledge and doctrines in Italy and throughout Western Europe. Of Olympia Morata, we are told that she "corresponded on equal terms with the most learned men of the day."

All these free, wide-reaching, and influential activities of Italian women in the promotion of humanist learning were in keeping with the very spirit of the Renaissance. In the third chapter of *Die Kultur der Renaissance,* Jacob Burckhardt, a renowned authority, says: "In order to understand the higher forms of social intercourse during the Renaissance, it is necessary to know that woman was regarded as in a position of perfect equality with man. One should not allow one's self to be deceived by the cunning and in part malicious researches respecting the presumptive inferiority of the beautiful sex. . . . Above all, the education of the woman among the higher classes is essentially the same as that of the man. There was not the slightest hesitation among the Italians of the Renaissance in according the same literary and even philological instruction to sons and daughters; for as they saw in this new classical culture the highest possession of life, so they assumed gladly that girls were welcome to it. . . . There was no question of a conscious 'emancipation' of woman or anything so out of the ordinary, for the situation was understood to be a matter of course. The education of the woman of rank, just as well as that of the man, sought the development of a well-rounded personality in every respect. The same development of mind and heart that perfected the man was necessary for perfecting woman."

Men of the Renaissance not only accepted as a matter of course this free and easy association with women in the advancement of learning and the civic spirit. Many writers of the period made a point of paying special tributes to women, if frequently in exaggerated form. Take, for example, Boccaccio (1313–1375), the fervent humanist, poet, story-teller, and friend of Petrarch. Besides writing *De Casibus Virorum Illustrium,* dealing with the troubles and vanities of illustrious men from the time of Adam to the fourteenth century, he wrote on illustrious women, *De Claris Mulieribus,* starting with Eve and coming down to Giovanna, queen of Naples; included were Cleopatra, Lucretia, Portia, Semiramis, and Sappho. This work passed through many editions and is esteemed as among the important texts of the Renaissance. It was translated into Italian by Joseph Betussi who "in the ardor of his zeal enriched it by fifty new articles."

About a hundred years later, Henry C. Agrippa (1486–1525), German writer, soldier, physician, architect, historiographer, doctor of law, and traveler in many lands, outdid Boccaccio. In 1509 Agrippa published a work on the nobility and superexcellence of women (*De nobilitate et praecellentia feminei sexus*), dedicated to Margaret of Burgundy. In this volume of thirty chapters, Agrippa employed the writings of fable-makers, poets, historians, and the canon law in efforts to prove the case, and resorted to theological, physical, historical, moral, and even magical evidences to support his argument. He declared that he was moved to write the book by his sense of duty and obligations to duty.

Many men wrote paeans to women, as Lucian the Roman had done and as men were to continue to do in the mood of the Renaissance, in many countries, for centuries. Finally, in 1774, just two years before the Declaration of Independence at Philadelphia, an account of such hymning of women was published at Philadelphia. This was a work in two volumes: *Essay on the Character, Manners, and Genius of Women in Different Ages* — enlarged from a French work of M. Thomas by Mr. Russell, an Englishman. It included a section on the "Revival of Letters and the Learning of Women, Of the Books written in Honour of Women, and on the Superiority of the Sexes, and the subject continued."

After giving an account of the work by Boccaccio and Betussi, the author of the *Essay* continued: "Philip de Bergamo, an Augustine monk, published a volume in Latin OF ILLUSTRIOUS WOMEN. Another performance on the same subject was published by Julius Caesar Capacio, secretary to the city of Naples; one by Charles Pinto, in Latin, and in verse; one by Ludovico Domenichi; one by James Philip Tomassini, bishop of Venice; and one by Bernard Scardioni, a canon of Padua, OF THE ILLUSTRIOUS WOMEN OF PADUA.

"Francis Augustine della Chiesa, bishop of Saluca, wrote

a treatise on THE WOMEN FAMOUS IN LITERATURE; Lewis Jacob de St. Charles, a Carmelite, wrote another on THE WOMEN ILLUSTRIOUS BY THEIR WRITINGS; and Alexander Van Denbusche, of the Low Countries, wrote one on THE LEARNED WOMEN.

"The celebrated Father le Moine published a volume under the title of GALERIE DE FEMMES FORTES; and Brantome wrote THE LIVES OF ILLUSTRIOUS WOMEN. But it is to be observed that Brantome, a French knight and a courtier, speaks only of queens and princesses. . . .

"After Brantome, Hilario da Costa, a Minim, published two volumes in quarto, each volume consisting of eight hundred pages, containing, as he tells us, the panegyrics of ALL the women of the fifteenth and sixteenth centuries, distinguished by their valour, their talents, or their virtues. But the pious ecclesiastic has, in fact, only given us the panegyrics of the CATHOLIC women of that period. He does not say a word, for example, of queen Elizabeth. . . .

"But all must yield to the indefatigable Italian, Peter Paul de Ribera, who published in his own language, a work entitled 'The Immortal Triumphs and heroic Enterprises of Eight hundred and forty-five women.' . . .

"Besides these large compilations dedicated to the honour of the whole sex, many of the writers of those times, men of taste and gallantry, addressed panegyrics to individuals, to women who were the living ornaments of their age. This practice was most common in Italy, where every thing conspired to favour it. . . . The courts of Naples, of Milan, of Mantua, of Parma, of Florence, and several others, formed so many schools of taste, between which reigned an emulation of glory and of talents. The men distinguished themselves by their address in war, or in love; the women, by their knowledge and accomplishments."

From Italy zeal for classical learning fanned out like rays from a sun. Queen Isabella of Spain became interested in it through her acquaintance with Vittoria Colonna and brought Italian men and women to Spain to instruct her courtiers and students in the universities. She studied the classics herself. She established a school of the classics in her palace. She attended examinations of students and watched with eagle eyes and sharp ears the progress of this education among her retinue. She collected texts for the courtiers to read and for students to use in the universities. One woman was commissioned to lecture on the classics at Salamanca; another on rhetoric at Alcalá. Later Philip II enriched this Spanish Renaissance by his patronage of Italian artists. He encouraged Spanish women to paint portaits as well as write letters, by inviting the Italian women portrait painter, Sophonisba Anguisciola, to his court. Of this portrait painter Van Dyck long afterward was to say that he learned more from her, even in her blind old age, than he had learned from many seeing men.

In France enthusiasm for classical learning was stimulated by Christine de Pisan — Italian in background — who grew up at the court of Charles V, in the late fourteenth century, where her father was installed as an astrologer. After the visit of Petrarch to France in quest of Greek and Latin texts possibly among the monastic treasures, monarchs began to accumulate a library for the French court. But Christine de Pisan did more than read texts there. She studied Plato and also Arab scientific learning in some books in the library. She shared Dante's interest in the State and urged the French to come to grips with their problem of national survival so seriously menaced by the invading armies of the English King. By coming to grips she meant more than war; she meant coming to realize the necessity of granting privileges to the middle class without which, she contended, France could not get up on its feet. Before Christine died, Jeanne d'Arc took the field as commander of French troops — her actual leadership financed by the great capitalist, Jacques Coeur, her will to lead inspired by her "voices," her acceptance as leader facilitated by French adoration of the Virgin.

Christine de Pisan tried to offset the influence of Jean de Meung's stereotype of the perfect lady in his *Roman de la Rose* by her *Le Livre des trois Vertus* (*The Book of the Three Virtues*) addressed especially to women. She hoped to arouse and develop political consciousness among French women. To this end she defended the spirit of the freer-thinking Italian women of her day in her *Cité des Dames* and awakened such interest that she was invited to the English court. She did not accept the invitation on the ground that her supreme duty lay in France, but this book was translated into English as *The City of Women*.

While the revival of classical learning was proceeding rapidly, the growing use of the vernacular languages in literary work gave another secular and even more realistic turn to intellectual interests. Women were very active in the creation of vernacular literature, especially in Germany and Italy — a literature of tales, romances, lyrics, songs, and commentaries on practical subjects. To devotional, theological, and classical books were now added works for men and women alike on contemporary life. More and more authors drifted away from religious theories and speculations to interest in human beings, in human life, and expressed new ideas in imaginative, descriptive, serious, and fantastic forms. After the invention of printing, the trickle of books in circulation became a broad stream and ever-larger masses of the people were drawn into the magic circle of the learned world and the world of creative thought.

To give the details necessary to support these generalizations respecting the spread of reading and learning among the men and women of the later middle ages would take a large number of volumes at a conservative estimate, for the historical documents run into thousands of pages. So again a single illustration must suffice here.

During the first half of the fifteenth century, a brilliant German scholar and monk, Johann Busch, wrote a chronicle of a monastery and a work on the reformation of monasteries. From the latter treatise, G. G. Coulton prints several excerpts in translation in his *Life in the Middle Ages*. According to this record, Busch heard that a certain Dominican reader or lecturer had preached in the town of Zutphen that "layfolk should have no books in the German tongue" and that no sermons should be preached save in churches and churchyards. Busch was startled by news of this lecturer's discourse, for, he said, he knew that there were more than a hundred congregations of Sisters and Béguines in the Utrecht diocese; that they possessed several books in the mother tongue and read them daily by themselves or publicly in the refectory;

and that "they read and heard German books of this sort in Zutphen, Deventer, Zwolle, Kampen, and everywhere in the cities and country districts [of the Netherlands]."

Resolved to correct the lecturer's error, Busch visited him and said: "Herein he hath preached ill, and he must publicly revoke it: for the princes of the land, the common people, men and women throughout the whole world, have many books written in the vulgar German tongue." Busch agreed with the lecturer that laymen and laywomen should not be reading "lofty and divine books" dealing with high questions of theological doctrines, but insisted that they had the right to read, and should read, books treating of vices and virtues and of a proper religious life. Having listened to Busch's arguments, the lecturer at length publicly revoked his command to the people and declared: "Ye may well and lawfully possess good and moral books in the German tongue, and read therein."

Reading was done in the middle ages — reading by men and women in many lands — and it undoubtedly increased as the centuries passed. Who were reading? Certainly not priests and men and women of religious orders alone. There is substantial ground for the statement that the teaching of youth in the castles of the rich, such as it may have been, was largely in the hands of the ladies of the castles. But reading was not confined to the upper classes, if mainly. The great English lawyer of the twelfth century, Ranulf Glanvill, declared: "The high-born of our country disdain letters, or delay to apply their children to them."

In what proportion were the men and women literate? G. G. Coulton, the life-long student of mediaeval history, gives a cautious answer: "Though very few women arrived at anything like the university stage in education, it seems probable that more of them could read and write than the men," especially in the upper classes "at the period when romances of adventure were offered in profusion."

CHRISTIANIZING THE HIGHER INTELLECTUAL INTERESTS

In the middle ages, as in other times, education, whether in schools or under the direction of private tutors, was marked by routine and discipline; and much writing, whether in Latin or the vernacular tongues, remained largely on the level of the practical, the descriptive, and the transcriptive. Paralleling these intellectual activities, however, were other concerns calling for the display of creative qualities — intellectual interests of a higher, or at least different, order. And it is a matter of positive record that among the persons of mediaeval society who wrestled with the moral, social, and intellectual problems of the period were numerous women, diligent, spirited, and influential. The highest of those problems, then as before and after, was "the riddle of our universe": how to discover unity, meaning, and instruction amid the diversities of physical nature and human life; how to find the very essence of human nature amid the multiplicity of its manifestations; how to comprehend and explain the conduct, experiences, and duties of men and women in relation to earth and society. Though the problem was not solved in the middle ages — nor has it been in any age — it was worked at with striking intensity of purpose in the time called mediaeval.

Among those who worked at it, two schools of thinkers or interpreters gradually took form and strove for supremacy. One school contended that intelligence, in sheer logical exercise, using pure reason, could explain the riddle or at least come nearest to an explanation. Writers of this school were, in most cases, men of the clerical world, professional thinkers, who composed monumental treatises on systematic theology and filled large libraries with their works. They had access to books which contained the philosophies of their forebears and they had leisure for speculations reaching high into abstract realms. Confined as a rule to cloister, study, library, or schoolroom, they had relatively little contact with the life of the mass of people — with the work, experiences, interests, and activities of the multitudes. They were speculative theologians, strictly speaking.

Members of the second school, on the other hand, thought that pure reason was not enough and in some cases that it was a false guide, at least to life. On their part they maintained that knowledge useful to life came from plain human experience and from insight into that experience — from intuitive comprehension of life's meaning. Persons of this mental outlook wrote less than the theologians proper, if they wrote at all. More often they were preachers to the multitudes and administered to their physical, moral, and spiritual needs. Such persons were commonly called "mystics" and their philosophy, if it deserves that name, was called "mysticism." Among the theologians and master logicians, Thomas Aquinas was an outstanding example in the thirteenth century; and among the mystics, Francis of Assisi was no less distinguished.

It must be borne in mind, however, that no absolute line separated the one school from the other. Aquinas, the great master of logic, of abstract reasoning, did not believe that he had attained Finality and Omniscience. He was a Dominican priest and, in the presence of the ultimate question of life in the universe, conceded that mysticism in its less extreme form revealed powers of discernment or understanding that went beyond sheer logic, or pure analysis and reasoning. On the other hand the mystics did not all eschew reason, or logic; they really had to use it to some extent in trying to bring their thought of life into verbal expressions.

The gulf that was made between the two kinds of thinking was a matter of emphasis. But a bridge across it was difficult to build, and in time terrible conflicts in theory and practice developed which finally split Christendom asunder. Nevertheless neither type of thinking eliminated the other type completely. The attitudes, methods, and instrumentalities of both schools — the one called rational or logical and the other irrational or mystical — survive as mental heritages into our own time and still struggle, if less violently today, for the right of superiority.

The differences between the two schools of mediaeval thinkers were more than intellectual and moral. The pure logicians tended to institutionalize religion and add power to the hierarchy. The mystics tended to socialize religion and life, to liberate it from the rule of the hierarchy, to carry ethical, as well as religious, teachings to the masses of the people, to ally themselves with and direct social unrest, to reach the ultimate individual in society and stir his or her latent force to moral and intellectual expression.

This is not to say that great mystics were not also orthodox Catholics: Bernard of Clairvaux and Catherine of Siena were both orthodox in matters of creed and both "constructive" mystics. Mysticism was manifest "not only in the personal experience of spiritual genius, but also in corporate and democratic movements. It profoundly influenced religion and art, and instigated both religious rebellion and religious reform," says Evelyn Underhill in a review of "Mediaeval Mysticism" in Volume VII of *The Cambridge Mediaeval History*. The major mystics were often highly educated and yet at the same time in close and intimate contact with life as lived by the lowliest people in the humblest communities, no less then with life as lived by the upper classes from whose riches the Church received enormous gifts of land and money. With mysticism was intimately associated the freeing of individuals from bondage to creed and classes, and the socializing of individuals for the necessities of the good life in society. In this form of reflective thinking rather than in the towering logic of theological speculation lay the democratic dynamics of the coming ages, which carried civilization forward.

If in the original records of the mystics and of contemporary critics of mysticism we seek to discover and order the features of that dynamism of thought and action, the following elements, or aspects, come repeatedly and emphatically to our attention. First are what may be called inner matters of the spirit. Mystics relied primarily upon the force of intuitive experience in the search for enlightenment; they laid stress on the inner spirit rather outward authority or power. While they often conformed to the requirements of authority, they preached spiritual liberty and unhindered communion with God, sometimes conceived as embodied in the human soul — "the spark of God," the "inner light," the "conscience of the individual." By some extremists among them — the great Ecstatics — Deism attenuated into a kind of Pantheism, thus challenging the God of the theologians and professional philosophers of the religious schools.

Second, the mystics' conceptions of life and God assumed particular outward manifestations. Activists among them, as distinguished from those who withdrew to contemplation, believed that their truths sprang from life, were designed for and applicable to life. They urged reforms of abuses in Church and State. They inveighed against luxury, wealth, and oppression of the people. To them, community or group or association was necessary to put the good way of life into effect. They emphasized care for the common people and preached to them in the style calculated to reach their minds and awaken their moral aspirations and powers.

Far more than the regular clergy, active mystics taught, wrote, and thought in the vernacular languages instead of Latin — thus coming closer to the people. In serving the poor many of them studied, wrote on, and made use of practical medicine. In the promulgation of their doctrines, mystics entered into social intercourse with one another and the public, thereby helping to break down barriers between the Church as an institution and its formal learning, on the one side, and the laity on the other. By traveling extensively even in times when travel was hard, they spread their doctrines of Christian living from one end of Western Christendom to the other, furnishing, if often inadvertently, fuel for popular movements such as peasants' protests and uprisings against feudal oppression.

A large number of the mystics, men and women alike, sprang from the humbler orders of people or identified themselves with the common life. Into the thinking and debating of the times they thrust leveling ideas derived from primitive Christianity, which were to become revolutionary in the later centuries. For example, take William Langland. Whether he was the sole author of *Piers the Plowman* is uncertain, but there is no doubt about the strain of mysticism in that book or the social drive of its thought, amid the confusions and digressions of the text. Langland above all emphasized the sufferings, poverty, and oppression of the masses. He assailed riches, luxury, and rapacity, whether in Church or State — corruption and avarice among clerics and laymen.

It was the levelling priest, John Ball, who in the middle of the fourteenth century brought out first principles:

> *When Adam delved and Eve span,*
> *Who was then the gentleman?*

He declared: "Good people, things will never go well in England so long as goods be not in common, and so long as there be villeins and gentlemen." If the origins of revolutionary doctrines of natural rights and equality in the Western world be sought, prime documents will be found in the records of mystics. While Thomas Aquinas taught the duties which members of classes owed to one another, revolutionary mystics taught what amounted to the abolition of classes.

In the movement of thought and action which marked the rise and growth of mysticism, so many-sided and complex in its ideas and expressions, women were prominent as thinkers, leaders, and disciples. Leaders among the men of the movement, no less than leaders among the women, strove to enliven spiritual interests in women. In turn, women leaders addressed their teachings to men no less than to women. And in the records of the middle ages are thousands upon thousands of pages which reveal the thought, power, and activities of women in this movement, from aristocratic women at the top to the plain women of the laboring classes at the bottom — many of them now enrolled among the saints of the Church.

Of the women leaders whose names appear only in the pages of most detailed histories, if even there in all cases, the following list is a selection:

Christina of Markyate
Hildegarde of Bingen
Angela of Toligno, called the
   Mistress of Theologians
Mechthild of Magdeburg
Christina Ebner
Adelaide Langmann
Margaret Ebner
Elizabeth of Schonau

Marguerite Porette,
   burned at Paris in 1310
Juliana of Norwich
Catherine of Siena
Catherine of Genoa
Bridget of Sweden
Catherine of Bologna
Colette of Corbie

Concerning the ideas, interests, journeys, and labors of these women in their manifold relations to men and society, little if anything is said in the general histories of the times — even in many of the larger works. But if we seek to find out all we can about a single one of these women, St. Catherine of Siena, for instance, we encounter not only the books written about her but eleven printed volumes of her own writings: *Opera* in five volumes and *Letere* in six volumes. Commenting on her *Book of Divine Doctrine,* a competent critic maintains: "It stands with the *Divina Commedia* as one of the two supreme attempts to express the eternal in the symbolism of the day. . . ." Among her letters are letters to kings, popes, cardinals, bishops, religious orders, political bodies, and numerous individuals of various ranks. Of them a careful critic has said: "By their historical importance, their spiritual fragrance, their literary value, and their beautiful Tuscan vernacular, the letters put the author almost on a level with Petrarch." If an evaluation of their historical significance and range be made the single test, they rank above the writings of Petrarch. The part Catherine played in Church politics, especially her role in restoring the unity of the Papacy, is more commonly known than her part in the intellectual, moral, and religious thought of the period; but that stress on her negotiations in papal politics is an emphasis on a single facet of her mind and purposes.

Another Italian woman, St. Catherine of Genoa (1447-1510), represented a different type of mystical thought and action. Catherine of Genoa came from the upper class and is correctly called "a lady of the Renaissance." She belonged to no religious order; she abstained from an active participation in the politics of State and Church. No miracles are ascribed to her. But she lifted "Christian Platonism to fresh levels of fertility." She taught her doctrines to a limited group of disciples, and according to Evelyn Underhill she established and ruled "with admirable common sense the first modern hospital."

WOMEN IN DISSENTING MOVEMENTS

There is still another phase of intellectual, moral, and religious history during the middle ages in which the ideas, interests, and activities of women bulk large in fact, if neglected in the written histories of the period in general circulation. This phase pertains to the important long series of heretical movements with which the Roman Catholic Church did battle, particularly from the twelfth century to the great crash of the sixteenth century when heresy flooded out in innumerable sects, denominations, religious uprisings, and popular movements — by which the founding and growth of the United States were so profoundly influenced. The history of heresy is, no doubt, highly controversial and is likely to be so as long as there are Catholics, Protestants, and free thinkers in the world. But whatever partisan and sectarian judgments may be rendered on heresy itself, women shared in and affected all the revolts of opinion, belief, and practice; and any written history which overlooks this fact is partial, fragmentary, untrue history.

It is inexcusable because a huge documentation exists relative to the ideas and doings of "heretical" women. Women taught, spread unorthodox opinions in numerous ways, and practiced their teachings. They were subjected to inquisitions, as were heretical men. Like men they were tortured and burned, displaying calmness and integrity amid the agonies of the rack and the stake. With men they perished by the thousands in the mass slaughters of religious wars.

Theologians and historians have disputed and still dispute whether the fate accorded to heretics was deserved or undeserved. Nevertheless, heresy was insistent among the intellectual, moral, and religious drives out of which emerged the modern world of thought, action, and institutions. Nor is there any doubt among students acquainted with the documents of history that women were prominent and invincible in the revolts which finally broke the sway of Roman Catholic authority over the Western mind and spirit.

Here again only illustrations are possible. Take, for example, the extract on a heretical woman from the chronicle of Ralph, Abbot of Coggeshall, given in Coulton's *Life in the Middle Ages*. The document narrates events in the days of Louis VII (1137–1180) when many heresies spread among the cities and provinces of France. A young cleric serving under the Archbishop of Reims, when walking in a vineyard one day, met a comely young maiden whom he tried to seduce — "prayed her love *par amours*." The maiden repulsed him and gave her views on the subject, indicating that she belonged to a heretical sect which regarded the sexual act as a mortal sin worthy of eternal damnation. The cleric then attempted to argue her out of her unorthodox theories and discovered that she had a mistress in the neighborhood who could argue with him. This mistress was seized and brought before the archbishop. Then a great verbal contest ensued.

In the course of the controversy the two women were condemned to the stake. The mistress shouted: "O man, men and unjust judges! Think ye to burn me with your fires?" In a trice she escaped them, fell through a window, and was borne away by evil spirits. But the maiden remained and stood fast by her doctrines. "No persuasion of reason, no promise of riches, could recall her from her foolish obstinacy," the chronicler recorded; "wherefore she was burned to death, to the admiration of many who marked how she uttered no sighs, no tears, no laments, but bore with constancy and cheerfulness all the torments of the consuming flames, even as martyrs of Christ (yet for how different a cause!) who were slain in old times by the heathen in defence of the Christian religion."

In the fourteenth century, to be very precise, in 1399, a number of Italian women at Florence, "certain daughters of Judas," as they were described in the record, "being instigated of the Devil," inveigled a Franciscan, Brother Michael, into expounding heretical doctrines which resulted in his death at the stake. When Friar Michael had come near to the place of execution, a faithful woman cried aloud, "Stand fast, martyr of Christ, for thou shalt soon receive they crown!" "I know not what he answered," the recorder noted, "but there arose much talk of this thing."

Far away, in England, about a quarter of a century later, Margery Backster, wife of a carpenter, was charged with heresy before the bishop of Norwich. The accusation lodged against her specified that she had spoken violently against "pope, cardinals, archbishops, and bishops" as persecutors of the people, and had repudiated many of the crucial doctrines and practices of the Church. She had scorned pilgrimages, graven images, holy water, feasts, and fasts. It was reported that she and her husband had been getting dangerous thoughts out of dangerous books, that "her husband read the law of Christ unto them, which law was written in a book that her husband was wont to read to her at night, and that her husband is well learned in Christian verity."

Whether Margery Backster was sent to the stake or escaped condemnation the documents do not tell us, but they do illuminate for a brief moment the religious life of little men and women in a little English community in the year 1428. Innumerable other records of inquisitions reveal similar scenes in widely scattered places of the Western world, from decade to decade, from century to century — until at length the Protestant revolt severed the unity of the Catholic Church, split into fragments itself, and facilitated, if unwittingly, the triumph of human interests over theology and authoritarianism.

In this iconoclastic and liberation movement, titled ladies and untitled wives of flaming Protestant preachers played invincible roles, the story of which is told in part in James I. Good's *Women of the Reformed Church.* Their sanction, their spoken and written words, and their activities were among the imperatives of this movement.

Chapter 12

Woman as Force in Long History

THOUGH THE modern age and the middle ages of Western history are but brief periods in universal history, the temptation to generalize about the whole of human time and universal history merely on the basis of that limited experience of human beings is almost irresistible. Publicists, popularizers, egoists confident of their knowledge, propagandists, patriots, revolutionists, feminists, antifeminists, explosivists of all kinds are wont to declare that "all history proves" this or that generalization about men and women or about man or woman.

"Universal history," asserted Thomas Carlyle, "is the history of what man has accomplished in this world, is at bottom the history of the Great Men who have worked here." If this be the truth of the matter, then, as the sage of Chelsea might remark, women are shot into the lumber room of the past.

"The history of the world," Georg Wilhelm Friedrich Hegel avowed, "is none other than the progress of the consciousness of freedom; a progress whose development according to the necessity of its nature [the progressive revelation of the spirit of God] it is our business to investigate." If so, then both men and women are pawns in the hands of God who planned it all and is all; and women go into the determinism which governs both women and men.

"The history of all hitherto existing society *(alle die bisherige Geschichte)*," Karl Marx proclaimed in the Communist Manifesto of 1848, "is the history of class struggles." In that case, class fights make all history; they have determined life and its events; man and woman, men and women, have been, or were up to 1848, in essence or substance victims of their stomachs' mandates, of the passion for material possessions and power, of greed and hatred, of oppression, revolt, oppression, revolt, ad infinitum. Mind has been only a reflection of economic interests. Since the rise of capitalism, capitalism has been the great oppressor. The revolt is to be the uprising of the proletariat. Agriculture and the political power of great landed families have made no history. But history can come to an end — that is, to an end of class fights — as a "spring into freedom" under the final dictatorship of the "working class."

In justice to the "great men" whose asseverations have just been quoted, it should be added that all of them did not in fact confine their thought of history wholly to these dogmatic statements. Elsewhere in his writings Carlyle, for instance, maintained: "You will find fibrous roots of this day's occurrences among the dust of Cadmus and Trismegistus; of Tubalcain and Triptolemus; the tap-roots of them are with Father Adam himself and the cinders of Eve's first fire." On another occasion in another mood he had another idea: "The time is approaching when History will be attempted on quite other principles; when the Court, the Senate, and the Battlefield, receding more and more into the background, the Temple, the Workshop, and the Social Hearth will advance more and more into the foreground." Yet the dictum of history as the work of a few masculine human beings had gone forth to the corners of the earth and there given vitality to a doctrine of history as all man-made in a "man's world."

Another view of long history interprets it as a movement of energy in ever-recurring cycles from barbarism through various stages to civilization and back again, with men and women carried irresistibly with the current. Although a limited theory of cycles was entertained among the ancients, it was an Italian scholar of the eighteenth century, Giambattista Vico, who gave it the modern verve. It was revitalized by an American, Brooks Adams, at the end of the nineteenth century, and again several years later by a German, Oswald Spengler. By Vico, all human beings are treated as abstractions; for Adams, women are persons, sharing with men the making of history both in the age of warriors and in the age of decay and degeneration — degeneration conceived as "effeminacy," or the loss of martial vigor. According to Spengler, woman *is* history, but man *makes* history.

A more optimistic and popular theory of history represents it as moving upward in a spiral, with progress rising higher and higher, while carrying a load of barbarism.

Another conception of history makes the everyday life of mankind unhistorical: "Happy are the people who have no history." Only the unique, the striking, the great crises in human affairs are deemed worthy of notice; such as the rise and fall of empires, the upthrusts of powerful religions — Judaism, Buddhism, Christianity, and Mohammedanism, the revolutions that have shaken societies to their foundations, from the collapse of the Roman Empire, through the American and French revolutions, to the rise of Bolshevism and Fascism in our day.

Less speculative, less controversial, disclaiming philosophy, is the type of historical research and writing generally followed by scholars of the academic profession; it is usually concentrated on some particular aspect or phase of history: political, military, economic, religious, artistic, scientific, or intellectual.

To pass over minor theories of historical construction and deal with another large generalization, history has been conceived — and with high justification in the records — as the human struggle for civilization against barbarism in different ages and places, from the beginning of human societies. To Condorcet and Guizot, in France, the systematic formulation of this interpretation must be ascribed.

This history of civilization so defined may be divided into two aspects, according to the scheme of Guizot: the external or outward aspects of civilization — visible expressions in institutions, habits, things, and agencies; and the interior — the intellectual and moral qualities of human beings which make for civilization, preserve its gains, and advance it. While it is generally agreed that the visible expressions and agencies are necessary instruments, civilization seems to depend far more

fundamentally upon the moral and intellectual qualities of
human beings — upon the spirit that animates mankind.

Trained scholars disciplined in the quest for truth contend
that only such generalizations as historic documents warrant
are permissible. But, being men as a rule, they tend to confine
their search for the truth to their own sex in history. This is
in accord no doubt with the caution of their professional training. Yet the caution which eliminates the quest for truth
about women in long and universal history may in fact limit
the ideas of such scholars about long and universal history or
any of its features, as they fasten their minds on males in
history. While exaggerating the force of men in the making
of history, they miss the force of women which entered into
the making of history and gave it important directions.

Certainly the original sources, which scholars use for the
study of men in long and universal history, often mention and
even recount stories or give elaborate data of many kinds about
women. For example, Herodotus, whom historians of the
modern age have called "the father of history," deliberately
included women in his history. Tacitus, the Roman, also
observed and commented on the women of his time. Indeed
ancient writers in various societies often thought it necessary
to consider women and among their works are to be found
statements respecting women's force of character, learning,
physical energy, military and political power, and creative
intelligence — statements made by the contemporaries of such
women.

Up to this point the evidence marshaled in preceding chapters from authoritative sources has certainly indicated that,
from modern times running back into and through the
mediaeval ages of Western feudalism and Christian contests
with barbarism, the force of woman was a powerful factor in
all the infamies, tyrannies, liberties, activities, and aspirations
that constituted the history of this stage of humanity's self-
expression. This is true, whatever plan of historical research
may be devised for the study of these ages, whatever descrip-
tions of modern or mediaeval life may be composed, whatever
popular writers may declare about human beings in this span
of time and this sector of the human habitat.

But as the human experiences of the modern age were
linked to those of the mediaeval period, so the human exper-

iences of that period were connected with those of previous history. In a few dramatic words, Pollock and Maitland tell us that "the oldest utterance of English law has Greek words in it. . . . If we would search out the origins of Roman law, we must study Babylon: this at least was the opinion of the greatest Romanist of our own day [Ihering]." Unquestionably there has been a high degree of continuity in history. There have also been cataclysm, change, reversion, change. But what change?

When an effort is made to answer this question by a serious study of historical documents, woman is discovered as a force so constant and general that forty volumes, if any number, would hardly suffice to give the record which sustains this generalization about women — the record found in excavated artifacts of a preliterate age, in folklore, in myths, in religious literature, in printed and unprinted manuscripts, in some general histories, in particular studies of women conducted by careful modern scholarship in universal history. Indeed it is hard to miss woman as force if one keeps one's eyes open and seeks, in the scientific spirit, the truth about woman as revealed in a documentation as diverse as it is ponderous, if one is not afraid to know her, if one really wants to know her.

STARTING CIVILIZATION

Where did human history begin? Long after the literate age opened, myths and speculations more or less lurid offered the only answers. After the triumph of Christianity and during the middle ages, the commonly accepted answer was that provided by the book of Genesis in the Bible. Indeed for centuries it was the fashion of chroniclers to start their histories with references to the Biblical account. That in truth Genesis presented two totally different accounts did not worry the answer-givers.

But with the spread of commerce, particularly after the discovery of the New World in 1492, sea captains, travelers, merchants, and missionaries began to bring back to Europe stories of primitive peoples found on distant islands and continents. By the middle of the seventeenth century the literature of travels and accounts of primitive societies had grown to an immense size. Then Europeans who were curious about how the human family started its career on the earth began to draw heavily on this literature and to construct images of human beginnings in "savagery," and peoples rising from savagery into civilization. French and English philosophers of a secular bent, in particular, gradually rejected the Biblical account and applied the spirit of natural science to their search for social origins.

As the nineteenth century matured, anthropologists, archaeologists, ethnologists, and other types of searchers explored the whole world for light on social origins. As a result of excavations in the Mediterranean regions even the archaic history of Greek and Roman societies was opened up, exposing primitive stages of culture utterly unknown to the oldest Greek and Roman poets, historians, and philosophers who had spun webs of theories about the "first" people. This knowledge, combined with the knowledge of other early societies unearthed or collected in other quarters of the globe, including the Occident, at length provided a substantial basis for drawing important conclusions respecting the prehistoric forms of human association and human work.

Two of these conclusions are stated by Robert Briffault in his monumental study of social origins, entitled *The Mothers* (1927): "One has reference to the form of primitive social organization, in which the most fundamental unit is not the state or the family, but a group of kinsmen having generally an animal or a plant for its badge. The other was the discovery that the part played in primitive society by women and their influence differed markedly from that which their place in civilized societies during historical times has assigned to them."

With regard to the part played by woman in primitive society, anthropologists of high standing, notably Mason, Briffault, Keller, Peake, and Dorsey, reached a verdict of fundamental significance: to woman must be assigned all or the main credit for having effected the first sharp distinction between the ways of human beings and the ways of great beasts of prey.

Of what did this sharp distinction first consist? Of cooking, making cloth, devising hand-made shelter, manufacturing domestic utensils of pottery and baskets for garnering seeds and grain, extending the diet and making meals attractive, budgeting the food supply, learning essentials about doctoring and nursing, making animals serve human beings, enlarging the communication of feelings or ideas by speech, song, and dance, and tilling the soil. When the discovery that crops could be produced by labor was made, nomads could settle on the soil, infancy could be prolonged, family life could evolve, the training of youth coud be advanced, and the conception of happiness find its place in the human consciousness. Instead of operating by rote, humanity could make progress in realizing its potentialities for a good and secure life.

Woman's success in lifting men out of their way of life nearly resembling that of the beasts — who merely hunted and fished for food, who found shelter where they could in jungles, in trees, and caves — was a civilizing triumph. It involved infinite experimentation with natural resources, infinite patience, especial responsibility for offspring, peculiar taste, a sense of esthetics, extraordinary manual skill, and the highest quality of creative intelligence. Early woman had to start from scratch. She had no instruction from the past when she began her researches and invented the domestic arts.

ORIGINS OF MAGIC

Given their origins and circumstances, early human beings had good grounds for thinking of woman as a goddess. Lacking knowledge about procreation and thus unable to understand how women brought babies into the world, especially mystified by woman's accomplishments with her digging stick in the earth, enchanted by her uses of fire and manufacture of useful commodities, appreciative of her arts of healing — in short, of her domestic science — her companions regarded her as a favorite of the unseen world. Everything she did was thought magical. She was worshiped, indeed, as magician. The deep regard for her leadership in all the amazing processes of creativeness expressed itself in efforts to appease her, if need be, to win her aid and comfort, in erecting temples for her honor and appointing priestesses and priests to serve her, to sing hymns, and praise her with harps and other instruments.

The goddess reigned far and wide in the distant past. Nor is her empire completely ended today; most Japanese still attribute their origin to the Sun Goddess who in one of her aspects is an agricultural deity, and in another aspect the ancestress of the race and patron of the ruling family. Woman was worshiped everywhere as Mother Earth, given various names such as Demeter, Ceres, and Isis, and symbolized in many ways, by mounds of earth or by stones for instance, until the age of image-making arrived when, as in the case of Athena, patron of the Greeks, she was given human form. When images were made, symbols of her handicrafts, especially the distaff, were commonly placed in her hands. She was thought to have the power of hypnotizing wild animals, even the king of beasts, and to the tamer of lions men sometimes went to pray for protection on the eve of their journeys through forests and jungles. In their reverence for maternity, early peoples frequently tucked infants into the arms of their goddesses, Isis holding her son Horus being one of the most famous examples.

Priestcraft developed in and around the temples dedicated to goddesses, and women sometimes made it a big business. High priestesses were customarily queens or princesses. Priestesses of a subordinate position were the musicians. They kept the books in which were registered gifts to the goddess and forms of revenue derived from the taxation of her adorers, received important worshipers with particular grace, handled the rites and ceremonies of the goddess cult. Priestesses of the lowest rank in the hierarchy, according to modern ideas of rank at least, were temple prostitutes who symbolized the worship of a sex while enlarging the income of the temples.

Men, however, were not obtuse to the values of priestcraft and men made their way into the profession. Eventually they proved exceedingly adept in emphasizing the importance of males elevated to the status of gods. But except for the ancient Hebrews, who finally reduced "idolatry" and made monotheism their ideal, with Jahweh (Jehovah) superseding Baal and Ishtar together as their supreme deity, men were seldom able with all their skill in priestcraft to eliminate the goddess completely. They did not try to do this in every case. They first made adjustments, compromises, and at the great temple of Delphi in Greece, for instance, both Mother Earth and Apollo the Sun God were worshiped. There the Oracle was a woman. But the persons who interpreted her sayings were male priests. In Egypt and in the days of the Roman Empire, goddesses and gods, it seems, had equal adoration.

The trend to masculine priestcraft was strengthened by priestly literature largely composed by men. In this writing men put women in places which they deemed most appropriate for them to fill or adorn. But the writing was writing and not a perfect picture-making of the lives which women actually always lived. In Christendom priests labored with might and main to uphold the authority of the Father God and His Son as against the long tradition of Mother and Son. But the strength of the mother-tradition was so tenacious that it could not be crushed. While the papacy forbade women to participate officially in the highest rites of the Church, the people-at-large and many priests insisted on paying their tribute of worship to Mary, the Mother of God.

Anything approaching an adequate impression of woman's force as ancient deity can only be gained by wide reading, in such works as *The Cambridge Ancient History* which carries phases of her divine role up to about 1000 B.C., in Egypt, Babylonia, and the Hittite Empires for example, and in works cited in the bibliography at the end of this volume. Since goddess functions ranged from guardianship of childbirth and all the arts of living to the patronage of kings and queens in empire building, the female was a potent deity indeed.

The goddess became a war goddess whenever a ruler wished to have her sanction — and thus popular sanction — for his aggressions against other peoples and rulers. How commonly she was so transformed may be realized by a study of that attribute of her potency which is elaborated in the first volumes of *The Cambridge Ancient History* dealing with the rise and fortunes of great historic States.

THE INTERVENTION OF WAR

The smooth flow and progressive development of the creative intelligence which had invented the arts of living, with domestic science as its core, was early interrupted by urges to violence and the organization of war bands.

How organized warfare started on its terrific historic career is not known, cannot be known. Malinowski, in his final work, published after his death, *Freedom and Civilization*

(1944), expressed the opinion that war is political and that the lowest primitive peoples are not warlike. Political scientists in modern times have traced the rise of the State to the war band. Current politics certainly demonstrate the intimate relation between politics and war, between States and their foreign policies. However this may be as to the union of War and State, the union has not been solely a masculine manifestation of power and values.

A German writer, signing the name of Sir Galahad, in a work published at Munich in 1932, *Mütter und Amazonen: Ein Umriss weiblicher Reiche (Mothers and Amazons: An Outline of Woman's Kingdoms)*, claimed by the author as the "first feminine culture history," described the highly explosive ways of belligerent females through long ages. And evidences of armed women have been discovered in the European excavations of ancient ruins, reinforcing the Greek contention that fighting women, the Amazons, were real women, not creatures of the imagination.

If, as often dreamed, the most remote days of humanity were idyllic, fights and wars certainly broke that harmony in very early times; and women were active in those conflicts in every way that men were, on some scale. Where they had power as rulers or in ruling families they often instigated and proclaimed wars and even marshaled their troops as they went into battle. They incited men to ferocity at the fighting fronts. They accompanied men on marauding expeditions. They fought in the ranks. They took up arms to defend their homes. They nursed men on battle fronts or kept households going while men were at battle, and they looked after the wounded on their return to civilian life.

There was not a type of war in which women did not participate. They were among the primitive hordes which went on looting expeditions against their neighbor or stood fast on their own ground in defense of their lives, herds, and fields. Old Roman records testify to the savagery of women in the Cimbrian tribes that swept down from the north into Rome. Among the Cimbrians, priestesses took charge of war captives. Standing on ladders which they carried with them to battle, they cut off the heads of prisoners, caught the blood in pots, and gave it to their men to drink, in the belief that it would double their strength.

Writing of the German tribes beyond the borders of the Empire, in the first century A.D., Tacitus devoted several passages to the "influence of women," especially in wars. He commenced this part of his *Germania* by saying that squadrons or battalions of soldiers were composed of families and clans. "Close by them, too," he went on, "are those who are dearest to them, so that they hear the shrieks of women, the cries of infants. They [women] are to every man the most sacred witnesses of his bravery — they are the most generous applauders. The soldier brings his wounds to his mother and wife. . . . Tradition says that armies already wavering or giving way have been rallied by women who, with earnest entreaties and bosoms laid bare, have vividly represented the horrors of captivity. . . . They [Germans] even believe that the sex has a certain sanctity and prescience, and they do not despise their counsels or make light of their answers. . . . They venerated Aurinia [as divinity], and many other women, but not with servile flatteries or with sham deifications."

One has only to go to Plutarch to discover how the Romans remembered their terrible encounters with barbarous hordes who were moving into their realm from the north. At Aquae Sextiae, 102 B.C., Plutarch stated, "the fight had been no less fierce with the women than with the men themselves. . . . They charged with swords and axes, and fell upon their opponents uttering a hideous outcry. . . . When summoned to surrender, they killed their children, slaughtered one another, and hanged themselves to trees." Dio Cassius declared that the Romans found the bodies of women in full armor among slain Marcomanni and Quadi. Other Roman writers said that several Gothic prisoners proved to be women and among the Varangians, who attacked the Byzantines, women were found wielding arms side by side with their men.

Women were no less vigorous in the defense of their homes, or their realms if they were rulers, against Roman imperial armies bent on conquest, subjection, and exploitation — the "civilized" Romans being about as brutal as the "barbarians" in their wars on other peoples. An illustration is provided in Roman accounts of the great British revolt against Roman tyranny, lust, and avarice, led by Queen Boadicea near the close of the first century A.D. Boadicea was the wife of a British king who died about the year 60, leaving his private property to his two daughters and to Nero, in the hope that the Roman Emperor would protect his kingdom and his family against Roman rapacity and cruelty; in vain, for the greed and ferocity of Roman administrators and military officers in Britain were unbounded.

According to Tacitus in *Agricola,* agitators went around among the Britons declaiming against the wrongs inflicted upon them by their Roman conquerors, and at length a revolt broke out. "Rousing each other by this and like language," Tacitus says, "under the leadership of Boadicea, a woman of kingly descent (for they admit no distinction of sex in their royal successions), they all rose in arms." The queen had herself been beaten by Roman officers or soldiers, her two daughters had been ravished, and the relatives of her late husband had been enslaved. So she was in a mood to fight the Romans to the last ditch.

For many days the Britons' uprising under Boadicea seemed to be on the verge of victory, but the tide turned. On the day of the last great battle, she made a flaming speech to her soldiers, reminding them of the evils inflicted on them by the Romans and urging them to defend their liberties. Her speech to the soldiers as reported by the Roman historian, Dio Cassius (epitome of John Xiphilinus), is to be found in the *Monumenta Historica Britannica,* pp. lv *ff.* Boadicea rode in a chariot with her two daughters to the front and took charge of the fighting. When her forces were finally overwhelmed by the superior military skill of the Romans, Boadicea committed suicide, thus sparing herself a worse fate at the hands of the Romans — representatives of the Augustan age of civilization.

Centuries before Boadicea undertook to defend her people against Roman oppression, another widowed queen far away on the borders of Persia, Tomyris, ruler of the Massagetae, a tribe called "savage" by some historians, took up arms against Cyrus, called "the Great," who wanted to add her patrimony to his dominions. Cyrus had proposed marriage but Tomyris suspected an ulterior motive — his hope of ruling her and her people — and she refused to marry him. Instead, she warned him that if he crossed the borders of her realm he would be slain. He ignored her warning and her army carried out her threat. Historians are not sure whether after the battle To-myris crucified Cyrus or hunted for his body and, finding it, cut off his head and plunged it into a sack filled with human blood, so that the would-be conqueror could have enough of his own medicine, so to speak.

Women of antiquity not only went to war with marauding war bands or in defense of themselves and their people; they often initiated or inspired great military enterprises under-taken for the conquest and subjugation of others.

In the opinion of Konrad Bercovici, one of the biographers of Alexander the Great, Alexander was driven from home to become the master of the world by his militant Epirote mother, Olympia, a priestess to whom his father, Philip, had been attracted when he saw her as maiden prancing to or from a temple with a snake, a god symbol, held high in her arms, and attended by a procession of other maidens. In Macedonia at the time of this family's sway the half-sister of Alexander, Cyname, was given military training — a cus-tom in other strong families for girls and boys. And some women gave it to themselves as fighters for the love of fighting.

However justifiable or unjustifiable Bercovici's explanation of Alexander's imperialist aggression may be must be left to a full exploration of documentary sources if there be any which can prove the "cause." But that Macedonian women of the governing élite were disposed to violence is beyond question, for the records prove it. Nevertheless women of Macedonian ancestry who became queens during the Ptole-maic regime in Egypt often took leadership of a constructive kind in that land, particularly in relation to improvements in agriculture.

The immortal queen of Egypt, Cleopatra, "by descent half Macedonian and (apparently) half Greek," must also be placed, in terms of power, among the defenders of a realm. Writers have made much of her "sex appeal," but historians familiar with the documents of her history go beyond this superficial judgment of her whole personality to her role as administrator and protector of her people. They tell us that she was not "especially beautiful" but attracted masterful men by other qualities. Then they emphasize other facts. "Apart from her attractions, she was highly educated, interested in literary studies, conversant with many languages, and a skilled organizer and woman of business. . . . The moral code had little meaning to her; she was her own law. . . . The keynote of her character was not sex at all, but ambition . . . bent to the pursuit of one object, power." And with all her mighty energies she followed that objective in her contests with Roman Caesars — to the bitter end, until the victory of Octavianus over Antony at Actium in 31 A.D. led her to take her own life, for it was then her nemesis that she could no longer hope to recover her realm.

Space does not permit even the barest review of efforts on the part of many other women in ancient times to use war as an instrument of policy in defending themselves and their realms against the overweening military power of imperial Rome. But if Cleopatra is to be singled out, so also must be Zenobia, Queen of Palmyra on the border of the Arabian desert. Zenobia admired Cleopatra but Zenobia operated more directly in actual military exploits, and was more spectacular in her flaming determination to extend her dominions. Zenobia came to the throne on the death of her husband about 266 A.D. Perhaps she expedited if she did not actually bring about his death. According to Nabia Abbott, a specialist in Arabian history, Zenobia's Semitic name was Bath-Zabbia, as recorded in inscriptions. Like Cleopatra, she was interested in learning, commerce, politics, and administration. She was familiar with Greek culture and had a broad knowledge of Egyptian letters.

Zenobia's husband had appeased the Romans by an alliance with them for defense. But Zenobia defied them. Not content with her dominion over Palmyra, she sought to bring all Syria, Western Asia, and Egypt under her scepter and thus justify the title she claimed as Queen of the East. In so doing she brought down upon her head the wrath of the Emperor Aurelian and ultimately the full weight of Roman power. She was however not an arm-chair strategist, for she donned martial attire, joined her troops, and "shared their toils on horseback and on foot." Besieged at last in Palmyra and refusing to make a compromise peace, Zenobia fell into Roman hands. "Loaded with costly jewels, fettered hand and foot with shackles of gold, she was led by a golden chain before the chariot of Aurelian, along the Sacred Way, while all Rome gazed, with eager curiosity, on the Arabian princess." After she had been used in a triumphal procession to demonstrate the prowess of her imperial captor and excite Roman crowds, Zenobia was allowed to retire and live quietly in a villa near Tivoli.

Nor were all women passive observers and silent victims of the numerous wars waged under the sanction of religion in far-off times and places. The love of power and strife that motivated Zenobia likewise characterized women of Arabia in the Islamic age. With a fury that may fairly be described as tigerish, women waged holy wars for and against the faith proclaimed by Mohammed. While the Prophet was still alive, one of his fiercest foes was a woman of a great clan called Hind, Hind al-Hunūd, "the Hind of Hinds." According to Nabia Abbott, in an article on "Woman and the State on the Eve of Islam," Hind al-Hunūd lived in the kingdom of Kindah, founded in the fifth century A.D. She sprang from a people known as the Quraish, who had long been dominant at Mecca, the great city of the Prophet. Tradition depicts her "as a woman holding to the heathen practices of Arabia, a wife whose virtue was not above suspicion, a mind that was quick to decisive actions."

One of the heathen traditions to which she adhered was the cult of the Lady of Victory. Its functions was to incite patriotism and lash patriots into ferocious fighting. The Lady of Victory was a woman of high social standing about whom the feminine cult members, likewise of high rank, gathered in the pavilion sacred to the local or tribal deity, within sight of the warriors whom they stirred to martial fervor by their war songs which they accompanied on their lutes. Around the Lady of Victory and her retinue the battle raged until it was lost or won.

In an armed contest between the Quraish and the forces of Mohammed, several of Hind al-Hunūd's relatives were engaged. That battle occurred at Badr. Her father, her uncle, and a brother were slain. But her husband, Abu Sifyan, survived and, with him, she prepared to wreak vengeance. When the time for the assault was ready, she as the Lady of Victory took her position in a sacred pavilion with fourteen or fifteen aristocratic women at her side. In the presence of these women the men were expected to fight, win or die.

This time the Quraish were victors. The story then runs to the effect that, standing on a rock, among the corpses of the foe, the Hind of Hinds "exultantly flaunted in the face of the fallen enemy the general victory and her personal revenge, in spontaneous satirical verse which drew answer from the women of Mohammed's party and later from Hassan ibn Thabit."

Despite this triumph, the Hind of Hind's husband afterward surrendered the city of Makkah to Mohammed. For that offense she wanted to kill her mate. But her husband defended himself by appealing to his people with the cry: "O people, become Moslems and be saved!" It was not long until Hind al-Hunūd had to accept the Prophet's religion herself. And her step-daughter, Ramlah bint Abi Sufyan, married Mohammed, as did other women, to forward their political designs or his, at least in part.

After the death of Mohammed, women waged contests over the succession to power and for centuries played an active role in conflicts and wars within the Islamic world and against Christians and pagans, in the name of the faith. Take a single example from the pages of history less known in the West, that of Turkan Kahtun, daughter of Tamghaj Khan, wife of Malik Shah dauntless leader of the Seljuk Turks whose empire extended, in the eleventh century A.D., from the Black Sea to the Persian Gulf and beyond.

In her quest for power, Turkan became an implacable foe of the Shah's grand vizier and, when a civil war broke out, largely as a result of her intrigues on behalf of her son over the succession to the throne, she took part in the maneuvers connected with the struggle. She secured the appointment of a vizier favorable to her plan; had her son, aged four, proclaimed Sultan; seized the city of Ispahan; sought allies; and started a war against the rival claimant. She offered to marry a brother-in-law if he would come to her aid and she cast about for other assistance. In the end she came to grief; she was captured and executed by her step-son, for whom she had risked everything.

East and West, wherever wars were fought, during the following centuries — wars of conquest or defense, of crusades or of self-protection — it was rarely, if ever, that women held entirely aloof. As long as the Eastern Empire lasted, they were intrepid, often masterful, in affairs of state that eventuated in armed conflicts. As the Empire of the East crumbled and feudal wars took the place of wars for imperial expansion, women belonging to aristocratic and royal families inspired wars, frequently initiated them, and sometimes used arms themselves, to say nothing of their share in the consequences of combats, favorable or disastrous. Indeed, as we shall now see, they were highly instrumental in building up the great states of the Western world which in time to come were to transform local contests-at-arms into global wars, with the assistance of women.

MAKING GREAT STATES AND SOCIETIES

The rise and growth of great States and great Societies, amid almost endless warfare, constitute perhaps the most elemental phase of long history. And in a measure not yet appreciated by historians, judging from their writings, the history of the State and Society, until the very edge of our living time, was the history of the family, clan, and tribe and of struggles among them for political and economic ascendancy. Class struggles were scattered all through this history; but great ruling families generally suppressed class uprisings or made use of one class against another in their contests for supremacy. These facts demand repetition and accent in every effort to get at the center of man and woman relationships connected with great social and political designs.

Casual bands of men collected from among members of a clan or tribe and directed by a chance leader, or *dux* as the Romans called him, did occasionally go out, conquer, and settle down upon neighboring peoples; but generally, in the building of great States and Societies, a family, clan, tribe or union of tribes extended its power by invading territories under its own chieftain and subdued other peoples to its authority.

Not only is this a fundamental datum of long history. Even the beginnings of human history, of those older aggregations of peoples over which great states were established, with which great societies were formed by consolidations, are to be found in associations of some kind — in groups of men, women, and children held together by loyalties to the groups.

The most primitive association may have been, as certain anthropologists maintain, a loosely organized and wandering
"pack," living almost on the level of wild animals; even so
it was not a collection of "free and equal *men*" struggling
along individually. Man was and is born of woman and
woman was and is the daughter of man; association of some
kind has been from the earliest times necessary to their existence. This is obvious, as Herbert Spencer once remarked
solemnly.

Nevertheless from the seventeenth century forward, political writers were fond of locating the origin of the State in a
primeval gathering of men who, in order to secure protection
of life and property, formed a permanent union and surrendered a part of their "original" liberty. This was the fiction
which Rousseau expounded with passionate rhetoric on the
eve of the French Revolution. It had hardly been discredited
by scientific research when the Darwinians, forgetting the
warnings of their master, Charles Darwin, made "all nature
red in tooth and claw" — an everlasting combat of individual
men for existence, wealth, and power. Then the economists
came along and reduced individualism to a "science," Society to a shadow, and the State to a mere policeman keeping
order over individual *men* battling with one another about
the acquisition of wealth. Except for traditionalists, however, these fictions have been exploded.

When the curtain begins to rise on history as recorded, we
see the play of families, clans, and tribes begin — not a play
of individuals scattered at random hither and yon on the
human stage. If the *Odyssey* and the writings of Hesiod (8th
century B.C.) give faithful pictures of early social practices
among the Greeks, as they presumably do in some respects,
the primary unit of society was composed of the clan-family
and the phratry. The larger political societies later formed
among the Greeks were aggregations of such primary units.

Similar groupings are found in the earliest days of Roman
history. The primary unit was the *familia,* the family, the
household. As in the course of many generations the family
grew in size, it became a *gens,* a blood union of men, women,
and children united by a comman name, an emblem, and
common religious rites. In time families were united in a
larger grouping known as the *curia; curiae* were joined to

make a tribe; and at length three tribes were joined to form the State — Roman Society with a political head.

Although mythology and fable are mingled in the accounts from which this picture of Roman associations is derived, although it may be too simple as thus starkly presented, there is good reason for believing that it is substantially true to life as history. The constitution of the early Roman kingdom was based upon such family groups. The *curiae* of the people, composed mainly of plebeians, each curia a society, were combined to make the Roman assembly, known as the *comitia curiata;* and men from about three hundred noble families formed the Senate. After 509 B.C., in the early days of the republic, the people were organized for military and political purposes into classes according to property, but the Senate was retained as a body of men drawn from the aristocratic families of Roman society.

As the Roman republic extended its territorial boundaries, Roman society became more populous, the estates of great families expanded at the expense of the small farmers, or plebeians, and extremes of wealth and poverty became a sign of a new order. Then class conflicts arose in Rome — conflicts between patrician families on one side, and plebeians on the other side, while the urban proletarians often served the upper class. Concerning the leaders of the aristocrats and of the people in many of these contests, the records of history give us little information; but we know that in the most famous of all such conflicts leadership in the plebeian cause was taken by two men connected with the oldest and highest of the nobility — Tiberius and Gaius Gracchus. Since this momentous struggle occurred in the second century B.C., it comes within the range of authentic history; and it is possible to obtain from documents clear if short accounts of families involved in it, of the two great leaders who espoused the popular cause, and of some of the Roman women who participated in the contest of ideas and interests that accompanied it.

Here, to borrow Carlyle's imagery, for a brief time as if by a flash of lightning the stage is flooded and we may see the actors and the drama before our very eyes. On their father's side the two leaders, the Gracchi, sprang from one of Rome's most illustrious families which had originated in the plebeian

Sempronian *gens*. On their mother's side they belonged to the powerful aristocratic family of P. Cornelius Scipio Africanus, ranked by some historians as "the greatest man of his age and perhaps the greatest man of Rome, with the exception of Julius Caesar."

Cornelia, the mother of the Gracchi, had married Tiberius Sempronius Gracchus, Roman censor, in 169 B.C. The plebeian origin of Gracchus made her patrician father hostile to this marriage and whether it took place before his death or afterward is among the disputed points of scholarship. Anyway, Cornelia insisted on marrying the man of her choice and to this union twelve children were born.

After the early death of her husband, Cornelia devoted herself to the education of her children. When Ptolemy offered to share his crown with her, she declined and kept to her self-appointed task. Presumably she was well prepared for it. In her girlhood she had been taught classical literature and philosophy by scholars installed in the household by her father, who was one of the earliest patrons of Hellenic teachers. She was familiar with the Greek language and spoke her Latin tongue with purity and elegance. "Her letters, which were extant in the time of Cicero, were models of composition, and it was doubtless mainly owing to her judicious training that her sons became in later life such distinguished orators and statesmen." Cicero acclaimed her, as he did his mother-in-law, for her literary talents, and Plutarch paid homage to her for her "parental affection and greatness of mind."

It is reasonably certain that Cornelia instilled in her children the principles of the republican tradition and a high sense of the public responsibilities attached to their citizenship. Positively, the mother was a close companion of the two sons who were to lead the revolt against aristocratic greed, and their respect for her is revealed in the records of their relation. In seems certain that Tiberius was induced to propose some of his agrarian reforms at the instigation of his mother and highly probable that her other son, Gaius, was moved by her intercession to drop one of his proposals. After the cause in which her sons were so prominent as leaders was lost and they had met tragic, premature deaths, Cornelia retired to a country estate where she was visited by men of affairs and men of letters who came from near and far to pay her honor and discuss with her philosophy, letters, and the times. Not long after her death the Roman people erected a monument to her, bearing the inscription now so memorable though now too lightly interpreted: "Cornelia, Mother of the Gracchi."

The two Gracchi, who sought to regenerate the republic and effect a better distribution of wealth among the people, perished by violence at the hands of their enemies — led by scions of great aristocratic families. In 133 B.C., when his farmer friends were at home busy with their crops, Tiberius was beaten to death by a mob, after a crowd of Senators, aided by their henchmen, had dissolved and broken up the popular assembly. In 121, inflamed by Opimius — a bitter foe of the Gracchi, leader of the high aristocratic party, powerful in the Senate, a man of violent temper — a mob of Romans murdered Gaius Gracchus and more than three thousand of his supporters. This chapter of family history was closed by the suppression of the plebeian class revolt.

At last rid of the two popular leaders, the nobles, monopolizing the Senate and all the highest offices, repealed the agrarian laws and used the expedient of cheap bread for the proletariat as a means of maintaining themselves in power. Nominally the greatest families of Rome, operating through the Senate, had triumphed over plebeians and proletarians; but they could keep no solid front against their foes. In the midst of social and foreign wars, they broke apart, preyed upon one another in terrible proscriptions, and kept Rome in fear and turmoil — until all noble families and the people as well were brought under the domination of Julius Caesar, nominally a leader of the people, unquestionably the scion of a great aristocratic family. Soon the despotism of empire under the sway of strong families put a brake on class conflicts, if not an end to them.

Upon the assassination of Caesar in 44 B.C., power of state passed for a time to two representatives of great families, Octavianus, nephew of Caesar, and Antony. But Antony fell victim to his own ambition and the charms of Cleopatra; after his fleet was defeated at Actium, 31 B.C., by that of Octavianus, Antony committed suicide, in the belief that Cleopatra had already taken her life. Having at last, in his own hands, all the symbols of state power, Octavianus in effect abolished the republic, reduced the senatorial families to impotence, and founded an authoritarian state on the ruins of popular institutions. Now government by anonymous masses and more or less anonymous nobles in the senate in reality drew to a close, though the republican tradition long continued as a formality. Now men and women bearing imperial titles assumed dictatorial might.

For nearly four hundred years, that is until 364 A.D., the Roman State was ruled by a long line of emperors who came to power in the competition among families, aided, abetted, or opposed by women of those families. Then the empire was divided into western and eastern parts, and each part had its own line of emperors, until 476, when the unhappy Romulus Augustulus laid down his symbols of an authority that had vanished and only the eastern empire with its capital at Constantinople survived. There, a succession of emperors, some weak, some mighty, ruled for nearly a thousand years, until 1453 A.D. when the Turks captured their imperial city.

For four hundred years in the West and for nearly ten centuries in the East, imperial power was ostensibly vested in some man at the head of some family clan. Actually, however, if not officially, his power was often shared by a woman or by several women. Frequently imperial power was exercised openly by one or more women.

With respect to the inner history of the older period when power was widely dispersed among men seated in the popular Assembly and among hundreds of family clans represented in the Senate, little was set down as its record. But after imperial centralization was effected and literacy had spread in Roman society, the documentation of politics and society became profuse and varied in its abundance. With the government of a great society concentrated in one great family after another, writing in many media — poetry, history, satire, eulogy — about Society and the State became phenomenal.

It is now possible, therefore, for modern inquirers to obtain detailed and often extensive knowledge concerning Roman families and Roman women in the imperial State — knowledge of women's operations, methods, and objectives as a force in that State. The documentation is immense. Biographies and histories written by moderns on the basis of that documentation are now available; they are positively staggering in the wealth of evidence they offer on this aspect of woman's historic force. Among such studies of ancient Rome are the 1,124 pages of the old work by J. R. de Serviez, *Roman Empresses . . . Wives of the Twelve Caesars,* first published in the eighteenth century — an age of despotism in Europe; and G. Ferrero's *Women of the Caesars,* published in 1911 when the power of European family clans was rapidly dissolving.

Of course the whole story of the rise and decline of the Roman empire, with the women of the Caesars included, cannot be told here. It is not all known. But phases of it can be illustrated. And we may properly begin with Livia Drusilla, wife of Augustus, the nephew of Julius Caesar and called "founder of the empire."

Livia was the daughter of Livius Drusus Claudianus, that is, a member of the Claudian clan, but she was later adopted into the Livian *gens.* Although it must be said that modern historians differ widely in their judgments of her character and activities, they are in agreement that her influence in Roman affairs was emphatic. Support for the verdict of her influence appears in the following account of her written by a scholar for William Smith's *Dictionary of Greek and Roman Biography and Mythology:*

"Livia never bore Augustus any children, but she continued to have unbounded influence over him till the time of his death. The empire which she had gained by her charms she maintained by the purity of her conduct and the fascination of her manners, as well as by a perfect knowledge of the character of Augustus, whom she endeavored to please in every way. She was a consummate actress, excelled in dissimulation and intrigue, and never troubled herself or her husband by complaining of the numerous mistresses of the latter. There was only one subject which occasioned any dissension between them, and that was the succession.

"Augustus naturally wished to secure it for his own family, but Livia resolved to obtain it for her own children; and, according to the common opinion at Rome, she did not scruple to employ foul means to remove out of the way the family of her husband. Hence she was said to be [by Tacitus], '*gravis in rempublicam mater, gravis domui Caesarum noverca.* The premature death of Marcellus was attributed by many to her machinations, because he had been preferred to her sons as the husband of Julia, the daughter of Augustus. But for this there seems little ground. The opportune death both of C. Caesar and L. Caesar seems much more suspicious. These young men were the children of Julia by her marriage with Agrippa; and being the grandchildren of Augustus, they presented, as long as they lived, an insuperable obstacle to the accession of Tiberius, the son of Livia [by her former husband]. But Lucius died suddenly at Massilia in A.D. 2, and Caius in Lycia A.D. 4, of a wound, which was not considered at all dangerous. It was generally suspected that they had both been poisoned, by the secret orders of Livia and Tiberius. She was even suspected of having hastened the death of Augustus in A.D. 14.

"Augustus left Livia and Tiberius as his heirs; and by his testament adopted her into the Julia gens, in consequence of which she received the name of Julia Augusta. By the accession of her son to the imperial throne, Livia had now attained the long-cherished object of her ambition, and by means of her son thought to reign over the Roman world. But this the jealous temper of Tiberius would not brook. At first all public documents were signed by her as well as by Tiberius, and letters on public business were addressed to her as well as to the emperor; and with the exception of her not appearing in person in the senate or the assemblies of the army and the people, she acted as if she were the sovereign. She openly said that it was she who procured the empire for Tiberius, and to gratify her the senate proposed to confer upon her various extraordinary honors.

"Thereupon Tiberius, perceiving that he was becoming a mere cypher in the state, forbade all these honors, and commanded her to retire altogether from public affairs; but she had gained such an ascendancy over him, that he did not feel himself his own master as long as he was in her neighborhood, and accordingly removed his residence from Rome to Capreae. Such was the return she was destined to receive for all the toil she had sustained and the crimes she had probably committed in order to secure the empire for her son. Tiberius no longer disguised the hatred he felt for his mother, and for the space of three years he only spoke to her once. When she was on her death-bed he even refused to visit her. She died in A.D. 29 . . . at a very advanced age, eighty-two according to Pliny, eighty-six according to Dion Cassius.

"Tiberius took no part in the funeral rites and forbade her consecration, which had been proposed by the senate, on the ground that she had not wished it herself. Her funeral oration was delivered by her great-grandson, C. Caesar, subsequently the emperor Caligula; but Tiberius would not allow her testament to be carried into effect. The legacies which she had left were not fully paid till the accession of Caligula; and her consecration did not take place till the reign of Claudius."

Contrary to this vision of Livia as consumed with personal ambition is Ferrero's view that she was a defender of republican virtues against the luxury-loving, indolent, or power-hungry aristocrats of her day.

Between the time of Livia and the last days of the Roman Empire, many families and dynasties had their turns at the exercise of State power. Among these families were all kinds of empresses and ambitious women who sought to make emperors, therewith influencing or directing the course of public affairs. Often women in this long list were highly praised by historians, poets, and philosophers. Lucian, of the second century, who enchanted many Roman audiences with witty and wise comments on various aspects of Roman life, wrote a panegyric to an unknown woman, supposed to be an empress, which for centuries served as a model for thousands of men who eulogized women. Other writers represented many women of the Caesars and women contestants for Caesar's power as vixens, murderers, and moral degenerates. Hence modern students are frequently baffled in trying to reach fair judgments. Undoubtedly, struggling for power, or merely holding it, was not soft business and the women engaged in it were tough.

Whether any of those women was or was not a viper cannot be determined alone from a study of Tacitus' writings. Modern scholarship has begun to check his works with reference to the writings of other Romans and their sources of data.

Tacitus had at hand the *Memoirs* of Agrippina I, wife of Germanicus, to consult in his treatment of the Roman campaign in Gaul and also the *Memoirs* of her daughter Agrippina II in his treatment of later events in Rome. But Tacitus is now suspected of having a special cause of his own to serve by his manner of relating events, reporting observations, and making judgments. Hence modern historians who rely on his accounts of the women of his time are likewise subject to questioning.

On the other hand Plutarch with his penchant for drawing murals from Roman history pictured many Roman women as models of virtue. G. Ferrero of the modern age, in building up the Roman background for Italian glory, also glorified certain Roman empresses whom Tacitus represented as amoral or deliberately vicious. Where does the truth lie as between Tacitus' account of Agrippina II, for example, and the recent account by Ferrero of this same empress?

Agrippina II was the daughter of Agrippina I and Germanicus and the mother of Nero. Through her influence, it seems to be agreed, Claudius was induced to dispose of his irresponsible, lewd, and corrupt spouse, Messalina, for whom no historians attempt seriously to apologize. When Messalina was slain, it also seems to be agreed, Agrippina II induced Claudius to marry her. In a little while after their wedding, Claudius was murdered and his death was attributed to her, the deed being ascribed by some writers to her resolve to get rid of him before he got rid of her. Upon the death of Claudius, Agrippina II, who had plotted to put Nero, her son by a former marriage, on the throne, succeeded in doing it and acted as regent for him. But what had been her purpose in having Messalina removed from the palace and in removing Claudius from the throne if she was responsible for that too? What did she do when power came into her possession with the accession of Nero as emperor?

Ferrero claims that the "zenith of her power" was reached when Nero, on her advice, restored the republic. "Most historians," he says, "hallucinated by Tacitus, have not noticed this [that Nero's power was severely limited], and they have consequently not recognized that in carrying out this plan Agrippina is neither more nor less than the last continuator of the great political tradition founded by Augustus. In the minds both of Augustus and Tiberius [Livia's son whom she seated on the throne] the empire was to be governed by the aristocracy. The emperor was merely the depositary of certain powers of the nobility conceded to him for reasons of state. If these reasons of state should disappear, the powers would naturally revert to the nobles. It was therefore expedient at this time to make the senate forget, in the presence of a seventeen-year-old emperor, the pressure brought to bear upon it by the cohorts, and to wipe out the rancor against the imperial power which was still dormant in the aristocracy. This restoration was not, therefore, a sheer renunciation of privileges and powers inherent in the sovereign authority, but an act of political sagacity planned by a woman whose knowledge of the art of government had been received in the school of Augustus."

Agrippina II recalled Seneca from exile and made him her own main councilor. She also appointed him as tutor to Nero. She drew about her several statesmen, such as Afranius Burrhus, and together she and they framed an economic and political program for the empire, which Nero placed before the senate with a preliminary oration in its support. The program embraced imperial free trade, a better adminstration of the corn supply, recognition of the senate as an important factor in a secure government, and measures for general welfare. Nero was not yet twenty-one years old at that time.

But what began so auspiciously ended disastrously for mother and son. Agrippina was soon opposed by a court party led by Seneca and Burrhus. Seneca's influence over Nero was not entirely wholesome; and Nero came under the spell of courtesans. At length he decided to throw off bondage to his mother, and when he discovered that she was plotting to oust him in favor of Britannicus, son of Claudius, Nero had his mother murdered.

In short, Ferrero gives these explanations of Agrippina's objectives: she was really laboring to reëstablish the old patrician line, the Claudian clan; to restore political integrity; to get rid of the freedmen whom Messalina had used for the promotion of her conspiracies; to recover the loyalty of the praetorian guards and the Roman legions for a limited rule by a responsible government; to reinstate Seneca and thus eliminate the terrorism which Messalina had turned against

the Stoics, leading Paetus and his wife, Arria, to plunge a
dagger into their own hearts before it was thrust there by
Messalina's agents; and generally to save the ruling family
from destruction.

In the strife for supremacy among great Roman families,
the poisoning or assassination of men, time and again, threw
the management of a ruling or competing family into the
hands of women. Some women became regents for sons too
young to wear the crown. Some of them gave up the governing task to their sons when they had attained their majority.
Others kept a tight hold of it until death carried them off.

Imperial power required the backing of physical force and
actual or potential warfare. Among the women who did not
shrink from war when their power was at stake was Julia
Maesa, aunt of Caracalla. He was murdered and he left no
adult male heir to the throne. For a moment Julia Maesa
took charge of the family's fortunes and governed the State.
But, knowing that a male must wear the crown, she proceeded
to get one for it. In 217 A.D. a challenger, Macrinus, seized
the throne for himself. But Julia Maesa refused to let him
keep it. She belonged to a different clan — a Syrian family.
Though beset by bitter rivals at Rome, she went to Syria
for her army, taking with her a huge sum, "the fruit of twenty
years' favor," to aid in mustering her soldiers. She also took
along her two widowed daughters, Julia Soemis and Julia
Mamaea, each of whom bore with her a young son who could
be acclaimed a proper successor to Caracalla the Syrian.

Julia Maesa knew how to procure her army and how to
hold the soldiers together and make them fight successfully if
attacked by the troops of Macrinus. When her men seemed to
be wavering in their allegiance to her, Maesa inflamed their
loyalty by ordering one of her daughters, Soemis, to hold aloft
in their presence her little lad, Varius Avitus, while the grand-
mother pronounced the child the son of Caracalla and thus
the lawful heir to the throne. Objectors were overcome by
bribes and finally even they saw in the face of this boy the
features of Caracalla. This helped in the winning of the battle
with the soldiers of Macrinus, which had to be fought if
Julia Maesa was to make her way to Rome. At a crucial point
in its course, Julia Maesa and her daughters left their chariots

and lashed their troops into a hotter tempo, if only by their tongues and frantically waving arms. At the end the day was won for Julia Maesa. Her grandson, Varius Avitus, was seated on the throne in place of Macrinus, who had held it for about fourteen months. Then the young man's mother, Julia Soemis, came to power as regent for her son.

In fact, Julia Soemis was now Augusta. She took a seat in the Senate at Rome and was the president of a woman's parliament which held sessions in the Quirinal and drafted codes of etiquette. But mother and son met terrible dooms. Varius Avitus, officially known as Marcus Aurelius Antoninus, preferred the name of the Syrian god, Elagabalus, whom he served as high priest. Moreover he spent so much time in this service and, with his mother, indulged in such gross religious rites in this connection that angry Romans killed the two and threw the mother's body into the sewer.

Meanwhile, Julia Maesa, fearing trouble, had a new candidate ready for the throne, Alexander Severus, the son of her other daughter, Julia Mamaea. After a brief contest, he was duly seated and his mother became his regent. Having turned to the Christian religion, Julia Mamaea had her son instructed in its tenets as well as in poetry, history, and pre-Christian philosophy. So eclectic did Alexander become in his intellectual interests as he grew up that, according to Gibbon, he made room in his chapel for all the religions of the wide Roman Empire, Christ thus mingling with Orpheus in the palace, while the Jews were granted broad liberties in life beyond its portals.

Julia Mamaea was thrifty and she apparently preferred peace to war. She withheld from the army sums of money which it craved and this was to plague her when she accompanied her son, Alexander, on a campaign against the Germans in Gaul. There she advised him to make peace. He had been all along so amenable to her advice that he was ready to take it again on this occasion. This infuriated the soldiers and in their resentment a small band of them slew Mamaea and killed her son. With his last breath, it is said, Alexander fumed against his mother as his evil genius.

Far away in space from the palace of the Caesars on the banks of the Tiber and across the centuries from the age of the first Augustus, another Roman empress, even more powerful in admitted fact than Livia, wife of Octavianus, seized and exercised sovereign power in her own right. She was Pulcheria, daughter of Arcadius, emperor of the East. In 408 A.D. Arcadius died, leaving a seven-year-old son, Theodosius, and three or four daughters. For a few years imperial affairs were in the hands of male regents, but in 414 one of the daughters, Pulcheria, aged fifteen, just two years older than Theodosius, took over the regency, was proclaimed Augusta, and until her death nearly forty years later was masterful in the direction of state affairs in the East.

In the pages of fifth-century documents and in scholarly monographs of the modern age, Pulcheria stands out with a distinctness given to few other women of that time. Even Hypatia, the great Neoplatonist teacher at Alexandria, a contemporary of Pulcheria, is more obscure in the pages of history though something about her is known — in part through letters in which her pupils paid her high compliments. Hypatia was a pagan and Egypt was officially Christian. Hypatia was thus out of order especially in her defiance of the Christian theology and her teaching of pagan philosophy. She paid an awful price for her temerity: death by assassination at the hands of a mob. Pulcheria, on the contrary, was a Christian by birth and Eastern Christendom has remembered her well on account of her services to the Christian Church. She was, however, neither responsible for the assassination of Hypatia nor pleased over it. She regretted it.

Pulcheria had been educated in pagan learning. She read and spoke Greek and Latin fluently. She was deeply interested in medicine and natural science. Though she had young Theodosius taught horsemanship and the use of arms, she instructed him in broader subjects and rhetoric. The charge was made that, in order to keep him like clay in her hands, she deliberately refrained from disciplining him in public matters which would have better prepared him for his role as emperor.

Pulcheria avoided such marital entanglements in politics as marriage might occasion. She took a vow of perpetual virginity and throughout the rest of her life made much of religious devotions. Meanwhile she was ever watchful and active in public affairs. When the time came for Theodosius

to marry, she chose a wife for him, Eudoxia, the daughter
of an Athenian sophist. After Theodosius became of age
and publicly assumed imperial authority, Pulcheria maintained her vigilance.

When in 450 he died as the result of a fall from his horse
while hunting, Pulcheria again took over the reins and appointed his successor, Marcian, chief of staff for the army.
Before the Senate, she placed the crown on Marcian's head,
and then to assure her grip on things she made him her husband, at least formally. Not until death cut her down three
years later was her firm grasp on the government broken. By
will she left all her vast estate to the poor, thus demonstrating the sincerity of her religious faith, and Marcian was careful to fulfill her final injunction. Later she was canonized
and her career was long celebrated by the Greek Orthodox
Church.

Before the death of Pulcheria in the East, the Roman
Empire of the West had begun to disintegrate. In 476 it
nominally came to an end. From the banks of the Tiber to
the borders of Scotland, it was invaded and overrun by barbarians from the north and east. In Italy, Gaul, Spain, and
Britain, Roman power dissolved; anarchy took the place of
law and order; and these once solid divisions of the Empire
split into fragments — cities, duchies, principalities, and petty
feudal estates. The great Roman families who had for so
long ruled in the Empire disappeared nearly everywhere, or
were merged with the barbarian invaders. In vain did Popes
at Rome seek to stem the tide of disintegration by substituting the authority and law of the Church for the power and
law of the old Roman State.

Once more darkness settled down on political history. For
centuries the chief historians were monks hidden away from
public life in their monasteries; they were cloistered dream-
ers, not men of public affairs, such as Tacitus, the Roman,
had been; and the so-called histories written by the monks
were made up principally of stories about the good or wicked
deeds of kings and princes, which they knew mainly or entirely from hearsay, interspersed with tales of miracles and
such curiosities of nature as a meteor shooting through the
sky. As far as the minor personalities, communities of peo-

ple, and social events of their times are concerned, their "histories" are of little aid in the search by modern scholars for knowledge of their age.

But in the relatively scanty documentation of the early middle ages is carried a good deal of information about the doings and sayings of many great warlords who tore the Roman Empire to pieces and of the Christian missionaries, monks, and nuns who labored to keep the faith alive and spread it to the ends of the still barbarian world. From the fragmentary records, chronicles, laws, lives of saints, and other sources, something can be gleaned about the labors, trials, and conditions of the anonymous multitudes that toiled at maintaining life and economy. By piecing fragments together, historians are able to describe today with some accuracy and fullness the general course of political and related events from the break-up of the Roman Empire to the rise of modern states and societies in Italy, France, Spain, England, and other parts of Western Europe.

In the general course of political events, in this large theater of history-making, one feature was continuous and clinching everyhere: the renewed competition of great families for power over territories large and small, each inhabited mainly by families of serfs. As the curtain of history rises higher and higher on the scenes of those endless conflicts, the names of the more powerful families — and of men and women who composed them — were entered in the records in ever-increasing numbers. Although hundreds, thousands, of the lesser families are lost forever in the oblivion of namelessness, modern scholarship in history has supplied evidence for the proposition that the political history of the West for centuries after the collapse of the Roman Empire was again the history of strife among feuding landed families for supremacy. The final triumph of the strongest families marked the creation of the modern states. Again women of ambitious families displayed their ambitions for power, for themselves and their clans.

In England this process culminated first. After about six centuries of feudal turmoil in this former province of the Roman Empire, William the Norman conquered England, centralized authority in a monarchy, and blazed the way for his successors to extend it over Wales and the rest of Great

Britain. Never again after the Norman conquest in 1066 did England fall back into the kind of feudal anarchy that had filled the Anglo-Saxon period with tumult. There were, to be sure, many struggles among English aristocratic families for power, but this ceased to assume the form of open and dangerous violence after the Wars of the Roses — the contests between the Yorkist and Lancastrian families, which were brought to a close on the field of Bosworth in 1485. There Henry Tudor, the Lancastrian claimant, under the banner of the Red Rose, slew Richard III, the Yorkist; and to seal the triumph Henry, as he had promised some of his supporters to do, married Elizabeth, daughter and heiress of Edward IV, the tragic woman whose two brothers had been murdered by Richard III.

The Tudor victor at Bosworth, duly crowned Henry VII, with the aid of his queen, Elizabeth, set about the work of strengthening the monarchy against grumbling malcontents and two pretenders. Lambert Simnel, impersonating the Earl of Warwick, aided by Margaret, Duchess of Burgundy, sister of Edward IV, and then Perkin Warbeck, impersonating Richard, Duke of York, also aided by Margaret, tried to raise revolts; but they were quickly suppressed.

In accordance with the customary method for building up family power by influential marriages, the eldest son of Henry and Elizabeth, Arthur, was married to Catherine, the daughter of Ferdinand and Isabella of Spain and, after Arthur's death a few months later, their second son Henry was married to Catherine. Meanwhile, with a view to a union with Scotland, they negotiated a marriage between their eldest daughter, Margaret, and James IV, king of Scotland; and out of this matrimonial union came at length, about two centuries later, the political union of England and Scotland.

It was under a succession of five great feudal families that the anarchy of France which followed the dissolution of Rome was overcome, and that the numerous provinces, duchies, principalities, and other feudal subdivisions were finally fused into one great society under a monarchy. These great families were the Merovingians, the Carolingians, the Capetians, the Valois, and the Bourbons.

From first to last, women were associated with men in this process of State and Society building. Clovis, first of the

Merovingians, was undoubtedly a valiant warrior, but his wife, Clotilde, was no less valiant in her way. As a modern scholar says: "For his part Clovis well understood that he never would bring Gaul beneath his scepter without the support of the Church and the Catholic Gallo-Romans who were tired of anarchy. Clovis laid the foundations of the French state by his conversion to Christianity, due to his wife, Clotilde, and to Remigius [archbishop of Reims] rather than by his victory over the Alemanni at Tolbiac." And when, after the lapse of twelve centuries, the French monarchy under the Bourbon Louis XVI was shattered, it was the vigorous if mistaken efforts of the queen, Marie Antoinette, daughter of the watchful Austrian empress, Maria Theresa, to save the throne, rather than the frailties and follies of Louis himself, that brought the revolution to its fateful climax in 1793.

The course of feudal anarchy in Spain after the disappearance of Roman government resembled that in England and France, until at length in 1469 the union of two great landed families, followed by the expulsion of the robust Moors, brought long-warring provinces under one crown and into one society. This union was the marriage of Ferdinand, crown prince of Aragon, and Isabella, heiress to the throne of Castile. The political relations of Ferdinand and Isabella were established by the terms of their marriage contract, later amplified by special regulations.

These regulations "created a kind of dyarchy, in which justice was to be exercised conjointly when they happened to be together in the same place, or by either of them separately if they happened to be separated. Royal charters were signed by both, and the coinage bore both heads upon it, while the seals also contained the arms of both kingdoms. Apart from this the administration of Castile was reserved to Isabella in her own right. Ferdinand raised some difficulties about accepting this arrangement, but eventually he gave way. The principle of equality between the two spouses which resulted from this system is expressed in the well-known formula, 'Tanto monta, monta tanto, Isabel como Fernando,' which is found so often on contemporary monuments. . . . On the other hand, Isabella was not recognized to have any rights in the government of Aragon; she never interfered in the concerns of her husband's kingdom." A more perfect "liberty and equality" would be difficult to imagine; moreover, the terms of the bond were observed by both till death separated them.

As fate would have it, the unity of Spain, the close bond between Castile and Aragon, was severed on the death of Isabella in 1504, and the rupture plagued Spanish politics on through the centuries despite the nominal authority exercised by Spanish rulers over the whole kingdom. But Ferdinand and Isabella had set the plan for centralization in the peninsula, Isabella being the more energetic of the two in this enterprise. Moreover, by arranging marriages for their children, they affected to a high degree the course of European history in general. The marriage of their daughter, Catherine, to Henry VIII of England with the subsequent divorce was a leading factor in the Protestant revolt in England and in many a quarrel and war that followed. Even more fateful for Spain, perhaps, was the marriage of their daughter, Joanna, to Philip of Austria, son and heir of the Emperor Maximilian. By this marriage Spain was taken into the stormy conflicts of continental Europe, with results little short of disastrous for the Spanish people.

In the work of constructing and consolidating all the other independent states and societies that came into being in Europe, within and outside the borders of the old Roman Empire, feudal, princely, and royal families were likewise instrumental — until the very dawn of our own times. In Italy, Germany, Russia, and other parts of Europe, the process started later and was slow in coming to fruition. In Italy unification was not effected until 1870, under the house of Savoy; in Prussia and Germany consolidation came to its climax in 1871, under the Hohenzollern family; and in Austria-Hungary it was the Hapsburg family that directed the methods of centralization, particularly in the eighteenth and nineteenth centuries. Building on the work of previous dukes and princes, the Romanoffs carried forward in Russia the expansion and coalescence of the older states and societies to form the vast Russian Empire, inherited by the Bolsheviki in 1917. The Romanoffs descended in the female line from the Russian Michael Romanoff, elected Tsar in 1613, and in the male line from a branch of the Holstein-Gottorp family in Germany.

If one strikes into periods of the tortuous diplomacy and wars as recorded in the first ten volumes of the *Cambridge Modern History* covering the time from the Renaissance to the restoration of the Bourbons in 1815, what does one learn about the force and work of women? Let us take three examples beginning, arbitrarily, with Henry IV of France. His second wife was Maria de' Medici, whom he married in order to win over to his side, as against the Hapsburgs, the grand duke of Tuscany, her uncle. After Henry's assassination in 1610, Maria seized power as regent for their son, Louis XIII, and ran affairs with a high hand. Resolved on a diplomatic union with Austria and Spain, she married the young king to Anne of Austria, daughter of Philip, king of Spain. Determined to have no interference with her plans, she dissolved the Estates General in 1614 and sent the parliamentarians home, on the ground, she alleged, that she needed their halls for a dance. Athough her son grew weary of her autocratic ways and eventually pushed her aside, her matrimonial adventure on his behalf proved to be almost ruinous for France.

Without pausing to deal with the War of the Spanish Succession and the War of the Austrian Succession, let us review two fateful family "deals" in which women were matchless actors. The first was the "diplomatic revolution" in which fortunes of the Austrian Hapsburgs and those of the French Bourbons were united by a firm alliance in 1756. This startling reversal of foreign policy for France and Austria was effected under the direction of Maria Theresa, Empress of Austria, with the aid of Madame de Pompadour, mistress of Louis XV; while Elizabeth, Empress of Russia, looked on benevolently, with an eye to her interests as against Frederick the Great of Prussia. The union brought about by the diplomatic revolution was sealed several years later by the marriage of the French dauphin, Louis, to Marie Antoinette, daughter of the Empress Maria Theresa. The second of the great diplomatic deals, known as the "Family Compact," brought about a close alliance between the Bourbon states of France, Spain, and the two Sicilies in 1761 — an arrangement that drew Spain into the Seven Years War then raging in the Americas and Asia as well as in Europe.

Students of history differ as to the exact part played by

women in these two diplomatic maneuvers. Did the Empress Maria Theresa initiate the diplomatic revolution and control her ministers in the negotiations that eventuated in the overturn? Was it the influence of Madame de Pompadour that finally led the King of France to the point of accepting it? Some documents support affirmative answers; others ascribe the achievement, if such it was, mainly to the ministers and other men who acted as agents in effecting the bargain.

At all events the two women were deeply involved in the intricate transactions; and "comprehensive and balanced" history — any history that purports to "explain" how the deal was made — must reckon with all the evidence in the case. While any decisions of these matters of feminine "influence" — one way or the other — could have made little difference to the thousands of men killed and wounded in the battles that followed the diplomatic revolution, there is no doubt that women were entangled in the business of diplomacy and that it was family, not merely men's, interests which were at stake.

Although in some countries of Europe, even in the middle ages, the power of the royal families was often checked more or less by parliaments or estates-general of one kind or another, it was on the other hand often strengthened by these legislative and taxing bodies. Such parliaments represented estates, rather than individuals counted by heads. The English Parliament, for example, consisted of the House of Lords — the great lay and clerical barons of the realm; and the House of Commons — made up of representatives of the county gentry and the burgesses in towns. But, by the middle of the eighteenth century, all the great States of continental Europe were unhampered, as a rule despotic, monarchies.

In fact, for more than a century before the eve of the French Revolution, despotism had been increasing rather than diminishing in strength. Great Britain was then actually governed by the king and a few hundred great families represented by the peers in the House of Lords. The House of Commons, it is true, still existed and its members were elected by men; but out of about eight million people only 160,000 men were qualified to vote; and elections to the House were largely controlled by the king and the members of the aristocracy.

Not without good reason was the period preceding the French Revolution kncwn as "the age of despots"; and at that time Catherine the Great of Russia was among the harshest of despots. In other words, Europe was dominated by royal families in which women wielded immense power even when they did not reign in their own right as Catherine did.

And it must be remembered that royal and aristocratic families were landed families. Occasionally, as in England, a great lord of land married the daughter of a rich merchant. Yet, generally speaking, marriages among royal families were confined to that circle and the same rule was applied among the families of the aristocracies. Kings and queens, of course, had large revenues from taxes, as well as incomes from their landed property, and they spent much of their time in the cities looking after affairs of state. But aristocratic families, while they often went to the capital for a season if they were rich enough to afford it, depended principally, if not entirely, upon their country estates for their livelihood and devoted a great deal of thought and energy to the management of their properties.

The relations and activities of men and women on the land — the prime source of economic support from the dissolution of the Roman Empire until the rise of modern commerce and industry — differed in many respects from the relations of men and women engaged in crafts and commerce in the towns. This is a fact usually neglected by the writers of letters, polite and serious, in our age.

In the first place, rural families — aristocratic, servile, and freehold — survived, often intact, through the centuries, while craft and mercantile families appeared and disappeared with the fluctuating fortunes of commerce.

In the second place, in the rural familes the men and women lived and worked together in almost uninterrupted association from season to season, from year to year. There the husband and wife each had heavy obligations connected with the economy of household and field; and when the man was away in wars, so often the case, the woman assumed responsibilities for keeping the family going by managing its land and household economy.

All in all, this is to say: In the royal and the aristocratic families which governed most of Europe for centuries, women displayed great force, directly and indirectly, in the affairs of state and in the management of the underlying economy which sustained the monarchy.

Not until the commercial and political revolutions, accumulating full force in the eighteenth century, actually disrupted the solidarity of royal and aristocratic families founded on a landed wealth did women alike with the great families to which they belonged lose most of the power which they had so long exercised in the affairs of State and Society. Not until then did the state pass to the control of parliaments composed of men and elected by men.

The date, 1789, when the French Revolution opened, dramatizes this transfer of power. Yet the acquisition of political power by men-at-large came slowly and tediously in the opinion of men seeking enfranchisement, that is, the right to help make laws and hold offices of government. Nearly a hundred years elapsed before all the adult men of France definitely won full parliamentary suffrage. It was not until 1871 that all adult males in Germany were granted the suffrage for members of the new imperial Reichstag; and this right amounted to little, owing to the power retained by the imperial and royal families of that country up to the débâcle in 1918. The extension of manhood suffrage in Great Britain, begun by the reform bill of 1832, was not completed until the close of the first world war. Even in the United States the struggle of white men for the vote was long and hard; the general victory did not come until more than fifty years after the Declaration of Independence had asserted that "all men are created equal" — and not full victory, at that, in view of poll tax and other qualifications then or later imposed in parts of the United States.

Furthermore, the period between the dissolution of woman's political power in royal and aristocratic families and the general enfranchisement of women was relatively short as measured against the long centuries of royal and aristocratic rule. When the movement for woman suffrage was formally launched near the middle of the nineteenth century, millions of men were still striving for enfranchisement throughout the continent of Europe. Women were winning the suffrage in the more progressive societies years before manhood suffrage had been won in other societies.

All things considered, men's monopoly over politics under systems of manhood suffrage, never complete, was brief, compared with the ages in which royal and aristocratic women exercised power in affairs of State and Society. Moreover, when women's campaigns for enfranchisement are contrasted with the violent and often bloody contests which masses of men had to wage for their enfranchisement, it is patent that women won the right to vote by men's consent with relative ease, including as ease a smaller span of time. To the women who spent their adult years in agitating for the ballot, the contest seemed so severe and so prolonged as to try their souls to the uttermost. Nevertheless man, the "tyrant" and "usurper" of 1848, yielded the suffrage to women quicker and with more grace than women of royal and aristocratic families had bowed to the tempest of rising democracy, with its cry of "votes for men."

BEGINNINGS OF WESTERN SOCIAL PHILOSOPHY

Older than the State was Society, though not the Great Society. Underlying and necessary to the process of state-building through the centuries were societies. Long before state-building families started their large-scale operations, ancient and simpler societies existed — associations of men and women held together by personal loyalties, common ties, and the requirements of mutual aid — all indispensable to human existence. Furthermore, throughout history such personal loyalties, common ties, and mutual aid perdured, serving everywhere among the forces which kept society going and developing, if it did develop, and providing forces of opposition to sheer power, to tyranny, in the state.

A search for the origins and nature of the moral and intellectual qualities that animate and sustain societies leads far back behind recorded history into the very beginnings of association in the pre-literate time. But, if we take the records that furnish information about early societies in which mother-right, or mother-law, was the binding social force and infer that this was the original social datum, then woman was the veritable center and principal director or administrator of the primitive social organization. On the other hand, if we accept patriarchy as the primitive social datum or the datum of early recorded history, nevertheless woman, as wife, mother, daughter, was at the center of and a force in the social organization so constituted — in practice whatever may have been the alleged power of the husband and father as set forth in the extant fragments of early *law*.

Eventually in the course of social development, social emotions, moral sentiments, and ethical views came to expression in formulated ideas, and such ideas were employed by reflective thinkers in the creation of thought-systems to which the term, "philosophy," became applied.

For the Western world it was in particular the Greeks who first enclosed the social emotions, sentiments, and ethical ideas in well-rounded systems of conceptual thought. It is true, certainly, that the Greeks borrowed ideas from other peoples, that conceptions from such sources were later fused with Greek conceptions. Still, Greek thought provided the main principles from which the social philosophies of the West stemmed, whatever metaphysical constructs were added to them. Did not Socrates and Plato provide the West with the first well-defined social Utopia — *The Republic?* Did not Aristotle, the critic of Plato's communism, declare that "man is a political animal" — meaning in fact a man within society, or a social animal — and start with the family "constitution" as the primary datum of "politics"? Was it not Greek Stoicism that later evolved the doctrine of universal humanity — the kinship of all human beings?

The systems of speculation and logic-manipulation constructed in subsequent times, insofar as they had meaning and use for life, were based on or took into serious account the social content of philosophy. It was only after thinking became professionalized that "the original practical purpose" of thought was gradually lost to sight and "practised for its own sake as theoretical thought" — as though unrelated to life as it is and must be lived, in society.

It was the "professional" thinkers who became the strange creatures of the earth described by Erasmus in his *Praise of Folly* — "the rhetoricians," "the scribbling fops," "the lawyers [who] will cite you six hundred several precedents," "the logicians and sophisters" who will "wrangle bloodily over the

least trifle," "the philosophers in their long beards and short
cloaks who esteem themselves the only favorites of wisdom,"
and at last the petty "divines" who inquire "whether God,
who took our nature upon him in form of a man, could as
well have become a woman, a devil, a beast, an herb, or a
stone."

But, all along, those thinkers who have been "practical"
and kept close to the idea of thought as related realistically to
the experiences and purposes of life have sought to carry
forward and develop the social content inherent in the oldest
and the final philosophies of the ancient Greeks.

One of the earliest — and perhaps the first — rivals of the
hymnology of war, hatred, and revenge made immortal by
Homer was the poetry of an Aeolian woman called Sappha
by her people but uniformly known to later times as Sappho.
Exactly when she lived is a matter of literary debate but there
is considerable agreement that she belonged to the sixth century B.C. and this puts her after Homer. Sappho wrote poetry
to be sung to the harp and some Greek writers said that she
invented a species of harp.

Much of Sappho's poetry was of a plaintive tenderness but
she had a fervid feeling for love as a saving grace. Several
of her feminine disciples also sang of the beauty and healing
force of love. Solon the law-giver and Plato the philosopher
were deeply affected by her hymns to the great idea of a
social power unrecognized by "the Bible of the Greeks":
Homer. Though Attic poets and playwrights tried to destroy
her by attacking her as a courtesan or "Lesbian" pervert, the
German classical scholar, Welcker, in his *Kleine Schriften,*
declares that such attacks were sheer calumny. Nor did they
succeed in their aim. More than twenty centuries have
honored the "sweet singer" of Aeolia.

To Pythagoras a legend attributes the invention of the word
"philosophy" (*philosophia* in its Greek form) and the use of
it "in its original and widest sense" is defined as "the love,
study, or pursuit of wisdom, or of knowledge of things and
the causes, whether theoretical or practical." Now under the
title "Pythagoras," in encyclopaedias and biographical dic-
tionaries, the whole case of Pythagoreanism is commonly
set forth.

After investigating some of the original sources, the "expert" author of the article captioned "Pythagoras" in the *Dictionary of Greek and Roman Biography and Mythology* remarked: "That there were several women among the adherents of Pythagoras is pretty certain. That any were members of the club of 300 [at Crotona] is not so probable. Krische considers that these female Pythagoreans were only the wives and relations of members of the brotherhood, who were instructed in some of the Pythagorean doctrines. These would doubtless be mainly with the religious part of his system." This admission that women were anywhere near the "brotherhood" goes beyond other articles in later and broader compendia which call the whole Pythagorean Order a "brotherhood," without so much as mentioning wives and other relatives "instructed" in its cult.

But after the foregoing statement in this compendium of knowledge is the note: "Comp. Menage, *Hist. de Mul. Philos.*" This refers to the work on the history of women philosophers by Gilles Ménage, written in Latin and published in 1765. And if one consults Ménage as advised, what does one discover? The names of twenty-eight women philosophers classified as Pythagoreans. And if one hunts for those names in this *Dictionary,* one gets clues to more than their instruction mainly in the religious part of "his" (Pythagoras') system. Pushing the inquiry back into ancient Greek sources brings those women to life as participants in the making of this philosophy. There one meets Theano, assumed from the weight of evidence to be the wife of Pythagoras. Who and what was she?

Theano was beautiful, devoted to medicine, hygiene, the arts of ethical living, physics and mathematics, a commentator on the art of healing, and a writer on virtue in its large Greek meaning, such as Socrates later associated with it when he spoke of virtue. There were daughters of this "love match," which captivated the imagination of the Greeks, and they too were philosophers who helped to spread the system of thought which was developed within this family and given to the Pythagorean Order.

The Dictionary sketch of Theano runs as follows: "The most celebrated of the female philosophers of the Pythagorean school appears to have been the wife of Pythagoras, and the mother by him of Telauges, Mnesarchus, Myia, and Arignote;

but the accounts respecting her were various. . . . Her traditional fame for wisdom and virtue was of the highest order, and some interesting sayings are ascribed to her by Diogenes Laërtius, and by Clemens Alexandrinus. Diogenes also informs us that she left some writings, but he does not mention their titles. . . . Several interesting letters are still extant under her name; and, though it is now universally admitted that they cannot be genuine, they are valuable remains of a period of considerable antiquity. They were first edited in the Aldine collection of Greek Epistles [at Venice in 1499, almost as soon as the printing press had been invented]; then in the similar collection of Cujacius, Aurel. Allob. 1606, fol.; then in Gale's *Opuscula Mythologica*. . . . Cantab. 1671, Amst. 1688; then, far more accurately in Wolf's *Mulierum Graecarum Fragmenta,* 1739 . . . ; and lastly in Io. Conrad Orelli's *Socratis et Socraticorum, Pythagorae et Pythagoreorum, quae ferunter Epistolae* . . . Lips. 1815 . . . ; the Greek text is also printed with Wieland's admirable translation of the letters, Leipz. 1791. Wieland's translation is reprinted at the end of Orelli's work. . . . Suidas mentions another Theano. . . . also a Pythagorean . . . who wrote works on Pythagoras, on Virtue addressed to Hippodamus of Thurium. . . . It is pretty clear, however, that this is only another account, somewhat more confused, of the celebrated Theano."

Elsewhere one learns that Theano corresponded with Callisto on child psychology and the best way to bring up a family; that her treatise on Virtue contained the doctrine of the "golden mean," renowned as a major contribution of Greek thought to the evolution of social philosophy. After the death of Pythagoras, which occurred at the end of the sixth or the beginning of the fifth century B.C., Theano carried on the central school of the Order. Just how many daughters she and Pythagoras had is a matter of guessing but some of them seem to be well established in the records — women who, as teachers, writers, and missionaries, disseminated the philosophy of their parents.

Concerning the belief that Pythagoras himself, alone, formulated the entire system of philosophy known as Pythagoreanism, F. M. Cornford, writing on "Mystery Religions and Pre-Socratic Philosophy" in Volume IV of *The Cambridge Ancient History,* makes this important statement: "Any reconstruction" of his system "is largely conjectural." At the same time Cornford refers to "the pious tradition whereby the school [of Pythagoreans] ascribed all discoveries to the founder." Indeed this is true. Pythagoras left no writing of his own for judging his leadership, but his personality must have been commanding to have given him the character almost of a god.

The Pythagoreans were in the beginning a society of families, and at the heart of their thinking was society. In time, as the Order expanded in numbers and in centers, an ascetic faction took form and it has become a common habit today among writers on this philosophy to call the whole Order a brotherhood." But this is to miss its original tenets. This oversight may be due to the intense interest in the mathematical system evolved by the Order — mathematics developed into a cult by the Order. Aristotle said in one comment on the Pythagoreans that, having been brought up in mathematical science, the Pythagoreans "thought that its principles must be the principles of all existing things." And the distinguished modern philosopher and mathematician, Alfred Whitehead, in the chapter of his *Science and the Modern World* headed "Mathematics," pays high tribute to "Pythagoras" as the first to grasp the fundamental principles of modern philosophic thought.

Since philosophic thought transcends or embodies the idea of order inherent in mathematics, if Pythagoreans "thought that its principles must be the principles of all existing things," then more than their mathematics must be studied if one would try to comprehend their system of philosophy in its fullness. The larger study requires attention to the social elements which played so essential a part in it and this really requires a close consideration of the women of the Order in its early career.

With their interests and impulses as wives and mothers, an ideal of harmonious family living was evolved and related to interfamily unity in their society. Simple living was a basic principle but it was not to be dull living. Health was to be cultivated by a hygienic diet; the rhythms of music, dancing, and song were to promote it; and apparel was to be suited to the satisfaction of esthetic taste rather than display, as a means of happiness. The Pythagoreans were at first Orphics and as such regarded themselves as companions of gods and goddesses, not frightened inferiors of the deities.

On this point Cornford says: "Pythagoreanism . . . begins, not with the elimination of factors that once had a religious significance, but actually with a reconstruction of the religious life. To Pythagoras . . . the love of wisdom was a way of life. He heralded and inspired all those systems — Socratic, Stoic, Neoplatonic — in which knowledge, no longer the child of wonder and of the unacknowledged desire for power over nature, became, if not a mere means to virtuous living, at least identified with the well-being and well-doing of the human soul. . . . The earlier form of Pythagoreanism must have been a construction of the 'seen order' capable of providing for the needs of the unseen."

Eventually within the Pythagorean Order an ascetic strain other-worldliness, became manifest, as the membership enlarged and more types of persons were included in it. On the other hand, exuberance of spirit occasionally went as far as extravagant license among some members and Dionysus became their cult god. For various reasons the Order encountered the antagonism of outsiders, at its center in Crotona, a Greek colony in southern Italy, and in Grecia Magna where branches were founded. By the middle of the fifth century B.C. it was generally stamped out as an organization, but several of its most effective exponents escaped from hostile mobs and carried on their teaching in Thebes and other places where they could be fairly safe from enemies. For example, Lysis found his way to Egypt and became the instructor of Epaminondas.

According to tradition, Philolaus was the first to write on the Pythagorean system and he lived at Thebes at the end of the fifth century. But he returned later with companions to Italy and refounded a school at Taras (Tarentum). At Taras lived Archytas, a friend of Plato, and Plato observed Pythagorean societies in Italy when he went there to visit his friend.

If Plato's story of Diotima, the priestess of Mantinea, is to be accepted as authentic and later writers are right in their assumption that she was a Pythagorean, this woman was an instructor of Socrates whom Plato says he called his teacher. Plato is somewhat specific as to what she imparted in philosophic thought. He says in his *Symposium* that she expressed "opinions on the nature, origin, and objects of life," and these opinions are the core of that dialogue. It is meaningful for the history of social thought that Plato represented a woman as worthy and competent to teach his own master initial elements of social philosophy.

Other women classified as Pythagoreans include Perictione, who may have been the mother or sister of Plato, a philosopher who wrote on the harmony of women and on wisdom. Aristotle spoke well of her. Aesara of Lucania was deemed so important that Alexander the Sophist made her the theme of lectures and the Roman poets Catullus and Horace, having discovered her in their time, sang her praises as a woman of letters.

From the Pythagorean philosophy many schools of philosophy sprang to emphasize one or more of its tanets, to reject some and expand others. For example, Parmenides, founder of the Eleatic School in the time of Socrates and now described as "the first philosopher who argues," had been trained in Pythagoreanism, but he detected what he believed to be contradictions within it. Troubled over the dilemma, he reported in a long narrative poem, he sought advice from a goddess whom he visited in the underworld where she dwelt. This advice she gave him: "Judge by reasoning the much-disputed proof. Pursue the Ways of Truth and the Ways of Untruth." This he decided to do.

In his account of "The Athenian Philosophical Schools," *Cambridge Ancient History*, Volume VI, F. M. Cornford says, with reference to Plato's Academy, that Plato founded it "on lines partly suggested by the Pythagorean societies Plato had seen in South Italy. He also found in Pythagoreanism the clue to the problem of knowledge." Elaborating that problem as one that bothered Plato, the author of this article goes on to say: "The possibility of knowledge had become a problem when Parmenides condemned as false the manifold world which 'seems' to the senses, and Protagoras had asserted, on the contrary side, that what seems to every man is real or true for him. . . . To a follower of Socrates the problem of knowledge presents a different aspect; it is, in the first place, the problem of that knowledge which is goodness." Then Cornford, turning to the *Metaphysics* of Aristotle, says:

"Platonism, as Aristotle saw, is a form of Pythagoreanism, modified by Socratic influence." The vitality in the philosophy of the Pythagoreans (not Pythagoras himself alone, who left no published writing and became a kind of vague god with the passage of time) becomes clear as it is traced from their thinking in the sixth century B.C. through the thinking of Plato and Aristotle into the thinking of the Hellenic and following ages.

In succeeding schools, offshoots of Pythagoreanism, women continued to be active as thinkers, writers, and teachers. Ménage names sixty-three women philosophers of the Hellenic age and classifies them by schools. Some became heads of philosophic schools, notably Arete of Cyrene who had urged her father Aristippus to set up a school at Cyrene and who conducted it after his death. She was interested in natural science and ethics and like her father she was concerned with a "world in which there would be neither masters nor slaves and all would be as free from worry as Socrates."

What a richness of ideas the Greek Philosophic speculations evolved! They embraced inquiries about such problems as these: the function of religion and the role of the goddesses and gods; war and peace and ways of attaining peace; religious and even scientific bigotry; naturalism and humanism; the dualisms of good and evil; family and social well-being; wealth and poverty; mind and matter; pantheism; the elevation of reason to supremacy in the mind; intellectual snobbery; contradictions within the formulated systems of philosophy; efforts to overcome the contradictions; whether the psychology of emotions explained conduct and mentality better than concern with conceptual thought; the place of virtue, pleasure, righteousness, and politics in the shaping of destiny; rhetoric versus fundamental knowledge; the laws of logic and their inadequacies; physics and its limitations; rules of oratory, playwriting, and poetry; citizenship and free opinion; simple living and restraint as opposed to ostentation and extravagance; sex and its significance; skepticism, cynicism, pessimism, sophistry, stoicism; mechanism; intuition; judgment based solely on the senses and its superficiality; traditional as inferior to investigatory, factual, and creative intelligence; educational theory and practice involving such questions as whether virtue can be taught, whether inspiration can spring out of ignorance, how aspiration can be promoted, what aspiration is. The Greeks pursued Truth in its fullest sense. They pushed scientific inquiries to considerable lengths. They sought after what is called culture; they analyzed it; some disowned it. Aristotle led the way in the encyclopaedic accumulation of exact knowledge as it existed by his time and for centuries was regarded in Christendom as "the master of them that know."

When their intellectually creative era closed, they had to their credit the collection, classification, and analysis of all the learning upon which they could lay their hands; the framing of educational systems and textbooks for instruction; the invention of every branch of literature with stylistic devices for each, established as immortal models.

To that broad and deep current of thought called philosophy which flowed from the Greek world down through the ages of the Roman world and on into Christendom, Roman thinkers made few if any original contributions. But their chief system of philosophy, borrowed from the old Greeks and reworked in the light of Rome's experience as "mistress of the world," centered reflective thought on things human, on the struggle between tyranny and liberty, within the human spirit and in history. That system was Stoicism, and its preëminent expositor was Lucius Seneca (4 B.C.-65 A.D.).

Lucius was the son of M. A. Seneca, a man of letters, and of Helvia of whose origins we know little except that her father had a low view of woman's talents. By some method Helvia acquired a liberal education and found in letters consolation for many afflictions. Despising the pride and show of the equestrian class to which she and her husband belonged, Helvia contributed to the education of her son and gave him the affectionate upbringing revealed to us in letters which are among the precious memorials of her age. To an aunt, whom he remembered with admiration, he was indebted for help in the beginning of his career. If his wife, Marcia, had less stoicism in her make-up than his mother, Seneca nonetheless found in her character continuous inspiration until that tragic day when, ordered by Nero to commit suicide, he bade her the last farewell.

The philosophy of life which Seneca developed "embraced

in the arms of equal charity all human souls, bond or free, male or female, however they might be graded by convention and accident, who have a divine parentage, and may, if they will, have a lofty, perhaps eternal future." To ranks and classes his ethics made no concessions; capacity for virtue was his only test of values. Women, in his view, were equals of men in culture and virtue: "Women have the same inner force, the same capacity for nobleness as men." In his letters to Helvia and Marcia, this breadth of view was recorded.

"It was not for nothing," wrote Samuel Dill in *Roman Society from Nero to Marcus Aurelius,* "that Seneca had been for five years the first minister of the Roman Empire. To have stood so near the master of the world, and felt the pulse of humanity from Britain to the Euphrates, to have listened to their complaints and tried to minister to their needs, was a rare education in social sympathy. . . . No one outside the pale of Christianity has perhaps ever insisted so powerfully on the obligation to live for others, on the duty of love and forgiveness, as Seneca has done. We are all, bond and free, ruler or subject, members of one another, citizens of a universal commonwealth. . . . The social instinct is innate and original in us. . . . It was only by combination and mutual good offices that men were able to repel the dangers which surrounded the infancy of the race, and to conquer the forces of nature. Man is born for social union, which is cemented by concord, kindness, and love. . . . Forgive if you wish for forgiveness; conquer evil with good; do good even to those who have wrought you evil. Let us copy the serene example of those Eternal Powers who constantly load with their benefits even those who doubt of their existence, and bear with unruffled kindness the errors of frail souls that stumble by the way."

Such were the great philosophic systems bequeathed from the ancient world to the middle ages. They entered into the thinking of the Italian Renaissance and in spirit became connected with the lofty teachings of those Christian mystics who preached the social gospel in mediaeval times, foreshadowing the day when democratic upheavals would usher in the modern era.

OPENING THE AGE OF ENLIGHTENMENT

Since the development of socialized philosophy and the relation of women to it in the mediaeval period has been treated in a previous chapter under the head, "Education and Intellectual Interests in the Middle Ages," the intellectual transition from feudalism to the concept of civilization in our own times is now to be considered. There is a consensus that France, after borrowing heavily from Italy, which in turn borrowed from classical culture, became the pioneer in enlarging the civilization of tastes, from matters of serving and eating food to the amenities of conversation. There is likewise general agreement that France also assumed the initiative in formulating or restating the chief ideas which incited the revolt against despotism on the continent of Europe, stimulated the movement for democracy, spurred zeal for reforms ranging from the revision of criminal laws to social reconstruction, and kindled anew the hopes for universal peace, such as had sustained Stoics in antiquity and inspired Christian idealists in the middle ages.

This transition, extending over more than two centuries, passed through three broad stages. The first was marked by the introduction and establishment of standards for "civility" reaching far beyond the standards of mediaeval chivalry, formalized in the Court of Love, to embrace more kinds of persons and broader social interests. The second was characterized by a skeptical attitude toward the claims of the State justifying its right to be tyrannical and cruel, toward the dogmatism and intolerance insisted upon by the Church with the support of the State. In the third stage, becoming marked early in the eighteenth century, constructive thinking emerged in efforts to evolve and give form and force to ideas pertinent to the release of thought and action in the interest of human happiness and general welfare.

These stages were not separated by sharp divisions. In some circles of the aristocracy, stress continued to be placed on civility and the refinement of social intercourse among the upper classes during the periods of skepticism and constructive philosophizing. Skepticism did not become a force until the new constructive ideas had been well delineated, for skepticism was itself the fruition of a search for better ways of conducting human affairs, and it continued after constructive proposals had become the chief topics of interest. But the variant emphases in fact led to such a revolution in thought that the three phases of the social and intellectual transition from feudalism to the modern age may be treated one by one.

At the opening of the seventeenth century, the manners and tastes of French noblemen and the bourgeois in general were still almost as crude as manners and tastes had been as a rule in the early days of feudalism. Powerful lords still kept their swords sharp, despised learning as effeminate and beneath the dignity of the strong man, spent more time with horses and dogs than with books or the arts, and looked on coarseness as a sign of strength. Like their forebears, many of them could scarcely read and write, if at all, and still fewer were interested in general ideas or arts or letters. Among the bourgeois the richest merchant families were often above the common run of nobles in degrees of gentility, more sensitive in tastes, and broader in their mental activities. But community life in French towns was marred by gross disorders and filthy habits. Dirty streets, open sewers, and epidemics bore outward witness to an inner state of disgrace. The very language spoken was a jumble of dialects, and confusion reigned in spelling, grammar, and meanings. Whatever colleges, universities, and lower schools had been trying to do for the improvement of manners, ways of living, and modes of intellectual intercourse, they had apparently made little impression on nobles, the average merchant family, and the masses of the people.

The government and the laws of France, civil and criminal, were despotic and brutal, and they grew worse rather than better as the decades passed. Under Louis XIV, despotism was regularized and glorified. After the revocation, in 1685, of the Edict of Nantes which had permitted some religious liberty, Protestants had no civil rights at law; they could not marry legally, have legitimate children, or bequeath property. By oath the successive rulers were pledged to extirpate all heresy and heretics. Books of every kind had to be submitted to censorship, and secret publication in defiance of it put guilty parties in jeopardy of harsh penalties. After

1614 the Estates General met no more — until 1789; and there were no official assemblies in which representatives could publicly and freely evolve, discuss, and promote ideas for reforming the despotic State administration and its laws or for reducing the coercive rights of the aristocracy and clergy.

In 1757 the death penalty was prescribed for persons who wrote, printed, or distributed any work in the nature of an attack on religion. Printed matter assailing or criticizing the government or its officials was forbidden and persons responsible for such publications were liable to fine and imprisonment. As some French writer has said of the old regime, only circumspect private conversations concerning such matters enjoyed considerable freedom from police interference. Practice seldom is as universally bad as repressive laws but it was bad enough in this time and place.

Under whose auspices and with what agencies was the campaign against the barbarisms and abuses of such a regime initiated and carried forward?

A struggle for civility in manners, tastes, language, and modes of association was deliberately started about 1608 by the Marquise de Rambouillet in her salon at Paris, and was continued there until her death in 1665. To her successive assemblies through the years she invited members of the court and of the aristocracy, writers, artists, musicians, and public officials in the upper ranges of the government. Under her skillful tutelage conversation was developed into a fine art, the French language was stripped of its grammatical monstrosities, its grossness, and its awkwardness; standards of literary and spoken communication were erected; and the enthusiasm for discriminative writing was stimulated, though encouragement was not given to radicalism or impiety.

The work for civility thus begun by Madame Rambouillet was taken up by other distinguished women, by the scores, who either followed the model she set or emulated her spirit; and it was maintained from generation to generation, until France became the arbiter of "good taste" and the exemplar of clear writing throughout the Western world. If some hostesses turned refinement into pallid preciosity and made their salons ridiculous, there can scarcely be any doubt that these feminine institutions of civility were, for a long time, the

greatest single influence in developing civilized social behavior, promoting lucidity of written expression, and inciting
talents to flower in arts and letters.

Although salons devoted entirely or mainly to matters of
taste in letters and arts continued to flourish, their monopoly
was invaded before the end of the seventeenth century by
newcomers especially concerned with critical thinking, while
by no means neglecting questions of literary and artistic excellence or of social philosophy. These newcomers founded
what may be called "salons of skepticism" and ushered in
the second stage of the transition from feudalism to the modern age. If authoritarianism in State and Church was to be
abolished or even mitigated, engines of criticism had to be
brought against it and applied again and again and again.
Yet to avoid the toils of the law, critics had to be wary in
shaping and stating their views. They had to be more or less
subtle. They could not be too blunt. They had too much
at stake to explode impulsively. They had to think of tactics.

Before the end of the seventeenth century, men and women
of critical inclinations, skeptics, began to gather at the homes
of prudent but hospitable women where wits were comfort-
able and could exercise their ingenuity in conversation while
at the same time saying what was on their minds. If they
were too lugubrious, they were boring. To be boring was to
be unwelcome. If they were unwelcome in the salons, the
alternative was to be denied self-expression unless they wished
in print to brave officers of the law.

Of all the salons open to skeptics at that period none was
more attractive to intellectuals than that of Ninon de Lenclos,
patron of bold thinkers. Concerning Ninon, Madame de
Sévigné exclaimed: "How dangerous is that Ninon! If you
knew how she dogmatizes on religion you would be horrified!"
By her personal appeal and her courage as hostess, Ninon gave
such measure, yet brilliance, to the conversations at her assemblies that the redoubtable memoirist, Saint-Simon, burst out in
an encomium over her receptions. Hearing of the *mots d'esprit*
exchanged there the king was accustomed to ask: "What is
Ninon saying now?"

Merely to list the names of the distinguished persons who
took part in Ninon's causeries would be to make an honor
roll of the age. High on it would be the names of Saint-Evre-

mond, master of irony; Scarron, poet and dramatist, whose wife was Madame de Maintenon; the great Condé, former regent of Louis XIV; dukes, professional men of war, diplomats, savants, poets, and writers of the first rank. La Fontaine, Boileau, and La Rochefoucauld enjoyed her confidence and found delight in her companies. The most acute women of the time were among her friends and guests. Indeed she made a point of selecting and inviting women of high spirit and skill in conversation — women who could be at ease with the men, participate in the play of thought, and exchange ideas for ideas. The sparkling clashes of minds made her salon far-famed.

To the end Ninon de Lenclos maintained her social independence and her skepticism. When a Jesuit priest begged her to offer to God at least her unbelief, she declined to make even that concession. Among her last visitors during her old age was a young man whose precocious intelligence so charmed her that she willed him 2,000 francs with which to buy books. He was François-Marie Arouet, known to posterity as Voltaire and destined to shake religious and political intolerance from center to circumference.

Skepticism implied the existence of ideals by which to test individuals, people, and institutions under review. Thus it led to the third stage, or emphasis, in the development of the salon — the recognition that formulated constructive philosophies were necessary to overcome what were deemed the barbarisms of the governing regime. In reflections on objectives and ways and means of attaining ideals, social philosophies were in time created and they furnished new directives for thought both in the later salons and in the great world beyond their halls.

Many salons continued to be primarily concerned with good taste in letters and arts. But all hostesses, even if they clung to receptions which attracted writers and artists of a conventional type, were not satisfied to be confined to those assemblies. Mme. Geoffrin had two assemblies a week in her home. She reserved Mondays for established artists and aspiring amateurs, and to her Wednesday rallies were invited only the savants, writers of the highest repute, and philosophers.

By the middle of the eighteenth century, the *philosophes* of the Enlightenment held sway in the meetings presided over by women devoted to the discussions of the perplexing issues which were being defined on the eve of the Revolution. The names of Voltaire, Diderot, d'Alembert, Rousseau, Turgot, Necker, and Condorcet led all the rest in distinction. Though Rousseau eventually flung himself out of the salon coteries and, jeering at civilization, advocated the freedom which he chose to envisage as primordial, he is to be associated, if only by his revolt, with the influence of these institutions of skeptical and philosophic civility.

Of all this movement the Goncourt brothers wrote enthusiastically in the nineteenth century, as French men and students of the records. "If one salon was closed," they said, "another was always open for a trial of theory. For example, after the death of Mme. de Lambert, the intelligentsia who had been her especial friends moved over to the salon of Mme. de Tencin, the *'bonne amie'* of Fontenelle who said to him one day as she placed her hand on his heart: *'Vous n'avez là que du cerveau.'* In this salon, the first in France to receive a man at his intellectual value, the littérateur began the great rôle he was destined to play in the society of that age; it was from here, from the salon of Mme. de Tencin, that he made his way to other salons and rose step by step to dominate a society which at the close of a century was to grant him so large a place in the state. . . . This woman hastened to the amusements of the mind, enjoyed comedy, novel or witticism, with a heart, a passion and a soul that seemed to escape from her life and abandon themselves utterly to the joys of her mind. What intellectual life, what movement, what vivacity of idea and idiom in the salon this woman collected exhaustively from among men of letters and quickened for her pleasure! Here Marivaux brought depth to subtlety; here Montesquieu awaited the passage of an argument to return it with swift or powerful hand. Here Mairan uttered an idea in a word, and Fontenelle commanded silence with one of the delicate stories he seemed to have found halfway between heaven and earth, between Paris and Badinopolis!"

Mme. de Tencin herself left a pen portrait of Louis XV which, admirers have declared, no historian will ever equal. And she was capable of criticism and fire of her own. Like Mirabeau she had a fierce combat with her father to escape burial in a convent all her life. And, like him, she was always at the center of strife. She played politics, she wrote, she served a term in jail. A product of conflict, both her turbulence and her intellect were of the French quality which was to bear the thinkers into revolutionary battles.

"Because they were continually occupied," wrote the Goncourts, "because they were forced by the exigencies of their domination, by their place in society, by the interest of their sex, and by their very inaction to carry on an incessant and almost unconscious work of judgment, comparison, and analysis, the women of that age attained a sagacity that gave them the government of the world. It permitted them to strike straight at the heart of the passions, interests, and weaknesses of everyone. The women of the day acquired this prodigious tact so speedily and at such slight cost that it appeared almost as a natural sense in them. It might well be said that there was intuition in the experience of so many young women with this admirable contemporary gift of knowledge without study, of that knowledge which caused the *savantes* to know a great deal without being erudite, of that knowledge which made women of Society know everything without having learned anything. 'Young intelligences divined far more than they learned,' said Sénac de Meilhan, in a profound epigram.

"This genius, this habit of perception and penetration, this rapidity and sureness of vision instilled in woman a rationale of conduct, a quality frequently hidden by the outward aspect of the eighteenth century, yet easily discernible in all the expressions that escaped it. This quality was the personality and property of judgment brought back to the reality of life: the practical spirit.

"What lessons this positivism of appreciation and observation, this imperturbable and apparently natural scepticism taught; how subtle it was, what terrifying depths and lengths it went to! It was this wisdom, without the illusion of God, of society, of man, of faith in anything whatever, builded of every mistrust and every disenchantment, clear and absolute as the proof of a mathematical operation, having only one principle, the recognition of fact, that placed this maxim in the mouth of a young woman: 'It is to your lover you must never say you disbelieve in God; but to your husband it does not matter at all, because with your lover you must leave yourself a way of exit. Religious scruples and devotion cut everything short.'"

Among the most versatile leaders of these numerous salons was Julie de Lespinasse. It was said of her that she united in her assemblies the Academy, the Encyclopedia, the State, the Army, and the Church, conducted a veritable laboratory of opinion, encouraged free discussions of pressing issues, all in the atmosphere of liberty. In her rooms men of the Encyclopaedia tried out their theories, read drafts of their articles before publication, and were subjected to criticism. Chastellux, social philosopher, tested his ideas at her parties. Able to speak English, as well as Italian and Spanish, Lespinasse was particularly inquisitive about English institutions of liberty and government and hospitable to members of the English parliament who visited France. Aware of the political and social storms brewing in France, she dedicated her talents to a search for "the possibility of avoiding a catastrophe."

From week to week, in some cases for twenty, thirty, or even forty years, energetic women of spirit, well educated and clever, directed these "republics of letters" under unwritten laws which they evolved through experience. They planned the intellectual strategy of the occasions, gently held discussions to the themes under consideration, raised questions for debate, encouraged young guests, courteously subdued monopolists of conversation, and drew out the interests of the shy or diffident. As Roger Picard says, the hostesses, although differing in character and talents, had certain qualities in common: good taste, urbanity, the art of leading each person to speak on the question about which he knew most or thought he knew most, or was thought by others to know most. Rival vanities were discouraged, the maladroit, offensive, and unjust word avoided, and minds firmly but graciously held to issues that had been joined. Instead of imitating the formalities and pedantry of schoolrooms, hostesses sought to promote the clearest possible thinking and forms of expression. To the influence of these women and the assemblies they directed was due in no small measure that literary grace which made French writing and conversing the admiration of the civilized world.

The spirit of the liberal and radical salons being cosmopolitan and friendly to English ideas, many Englishmen attended their assemblies by invitation from the hostesses or after having sought this privilege on their own motion. Among the English visitors were Hume, Bolingbroke, Chesterfield, Horace Walpole, Gibbon, and Adam Smith. Benjamin Franklin and Thomas Jefferson from America were sometimes guests. Continental princes now and then sent agents to attend the assemblies and report on the opinions voiced there. The commingling of professional soldiers, bankers, diplomats, statesmen, and other men holding positions of prominence in public life with historians and philosophers gave to these forums intellectual brilliance and a challenge to good thinking, not to be found in the confines of the court or of an ordinary political parliament.

At a time when censorship bore down hard on freedom of speech and press, in a country that had no open forum such as the English parliament, under the protection of the salons all the institutions and projects that were to figure in the Revolution were brought under persistent and rigorous scrutiny: constitutional government and liberty, representative government, separation of State and Church, natural rights, the release of economy from the strangle-hold of provincialism and mercantilism, sovereignty of the people, programs of liberty, equality, and fraternity. If, as has often been remarked, these men and women were "playing with fire," it may be justly added that they were also seeking ways and means of grappling with the inevitable in the hope of escaping disaster.

FORMULATING THE IDEA OF CIVILIZATION

In such associations of minds with minds, two revolutionary ideas — social philosophies — were developed and propagated in the eighteenth century. Their revolutionary character lay in their interpretations and evaluations of long history — past, present, and in the coming centuries. The first was the idea of progress; the second was the idea of civilization. By their nature and influence they have long separated the thought and practice of the Western world from the thought and practice of the Eastern world — one might almost say from the world east of the Rhine. Both are opposed to the static conception of the human universe, dominant in the middle ages, and to the static conception of utopian communism, so rampant in our age, as a final "spring into freedom," good everywhere and for all time.

The first of these world views — the idea of progress — rejected that theory of the world which regarded it as a vale of tears where human beings, under a divine plan, are trained, disciplined, and tested for happiness, not here, but in heaven; or, if unrepentant and sinful, are sent into everlasting awful punishment. To this world view, the idea of progress opposed an optimistic conception of human history and opportunity — the progressive improvement of social and individual life on earth by the utilization of the natural and moral sciences in realizing lofty, but ever-advancing, ideals for human aspiration.

The idea of progress was set forth in its original form in 1737 by Abbé de Saint-Pierre in his *Observations on the Continuous Progress of Human Reason.* "Here," says J. B. Bury, in his study, *The Idea of Progress,* "we have for the first time, expressed in definite terms, the vista of an immensely long progressive life in front of humanity. Civilization is only in its infancy. Bacon, like Pascal, had conceived it to be in its old age. . . . The Abbé was the first to fix his eyes on the remote destinies of the race." By its necessary commitments this idea was dynamic, and it lent inspiration to the salons engaged in exploring the possibilities and prospects for radical, if steady, reforms in the old régime of State and Church.

Accepting the idea of progress, the Marquis de Condorcet incorporated it in a larger idea which had appeared in France near the middle of the eighteenth century — the idea of civilization — and gave the result of a systematic formulation in his *Esquisse d'un tableau historique des progrès de l'esprit humain,* published in 1795, posthumously. Although Mme. Condorcet did not conduct a salon in the grand manner, her home was one of the most important intellectual centers of France on the eve of the Revolution. Among the friends of the Condorcets were Adam Smith, Benjamin Franklin, Thomas Jefferson, and Thomas Paine. Madame Condorcet translated Smith's *Theory of Moral Sentiments* and Paine's speeches to the convention. When her husband was being hunted by the police she supported him by "painting miniatures and selling lingerie"; when he thought of writing his memoirs, she besought him to write, instead, his philosophy of history and society, which on her advice he incorporated in his *Esquisse* — rendering effective aid in advancing the idea of civilization on its way to a place of power in Western thought.

As the Beards show in *The American Spirit: A Study of the Idea of Civilization in the United States,* this idea, wrought out by French thinkers in the age of, and under the influence of, the salons, became the highest synthesis of liberal thought, as distinguished from fixed utopias and ideologies, in the Western world including the United States, and it is today the idea to which leaders in education, social improvement, and statecraft most commonly turn for sanction and inspiration. In its composite formulation it embraces a conception of history as the struggle of human beings for individual and social perfection — for the good, the true, and the beautiful — against ignorance, disease, the harshness of physical nature, the forces of barbarism in individuals and in society. It transcends conservative "civility" by making civility serve a universal civilizing process. Inherent in the idea is the social principle. That is to say, the civilization of men and women occurs in society, and all the agencies used in the process — language, ideas, knowledge, institutions, property, arts, and inventions — are social products, the work of men and women indissolubly united by the very nature of life, in a struggle for a decent and wholesome existence against the forces of barbarism and pessimism wrestling for the possession of the human spirit.

With what upshot for theory and practice, for education and for life, individual and social, in a world torn open by wars and revolutions today?

Despite the barbaric and power-hungry propensities and activities in long history, to which their sex was by no means immune, women were engaged in the main in the promotion of civilian interests. Hence they were in the main on the side of *civil*-ization in the struggle with barbarism.

If this phase of woman's force in history is to be capitalized as against barbaric propensities and activities, then an understanding of women's past history in both connections must be regarded as indispensable to the maintenance and promotion of civilization in the present age.

But this is no "woman question" alone, as social philosophers — women and men — have understood from the dawn of reflective thought. It is a human problem — a problem of knowledge, intelligence, and morals — for individuals, families, communities, and states. For centuries, judges of equity in the Anglo-Saxon world and makers of enlightened legislation everywhere have recognized it as such. So have all the men and women arrayed on the side of civilization.

Upon the truth of this matter and the uses made of it will depend forevermore the power of men and women to control themselves and the instrumentalities at their hands in the struggle *against* disruptive forces of barbarism and *for* the realization of the noblest ideals in the heritage of humanity.

Chapter 13

An Illustrative Bibliography

"NO DOCUMENTS, no history," said Fustel de Coulanges. All the documents for all the history would be the acme of equipment for the study of history. Though all history has not been documented, what has been recorded is too voluminous for any individual or circle of individuals to know in its completeness. Only in narrow phases of history have scholars apparently satisfied themselves that they have discovered all the existing documents.

The subject of woman in history is as gigantic as the subject of man in history, one learns merely by dipping into the files of any major library of the world, such as the Congressional Library at our national capital.

For the aspect of woman as force, variously comprehended or ignored, and reflective thought about her force, the following bibliography provides some materials for students and less serious readers. Owing to the limitations of space here, this bibliography is fragmentary, merely selective from the resources of American libraries. Yet it is highly illustrative and suggestive of the amount of documentation and reflection respecting woman in history.

With a few exceptions, titles which appear in the body of this volume are not repeated here. The emphasis on French and German titles among foreign works is due to the idea of confining foreign titles to languages most widely used in the United States. Among serious omissions is a list of works on woman's historic force as musician; this must wait on the findings of a competent exploration now on the verge of completion by an adequate musicologist.

GENERAL WORKS

Cambridge Ancient, Medieval, and Modern History. 33 vols. These volumes are very uneven in the recognition of women as makers of history but in places this aspect of history is superbly treated. *To the volumes are attached treasures of bibliographical sources.*

Dictionary of Greek and Roman Biography and Mythology. Edited by William Smith. 3 vols. London, 1873. *Bibliographies* for every feature.

The Mothers. By Robert Briffault. 3 vols. Macmillan, 1937. Indispensable monumental history of women in many relations, from the dawn of society to its expression in the Renaissance. *Extraordinarily rich in its bibliography.*

Pauly's *Handwörterbuch der Alterwissenschaft.* Edited by Georg Wissowa, Stuttgart.

Monumenta Historiae of Germany, Denmark, Norway, etc.

Harvard Oriental Series.

Sacred Books of the East. Clarendon Press.

The Temple Classics. London.

Literatures of the World. Appleton.

The History of Human Marriage. By Edward Westermarck. 3 vols. 5th ed., Macmillan, 1921. See different interpretation by Briffault.

General History of Women. By Thomas Heywood. London, 1657.

Essay on the Character, Manners, and Genius of Women in Different Ages — Enlarged from the French of M. Thomas by Mr. Russell. 2 vols. Philadelphia, 1774.

Woman Through the Ages. By Emil Reich. 2 vols. London, 1908.

History and Condition of Women in Various Ages and Nations. By Lydia Maria Child. Boston, 1835.

Les Femmes dans l'Histoire. By Mme. de Witt-Guizot. Paris, 1888.

Das Weib. By Hermann H. Ploss and M. Bartels. First ed., 1876. Later ed., 1891. Stuttgart.

A Moral History of Women. By Dr. Sarah P. White. Doubleday, Doran, 1937.

Woman's Share in Social Culture. By Anna Garlin Spencer. Lippincott, 1925. An historical review.

The Book of Woman's Power. By Ida M. Tarbell, 1911; The Business of Being a Woman, 1912. Macmillan.

History of Women. By Stephen W. Fullon. London, 1855.

Gedanken and Einfälle. By Heinrich Heine. 1845-56. Woman called the secret spring of history.

De l'Influence des Femmes sur les Moeurs et les Destinées des Nations. By Mme. F. Montgeltaz. Paris, 1828.

Vom Einfluss der Frau auf die Geschichte. By José Ortega y Gasset. Trans. into German from the Spanish by Fritz Ernst. Stuttgart, 1930. Cited as a German work to show its wide appeal in Europe.

The Influence of Women on the Progress of Knowledge. By Henry Thomas Buckle. Fraser's Mag., April, 1858, and reprinted in the first volume of the Miscellaneous and Posthumous Works. This was the only public speech Buckle made.

Woman and Society. By Meyrich Booth. Longmans Green, 1929.

Erkenntnisgeist und der Muttergeist. By Ernst Bergmann. Leipzig, 1933. Note date and country of publication.

The Ancient World. By W. E. Caldwell. Farrar and Rinehart, 1937.

Roman Society. By Samuel Dill. 3 vols. Macmillan, 1920-26.

Hellenistic Civilization. By W. W. Tarn. London, 1927.

Die hellenistisch-römische Kultur in ihren Beziehungen zu Judentum und Christentum. By Paul Wendland. Tübingen, 1907.

The Birth of China. By Herlee G. Creel. John Day, 1937.

The Four Hundred Million. By Mary A. Nourse. Bobbs-Merrill, 1935. A history of China.

Das Weib im Altindischen Epos. By J. J. Meyer. Leipzig, 1915.

Women in Ancient India. By Clarisse Bader. Moral and literary studies. London, 1925. A work crowned by the French Academy.

Women under Primitive Buddhism; Laywomen and Almswomen. By Isaline B. Horner. Dutton, 1930.

Woman in the Sacred Scriptures of Hinduism. By Mildred W. Pinkham. Columbia Univ. Press, 1941.

Outlines of the History of Ireland. By Patrick W. Joyce, Dublin, 1894.

Illustrious Irishwomen. By Elizabeth Casey. 2 vols. London, 1877. From the early period, with sources cited.

Medieval Slavdom and the Rise of Russia. By Frank Novak. Holt, 1930.

Grosse Frauen der Heimat. By Käthe Braun-Prager. Vienna, 1936. Includes studies of Maria Theresa, Ida Pfeiffer, Antonie Adamberger, Kathi Fröhlich, Marie von Ebner-Eschenbach, Pauline Metternich, Bertha von Suttner, Helena Langner, Tina Plan.

AUTOBIOGRAPHIES, DIARIES, JOURNALS

Peregrinatio ad Loca Sancta. Ed. by Wilhelm Heraeus. Heidelberg, 1908. Trip of a Spanish nun to the Holy land in the fourth century.

A Journey through the Crimea to Constantinople. By Lady Elizabeth Craven (Princess Berkeley of the Holy Roman Empire, 1750-1828.) Ed. by Broadley and Melville. London, 1914.

Persian Pictures. By Gertrude Bell. Liveright, 1928.

The Road to Salem. By Adelaide L. Fries. Univ. of North Carolina Press, 1944. Drawn mainly from her autobiography written in 1803 by a woman who became a deaconess in the Moravian Church.

Journal of Narcissa Whitman. In the Souvenir of Western Women edited by Mary Osborne Douthit of Portland, Oregon. Memoir of a missionary to the Oregon country.

On Journey — autobiography. By Vida Scudder. Dutton, 1924. A memoir of a mind.

A Woman's Quest. By Maria Zakrzewska. Appleton, 1924. Story of a Polish-American physician's career, in the nineteenth century.

Eliza Pinckney. Her diary and letters edited by Harriott Horry. Scribner's, 1926. Experiences and ideas of a woman planter in colonial America.

Facing Two Ways. By Baroness Shidzue Ishimoto. Farrar and Rinehart, 1935. Autobiography of a Japanese woman of the middle class married to an aristocrat; educated in part in the Orient and in part in the Occident.

My Fight for Birth Control. By Margaret Sanger. Farrar and Rinehart, 1931.

Fighting for Life. By Dr. Sara Josephine Baker. Macmillan, 1939. Personal account of public work for child hygiene.

A Woman of Genius. By Mary Austin. Houghton Mifflin, 1917. A fictional autobiography of a great American actress and the role of love in her career.

A Great Love. By Alexandra Kollontai. Vanguard, 1929. Her own story told by a leading participant in the Bolshevist Russian Revolution.

Lights Vanished. By Lydia Kniagevitch. Snellgrove Publications, New York, 1940. A Russian mine-owner's story.

Testament of Youth. By Vera Brittain. Macmillan, 1933.

Unveiled. By Selma Ekrem. Washburn, New York, 1930.

My Life and History. By Berta Szeps. Trans. from the German by John Sommerfield. Knopf, 1939. Related to the history of her country, Austria, in its last half century or more.

Memoiren einer Sozialistin. By Lily Braun. Munich, 1909-11.

West with the Night. By Beryl Markham. Houghton Mifflin, 1942. "Adventure-packed" autobiography of an English girl reared in Africa.

Winter's Tales. By Isak Dinesen. Random House, 1943.

ART

Women in the Fine Arts from the 7th Century B.C. to the 20th Century A.D. Ill. Houghton Mifflin, 1924. More than a thousand women discovered as worthy of mention and author thinks an exhaustive research would increase the number largely. An Introduction of 50 pages on the history of art.

Women Painters of the World from the Time of Caterina Vigri (1413-1563) to Rosa Bonheur, and to the Present Day. Edited by Walter Shaw Sparrow. Art and Life Library, Vol. 3. London, 1905.

The Women Artists of Bologna. By Laura Ragg. London, 1907.

Die Frauen in der Kunstgeschichte. By Ernst Guhl. Berlin, 1858.

Women Artists in All Ages and Countries. By Elizabeth F. Ellet. Harper, 1859. Based on *Die Frauen in der Kungstgeschichte* by Ernst Guhl, but with additions, since that work closed with the eighteenth century. Also used works of Vasari, Descompes, and Fiorillo. Deals more strictly than Clara E. C. Waters with what the women artists had done, and issued before her volume.

Die Frau als Kunstlerin. By Hans Hildebrandt. Ill. Berlin, 1928.

English Female Artists. By Ellen C. Clayton. 2 vols. London, 1876. These two volumes are more biographical than interpretative. The author begins with early painters and ends with the second half of the nineteenth century.

Woman in Science. By H. J. Mozans. Appleton, 1913. Also contains important historical data on women in art.

BUSINESS

The Native Races of the Pacific States. By Hubert Howe Bancroft. A. L. Bancroft & Co., San Francisco, 1882. Vol. III, p. 145.

History of the Oregon Territory. By J. Dunn. London, 1844. Page 108, on women traders.

History of the Indian Tribes of the United States. By Henry Rowe Schoolcraft. Vol. V, p. 176, on women traders. Lippincott, 1851-57.

History, Manners and Customs of the Indian Nations. By John Gottlieb E. Heckewelder. Hist. Soc., Philadelphia, 1876.

Burma, Past and Present. By Albert Fytche. London, 1878. Vol. II, p. 72, on women traders.

The Chinese Repository. Printed for the proprietors, Canton, 1832-51.

The Mothers. By Robert Briffault. Vol. I, pp. 483 ff.

Women Traders in Mediaeval London. By Eileen Power. Econ. Jr., pp. 276 ff., June, 1916. London.

Studies in English Trade of the 15th Century. By Eileen Power. Women Traders in Bristol. London, 1933.

Women Traders in Mediaeval London. By A. Abram. Econ. Jr., Vol. 28, pp. 276-285. 1916, London.

The London Silkwomen of the Fifteenth Century. By Marian K. Dale. Econ. Hist. Rev., Vol. IV, pp. 324-35. 1933, London.

The Working Life of Women in the Seventeenth Century. By Alice Clark. Harcourt, Brace, 1920.

Colonial Women of Affairs. By Elizabeth Dexter. Houghton Mifflin, 1924.

The Employments of Women: A Cyclopaedia of Women's Work. By Virginia Penny. Boston, 1863.

The Land of the Lamas. W. W. Rockhill. Century, 1891.

ECONOMY

Hunger and History. By Ezra Parmalee Prentice. Harper, 1939.

Women in English Economic History. By F. W. Ticknor. Dutton 1923.

Social England in the Fifteenth Century. A study of the effect of economic conditions. By Annie Abram. Dutton, 1909.

English Life in the Later Middle Ages. By Annie Abram. Dutton, 1913.

Persian Women and Their Ways. By Clara C. Rice. London, 1923.

Historic Farms of South Africa: the wool, the wheat, and wife, of 17th and 18th centuries. By Dorothy Fairbridge. Oxford Univ. Press, 1931.

Women and the Land. By Frances G. Wolseley. London, 1916. An account of twentieth century land uses by English women.

Mobilization of Women in Industrial Japan. Institute of Pacific Relations, New York, 1941.

History of Slavery. By W. O. Blake. Columbus, Ohio, 1857.

The Romance of the Lace Pillow. By H. H. Armstrong. 1917. History of lace-making industries in Devon and Ireland.

Women in English Life from Mediaeval to Modern Times. By Georgina Hill. 2 vols. London, 1896. Many aspects of economy covered, such as women in gilds, as petitioners to Parliament, political influence, the gentlewoman in trade.

Middle-Class Culture in Elizabethan England. By Louis B. Wright. Univ. of N. Carolina Press, 1935. Shows women in many crafts and trades.

Six Thousand Years of Bread. By H. E. Jacobs. Doubleday, Doran, 1944. "Man" used generically in large part, perhaps, but explicitly attributes to woman discovery of agriculture and early knowledge of herbs.

A History of Agriculture in Europe and America. By Norman S. B. Gras. Crofts, 1925. Important recognition of women from early stages.

Schaffende Arbeit und Bildende Kunst. By Paul Brandt. 2 vols. Pictorial history of industries and mechanical arts with data on women.

Household Manufactures in the United States, 1640-1860. By Rolla M. Tryon. Univ. of Chicago Press, 1917.

Guilds in the Middle Ages. By George François Renard. Trans. by Dorothy Terry and edited with intro. by G. S. H. Cole. London, 1919.

The Dogaressas of Venice. By John Edgcumbe Staley. Venice guilds under patronage of the Dogaressas. London, 1910.

Guilds of Florence. By John Edgcumbe Staley. London, 1906.

Les Corporations ouvrières de Paris du XIIe siècle au XIIIe siècle. By Alfred L. A. Lunt. Paris, 1884. Includes account of women seamstresses.

The English Craft Gilds; Studies in Their Progress and Decline. By Stella Kramer. Columbia Univ. Press, 1905.

The Women Silversmiths of England. By T. H. Ormsbee. Amer. Collection. May, 1938, pp. 8-9.

Nordwesteuropas Verkehr, Handel und Gewerbe im frühen Mittelalter. Vienna, 1924.

La Femme dans la Société capitaliste. By Marguerite Faussecave. Paris, 1926.

A Documentary History of American Industrial Society. Ed. by John R. Commons and Associates. 10 vols. A. H. Clark, 1910-11.

Women and Wealth. By Mary S. Branch. Univ. of Chicago Press, 1934.

EDUCATION

The Primitive Family as an Educational Agency. By A. J. Todd. Putnam, 1913.

Cannonesses and Education in the Early Middle Ages. By Sister Mary Pia Heinrich. Catholic Univ. Press. Washington, D. C., 1924.

De ingenii muliebris ad doctrinam et meliores litteras aptitudine. By Anna van Schurman. Leyden, 1641, Trans. into English by Clement Barksdale as "The Learned Maid, or Whether a Maid may be a Scholar." London, 1659.

Anna Van Schurman: Artists, Scholar, Saint. By Dame Una (Birch) Pope-Hennessy. Longmans, Green, 1909. This woman is said to be the "most famous learned woman of the 17th century."

Education of Women during the Renaissance. By Mary A. Cannon. National Capital Press, Washington, 1916.

Studies in Education During the Renaissance. By W. H. Woodward. Macmillan, 1906.

The Learned Lady in England, 1650-1760. By Myra Reynolds. Houghton Mifflin, 1920.

Elizabeth Footon, First Quaker Woman Teacher (1600-72). By Mrs. Manners. London, 1914.

A Serious Proposal. By Mary Astell. London, 1694.

Mary Astell (1666-1739). By Florence Smith. Columbia Univ. Press, 1916. Full presentation of the life and works of Mary Astell, a pronounced advocate of higher education for women, and well-educated herself.

The Ladies' Library. 3 vols. London, 1714. Compilation from seventeenth century authors. It was received at the time of its publication as a judicious collection of the best passages from authoritative sources. The book aimed to give "recognition of woman's ability to think on important and difficult questions," thus obtaining for her a "more honorable place in the home, social and church life."

The Wandering Scholars. By Helen Waddell. London, 1927.

A History of the Family As a Social and Educational Institution. By Willystine Goodsell. Macmillan, 1927.

La Pedagogie Féminine; Extraite des principaux Ecrivains qui ont Traité de l'Education des Femmes depuis le XVIe Siècle. By Paul Rousselot. Paris, 1881.

Histoire de l'Éducation des Femmes en France. By Paul Rousselot. Paris, 1883.

Nu Chien or Lessons for Women. Formulated by Pan Chao, foremost woman scholar of China. By Nancy Lee Swann. Century, 1932.

GOVERNMENT AND POLITICS

Queens of Egypt. By Janet R. Buttles. Preface by Maspero. London, 1908.

Cleopatra. By Baston Delayen. Dutton, 1934.

Queen Eurydice and the Evidence for Woman-Power in Early Macedonia. By G. H. Macurdy. Am. Jr. of Philology. Vol. XLVIII, pp. 201 ff. 1927.

The Age of Pericles: An Interpretation. By Wallace E. Caldwell, South Atlantic Quarterly, 1929.

Greek Life and Thought. From the Age of Alexander to the Roman Conquest. By J. P. Mahaffy. Macmillan, 1887.

Hellenistic Queens; A Study of Woman-Power in Macedonia, Seleucid Syria, and Ptolemaic Egypt. By Grace H. Macurdy. Johns Hopkins Press, 1932.

The Roman Empresses. The History of the Lives and Secret Intrigues of the Wives of the Twelve Caesars. By T. R. Nicholas de Serviez. 2 vols. Nichols, New York, 1913.

The Women of the Caesars. By Guglielmo Ferrara. Loring & Mussey, New York, 1911.

Vassal Queens and Some Contemporary Women in the Empire. By Grace H. Macurdy. Johns Hopkins Studies in Archaeology, No 22, 1937.

Imperial Byzantium. By Bertha Diener. Trans. from the German by Eden and Cedar Paul. Little, Brown, 1938.

Byzantine Portraits. By Charles Diehl. Trans. by Harold Bell. Knopf, 1927.

The Dogaressas of Venice. By Edgcumbe Staley. Scribner, 1910.

Mont-Saint-Michel and Chartres. By Henry Adams. Houghton Mifflin, 13th imprint, 1924.

The Queens of Aragon, Their Lives and Times. By E. L. Miron. Brentano, 1913.

Queens of Old Spain. By Martin A. S. Hume. London, 1906. Author peculiarly competent as editor of Calendar of Spanish State papers and close student of Spanish history.

So many biographies of Spanish, French, and English or British women rulers have been written that it is impossible here to do much more than call attention to this fact. Maria Theresa, Christina of Sweden, and rulers of Russia, especially Catherine the Great, have also been favorite subjects for biographers. Many interpretations naturally appear in works on such state-makers as Jeanne d'Arc (Joan of Arc), Isabella of Spain and Elizabeth of England. Catherine de' Medici, Marie Antoinette, and Mary Queen of Scots have had peculiar fascination for writers as figures in tragic drama. The long-reigning Victoria, British empress, has been a challenging theme of more recent times. The following titles are given merely to indicate some distinctly informative writing by recognized scholars, types of lesser-known writing about women sovereigns of the modern age, or collections of sketches.

The following titles are given merely to indicate some distinctly informative writing by recognized scholars, types of lesser-known writing about women sovereigns of the modern age, or collections of sketches.

Isabella of Spain, the Last Crusader. By W. T. Walsh. McBride, 1930.

Queen Elizabeth. By John E. Neale. Harcourt, Brace, 1934.

Geschichte Maria Theresias. By A. von Arneth. Vienna, 1863-79.

Two lives of Jeanne d'Albret, Queen of Navarre: *Histoire de Jeanne d'Albret* by T. G. Murat, Paris, 1862; and The Life of Jeanne d'Albret by Mabel W. Freer. London, 1885.

Secret History of the French Court under Richelieu and Mazarin — The Life of Marie Chevreuse. By Victor Cousin. Paris, 1877.

Louise de Savoie et François I. By Marie Alphonse René de Maulde la Clavière. Paris, 1895.

The Last Empress. By Daniel Vare. Doubleday, Doran, 1936.

The Motherly and Auspicious. By Maurice Collis. Putnam, 1944. A study of the Empress Dowager of China, Tzu Hsi, by an Irish scholar and British civil servant.

The Flight of an Empress. As told by Wu Yung. Transcribed by Liu Kun. Trans. and ed. by Ida Pruitt. Introduction by Kenneth S. Latourette. Yale Univ. Press, 1936.

Zhinga, Negro queen of Angola, born 1582. Brief sketch in Lydia Maria Child's Appeal in Behalf of that Class of Americans called Africans, 1833.

Famous Women, as Described by Famous Writers. Trans. and Ed. by Esther Singleton. Dodd, Mead, 1904. Selected on the basis of their political influence. The women are Mary, Queen of Scots; Mme. de Maintenon; Queen Elizabeth; Mme. Roland; Lady Hamilton; Agnes Sorel; Bianca Capello; and Mme. de Pompadour.

Recherches sur la Condition Civile et Politique des Femmes depuis les Romains jusqu'à nos Jours. By E. S. Laboulaye. Paris, 1843.

The Conquest of Brazil. By Roy Nash. Harcourt, Brace, 1926.

The foregoing have to do with women of the pre-democratic modern age in positions of governing and political power. Coming now to the democratic age, the following works suggest its literature dealing with women.

The Leveller Movement. By T. C. Pease. Oxford Press, 1916. A study of the history and political theory of the English civil war in the seventeenth century.

Puritanism and Liberty. Being the Army Debates of 1647-49 from the Clarke Manuscripts with supplementary documents, selected and edited with an Introduction by A. S. P. Woodhouse. Foreword by A. D. Lindsay. London, 1938. Chapter VIII contains a Petition of Women to Parliament. Woodhouse in a footnote presumes to question women's writing of this petition but without positive knowledge of the matter.

English Democratic Ideas in the Seventeenth Century. By G. P. Gooch. Cambridge Univ. Press, 1927.

Studies in the English Social and Political Thinkers of the Nineteenth Century. By R. H. Murray. 2 vols. Cambridge, 1929. Mary Wollstonecraft included.

Letters of Mrs. (Abigail) Adams, the wife of John Adams. Boston, 1840. This edition of her letters includes those written from England.

Madame Roland. By Ida Tarbell. A biography in approval of her conception of government at the time of the French Revolution. Scribner, 1896.

A Woman's Philosophy of Woman; or Woman Affranchised. By Mme. Jenny (Comtesse d') Héricourt. Trans. from the French anonymously. New York, 1864. Replies to Michelet, Proudhon, Girardin, and Comte in behalf of equal rights for women.

History of Woman Suffrage (in the United States). Ed. by Ida H. Harper, Elizabeth C. Stanton, Susan B. Anthony, and Matilda J. Gage. 6 vols. Based on source materials. Fowler & Wells publishers of first three volumes, 1881-87; National American Woman Suffrage Association, publisher of next three volumes.

Political Women. By Sutherland Menzies. London, 1873.

Tocqueville and Beaumont in America. By G. W. Pierson. Oxford Press, 1938. Their letters from America.

Democracy in America. By Alexis de Tocqueville. Gilman edition, Century, 1898.

My Dear Lady, the Story of Anna Ella Caroll. By Marjorie W. Greenbie. Putnam, 1940. A great figure in the democratic movement of the U. S. at the period of its civil war.

Gertrude Bell. By Ronald Bodley and Lorna Hearst. Macmillan, 1940. Her extraordinary political achievements in the Near East, in our time.

Anna and the King of Siam. By Margaret Landon. John Day, 1944.

Women in the Young Turks Movement. By D. K. Brown. Atlantic Monthly, May, 1909.

The Christian Attitude toward Private Property. By Vida D. Scudder. Milwaukee, 1934.

Our revolutionary age with its threefold contest over forms of government — democratic and capitalistic, facist, communistic — has also its important literature relative to the force of woman as activist and thinker, such as the following works.

The Theory of the Democratic State. By Marie Collins Swabey. Harvard Univ. Press, 1937.

Bacon's New Atlantis and Campanella's *Civitas Solis:* A Study of Relationships. By Eleanor D. Blodgett. Modern Language Association of America, Vol. 46, 1931. This article interprets the work of Campanella which introduced a society of communism, organized under priest-magistrates who earned their offices through training and education. Women have their place and are important in the family.

Communism in Central Europe in Time of Reformation. By Karl Kautsky. Trans. by J. L. and E. G. Mulliken. Tied up with problem of marriage, proportion of sexes, philosophy of Plato, etc.

Socialism and Communism in Their Practical Applications. By M. Kaufmann. London, 1883.

The Friends of the People. By Alfred Neumann. Trans. from the German by Countess Nora Wydenbruck. Macmillan, 1942. A story of Paris during 1870-71.

Lenin on the Woman Question. By Klara Zetkin. International Publishers, New York, 1934.

Reminiscences of Lenin. By Klara Zetkin. Modern Books, 1939.

Russian Women in the Building of Socialism. By Anna Razumova. Workers Library, 1930. Exposition of the Five Year Plan by a Russian working woman.

Woman in Soviet Russia. By Fannina W. Halle. Viking Press, 1933. Background described as far as pre-Christian time. And Women in the Soviet East. Dutton, 1938.

Factory, Family and Woman in the Soviet Union. By Susan M. Kingsbury and Mildred Fairchild. Putnam's, 1935.

Lenin and Krupskaya. By C. Bobrovskaya. Workers Library, New York, 1940.

The Workers' Opposition: Material and Documents, 1920-1926. By Alexandra Kollontai, a party to it. See The Russian Revolution by William H. Chamberlin, Vol. I, p. 377. Macmillan, 1935. Other Russian women revolutionists appear in his two volumes. Dictatorships in the Modern World. Ed. by Guy Stanton Ford. Univ. of Minnesota Press, 1939. Includes "Women under the Dictatorship," by Mildred Adams.

Women Must Choose. The Position of Women in Europe To-Day By Hilary Newitt. Preface by Storm Jameson. London, 1937.

Do We Want Fascism? By Carmen Heider. John Day, 1934.

Women under Fascism and Communism. By Hilda Browning. London, 1934.

The Fascist Movement in Italian Life. By Pietro Gorgolini. Preface by Mussolini. Trans. by M. D. Petre. Little, Brown, 1925.

Italian Women. By Maria Castellani. Rome, 1939. A defense of Italian fascism.

Women of Fascism. By Margherita G. Sarfatti, author of the Official Biography of Mussolini and editor of *Popolo d'Italia*. Featured article in N. Y. Herald Tribune, November 12, 1933. See also the article, The Woman Behind Mussolini, Pictorial Review, September, 1934.

Countess Edda Ciano. Time Mag., May, 1922.

Die Frau im dritten Reich. By Else Frobenius. Berlin, 1933.

Geschichte eines Hochverraters. An autobiography. By Ernst Roehm. 7th ed., Munich, 1934. Story of a major exponent of man's right to direct the world, by one of the men whom Hitler early "purged."

Die Deutsche Frau und der National-Sozialismus. By Guida Diehl. Eisenach, 1933. A plea in behalf of Hitlerism.

My Battle (*Mein Kampf*). By Adolf Hitler. American edition in translation. Houghton Mifflin, 1933.

Die Frau. Leading woman's journal of Germany. Its issues reveal the trend from liberalism to dictatorship.

Counter-attack in Spain. By Ramón José Sender. Trans. from the Spanish by P. C. Mitchell, Houghton Mifflin, 1937.

I Must Have Liberty. By Isabel de Palencia. Longmans, Green, 1940.

Red Spanish Notebook. By Mary Low and Juan Brea. London, 1937.

Women and the Fall of France. By Konrad Bercovici. The Woman's Digest, New York, October, 1943.

LAW

To indicate what can happen to assumptions when attention is turned from textbooks and other secondary works to original sources, a single volume of documents is named first in this list of legal materials: *Monumenta Historica Britannica*. It contains the fundamental facts about early law in England.

History of English Law. By Pollock and Maitland. 2 vols. 2d edition, Cambridge Univ. Press, 1918. Before the time of Edward I.

British Freewomen: Their Historical Privilege. By Charlotte Carmichael Stopes. Soc. Sci. Series. London, 1894.

Brehon Laws. Encyc. Brit. Women freed from military service.

Commentaries on American Law. By James Kent. 4 vols. 14th edition, ed. by John M. Gould. Little, Brown, 1896.

Commentaries on Equity Jurisprudence. By Joseph Story. 2 vols. Little, Brown, 1839.

Studies in the History of American Law, with Special Reference to the 17th and 18th centuries. By Richard Brandon Morris. Columbia Univ. Press, 1930.

Two Centuries' Growth of American Law, 1701-1901. By members of the faculty of the Yale Law School. Scribner, 1901.

The Code of Hammurabi. Cambridge Ancient History, Vol. I, Ch. XIII. See also translation of the Code, by Robert F. Harper. Univ. of Chicago Press, 1904.

Modern Customs and Ancient Laws of Russia. By Maxsim Kovalesky. London, 1891. Treatise by a professor of Jurisprudence at the University of Moscow.

Hindu Law and Usage. By J. D. Mayne. 9th ed., London, 1922.

Mohammedan Law. By Syed Ameer Ali. 4th ed., London, 1917.

A Comparison of the Political and Civil Rights of Men and Women in the United States. Compiled by the Inter-American Commission of Women. U. S. Govt., 1936.

Justice and World Society. By Laurence Stapleton. Univ. of N. Carolina Press, 1944. Study of universal idea of justice known as "Law of Nature."

LETTERS

Perhaps the most astounding statement about women ever made by a thoughtful scholar was that of Henry Adams who declared that only Mme. de Sévigné and Abigail Adams had ever revealed themselves in their letters. On the contrary women have been exceedingly prolific letter writers. In quantity, the Sévigné letters may have led all the rest and a Dictionary of them was published by Macmillan in 1914 in two volumes. A large bibliography of literature on this woman is attached to her sketch in the Encyclopaedia Britannica. But such attention to this woman tends to obscure both the number and the value of other women letter writers in all ages. For instance letters of Mme. du Deffand, Louis Colet, Ninon de Lenclos, and Julie de Lespinasse are equally or more important for understanding the intellectual force of women and their relations with great contemporaries. In addition to the following items, accordingly, the section on REVOLUTIONISTS and SALONS should be consulted. What is not here is a list of works called "Literature," that being beyond the scope of this treatise.

Griechische Dichterinnen, ein Beitrag zur Geschichte der Frauen Literatur. By J. C. Poestion. Vienna, 1876.

The Contribution of Women to Sanskrit Literature. By Jatindra Bimal Chandhuri. Ed. with critical notes, etc. Calcutta, 1940.

Cultural Interests of Women in England from 1524 to 1640. Indicated in the writings of women. By Ruth W. Hughey. Ithaca, 1932.

Women as Letter Writers. By Ada M. Ingpen. New York, Baker and Taylor, 1909. A collection of women's letters from the fifteenth to the nineteenth century.

Frauenbriefe aller Zeiten. By B. Ihringer. Stuttgart, (no date).

Anthologie des Lettres de Femmes. By Henri Guyot. From the sixteenth century to our days. With sketches of the letter-writers. 2 vols. Paris, 1923.

Feminead, or Female Genius. By John Duncomb. London, 1751.

Memoirs of Several Ladies of Great Britain Who Have Been Celebrated for their Writings or Skill in the Learned Languages, Arts and Sciences. By George Ballard. Oxford, 1752.

Distinguished Women Writers. By Virginia Moors. Dutton, 1934. In her fifteen sketches are these women: Marie Bashkirtseff; Christine Rosetti; Sappho; Jane Austen; St. Teresa; Elizabeth Barrett Browning; George Eliot; Katharine Mansfield; Mme. de Sévigné; Dorothy Wadsworth; George Sand; Emily and Charlotte Brontë; Emily Dickinson; Charlotte Mew; and Elinor Wylie.

Saint Catherine of Siena as Seen in Her Letters. By Vida Scudder. Dutton, 1905.

A Great Lady's Friendships. Letters to Mary, Marchioness of Salisbury, Countess of Derby, 1862-90. Macmillan, 1934.

English Women in Life and Letters. By Margaret Phillips and W. S. Tomkinson. Oxford Univ. Press, 1926. Seventeenth and eighteenth century women in town and country, their education, their writing, in industry, in professions.

Letters of a Diplomat's Wife. By Edith O'Shaughnessy. Harper, 1916. Informed and broad study of Mexico.

Memoirs of the Life of Agrippina. By Elizabeth Hamilton. London, 1804.

Critique et Portraits littéraires. By C-A. Sainte-Beuve. Paris, 1836-39.

Honoré de Balzac: Unpublished Correspondence with Mme. Zulma Carraud. Armand Colin, Paris, 1935.

Letters of Charlotte Elizabeth, Mother of Philip of Orleans. Ed. by Frederick L. Jones. London, 1889.

The Letters of Mary W. Shelley. Ed. by Frederick L. Jones. Univ. of Oklahoma Press, 1944.

The Lost Art. Letters of Seven Famous Women. Ed. by Dorothy Van Doren. Coward-McCann, 1929.

French Women of Letters. Julia Kavanagh. London, 1862.

Letters to Her Companions. By Emily Malbone Morgan. South Byfield, Mass., 1944.

The Great Victorians. Ed. by Hugh and H. J. Massingham. London, 1932. Among about forty men are four women: Charlotte Brontë, Emily Brontë, George Eliot, and Florence Nightingale.

Letters of Jane Welsh Carlyle to Joseph Neuberg, 1848-62. Ed. by Townsend Scudder. Oxford Univ. Press, 1931.

MEDIAEVAL AFFAIRS

Of Six Mediaeval Women. By Alice Kemp-Welch. London, 1913. The six women are Roswitha the Nun; Marie de France; Mechthild of Magdeburg; Mahaut, Countess of Artois; Christine de Pisan; and Agnes Sorel.

The Mediaeval Village. By G. G. Coulton. Cambridge Univ. Press.

Mediaeval England. By Mary Bateson. Study of the Nations Series, London, 1904. Ill. From Norman Conquest, 1066, to middle of fourteenth century.

Town Life in the Fifteenth Century. By Alice Stopford Green. 2 vols. Macmillan, 1894, 1907.

MEDICINE AND NURSING

Mémorial de L'Art des Accouchements. By Marie Anne Boivin. 1824.

A History of Women in Medicine. Ill. By Dr. Kate Campbell Hurd-Mead. The Haddam Press, Haddam, Conn., 1933.

Les Femmes et le Progrès des Sciences Médicales. By Melina Lepinska. Paris, 1930.

A History of Nursing. — From the Earliest Times to the Present Day. By Adelaide Nutting and Lavinia Dock. 4 vols. Putnam, 1907-12.

Heroic Lives. By Rafael Sabatini. Houghton Mifflin, 1934. One life so interpreted is that of Florence Nightingale.

Alice Hamilton, M.D., Crusader for Health in Industry. By Elizabeth S. Sergeant. Harper's Mag. May, 1928.

Catholic Women in Medicine. Catholic World, Vol. 141, p. 222 ff.

MONASTICISM

Women under Monasticism. Saint-lore and Convent life between A.D. 500 and A.D. 1500. By Lina Eckenstein. Cambridge Univ. Press, 1896.

Histoire des Ordes Monastiques. By Pierre Helyot. Paris, 1714-19. 8 vols. The author was a Franciscan friar and historian and traveled extensively on monastic business.

Mediaeval Nunneries (1275-1535). By Eileen E. Power. Cambridge Univ. Press, 1922. Chapter heads include Education, Private Life and Private Property, The Machinery of Reform, The Nun in Mediaeval Literature, List of English Nunneries. Bibliography.

NOVELS

Immortal Marriage. By Gertrude Atherton. Boni and Liveright, 1927. Aspasia, Pericles, and their time.

The Joseph series. By Thomas Mann. Trans. by A. T. Lowe-Porter. Knopf, 1934-44.

The Street of the Sandal Makers. By Nis Petersen. Trans. from the Danish by Elizabeth Sprigge and Claude Napier. Macmillan, 1933. A tale of Rome in the time of Marcus Aurelius.

Basilissa. By John Masefield. Macmillan, 1940. A tale of Theodora and Justinian.

The Tale of Genji. By Lady Murasaki. Trans. from the Japanese by Arthur Waley. 2 vols. Houghton Mifflin, 1936. Called a world classic — a picture of Court life in the late eighth centuries of Japan.

Not Made with Hands. By Helen White. Macmillan, 1935. Mathilde of Tuscany, a central figure.

The Raven's Wing. By Elizabeth Sprigge. Macmillan, 1940. Built around Empress Elizabeth of Austria.

A Woman of Genius. By Mary Austin. Houghton Mifflin, 1917. A fictional autobiography.

Woman under Glass, Saint Teresa of Ávila. By Virginia Hersch. Harper, 1930.

Mère Marie of the Ursulines. By Agnes Repplier. Her personality and work in Canada in the colonial era. Literary Guild of America, 1931.

The Faithful Wife. By Sigrid Undset. Knopf, 1937. A dramatization of Marriage versus career, etc., by fictional treatment. Also see her other novels on other themes.

River Supreme. By Alice Tisdale Hobart. Bobbs-Merrill, 1934. First of her series of novels dealing with race relations, in this case with Westerners and Chinese.

Immortal Wife. By Irving Stone. Doubleday, Doran, 1944. Fictional biography of John and Jessie Benton Frémont.

The Rainbow. By Wanda Wasilewska. Simon and Schuster, 1944. Stalin Prize award.

French Novelists from the Revolution to Proust. By Frederick C. Green. Appleton, 1931. Chapter I discusses women novelists.

Gone with the Wind. By Margaret Mitchell, 1936. Theme: The American civil war.

PEACE

The Hopi Way. By Laura Thompson and Alice Joseph. Univ. of Chicago Press, 1945.

Life of Clara Barton. By Percy H. Helper. Macmillan, 1905. Her attitude toward war gained by her experience as nurse in the American civil war.

Reminiscences. By Julia Ward Howe. Houghton Mifflin, 1899. Composer of "Battle Hymn of the Republic" turned to work for world peace in 1870.

The Peace Movement in America. By Julius Moritzen. Intro. by J. J. Tryon. Putnam, 1912.

Proceedings of the Cause and Cure of War Conferences in Washington, D.C., 1925-34.

Die Waffen Nieder, or Ground Arms. By Berta von Suttner (Countess Kinsky). McClurg, Chicago, 1906. Background of the Nobel Prize.

Women, World War, and Permanent Peace. By May E. Wright Sewall. John J. Newbigin, San Francisco, 1915.

Publications of Women's International League for Peace and Freedom. Washington, D. C.

Women and the War System. By Lucia T. (Ames) Mead. World Peace Foundation, Boston, 1912.

Women at The Hague. By Jane Addams and Associates. Macmillan, 1915. Account of international conference of women who tried to bring the first world war to an end in 1915.

The History of the Woman's Peace Party. By Marie L. Degen. Johns Hopkins Studies, Series LVII, No. 3, 1939.

A Footnote to Folly; Reminiscences of Mary Heaton Vorse. Farrar and Rinehart, 1935. Includes memory of her observations of women in conferences in Europe after first world war.

Effects of War and Militarism on the Status of Women. By Emily Balch. Amer. Sociological Publications, Vol. 10, 1915.

Women, War and Fascism. By Dorothy McConnell. American League Against War. 1935.

PHILOSOPHY

Die Frauen in der Philosophie. By K. Joel. Ein Vortag. Hamburg, 1896.

Sappho of Lesbos. Her Life and Times. By Arthur Weigall. Stokes, 1932.

Dictionary of Greek and Roman Biography and Mythology. Ed. by William Smith. 3 vols. Ill. London, 1873. Here are to be found sketches of Greek and Roman women philosophers and sources for extending knowledge of them.

A Manual of the History of Philosophy. By Wilhelm G. Tennemann. Trans. from the German by Arthur Johnson. Oxford, 1832. On the Pythagorean women, see Vol. XXIV.

Life of Pythagoras. By Iamblichus of Chalcis. Trans. by Thos. Taylor. London, 1818. Gives names and identification of many Pythagorean women philosophers.

Femmes Pythagoriciennes. By Mario Meunier. Paris, 1932. Translation of fragments and letters, with notes.

Prolegomena to the Study of Greek Religion. By Jane Ellen Harrison. Cambridge Univ. Press, 1932. Chapter XII gives important interpretation of the role of women in the Pythagorean philosophic movement.

Griechische Dichterinnen; und Griechische Philosophinnen. By J. C. Poestion. Vienna, 1876.

Historia Mulierum Philosopharum. By Gilles Ménage. London, 1765.

Hellenica — Essays on Greek Poetry, Philosophy, History, and

Religion. Ed. by Evelyn Abbott. Longmans, Green, 1898. One of the essays is on the Oracle.

The Greek Philosophers. By Alfred William Benn. Dutton, 1914. Individual women philosophers not treated at length but a few are really discussed and as influence they are made important.

Pluto, Aristotle, and the Greek playwrights, Aeschylus, Euripides, and Aristophanes are essential sources.

De Arete Philosopha. By J. G. Eck. Leipzig, 1775.

Abhandlung über Diotima. By Friedrich Schlegel. Vienna, 1822.

The Greek Sceptics. By Mary H. Patrick. Columbia Univ. Press, 1929. Some mention of women.

Thaïs. By Anatole France. Trans. by R. B. Douglas. Lane, New York, 1909. Summary of Greek philosophy.

Geschichte der Philosophie. By Heinrich Ritter. 12 vols. Hamburg, 1836-53.

Dante et le philosophie catholique du treizième siècle. By A. F. Ozanam. Paris, 1845. Part IV, Ch. II. Influence of women on Catholic philosophy.

Mme. Condorcet (Marie-Louise-Sophie de Grouchy). Nouvelle Biographie General, Vol. II. Paris, 1856.

Féminisme et Positivisme. By Louise-Marie Ferré. Paris, 1938.

Auguste Comte — Thinker and Lover. By Jane M. Style. London, 1928. Influence exerted by Clotilde de Vaux.

Roots of Change. By Joseph H. Fichter. Appleton-Century, 1939. Fifteen leaders during three centuries. A Catholic exposition of lives, ideas, and dreams.

See *Religion.*

PIONEERS AS MIGRANTS

Voyages to Vinland. The First American Saga. Trans. and Interpreted by Emar Hangen. Ill. by Frederich Trench Chapman. Knopf, 1942.

The Women of the Mayflower. By Ethel J. R. C. Noyes. Memorial Press, Plymouth, Mass., 1921.

The Women Who Came in the Mayflower. By Annie Russell Marble. The Pilgrim Press, Boston and Chicago, 1920.

Emigrés in the Wilderness. By T. Wood Clarke. Ill. Macmillan, 1941. The movement to the new world from the old world by men and women, both personalized.

Pioneer Mothers. By Harry Clinton Green and Mary Walcott Green. 3 vols. Putnam, 1912.

Pioneer Women of the West. By Elizabeth F. Lummis Ellet. Scribner, 1854. Based almost wholly on original sources. Story of settlement from Tennessee to Michigan in North America.

PRIMITIVES

Woman's Share in Primitive Culture. By Otis T. Mason. Appleton. 1st ed., 1900.

The Mothers. By Robert Briffault. 3 vols. Macmillan, 1929. A study of the Origins of Sentiments and Institutions. Consult his bibliography.

The Primitive Working Woman. By Anna Garlin Spencer. Forum, Vol. 46, pp. 546-58, 1911.

The Seri Indians. By W. L. McGee. 17th Annual Report of the Bureau of Ethnology, Smithsonian Institution, Washington, D.C. Part I. Management of the economy and industrial arts by women.

Status of Women in Iroquois Polity before 1784. By John N. Hewitt. Smithsonian Annual Report, pp. 475-488, 1932.

The Age of Mother-Power. By C. Gasquoine Hartley (Mrs. Walter M. Callichan). Dodd, Mead, 1914.

9th Annual Report, Bureau of Ethnology, Smithsonian Institution. Washington, D.C., 1892. Articles on division of labor among American Indians by Parry, Nordenskjold, and Simpson.

Annual Reports of the Geographical and Natural History Survey of Canada. Ottawa.

On the Social and Political Position of Women among the Huron-Iroquois Tribes. By Lucien Carr. Report of the Peabody Museum of Amer. Archaeology and Ethnology. Vol. 3, pp. 207-232. Harvard Univ. Press, 1880-1887.

Iroquois Women. By W. M. Beauchamp. Jr. Amer. Folk-Lore, Vol. XIII, Boston, 1901.

Native Races of the Pacific States of North America. By H. H. Bancroft. 5 vols. New York, 1875.

Sachems of the Narragansetts. By Howard M. Chapin. Rhode Island Hist. Soc., Providence, 1931.

Cheyenne Woman Customs. By Geo. N. Grinnell. The Amer. Anthropologist, Vol. IV, 1902.

Tales of the North American Indian. By Mary Austin. Harvard Univ. Press, 1929.

The Story of the Red Man. By Flora Warren Seymour. Longmans, Green, 1929. Gives account of Sarah Winnemucca, daughter of Shoshone chief, spokesman for her tribe, diplomat, and writer following troubles of 1878 between her people and the whites.

Life among the Piute. By Flora Warren Seymour. Ed. by Mary Mann. Boston, 1883. Early appearance of a North American Indian woman in literature.

Der Germanische Mutter und Matronenkult am Niederrhein. By Ernst A. Philippson. Germanic Review, April, 1944.

Aboriginal Woman. By Phyllis M. Kaberry. Ill. The Blakiston Co., Philadelphia, 1939.

Handbook of American Indians North of Mexico. Ed. by F. W. Hodge. Smithsonian Institution. Bureau of American Ethnology. Bull. 30, 2 vols. Washington, 1907-10.

Studies in Comparative Ethnology. By Elie Reclus. Scribner and Welford, 1891. Observations of the Western Inoits, especially the Aleutians. Gives women great credit for launching civilization.

The Individual and His Society. The Psychodynamics of Primitive Social Organization. By Abram Kardiner. California Univ. Press, 1939. Union of psychology and social anthropology in study of the Indian.

RELIGION

The Age of the Gods. By C. Dawson. London, 1928.

Silk Goddess of China and Her Legend. By Terrien de Lacouperie. Trans. by E. J. Albert. London, 1891.

Ancient Celtic Deities. By Sir Edward Anwyl, Transactions of the Celtic Society of Inverness, Vol. XXVI. Inverness, 1921.

The Cults of the Greek States. By L. R. Farnell. 5 vols. London, 1896-1909.

The Dawn of Civilization. By G. Maspero. Appleton, 1894. In Egypt and Chaldaea.

The Gods of Northern Buddhism. By A. Getty. Clarendon Press, 1914.

Sumerian Mythology. By S. H. Kramer. American Philosophical Society, Philadelphia, 1944.

Mythes et Symboles Lunaires. By C. Hentze. De Sikkel, Antwerp, 1932.

Biography of the Gods. By A. E. Haydon. Macmillan, 1943.

The Cultural Heritage of India. By One Hundred Indian Scholars. Ill. 3 vols. Ramakrishna — Vivekananda Center, New York, 1917. See especially treatment of Ramakrishna, priest of Kali, worshiper of divinity in the Mother.

Woman in World History: Her Place in the Great Religions. By Ebe Minerva White. London, 1924.

Prolegomena to the Study of Greek Religions. By Jane Ellen Harrison. London, 1903. Attention drawn to elements long neglected, to that date.

Delphic Woman: Twelve essays reprinted from The New Image and Old Lamps for New. By Claude Bragdon. Knopf, 1936.

The Religion of the Ancient Celts. By J. H. MacCulloch. Edinburgh, 1911.

A Theory of Civilization. By Sholto O. G. Douglas. Macmillan, 1914.

The Apostle. By Sholem Asch. Putnam, 1943.

Woman under Primitive Buddhism. By L. B. Horner. Dutton, 1930.

Women Leaders of the Buddhist Reformation. By Mabel Bode. Royal Asiatic Society Jr., 1893. London.

Priesthoods of Women in Egypt. By Margaret Alice Murray. International Congress of History and Religions. Vol. I, pp. 22-224. Oxford, 1908.

History of Oracles. By Bernard Le Bovier de Fontenelle. Amsterdam, 1687.

The Women of Early Christianity. By Lina Eckenstein. Revised and edited by Ceili Roscoe, 1935.

Christianisme et Culture Féminine. By Lucie Goyau. Paris, 1914.

Encyclopaedia Theologique. Ed. by J. P. Migne. Am. ed. with Introduction by Vida Scudder. Dutton, 1916. Important references to early English women Christians.

Women in the Early Christian Ministry. By Ellen B. Dietrick. Alfred J. Ferris, Philadelphia, 1897.

Saint Catherine of Siena as Seen in Her Letters. By Vida Scudder. Dutton, 1905.

The Soul Afire. Revelations of the Mystics. Edited by H. A. Reinhold. Pantheon Books, 1945.

The Mystics of Siena. By P. Misciatelli. Appleton, 1931.

A Dictionary of Saintly Women. By Agnes B. C. Dunbar. 2 vols. London, 1904-5.

The Decline of the Mediaeval Church. By A. C. Flick. Knopf, 1930.

Women of the Reformed Church. By James I. Good. The Sunday School Board of the Reformed Church in the United States. Philadelphia, 1901. Historical study.

Mont-Saint-Michel and Chartres. By Henry Adams. Houghton Mifflin, 1936.

Life of St. Macrina. By St. Gregory of Nyssa (her brother). London, 1916.

The Life of Mahomet. By W. S. Muir. London, 1858.

Aishah, the Beloved of Mohammed. By Nabia Abbott, Univ. of Chicago Press, 1943.

An Ancient Salvation Army, Second century A.D. By V. E. C. M. Rosemary Mag., Vol. 39, pp. 499-513, 1911. Somerset, Ohio.

An Historical Character, Relating to the Holy and Exemplary Life of the Lady Elizabeth Hastings. By Thomas Barnard. London, 1742.

The Influence of Women in Islam. By Ameer Ali. The Nineteenth Century Mag., pp. 755-774, May, 1899.

The Rise of the Huguenots of France. By H. M. Baird, 2 vols. Scribner, 1879.

Great American Foundresses. By Rev. J. Code. Macmillan, 1929.

Reform Periodicals and Women Reformers, 1830-60. Amer. Hist. Rev., Vol. 37, p. 678 ff. July, 1932.

Quaker Women, 1650-1690. By Mabel Richmond. London, 1915.

Religion in Colonial America. By W. W. Sweet. Scribner, 1942.

THE RENAISSANCE

The Civilisation of the Renaissance in Italy. By Jacob Burckhardt. Trans. by S. G. C. Middlemore. Macmillan, 1909.

Women of Florence. By Isadora del Lagno. Trans. from the Italian by Mary Steegman. Chatto and Windus, 1907.

Theorien über Frauenbildung im Zeitalter der Renaissance. By W. Ruhmer, Bonn, 1915.

The Golden Days of the Renaissance in Rome. From the pontificate of Julian II to that of Paul III. By Rudolfo Lanciana. Houghton Mifflin, 1906.

The Life of Michael Angelo Buonarroti. By J. S. Harford. London, 1858. Includes memoirs of Vittoria Colonna.

The Life of Vittoria Colonna. By T. A. Trollope. New York, 1859.

Woman in Italy. By William Boulting. London, 1910. From chivalrous services of love to the appearance of the professional actress.

The Court of Ferrara. By Casimir von Chledowski. Trans. from German by Rosa Shapire. Berlin, 1910. Also his The Men and the Women of the Renaissance. Munich, 1912.

La Femme Italienne à l'Epoque de la Renaissance. By E. Rodocanachi. Paris, 1907.

Isabella d'Este, Marchioness of Mantua. By Julia Cartwright (Mrs. Ady. London, 1903; Beatrice d'Este, 1912; Christine of Denmark, 1913.

Louise de Savoie et François I. By Maulde la Clavière. Paris, 1895. His The Women of the Renaissance, trans. by G. H. Ely, Putnam, 1900.

Lucrezia Borgia. By Ferdinand Gregorovius. 2 vols. Stuttgart, 1875. Based on documents and correspondence of her day.

Mantova E. Urbina. Isabella d'Este. By A. Luzio and A. Renier. Ed. by Elizabetta Gonzaga. Turin, 1883.

The Renaissance and Its Makers. By J. D. Symon and S. L. Bensusan. London, 1913.

The Renaissance. By Edith Sichel. Holt, 1914.

Das Weib in der Renaissance. By Hans Floerke. Munich, 1920.

The Three Estates in Mediaeval and Renaissance Literature. By Ruth Mohl. Columbia Univ. Press, 1933.

Middle-Class Culture in Elizabethan England. By Louis B. Wright. Univ. of N. Carolina Press, 1935. Chapter 13 deals with the popular controversy over women at that time.

Moulders of Destiny: Renaissance Lives and Times. By Lloyd W. Eshleman. Covici, Friede, 1938. Catherine de' Medici is number 9 in this list.

Nobyltie off Women. By William Bercher. 1539.

Agrippa's *De Nobilitate et Praecellentia Foeminei Sexus.* Trans. by David Clapham. 1542.

Defense of Good Women. By Sir Thomas Elyot. 1545. His wife was educated in the school of Sir Thomas More. He called himself a democrat — that early.

Defense of Women. By Edward More. 1560.

Women in the Cycles of Culture, A Study in "Women's Power" through the Centuries. By Anna de Koven. Putnam, 1941.

Italy After the Renaissance; decadence and display in the seventeenth century. By Lacy Collison-Morley. London, 1930.

REVOLUTIONISTS

Seven Women Against the World. By Margaret Goldsmith. Methuen, 1932.

Pioneer Women. By Harry C. Green and Mary W. Green. 3 vols. Putnam, 1912.

The Women of the American Revolution. By Elizabeth L. F. Ellet. Scribner, 1848, 1850.

Portraits of Jews. By Hannah R. London. 1927. About Jewish women who took part in the American Revolution.

Women of the French Revolution. By J. Michelet. Paris, 1855.

Women of the French Revolution. By Winifred Stephens. Dutton, 1932.

Memoirs of a Revolutionist. By Vera N. Figner. Trans. from the Russian by Martin Lawrence. International Publishers, New York, 1927.

Spiridonova, Revolutionary Terrorist. By Steinberg. Methuen, 1936.

Prison Letters of Constance de Markiewicz. Ed. by Sean O'Faolain. Longmans, Green, 1934.

Prison Letters of Rosa Luxembourg. Authorized collection.

Written to Karl and Louise Kautsky from 1896 to 1918. Ed. by Louise Kautsky. Trans. from the German by Louis P. Lochner. McBride, 1925.

La tour de Constance et ses prisonnières; liste générale et documents inédits. By Charles Sagnier. Paris, 1880.

Marie Durand, Prisonnière à la tour de Constance (1715-68). *Son temps, sa famille, ses compagnes de captivité.* By Daniel Benoît. Paris, 1935.

My Disillusionment in Russia. By Emma Goldman. Doubleday Page, 1923.

In Prison. By Kate Richards O'Hare. Knopf, 1923. Memoir of an American socialist-pacifist.

Two Letters written by a Noble Roman lady in prison under Diocletian. See Suidas.

Woman. By Madeleine Marx (Magdeleine Legendre Paz). Trans. from the French by Adele Szold Seltzer. Thos. Seltzer, 1920. Introduction by Henri Barbusse who ranks the author among the "loftiest poets of our age."

Pasionaria, the People's Tribune of Spain. Workers' Library, New York, 1938.

SALONS

For the history of the French salons in the seventeenth and eighteenth centuries, two monumental collections of *Mémoires* were assembled by the French. One is the collection of Barrière and Lescure in 32 volumes. The other is the collection of Petitot and Monmerque consisting of 131 volumes. For vividness with respect to great salonières, their correspondence must be read and for this contention, see introduction to section on LETTERS.

Les Salons Littéraires et la Société Française (1610-1789). By Roger Picard. Brentano, 1943.

The Women of the 18th Century. By Edmond and Jules de Goncourt. Balch, 1927.

The Women of the Salons. By S. G. Tallentyre (Evelyn Hall). Putnam, 1926.

Woman in France. By Julia Kavanagh. 2 vols. Putnam, 1893. Deals with the Regency, the reigns of Louis XV and Louis XVI, and the Revolution.

Petit Traite de l'Égalité des hommes et des femmes. By Mlle. de Gournay. Paris, 1622.

Les Femmes Philosophes au 18ème Siècle. By M. de Lescure. Paris, 1886.

The Salon. By Helen Clergue. Putnam, 1907.

La Salon de Mme. Necker. Ed. by Vicomte d'Haussonville. 2 vols. Paris, 1882.

Julie de Lespinasse. By P. de Segur. Trans. from the French by P. A. L. Warnel. Holt, 1907.

The Great Literary Salons. Lectures delivered at the Musée Carnavalet. London, 1830.

Salons. Pictures of Society through Five Centuries. By Valerian Tornius. Trans. by Agnes Platt and Lillian Wonderley. Cosmopolitan Book Corp. New York, 1929.

An Eighteenth Century Marquise: A study of Emilie du Châtelet and her times. London, 1910. This marquise was the close friend of Voltaire.

Women and the French Tradition. By Florence Ravenel. Macmillan, 1918. Chapter V on Mme. de Staël, "the Great Salonière."

The Salon, Its Rise and Fall. By Valerian Tornius. Trans. by Agnes Platt. London, 1929.

The Salon and English Letters. By C. Tinker. Macmillan, 1915.

Some German Women and their Salons. By Mary Hargrave. London, 1912.

Les Salons de Vienne et de Berlin. By Blaze de Bury. Paris, 1861.

SCIENCE

Die Heilige Hildegard von Bingen, die Erste Deutsche Naturforscherin und Aerztin, ihr Leben und Werk. By Hermann Fischer. Munich, 1927.

Les Femmes dans la Science. By A. Rebière. Paris, 1894. Brief biographical sketches.

Women in Science. By H. J. Mozans. Appleton, 1913. An historical review.

Agnesi. By Luisa Anzoletti. Milan, 1900.

Women in the Realm of Science. By Morris Goldberg. American Hebrew, Vol. 126, 1930.

The Rise of Modern Physics. By Henry Crew. Baltimore, 1935. In the introductory review of science, Hypatia is considered.

Studies in the History and Method of Science. Edited by Charles Singer. 2 vols. Clarendon Press, 1917-1921. Volume I contains an exceptionally comprehensive treatment of the Abbess Hildegard's contribution to science in the twelfth century and reproductions of her own colored drawings. Fully footnoted.

The Sexes in Science and History. By Eliza R. Gamble. Putnam, 1916.

Madame Curie. A Biography. By Eve Curie. Trans. by Vincent Sheean. Doubleday, Doran, 1939.

The Jewish Woman in Science. By Ida Welt. Hebrew Standard, April 5, 1907, p. 4. Includes an alchemist of the fourth century B.C.

WAR

Les Guerrières. By Col. Charles Armand Romain. Paris, 1931. Sketches the woman warrior in legends, in antiquity, in the middle ages, in modern times, with emphasis on the French woman. Gives his sources.

Deutsche Alterthumskunde. By C. von Mullenhoff. Vol. IV, p. 205.

La Mère chez Certains Peuples dans l'Antiquité. By Giraud-Theulon Fils. Paris, 1867.

Mütter und Amazonen. By Berta-Eckstein Diener. *Ein Umriss weiblicher Reiche.* Albert Langen Verlag, Munich, 1932.

L'Origine des Amazones. By Adolphe Reinach. Paris, 1913.

Les Déesses Armées. By Denyse Lelasseur. Paris, 1919.

Les Femmes en Guerre. By Fernand Corcos. Montaigne, 1926.

La Femme Soldat. By Comte Em le Las Cases. Rouen, 1900.

La Femme et les Armées de la Révolution et de l'Empire (1792-1815). By Raoul Brice. Paris, 1913.

Les Femmes Militaires de la France. By Tranchant and Ladimir. Paris, 1866.

Les Femmes de France pendant l'Invasion (1870-1871). By Joseph Turquan. Paris, 1893.

Histoire de Jeanne d'Arc. By Vallon, Anatole France, and others.

Women and Soldiers. By Ethel B. Tweedie. London, 1918.

War and Woman. Henry Clay Hansbrough. Duffield, 1915.

The Rise of Fernando Cortes. By Henry R. Wagner. Pub. by the Cortes Society, Bancroft Library, Berkeley, Calif. New Series, No. 3. Important data about Dona Marina whose aid was so vital in Cortes' conquest of Mexico.

Histoire de la Gaule. By Camille Jullian. Paris, 1918.

Histoire Militaire des Femmes. By De la Barre Duparcq. Paris, 1869.

Les Femmes Décorées de la Légion d'Honneur et les Femmes Militaires. By Jean Alesson. Paris, 1888.

Madame Sans-Gêne et les Femmes Soldats. By Émile Cère. Paris, 1894.

The March of the Barbarians. By Harold Lamb. Doubleday, Doran, 1940.

Women in War. By Francis G. Gribble. Dutton, 1916.

Women of the War: Their Heroism and Self Sacrifice. By

Frank Moore. Ill. Hartford, Conn., 1867. Women of the American civil war.

Reminiscences of Peace and War. By Mrs. Roger A. Pryor. Macmillan, 1905. Her memory of the American civil war from the Southern side.

U. S. Council of National Defense Commission on Woman's Defense Work. Govt. Printing Office, Washington, 1918.

Women and War Work. By Helen Fraser. London, 1918.

Society at War. By Caroline E. Payne. Houghton Mifflin, 1931.

American Women and the World War. By Ida Clyde Clarke. Appleton, 1918.

Yashka. By Isaac Don Levine. Transcription of autobiography of Maria Botchkareva, Commander of Russian Women's Battalion of Death. Stokes, 1919.

The Armed Horde. By Hoffman Nickerson. Putnam, 1940.

It's A Great War. By Mary Lee. Houghton Mifflin, 1929. Memoir of an American nurse at the front in the first world war.

Women and Cruelty. By E. de Beaumont. London, 1905. The sword and womankind; soulless women; women of gigantic stature; lady duellists.

Lincoln's Daughters of Mercy. By Marjorie Barstow Greenbie. Putnam, 1944.

Spies and Traitors of World War II. By Kurt Singer. Prentice-Hall, 1945.

INDEX